OLD DERBYSHIRE AND NEW WORLDS:
THE JEFFERYS OF HUNGRY BENTLEY

This iconic photograph of Mary (nee Robinson) Jeffery and thirteen of her fifteen children, taken in 1882 outside the Riddings features the main characters whose lives and descendants will be traced in the chapters that follow

OLD DERBYSHIRE AND NEW WORLDS:

THE JEFFERYS OF HUNGRY BENTLEY

by

Valerie Hardy

Dedicated to the memory of my father Jeffery Hellaby
and grandmother Ellen née Jeffery
and
To my daughter Clare and granddaughters Isabel and India de Bono

First Published privately in Great Britain in 2010 by Valerie Hardy

Second edition published in Great Britain in 2022 by

Woldscot
Water Lane
Brimscombe
Glos GL5 2ST

ISBN: 978-1-3999-1751-3

A CIP catalogue record for this book is available from the British Library

Edited by Rosalie Vicars-Harris
Designed by David Fordham
Photographs retouched and Family Trees designed by Malcolm Lewis
Design of the additional material for the second edition by Malcolm Lewis

Printed in Great Britain by Biddles Books Limited, Kings Lynn, Norfolk

CONTENTS

PREFACE AND ACKNOWLEDGEMENTS

'The past is a foreign country; they do things differently there.'
L.P. Hartley (The Go-Between)

The Jeffery story tells of a vanishing world: of a family through thirteen generations with its roots in the land and whose members are now spread around the globe. The story focuses on the lives of the fifteen children, their predecessors and descendants, of my great grandparents, Thomas and Mary Jeffery, of the *Riddings Farm*, Hungry Bentley, Derbyshire.

I was born on the Staffordshire bank of the middle Dove Valley but my roots are on the opposite side of the river in Derbyshire. This is land where Jefferys and their descendants have lived and farmed for nearly four hundred years. Although I have researched the other branches of my family, the Hellabys, Websters and Robinsons, it is the Jefferys, my paternal grandmother's family, who captured my imagination. Researching the Jeffery story has been an odyssey of the heart as well as the mind: it is a story which I have felt compelled to write. The family's story is one whose history gazes

out of old photographs, lingers in letters and remains vivid and immutable in the memories of many older members of the family who recall those earlier generations of a vanished world. It is a story which dwells in the land of my roots. In writing the Jeffery story I have been fortunate to walk hand in hand with serendipity in the footsteps of my ancestors.

The seeds for the Jeffery story were sown on a summer afternoon seventy years ago. I was four years old and my sister and I were staying at *Bentley Fields Farm* when we walked across the fields to visit our Jeffery cousins at the *Riddings*, our grandmother's old home. From my earliest days it was through my much loved father, Jeffery Hellaby, that I became aware of his abiding interest in his Jeffery cousins and the closeness which he felt to his mother's family. The *Riddings*, had a very special place in his heart. It was through him that I learnt of his uncles and aunts, the eight brothers and six sisters of his mother who had been born at the *Riddings*. He explained that his cousin Thomas Jeffery, son of his mother's brother Owen, was the fifth generation of Jefferys to farm at the *Riddings*.

The Riddings in 1928

LEFT *The author in Yeaveley Churchyard*

RIGHT *In the mud at Stydd*

My father's mother, Ellen nee Jeffery Hellaby, was the only grandmother I knew. She would make her home with us at *Fauld House Farm*, near Hanbury, during the late summers of the 1930s and 1940s. I have vivid childhood memories of the many occasions when she would take my hand and we would walk together along Fauld Lane to post her letters to her brothers' families in America. As a child, it seemed magical that these letters could be going to a far away land and that my Granny and I had family who lived there. It was the dawn of a realisation that my father had American cousins and that the world was a much larger place than the area around my own home. Years later, I discovered that my grandmother had visited her family in America at the end of the nineteenth century many years before a flight across the Atlantic made such a trip relatively commonplace. After my father's death I found that he had kept the letters from America to which his mother had not been able to respond in the months before her death.

My father and grandmother fired my interest in the Jeffery family story: their influence has been inspirational. Through them my imagination was captured by the discovery that the *Riddings* has continued to be home

to six generations of Jefferys from the late eighteenth century and that also, a number of my great uncles had left the *Riddings* for the New World during the nineteenth century.

Later, after my grandmother's death in 1950, my cousin Dorothy Jeffery, also of the *Riddings*, continued the correspondence with the families of our pioneering great uncles. During the year 1951-52, whilst on a teaching exchange, Dorothy visited many of them. On her return, I recall being completely enthralled when she showed pictures, told of her travels and of her meetings with our cousins across America. Sixteen years later during a year spent in America I too was privileged to meet many of these descendants. It was that experience which further fuelled my desire to write the Jeffery family story: it was a story which was waiting to be told. However, it was not until October 2008 following my retirement that I began to write.

Not surprisingly, as a geographer, my research has reinforced the importance of the concept of place in the history of the Jeffery family. Fieldwork has involved walking the 'streets' of the lost village of Hungry Bentley and the ancient pathways of my childhood that stitch

together *Bentley Fields*, *Bentley Hall* and the *Riddings*; ploughing along muddy tracks to *Stydd Hall* and remote farms in the Somersal Herbert area together with recording and photographing in churchyards in the drizzle under dripping yew trees.

Tracing the family back to the seventeenth century is clearly an endeavour fraught with many perils. The data I include is accurate to the best of my current knowledge. There may, however, be some errors for which I take full responsibility. In addition to time spent in country churchyards, visiting family farms and garnering information provided by others working on Jeffery genealogy, my research has included many hours spent in the archives with the parish records. I am most particularly grateful to Margaret Walker who has spent much time in confirmation of my earlier studies of these records.

The Jeffery family story is traced back through thirteen generations. However, generations eight, nine and ten form the main focus of the story covering nearly two hundred years of Jeffery history from 1817 to the present day. Central to the story are the fifteen children, born between 1844 and 1865, of my great grandparents, Thomas Jeffery (1823-1876) and Mary Robinson (1817-1906) of the *Riddings*, Hungry Bentley in Derbyshire. They are the eighth generation. The story is taken through to their grandchildren with occasional references to their great grandchildren. I have personal memories of the two youngest daughters of the fifteen children: my Grandmother Ellen and my Great Aunt

Clara. Sixteen of Thomas and Mary's fifty-two grandchildren, both in England and America, have been a part of my own life and a number of them have contributed oral history to this book. At the time of writing, there are ten remaining grandchildren. There are at least ninety-six great grandchildren as well as their innumerable descendants.

Some of the later generations of Jefferys may be disappointed in not finding themselves named in this book. To them I apologise and encourage them to trace further their own family lines. The diagrams of the family trees have of necessity been curtailed. Following the Jeffery family story back through thirteen generations has necessitated addressing the practical problems of great numbers and family names. The blood descendants of seventeenth century Thomas Jeffery baptised on 11 December 1653 and his father William born over twenty years previously now number in the thousands and many of them, through marriage, no longer carry the Jeffery name.

In writing the family story I have become acutely aware of a number of themes which persist through generations of Jefferys. There appears to be a Jeffery gene for longevity probably inherited from Mary Robinson: the reader will discover a significant number of nonagenarians, on both sides of the Atlantic, including some who were not far short of achieving their century. A 'gene' for adventure and travel is also apparent from the nineteenth-century American pioneers to the twentieth and twenty-first-century travellers and emigrants to South Africa, Australia and New Zealand. In many cases, this has been matched by a strong worldwide sense of family and the maintenance of links with their Derbyshire roots. Additionally, qualities of gentleness, generosity and public responsibility together with a reserved, unassuming demeanour, an independence of spirit, good looks and a sense of style appear to be characteristics repeated down the generations. Many Jefferys are reticent but deep thinking: they feel much but display little. The old adage – 'when all's said and done, there's a lot more said than done' is reversed for Jefferys who do much and say little.

It is also interesting to observe the genetic inheritance in family likenesses. I recall my first meeting in California, with John Arthur Jeffery, the grandson of my grandmother's eldest brother Thomas. I found his strong resemblance to my father quite remarkable. The resemblance, seen in photographs, of John Arthur's father, John Arthur the first and son of Thomas Jeffery and my father's first cousin, is also remarkable. Additionally, on one special occasion my father remarked how like his mother Ellen I am. I have observed many other quite distinctive resemblances in working with such a great wealth of family photographs including the resemblance shown by Fred Jeffery of the *Riddings* to his great grandfather Thomas Jeffery also born at the *Riddings* over a hundred years before him.

In writing the stories of the fifteen children, their predecessors and their descendants I have tried to see them in the context of the times and events through which they lived and to which they have contributed. It has been a privilege to incorporate oral testimony, material from written records including memoirs, diaries, letters, wills and newspaper reports together with a wealth of photographs from the family. I acknowledge and am indebted to the many members of the extended Jeffery family who have made their own distinctive and individual contributions.

Whilst it is very difficult indeed to single out individuals, I do owe very special and warm thanks to Geoff Jeffery, now in Georgia and Michael Jeffery in Alaska, USA: they have been very generous in providing a wealth of information enabling me to piece together the stories of my grandmother's pioneering brothers Joseph and Thomas and their descendants. The story of the oldest emigrant brother, Thomas, has been further enriched by the treasure trove of photographs which Michael's elder brother, John Arthur Jeffery the third, in California, also very kindly provided for me. Some of these photographs from John Jeffery do appear in the text of the story of pioneering Thomas Jeffery who emigrated in 1865. Many more than could be incorporated into this text are included in a special section at the end of the book.

I also wish to offer my warmest thanks, most particularly for their contributions by way of photographs and oral history, to Audrey (nee Jeffery) Bates in South Africa; Peggy (nee Poyser) Halton of Roston, Derbyshire; Irene Jeffery of London; Margaret Jeffery of the *Riddings*, Hungry Bentley; Mary Jeffery of the *Home Farm*, West Broughton; Vivian Lowe of Abingdon, Oxfordshire; Kathryn O'Malley of New Zealand and America; Marjorie Snow (nee Hellaby), my sister, of

Field House, Marchington; Elizabeth Watson of Mayfield, Derbyshire; Stella, Richard and Rosemary Spencer of *Bentley Fields*, Hungry Bentley and Elizabeth Spencer of Clifton, Ashbourne. Additionally I am indebted to the late Arthur Jeffery of Roston, Frank Jeffery of Mickleover, Derby and Jeffery Spencer, of *Bentley Fields*.

Sincere thanks and acknowledgements are also due to Connie Bradley; Philip Brown; Angela and Nigel Collingwood; Brenda Garner; Henry Hand; Noreen Haselwood; John Hidderley; Sally and Ken Houghton; John Jeffery (son of Wilson Jeffery); Lu Jeffery; Jane McKirdy; Beryl Page; Simon Rawson; Ralph Selby; Margaret Walker. My thanks are also due to the late John Jeffery of Denby, Derbyshire and the late Marjorie Pirie-Fellows of California. My thanks are also due to the staff of the Derbyshire Local Record Office in Matlock and also to Lorie Nuge in the library in Sarasota, Florida.

Special thanks are due to my designer, David Fordham. I have admired David's consummate skills in meeting the challenge of combining such a wide range of sources and illustrations. Warmest thanks are also due to my cousin Rosalie (nee Jeffery) Vicars-Harris and her husband Malcolm Lewis (Lew) for their patience, unfailing good humour, advice and very considerable talents in their brilliant editing of both the text and photographs and designing the family trees. Rosalie has, in addition, contributed many family photographs and I have very much appreciated her superb management skills in organising the printing and production of this book.

Very special thanks and deep appreciation are due to my husband Colin. Through our innumerable discussions across the dining table he has helped me to see the wood from the (family!) trees and shape this history. I have valued his forensic mind and insistence that I clarify ambiguities and close loose ends. He has given me the most tremendous support and encouragement throughout the preparation of this book.

PART ONE

THE
PLACES

THE PLACES

Sketch Map of Jefferyland

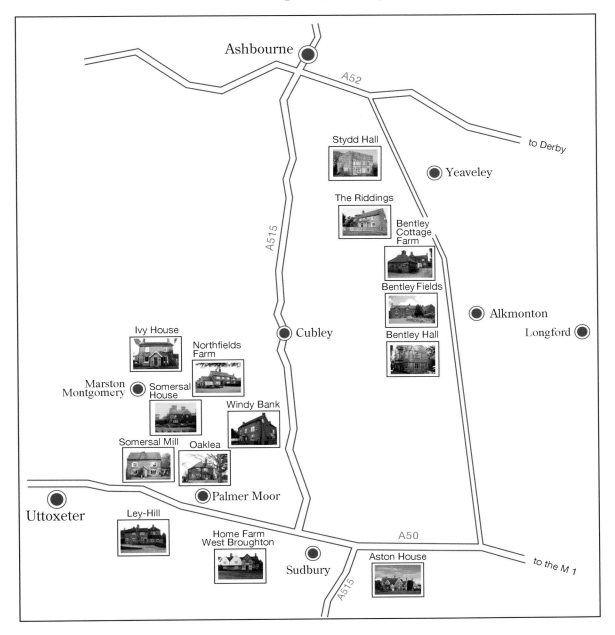

Ashbourne

A52

to Derby

Stydd Hall

Yeaveley

The Riddings

Bentley Cottage Farm

Bentley Fields

Alkmonton

Bentley Hall

Longford

A515

Cubley

Ivy House

Northfields Farm

Marston Montgomery

Somersal House

Windy Bank

Somersal Mill

Oaklea

Palmer Moor

Uttoxeter

Ley-Hill

Home Farm West Broughton

A50

Sudbury

A515

Aston House

to the M 1

Jefferyland

Lane to Windy Bank Farm, Somersal Herbert

The Derbyshire Jefferys have their roots in the heart of the county. They have farmed here for over four hundred years. The area was also the springboard from which the pioneers of the family launched themselves to 'fresh woods and pastures new' during the nineteenth century. For those, the lure of the New World was only matched by the pull exerted by the land of their roots. This remains in many of their descendants today.

This area, 'Jefferyland', is a hidden and secret place. It is roughly triangular in shape and lies between Derby, Uttoxeter and Ashbourne. The River Dove marks its western and southern border. It will be avoided by hasty travellers on the A50 on their way from Derby to the Uttoxeter Races or further afield to the Alton Towers Pleasure Park. Those heading to Ashbourne along the A52 bound for Dovedale and the Peak District will bypass the area. Should travellers drive along the A515, which bisects Jefferyland, between Sudbury and Ashbourne, they will not pass through any villages. They will only witness the signposts to right and left. (See map).

Strangers who leave the main roads will soon find themselves in a maze of narrow, winding, often sunken lanes bound by hedgerows. These link the scattered villages east and west of the old turnpike road. Should the visitors' destination be one of the family farms then they may well find themselves on farm tracks across fields, some distance from even these minor roads.

However, the visitor is rewarded by the area's understated beauty. It is an ancient landscape underpinned by its geology of glacial soil overlying sandstone and shale. Although few places are higher than 150 metres, there remains a distinct sense of elevation as the area overlooks the plains of the River Dove. The area marks the northern limit of the Midland Plain where it abuts the Derbyshire Peak District and Staffordshire Moorlands. A network of post-glacial rivers, now much reduced to small streams, has shaped the shallow valleys and low ridges of this land.

Whilst the wayward visitors will always be greeted by hospitable people, they nevertheless remain outsiders. The secret nature of Jefferyland is aided by a network of close family links. Village, church, chapel and school have reinforced these relationships as has the shared livelihood of farming. In the recent past, cousins would meet and prod fat cattle with walking sticks at Uttoxeter market. Their wives shared family and neighbourhood news over lunch at Pakemans. It would be a rare occasion during a visit to the bank or the shops in Ashbourne if time was not spent greeting some relation on the street. Jefferyland is also 'cousins country'.

It is a pastoral landscape. Villages such as Alkmonton, Hungry Bentley, Yeaveley, Cubley, Longford and Shirley were originally nucleated settlements surrounded by open fields where, today, the ridge and furrow pattern in the fields provides evidence of the ancient strip farming.

The number of villages which were already present by the time of the Domesday survey and the place names are indicative of a settlement pattern already established by Anglo-Saxon times. In the Middle Ages, the density of settlement was greater than it is today. This is reflected in the remnants of deserted and shrunken villages, such as Alkmonton and Hungry Bentley.

The footpaths and track-ways, which remain to this day, linked the villages and scattered farmsteads. By the early seventeenth century, some areas were already enclosed. The hedgerows and scattered boundary trees indicate a long history of enclosure and add to the sense of antiquity to the landscape. It is an ancient landscape revealing a land resonant of Hoskin's words as: *the richest historical record we possess and where there are discoveries to be made for which no written documents exist.*[1] Although written records do provide evidence of the Jeffery ancestors who have lived in the area over the past few hundred years, it is the landscape itself that reveals a wealth of evidence of settlement in the area from former times. These settlers were the earliest ancestors.

The name Bentley is derived from the Old English *beonet-leah* meaning 'clearing overgrown with bent grass'. The addition of Hungry was first seen in the mid-fifteenth century. It has been suggested that this could be a reference to relatively poor quality soil. However,

[1] W.G. Hoskins: The Making of the English Landscape.

this could be misleading as the land is not particularly infertile.

Earthworks, showing the pattern of the 'lost' medieval village of Hungry Bentley are revealed on *Bentley Fields Farm*. The original manor house of this deserted village was located close to where the seventeenth-century *Bentley Hall* now proudly stands alongside the old Roman road midway between Alkmonton and Cubley. The original manor house was surrounded by a moat (which sadly has now been filled in) and closer to the 'lost' village. Hungry Bentley lies at the heart of Jefferyland and it is the farm at the *Riddings*, which has been home to Jefferys for at least five generations, that is its hearth.

Hungry Bentley Heartland. View from Bentley Fields Farm to the Riddings with the Weaver Hills in the background

At the time of the Domesday survey of 1086, there were seventeen landholders in Derbyshire: King William together with sixteen of his Norman noblemen. It was Henry de Ferrers, ancestor of the Earls of Derby, who held a significant proportion of the land in the area. Henry was King William's largest tenant-in-chief in Derbyshire with Tutbury Castle, in neighbouring Staffordshire, as one of his main seats. He kept only one-third of his Derbyshire manors under direct management; the rest were tenanted by knights, including those of his own family, most of whom had accompanied him from Normandy. Ralph de Bagpuize, held Barton, Alkmonton and Hungry Bentley. The descendants of the Bagpuizes became prominent landholders in this part of Derbyshire during the three centuries following the Norman Conquest.

At the time of the Domesday survey in 1086, Hungry Bentley was held by Ralph de Bagpuize, under Henry de Ferrers. At this time it was deemed 'waste' and maybe this is where the tag 'hungry' originates. Domesday records:

In BENELEI (Bentley) Wulfgeat and Ulfkell had one carucate (equivalent of around 120 acres and based on the amount of land a team of oxen could plough in a season) of land taxable.
Land for one plough. Waste
Value before 1066, 20 shillings; now 11 shillings

Clearly the value of the land since the time of Edward the Confessor had declined significantly. In neighbouring Alkmonton, also held by Ralph de Bagpuize under Henry de Ferrers, the value had also declined but only by a third instead of almost a half at Hungry Bentley.

The present day Alkmonton lies about a mile to the north, north-west of the 'lost' village of Alchementune of Domesday record.

The Bagpuize family were prominent in the area during the three centuries following the Norman Conquest. In 1100 AD, Ralph's son, Robert, founded St Leonard's hospital for female lepers, which was sited north of the deserted medieval village but south of the present village of Alkmonton. The chapel of the leprosarium was dedicated to St Nicholas and it was probably the site where the old Norman font (now in St John's Church, Alkmonton) was found at Cockshut Croft on the north side of Alkmonton *Old Hall Farm* in 1844. The point on the Six Inch Ordnance map, which marks the site of a chapel, is the point where the Norman font was unearthed. The old Roman road, now known locally as Long Lane, connecting Derby to Rocester, originally went through Alkmonton. It was diverted from the Romans' route westwards as travellers doubtless wished to give the leper hospital a wide berth.

Alkmonton and Hungry Bentley remained with the Bagpuize family (Ralph and his descendant Galfrid) until late into the fourteenth century. With the death of the last male representative, William de Bagpuize, about 1381, the bulk of the property was sold to Sir Walter Blount, Lord Mountjoy of Thurvaston, who was a member of John of Gaunt's retinue and holder of land in seven counties. The Bentley manor, however, continued to be held as dower land by Joan, Lady Bagpuize, as late

as 1397 and the family who held it under them were the Bentleys. Edward Bentley Esq. was the last of the Bentleys to inhabit the Hall in 1586.

The deserted medieval villages of Hungry Bentley and Alkmonton were not alone in Derbyshire. The Black Death, which peaked in England between 1348 and 1350, weakened all village communities with such severity that the old methods of communal farming were regularly discontinued as the population fell.

The minority of villages, that eventually became totally deserted, probably shrank to extinction over several generations and it may well have been in the middle decades of the fifteenth century, up to a hundred years after the Black Death, that Hungry Bentley and Alkmonton were finally deserted. However, in the absence of conclusive evidence, the timing and even the contribution of the Black Death has to remain in the realms of speculation although the probability does remain quite high.

There is an alternative theory relating to the location of both deserted villages. Both are sited on relatively higher plateau land topped by glacial drift: climatic fluctuation to drier conditions may have provoked a serious problem of water supply. Again, this has to be speculative but it could be that both factors contributed to the desertion of both medieval villages. What is clear is that both villages were still extant in the third decade of the fourteenth century as, in 1334, the township of Alkmonton was paying a tax of £1 2s 6d and the poorer village of Hungry Bentley paid a tax of 13s 5d.

The earthworks revealing the pattern of the lost village of Hungry Bentley, which are clearly shown in the fields of *Bentley Fields Farm*, have been surveyed by Peak and Trent archaeologists for English Heritage in addition to being studied by the Universities of Cambridge and Nottingham.

Bentley Fields today is farmed by Richard Spencer, as it was by his father, Jeffery Spencer, his grandfather, Percy Spencer and his great, great uncle, Owen Jeffery, before him. Richard is the great grandson of Mary Jeffery, sister of Owen and daughter of Thomas (1823-1876) and Mary (1817-1906) Jeffery of the *Riddings*. Thomas and Mary (nee Robinson) Jeffery were the parents of the fifteen children born at the *Riddings*. (See PARTS THREE and FOUR).

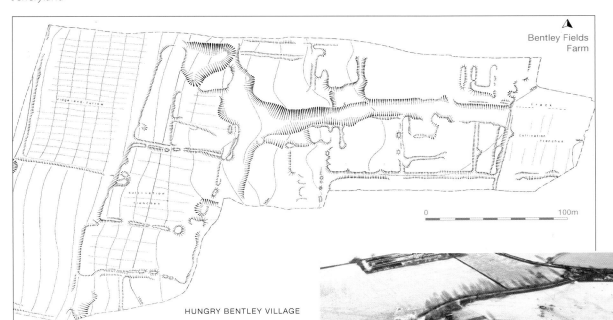

HUNGRY BENTLEY VILLAGE

Lost Village of Hungry Bentley surveyed by Trent and Peak Archaeology for English Heritage and reproduced with their permission

The photographs illustrating the lost village, as it is revealed today, show Richard's sheep with a whole medieval village to themselves. It is quite a moving and strange experience to walk through his fields on a sunny morning in late spring, viewing the earthworks revealing the village. The well-defined street pattern, marked

Main Street Lost Village

TOP *Aerial photograph of Bentley Fields Farm and lost village in the snow*
BELOW *Snow covered lost village*

Side Street Lost Village

by linear hollows and the buildings marked by grass covered house platforms, make it just possible to imagine what the village might have been like a millennia ago.

The elevated site of this 'lost' village becomes immediately apparent if one walks its ancient turf-covered streets. The footpaths westwards reveal the wonderful setting of the farm at the *Riddings* on the other side of the Bentley Brook valley and the footpath southwards leads to *Bentley Hall*.

Both of the original medieval villages of Hungry Bentley and Alkmonton, have been deserted now for around five hundred years. Today, the ecclesiastical parish of Alkmonton embraces both these ancient townships.

The Manor of Hungry Bentley was held by the Bentley family until 1586 when Edward Bentley became involved in the Babington Plot to remove Queen Elizabeth from her throne. As a result, he paid the ultimate penalty and the estate was forfeited to the Crown.

A decade after the death of Queen Elizabeth, James 1 granted Hungry Bentley Manor to Thomas Browne of Shredicote, Staffordshire. The record states:

An epitome of title with the deeds recites as follows: 20 April 1613. By deed enrolled Lord Windsor in consideration of £2.600 grants the Manor of Hungry Bentley to Thomas Browne and his heirs.

Thomas Browne's son, Edmund, married Dorothy Vernon, second daughter of Sir Edward Vernon of Sudbury Hall. It was Edmund and Dorothy's eldest son, Thomas, who inherited. However, Edmund, was found guilty of plotting with his father-in-law, Sir Edward Vernon, against Oliver Cromwell. Consequently, they were both imprisoned in the Tower of London. The Hungry Bentley Manor remained with the Brownes through five generations.

In 1749, Thomas, great, great-grandson of the first Thomas Browne, conveyed the whole of the estate, for £12,000 to Edward Wilmot Esq. M.D. of Jermyn Street, London. Up until this point, the lord of the manor had lived at *Bentley Hall*. Under the Wilmots, who remained as lords of the manor for four generations, *Bentley Hall* was to become a tenanted farm.

During the early nineteenth century, the 1074 acres that comprised the estate of Hungry Bentley Manor, had a population of around eighty people in thirteen households. It had a rateable value of £1,473 in 1857.

White's Directory of 1857 paints the following picture:

BENTLEY HUNGRY liberty, a township, and a scattered village, 5 miles from Ashbourne contains 1,074 acres 1 rood 28 perch of fertile loam, of which one fourth is arable, 13 houses, and 84 inhabitants, of whom 51 were males, and 33 females; rateable value £1, 473. Sir Henry Sacheverel Wilmot, Bart., is lord of the manor, held for an unexpired 830 years, granted by Robert Jackson to William Woolley, on 26th March, 1686, for 1,000 years, without impeachment of waste, at the yearly rent of £10, subject to land tax. The Rev German Buckston is the present owner of it. The tithe was commuted in 1839, for £67 10s. Formerly here was a chapel, of which nothing remains. The Bentley estate was purchased by Sir Edward Wilmot, great grandfather of the present Baronet, on the consideration of having a deer leap, considered to be seven feet from the boundary of the liberty, the timber growing on which, with the minerals, are the property of the owner of the Bentley Estate. Bentley Hall, an ancient building (now a farm house) is in the occupation of Mr. Daniel Oakden, and Middleton Park, another Farmhouse, is in the occupation of Mr. Thomas Oakden.

The farmers at this time included Thomas Jeffery at the *Riddings*. The *Riddings* household would have contributed fifteen of the eighty-four Hungry Bentley inhabitants by the end of 1857.

In 1857, Sir Henry Sacheverel Wilmot, Bart., determined to sell the manor of Hungry Bentley. In *THE TIMES* of Monday, 9 November 1857 and the *DERBY MERCURY* of 11 November 1857, the following advertisement appeared.

Derbyshire – A very valuable and manorial estate, comprising the township of Hungry Bentley and 1000 acres of very rich and fertile land, divided into several very convenient farms, including the well-known Bentley Hall and Middleton Park Farms.

Messrs. Moody and Newbold have much pleasure in announcing that they are instructed to offer by auction, in the one lot, at the King's Head Hotel, Derby, on Friday, November 13th, that most desirable and freehold manorial estate, comprising almost the entire township of Hungry Bentley, lying in a ring fence, with above a 1000 acres of rich and fertile land, exceedingly well tenanted in a high state of cultivation, and situated about 12 miles from Derby, six from Ashbourne, six from Uttoxeter and six from Rocester, a first class situation on the North Staffs Railway. The above estate is well timbered, situated in a most beautiful district, and approached on every side by good roads: and to either the country gentleman, sportsman or capitalist, affords an opportunity for investment rarely to be met with.

Particulars for sale will shortly be detailed and may be had from the newspaper offices; the inns in the neighbourhood; the auctioneers, Derby; Messrs. Simpson, Solicitors, Derby and E.W Wilmot Esq. Burton.

At the time of the advertisement for the sale of the estate, the principal farms were tenanted by Daniel Oakden of *Bentley Hall*, Thomas Oakden at *Middleton Park*, Thomas Jeffery at the *Riddings* and John Jeffery at *Bentley Cottage Farm*.

It was on 27 March 1860 that the Hungry Bentley estate was sold to the trustees of Lord Vernon.

In 1878 Hungry Bentley Manor was conveyed by Lord Vernon to S.W. Clews Esq., of Norbury Hall. The estate consisted of around 1042 acres with a total rental from eight farms of about £2,000 per annum.

In 1876 John Massey, grandson of Philip Oakden, was farming at *Bentley Hall* and by 1887 Samuel Hidderley was the tenant. By the turn of the century, the widowed Mary Jeffery continued at the *Riddings* with her son, Owen, farming both the *Riddings* and *Bentley Fields* farms.

Bentley Estate Sale, 1920

By 1916, Kelly's Directory confirms that Owen's son, eighteen-year-old Thomas Jeffery was farming at the *Riddings*, my grandmother Ellen (nee Jeffery) and grandfather, William Hellaby, were farming at *Bentley Hall* and Owen Jeffery's nephew, Percy Spencer, was farming at *Bentley Fields*.

Following the end of the First World War, many of the landed estates found themselves in difficulty. In 1920 the Hungry Bentley Estate was sold by the Clews family. The estate now totalled 1042 acres with a total rental from eight farms of £1,222 10s. The eight farms were *Bentley Hall*, *Middleton Park*, *The Home Farm*, *Bentley Fields*, the *Riddings*, *Bentley Cottage Farm*, *Small Holding*, *Cottage Holding*. The estate was split up and a number of the farms, including the *Riddings* and *Bentley Fields*, were purchased by the Jeffery and Spencer tenants.

Family Farms

The homes of the Jeffery family and their descendants roughly occur in three groups, principally in Derbyshire but straying into eastern Staffordshire. One generally common factor is that many of them lie some distance from main roads and are only accessed by narrow lanes and farm tracks.

One cluster, to the east of the A151, in the Hungry Bentley and Yeaveley heartland, includes the *Riddings*; *Bentley Fields*; *Bentley Cottage Farm*; *Bentley Hall* and *Stydd Hall*.

To the west of the old turnpike road, there is another cluster in the Somersal Herbert, Doveridge and Sudbury area. These include the *Home Farm, West Broughton*; *Somersal House*; *Somersal Mill*; *Northfields* (formerly Potter Somersal); *Windy Bank*; *Ley Hill*; *Palmer Moor, Oaklea* and *Aston House*.

The third group occurs on the periphery of Jefferyland. These include *Snitterton Hall*, further north, near Matlock; *Holly Bush Farm* between Ashbourne and Matlock; *Lower House Farm*, Roston on the Staffordshire borderland; *Shardlow House* in the south of the county; *Donington Park*, just across the border in Leicestershire and *Parkside* on the edge of the Staffordshire Moorlands.

A number of these places remain as the homes of the descendants of five of the fifteen children of Thomas and Mary Jeffery of the *Riddings*. They will feature in the following pages, principally in PART FOUR: THE PEOPLE WHO STAYED.

A number of the Jeffery homes which are described below are those with which I have longstanding personal connections and which, in a number of instances, featured significantly during my early years. On the other hand, *Snitterton Hall*, on the periphery of Jefferyland, is a home where I have only relatively recently discovered family connections.

The *Riddings* has been home to Jefferys for at least five generations. It was home to Thomas and Margaret (nee Coxon) Jeffery together with their daughter Fanny and sons Thomas and John. It is also likely that it was the home of Thomas's parents, Thomas and Fanny (nee Harrison) Jeffery and their seven children. The evidence suggests that it has been a Jeffery home for six generations and close on three hundred years.

The Riddings from Bentley Fields Farm

On the death of Owen Jeffery of the *Riddings*, in 1919, his obituary stated that:

The late Mr. Jeffery, who was 67 years of age, was a member of a family which had occupied that farm for about 200 years.

It was the home where Thomas and Mary Jeffery's fifteen children were born between 1844 and 1865. It was my Grandmother Ellen Jeffery's home until her marriage in 1897 and the home for which her eldest son, Jeffery Hellaby, always had a very special affection. It remains home to Margaret and Frederick Jeffery to this day.

The *Riddings* has a remarkable setting. It lies isolated and remote from the nearest villages of Alkmonton, Yeaveley and Cubley. Its only access from the road is by an unfenced lane of over half a mile, across the fields. A path, more regularly used in earlier centuries than today, links the *Riddings* to *Stydd Hall*, another of the homes with Jeffery family connections and which, like the *Riddings*, remains with the Jefferys.

TOP *The Riddings in the nineteenth century*

ABOVE *The Riddings in the twentieth century*

RIGHT *The Riddings kitchen, late nine-teenth century*

ABOVE *Approach to the Riddings*
LEFT *The Riddings in 2009*

The Homestead is situated in the centre of the Holding and comprises a well-built Brick and Tiled Dwelling House, containing two Sitting Rooms, Kitchen, Dairy, Pantry and Store Room, Cellar, Scullery and six Bedrooms.

Capital Brick and Tiled Buildings most conveniently ranged around the Farm Yard, comprising Loose Box, three-stall Stable with Loft over, Tying for 34 cows with Fodder Bing, Calf House, Loose Box with Loft over, Mixing Place with Loft over, Cart Shed and Trap House, a six-bay Dutch Hay Barn, two Grain Holes, a Wood and Corrugated-roofed Shed for 12 yearlings with Fodder Bing, Brick and Tiled Piggery and Fowl House.

There is a Paved Yard with Milk Cooling Shed and pump, Good Garden, Orchard, and EXCELLENT OLD TURF AND ARABLE LAND embraces an area of 223 acres 1 rood 4 perches.

At the time when the Bentley Estate was sold in 1920 and Thomas Jeffery became the owner occupier, the *Riddings* was described:

A Capital Dairy Farm, with an Excellent House, and Buildings, and Good Sound Land, well watered and in good heart.

Situate (sic) in the Parish of Bentley, approached from the Cubley Road, and bounded on the East Side by the Bentley Brook.

. . . . . Well Dolly, you know, Stydd Hall could be bought but it's very out of the way.

Stydd Hall, Yeaveley, had been home to Mary Robinson, before her marriage to Thomas Jeffery of the *Riddings*, in 1843. The Robinsons were tenants at *Stydd* from the 1840s until the death of Samuel Robinson at the Hall on 1 April 1912. In 1919 Thomas and Mary Jeffery's sixth son, Owen, who was then farming at the *Riddings*, bought *Stydd Hall* for his daughter, Dorothy Jeffery.

Mary Jeffery, of the *Home Farm*, *West Broughton*, grand-daughter of Owen Jeffery's elder brother John, recalled a conversation between the brothers, before Owen's daughter Dorothy, married Ernest Hand. Dorothy was always known as Dolly.

BELOW *Stydd Hall*

I remember Grandpa talking to Uncle Owen about Dolly. Well Dolly, you know, Stydd Hall could be bought but it's very out of the way. Dolly replied – I've always lived off the beaten track.

Stydd Hall Farm borders *Riddings* land. Robinsons had farmed at *Stydd* over a number of generations and there were many family links between Jefferys, Robinsons and Poysers (Margaret Jeffery of the *Riddings* married John Poyser) with *Stydd Hall* throughout the nineteenth and twentieth centuries.

Stydd Hall, said to have once been moated, has been described as *enigmatic house on an enigmatic site*.[2] Remote like the *Riddings*, it is accessed by a farm track across the fields. It is a house with a very long and fascinating history and has a monastic foundation.

The Hall was originally a medieval fortified preceptory of the Knights Hospitallers founded in 1190, during the reign of Richard the Lionheart. Today, all that remains of the thirteenth century chapel of St Mary and St John

[2] Maxwell Craven & Michael Stanley, The Derbyshire Country House

Remains of the chapel at Stydd Hall

the Baptist, which was attached to the monastery, is some of the walls and a stone font. The seventeenth-century brick tower house was built on the foundations of the domestic part of the old monastery. At the monastery's dissolution, in 1541, Henry V111 granted it to Thomas Chard, who was in the household of Anne of Cleves, Henry's fourth wife. However, the following year it was sold on to Charles Blount, the fifth Lord Mountjoy.

A substantial quantity of medieval masonry remains in the south wall of the present house, which is thought to be mainly late Elizabethan or Jacobean in date. However, the Hall underwent substantial remodelling in the 1860s. By this time it was operating as a farm-house, where the Robinsons were tenants, until it was purchased, as we have seen, by Owen Jeffery in 1919, when it became a family home for his daughter and her family in the 1920s.

There is a family legend of an underground passage linking *Stydd Hall* to *Bentley Hall*, during the sixteenth and seventeenth centuries. Romantic as this tale may be, the distance of two miles, with the Bentley Brook between the two Halls, would seem to belie the story. However, it is a story which continued to gain credence into the nineteenth century, when Hannah Hidderley as a child at *Bentley Hall*, playing with her Robinson cousins, claimed to have found the bricked-up entrance to the tunnel to *Stydd Hall*.

Bentley Hall is an extraordinarily beautiful old manor house which has played a prominent part in the Jeffery family story from the eighteenth and through much of the nineteenth and twentieth centuries. It was the home of my grandparents, William and Ellen (nee Jeffery) Hellaby for around thirty years in the early twentieth century and my father carried a photograph, of this much loved home of his youth, in his wallet until the day he died.

Over a century earlier, it was the home of Philip Oakden. He was born on the neighbouring farm of *Middleton Park* in 1759. By the early 1820s, he was farming at *Bentley Hall* and his son, Daniel Oakden, continued there until 1858.

It was, however, through Philip Oakden's daughter, Elizabeth, that the family link with *Bentley Hall* was triggered. Elizabeth married William Robinson of *Stydd Hall*. Elizabeth and William's second daughter, Mary, married Thomas Jeffery of the *Riddings* in 1843. When Elizabeth, my great, great-grandmother, was a young girl growing up at *Bentley Hall* at the end of the eighteenth and early nineteenth centuries, she would little realise that one of her own granddaughters, Ellen, would return as its mistress at the dawn of the twentieth century. Even less could she have dreamt that the imagination of one of Ellen's own granddaughters would be fired, by the way that this beautiful and historic old house, has featured in the history of the Jeffery family for nigh on two hundred years. Elizabeth Oakden was to become the grandmother of Thomas and Mary Jeffery's fifteen children of the *Riddings* but sadly, as she died in March 1832, none of them were to know her.

A very great deal has been written about *Hungry Bentley Hall*, as it was originally named. At this point, however, it is interesting to note an item published in the *Derbyshire Miscellanea Genealogica et Heraldica* Volume Two on page 268 under a heading of 'Hungry Bentley Hall' where Francis Fisher describes a visit he made in August 1884:

LEFT *Bentley Hall in the 1980s*

BELOW *Bentley Hall – late nineteenth / early twentieth century. From my father's wallet*

The ancient residence of Bentley Hall faces the high-road from Longford to Cubley. It stands upon the manor of Hungry Bentley. ……………. The principal portion of the house is brick-quoined with stone and stone-mullioned windows. The Hall proper was built in the earlier part of the 17th century, most probably by the purchaser Thomas Browne. It is now used as a farmhouse, and at the time of my visit in August 1884 was tenanted by the late John Massey, (John Massey died in September 1884) *whose grandfather and uncle* (Philip and Daniel Oakden) *had held the farm in the same way. The fireplace in the hall, partly bricked up in 1848, measures 10 feet across and 4 feet in recess. There is a very massively carved-oak staircase in the old portion of the house about five feet wide. The staircase in the later portion is about 8 feet in width, built of plain oak with oaken balustrade and balusters of curiously twisted wrought iron. The entrance door to this later hall is 12 feet high. Inside this hall there still hang several large old allegorical paintings in oil and in distemper. One of them, I ascertained represented 'Joan of Arc'. These relics of former grandeur, in their tarnished gilt frames, have a very melancholy appearance in the old house, which is now fast going into decay. I could not learn anything of their history beyond the fact that they had ' always been there'.*

At the time of his visit, my grandmother was a young woman at the *Riddings*. It would be eighteen years before she moved to *Bentley Hall* with her husband William Hellaby.

In 1920, the description of this *Important Agricultural Holding situate (sic) at HUNGRY BENTLEY on the road leading from Cubley to Alkmonton* stated:

The Farm House comprises a superior Jacobean Residence, principally built of Brick and Slated, with Stone Mullioned Windows with Latticed Panes, containing Entrance Hall laid with Minton Tile, approached from a Porch with two Stone Columns through a fine massive Iron-studded Oak Door; a Handsome Dining Room with Marble Mantel, Sitting Room, Large Kitchen, Pantry, Scullery, Side Entrance and Cellar. There is Fine Oak Staircase and another Staircase with twisted Iron Banisters leading to Six Bedrooms Bath Room (H. and C.) with Lavatory Basin, W.C., and three Attics. There is a Milk Cooling Shed, Washhouse, Tick House, and Coal House.

The Farm Buildings are adequate to the Holding and comprise: a range of four brick and tiled Piggeries, a brick and tiled Range, tying 30 cows, with Fodder Bing, Chop House and Calf House. Another Range, comprising Mixing House, two Bull Houses, Tying for 41 Cows with centre Bing, Lofts over and a Pigeon Cote. A five-bay Dutch Hay Barn, and two four-bay Dutch Hay Barns, Grain Hole. Another set of Farm Buildings comprising: a Brick, Wood and Tiled Range, tying 24 Yearlings and Fodder Bings, Loose Place, tying for 10 Yearlings, a four-bay Implement Shed, a Large Barn and an excellent Sheep Wash. Round the Stable Yard is a brick and Tiled Range comprising: Harness Room, three bay Wagon Hovel, three loose Boxes, five-stall Stable, Loft and granary over, a four-bay Cart Hovel.

ORCHARD and OLD TURF AND ARABLE LAND comprises an area of 249 acres 1 rood 23 perches.

Bentley Fields Farm has been home to Jefferys and Spencers for one hundred and twenty years. Owen Jeffery, Thomas and Mary Jeffery's eighth child, farmed both the *Riddings* and *Bentley Fields* land from 1895 until 1914. From 1914, when Owen and his family returned to the *Riddings*, his nephew, Percy Spencer, took over at *Bentley Fields*. Percy Spencer was the son of his sister Mary Jeffery, who had married Herbert Spencer in 1888.

ABOVE *Bentley Fields – early twentieth century*
BELOW *Bentley Fields 2009*

The Home Farm, West Broughton

In 1920 *Bentley Fields* was described as: *A desirable Compact and Arable Farm* with:

The Farm House comprises a substantial Brick and tiled Dwelling House, containing Drawing room with Two China Closets, Dining room, Kitchen, Back Kitchen with glazed Sink, Larder, Two Cellars, Milk Cooling House with large zinc Tank and Water laid on, five bedrooms on the first floor and two Men's bedrooms, Three Attics, Principal and Secondary Staircases, Paved Yard with Pump, Washhouse, Dairy and Coal House.

The Capital Farm Buildings Brick Built and Tiled, are conveniently arranged around three sides of the Yard, and includes Calf House, Young Stock Shed for 17, Tying for 51 Cows with Fodder Bings, Mixing Place with Loft over, Engine House, Covered Grain Hole, Tying for 16 Yearlings, Barn, Calf House and Implement Shed. Another Range includes five-stall Stable, trap House, Man's room and Lofting over, a Range of four Brick and Tiled piggeries, Another range comprising Large Loose Box, four-bay Cart Hovel, Wood and tiled Poultry Houses, a nine-bay Dutch Hay Barn, Grain Hole.

EXCELLENT OLD TURF AND ARABLE LAND embraces an area of 223 acres 1 rood and 4 perches.

The *Home Farm, West Broughton*, formerly known as *West Broughton Hall*, stands on a knoll in the midst of the shrunken settlement of West Broughton, Doveridge. It has been a Jeffery home for one hundred and twenty-one years. John Jeffery, born in 1849, was the fourth son of Thomas and Mary Jeffery of the *Riddings*. John married Maria Wilson in 1880 and their three children were born at *Somersal Mill*. In 1889, John and Maria, with their young family, eight-year-old Mary, five-year-old Offley and three-year-old Katie, moved to the *Home Farm, West Broughton*, on the Vernon Estate.

John and Maria's children, and later Offley's children, grew up in this beautiful old house. The oldest parts, above the front entrance porch, date back to the four-teenth century. Much of the house is sixteenth century with eighteenth-century additions. To this day, it remains the home of John Jeffery's youngest grand-daughter, Mary Jeffery.

BELOW TOP LEFT *Somersal Mill*
BELOW TOP RIGHT *Somersal House*
BELOW BOTTOM *Northfields Farm, formerly Potter Somersal*

When John and Maria Jeffery and their family moved to the *Home Farm, West Broughton* in 1889, Margaret and John Poyser, with their family of nine children, moved into *Somersal Mill* from *Parkside Farm*, Ramshorn in the Staffordshire Moorlands. Margaret, also born at the *Riddings*, was John Jeffery's eldest sister. The Poyser children were to grow up close by their Jeffery cousins at the *Home Farm, West Broughton*, and also, close by their nine cousins at *Northfields* and *Somersal House*,

Northfields Farm, formerly known as *Potter Somersal*, was farmed by Thomas and Mary Jeffery's second son, William. William's son, William Charles, continued at *Northfields* when his father took over neighbouring *Somersal House*, which remained with the Jefferys and their descendants until 1975.

In 1920 William Charles Jeffery, with his wife Mary and their young family, twelve year-old Constance,

Aston House in the 1940s

nine-year-old Henry and six-year-old Frank moved to *Aston House*, Sudbury. *Aston House*, built in 1861, has been a Jeffery home for ninety years. William Charles's son Henry continued farming there and his grandson, Robert Jeffery, will continue to farm there until the spring of 2011. Like the *Home Farm,* West Broughton, *Aston House*, is part of the Vernon Estate.

A few years before William Jeffery moved to *Aston House,* it was farmed by Frederick Snow (who was to become father-in-law of Ellen Jeffery's granddaughter, my sister Marjorie). At this time, it was described in a farming article in the *DERBYSHIRE ADVERTISER* of 17 June 1913:

Aston House it is named, and the homestead, with its surroundings of many acres of some of the choicest of Derbyshire pasture, is one of the best and most expansive, under the Vernon's rule.

It was a house which William's daughter-in-law, Vera Jeffery, came to love and described in her memoirs as

'written on my heart'. It was also a home that I came to know as a child when my father visited his Jeffery cousins.

❦

Snitterton Hall was a Jeffery home between 1895 and 1905. It was the home of my grandmother's elder sister Clara of whom I became very fond when she lived with us during the winter of 1940. Thomas and Mary Jeffery's sixth daughter, Clara, had married Arthur Cook in 1882. *Snitterton*, an extraordinarily beautiful old house, was also the home from which Mary Ellen Jeffery, daughter of my grandmother's brother George, married in 1902.

Snitterton Hall in 2008

Snitterton Hall, lying west of Matlock, is an Elizabethan manor house, built in the 1630s, on the site of a medieval manor which appeared in Domesday. It has recently been restored and is now once again a family home. At the time when my Great Aunt Clara Cook (nee Jeffery) was there with Arthur Cook and their family, it was a tenanted, working farm.

Mary Jeffery from the *Home Farm, West Broughton*, who has been very generous with sharing her memories with me, recalled:

I remember taking mother and father up to Snitterton Hall to see where the Cooks had lived. Father (Offley Jeffery) *used to go as a boy to visit them. I remember Cousin Ida* (daughter of Arthur Wood Jeffery and her father's cousin) *talking about Cousin Gertrude Mary Cook.*

The *Riddings*, *Stydd Hall*, *Bentley Fields*, *Home Farm, West Broughton* and *Somersal Mill*, remain with Jefferys and their descendants, Spencers and Poysers, to this day.

PART TWO

THE
PREDECESSORS

THE PREDECESSORS

Two Hundred Years and
The First Seven Generations

The Early Forebears

JEFFERYS: The First Six Generations

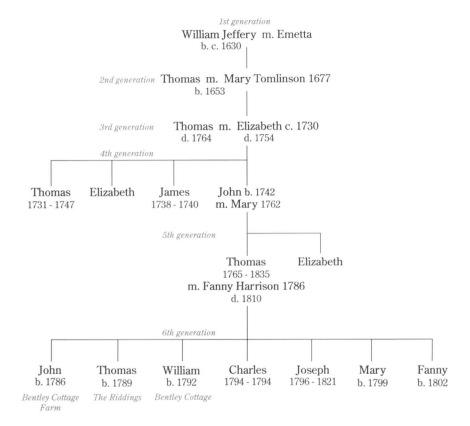

1st generation
William Jeffery m. Emetta
b. c. 1630

2nd generation Thomas m. Mary Tomlinson 1677
b. 1653

3rd generation Thomas m. Elizabeth c. 1730
d. 1764   d. 1754

4th generation

Thomas   Elizabeth   James   John b. 1742
1731 - 1747   1738 - 1740   m. Mary 1762

5th generation

Thomas   Elizabeth
1765 - 1835
m. Fanny Harrison 1786
d. 1810

6th generation

John   Thomas   William   Charles   Joseph   Mary   Fanny
b. 1786   b. 1789   b. 1792   1794 - 1794   1796 - 1821   b. 1799   b. 1802
Bentley Cottage   *The Riddings*   *Bentley Cottage*
Farm

The Jeffery family is traced back over thirteen generations. Our story starts in the seventeenth century with FIRST generation WILLIAM, who was born around 1630, at the time when King Charles I was on the throne. William grew up during the time of the Civil War between 1642 and 1649. During the Civil War Derby, and parts of the south of Derbyshire, supported the Parliamentarians. However, much of the centre and north of the county were Royalist strongholds where many of the principal landowning families, including the Vernons, the major land-owning family in our area, declared for the King.

William would have been about twelve years old when the King visited Derby on 15 September 1642 and when in December in 1642, the Earl of Newcastle invaded Derbyshire and raised a Royalist force. He would have been about fourteen when, during February 1644, Royalists from Bakewell and other parts of the county, assembled daily in Ashbourne in such force as to obstruct all communication between the town and neighbouring villages. This would have caused enormous hardship in the area. There were a number of skirmishes between Royalists and Roundheads and also, in 1644, a detachment of royalist troops sought shelter in Boyleston Church, less than three miles from Alkmonton. Parliamentary forces surrounded the church and captured the whole regiment.

The church registers for Longford parish, which are preserved from 1538, include two entries for the burial of soldiers in August 1645 and in November 1645 that of a local man who had been murdered by soldiers:

John Malley who had his house broken in sundry places, the first November the night, and because they could not get in, and would not yield, they fired at him with a slugge into the head. He died and was buried, the second day of November, 1645.

In August 1645, shortly after the fatal battle of Naseby Charles I with the remnants of his army of only 3000 men, visited Ashbourne and attended a service in St Oswald's Church, known as the Cathedral of the Peak. An extract from the church register states:

1645, August. King Charles came to church, and many more, and talked with Mr. Peacock, the vicar.

However, the impact of the Civil War was not the sole matter of serious concern for the people of Ashbourne and the surrounding villages at this time. Later in the very same month of August following the King's visit, when the parish church had been packed with a very large congregation, Ashbourne and neighbouring Clifton were visited by the horrors of the Plague. In the accounts of the churchwardens and constables of Uttoxeter, the following items occur:

1645. August 26th: Paid to Ashbourne by the Churchwardens of Uttoxeter when the town was infested with the Plague, £5.
Paid to the inhabitants of Clifton, when the Plague was there, £5.

A monumental inscription in Chesterfield Church, to the memory of Paul Webster, a native of Ashbourne, states that 'his removals from Ashbourne were occasioned by the plague and civil wars'.[1]

When King Charles was executed in 1649, William Jeffery would have been a young man. He had married by the time Oliver Cromwell became Lord Protector in 1653. William married Emetta and their son, Thomas, was born at the end of 1653 during the Commonwealth period when, for eleven years, England was a Republic

---

[1] Dawson and Hobbs 1839

and a military dictatorship. The name 'Thomas' was carried forward in the Jeffery family through the next four hundred years.

⁂

The SECOND generation was marked by William and Emetta's son, THOMAS Jeffery, who was baptised on 11 December 1653, at Brailsford, Derbyshire. During the decade of the Commonwealth, the area remained a Royalist stronghold. In 1654, Edmund Browne of *Bentley Hall*, together with his Vernon in-laws, was implicated in a conspiracy against Oliver Cromwell. An extract from the *Mercurious Politicus*, a newssheet of 1654 states:

Last week a new conspiracy was detected against his Highness, Oliver Cromwell, and the present Government. Five chests and two trunks of arms were discovered in one place in London which were to be conveyed to the country. Divers persons are apprehended and in the Tower ……………… Divers arms were conveyed to Derbyshire to the house of one Mr. Edward Vernon, who is brought up and committed also, and with him was brought up his uncle of Stockley Park and one Mr. Browne of Hungry Bentley in the county of Derby.

Edmund Browne's home was *Bentley Hall*. (*See* PARTS ONE and FOUR)

One is led to suspect, that the Restoration of Charles II in 1660 was greeted joyously in this part of Derbyshire.

Thomas Jeffery would be six years old when the monarchy was restored on 29 May 1660. The Restoration provided an opportunity for widespread jubilation. The tradition of ringing the church bells on 29 May, called Oak Apple Day, to commemorate Charles II's successful escape by hiding in an oak tree after the Battle of Worcester, survived in several places in Derbyshire for many generations. Indeed, my own mother told me of her own childhood memories of its celebration in Cubley, in the early twentieth century. For Thomas and his family, May 29 was probably a fete day throughout his life.

When Thomas married Mary Tomlinson, on 29 September 1677 in St Oswald's Church, Ashbourne, Charles II had been restored to the throne for over seventeen years. Thomas and Mary went on to have a son, THOMAS, marking the THIRD generation. About 1730, Hanoverian Derbyshire saw this Thomas married to

Elizabeth and generations three, four and five take the Jefferys through the eighteenth century.

❦

The children of Thomas and Elizabeth mark the FOURTH generation. Their four children were all baptised in St Chad's Church, Longford. Their first-born son, also christened Thomas, was baptised on 7 March 1731. Their daughter, Elizabeth, was baptised on 29 July 1736 and two years later, their second son, James, on 29 July 1738. These three children were born during the reign of George II. However, Thomas and Elizabeth's son James died young: he was just two years old when he was buried in Longford, on 10 August 1740. On 6 April 1742, another son, JOHN, who carried the line through the FOURTH generation, was baptised at Longford.

Thomas and Elizabeth's son John was only three years old when, in 1745, Charles Edward Stuart, the Young Pretender also known as Bonnie Prince Charlie, advanced through the north of England to Ashbourne with an army of 5000 men. The advance of this victorious Scottish army, seeking the restoration of the Stuarts, created mayhem in the area. The church registers of Longford parish for August 1745 record the burials of several soldiers slain in these civil wars.

The *DERBY MERCURY* for 12 December 1745 reported:

During their stay in Ashbourne, the rebels plundered some gentlemen's houses to a great value. Two of them went to Clifton, near Ashbourne, and demanded a horse of one Humphrey Brown; upon his refusal, they shot him dead on the spot, and then took to their heels. They also shot an innkeeper at Hanging Bridge, and plundered and robbed all around the country.

These tumultuous times are associated with the family legend of *Stydd Hall*, Yeaveley, when a French soldier, who supported the Jacobite cause, is alleged to have sought sanctuary at the Hall and solace with a Derbyshire maid! The story goes, that a soldier with the name of Jeffery (Old French 'Jeufroi' or 'Jeffroi') was somewhat waylaid by the charms of a young girl at *Stydd Hall*. He was said to have hidden in a well and thus avoided returning with the retreating Jacobite army. As yet, there remains no firm evidence for this story, but it is intriguing to speculate on its origin. (For Stydd Hall *see* PARTS ONE and FOUR).

A court martial was instituted to enquire into the case, and the spirit dealer being adjudged guilty, was sentenced to lose his ears.

A curious incident in relation to the Pretender's visit to Ashbourne was still in circulation towards the middle of the nineteenth century:

A private, passing through the market place, requested a lad to direct him to a shop where he might purchase spirit. The lad accordingly pointed out a spirit-shop, the proprietor of which happened to be standing by at the time. He, fearing the visit of the Highlander, thought proper to deny the fact, and accused the lad of lying. The Highlander, having ascertained that the person did keep a spirit-shop reported the occurrence to his commanding officer. A court martial was instituted to enquire into the case, and the spirit dealer being adjudged guilty, was sentenced to lose his ears. His wife, a beautiful woman, was horror-struck at the barbarous sentence. She flew to the Chevalier, and by her tears and urgent entreaties, succeeded in gaining her husband's pardon.[2]

For Thomas and Elizabeth Jeffery with their three young children, Thomas, Elizabeth and John, the turmoil in the area was compounded when, five years after the birth of their youngest son, John, their first-born son, Thomas, died. He was buried on 16 April 1747 in Longford churchyard.

Only two of Thomas and Elizabeth's children, Elizabeth and John, survived into adulthood. Their eldest daughter, Elizabeth, was eighteen and their son, John, only twelve, when their mother, Elizabeth, died in 1754. She was buried on the first of October. Six years later, daughter Elizabeth married Thomas Ryde on 23 September 1760. Elizabeth's bridegroom, Thomas, came from the village of Edlaston south of Ashbourne. Thomas and Elizabeth's son, John, married Mary in 1762. It is this JOHN who was to continue the direct line into the FOURTH generation. His father, Thomas, remained a

[2] The History of the County of Derby by Stephen Glover & Thomas Noble. Pub. by H. Mozeley & Son 1829

Longford Church

widower for ten years. He died in 1764, during the early years of the reign of George III and was buried on 17 May in Longford churchyard.

The two children of John and Mary carried the line into the FIFTH generation. They were named after their grandparents. John and Mary's daughter Elizabeth was baptised on 20 March 1763 and their son THOMAS on 5 September 1765, at Longford. It was Thomas who carried the direct line for the FIFTH generation. It was during this generation that the *Riddings* began to feature in the family story. It was also the period when Colonial America gained independence following the Revolutionary War. Exactly one hundred years later, in 1865, another Thomas Jeffery, a direct descendant, was to leave the *Riddings* to make his life in America.

On 15 October 1782, John and Mary's nineteen-year-old daughter, Elizabeth, married Joseph Smith of the *Riddings*. In the spring of 1786 their daughter Mary was born. Sadly, in May, she was both baptised and buried at Longford. The following year, their son Joseph was born in 1787. He was baptised on 22 March. Five years later, in 1792, a second daughter, Margaret, was born. All three children are recorded in the Longford parish register as the daughter or son of Joseph Smith of the *Riddings*, Bentley.

Twenty-year-old THOMAS, son of John and Mary Jeffery, who marked the FIFTH generation, married Fanny Harrison on the last day of January 1786 at Somersal Herbert Nonconformist Chapel. Fanny, daughter of John and Mary Harrison of Somersal Herbert, was a young bride. She did not reach her sixteenth birthday until four months later, on 27 May. Thomas and Fanny had seven children during the following fifteen years. Of their two elder sons, John, born in 1786, farmed at *Bentley Cottage Farm* and Thomas, born two years later, farmed at the *Riddings*.

Thomas and Fanny's family comprised five sons and two daughters. Their two elder sons, John baptised on 3 January 1786 and Thomas, on 9 September 1789, were followed by three more boys: William, baptised on 29 February 1792 and Charles on 2 June 1794. Charles survived for less than three months. He was buried at Longford on 22 August 1794. These were the years of the French Revolution and the beginning of the Napoleonic Wars. Their youngest son, Joseph, was baptised on New Years Day 1796. However, Joseph's life was also relatively short. He died as a young man twenty-five years later. He was buried in Longford on 8 November 1821. Their two daughters, Mary, baptised 11 February 1799 and Fanny, baptised on 3 March 1802, completed their family.

Thomas and Fanny's family did not continue long as a unit. Some years following their youngest daughter, Mary's, birth, Fanny's health began to fail and she developed tuberculosis. Her decline was slow but she finally succumbed on 22 October 1810. Her two young daughters, Fanny and Mary, were only eight and eleven and her younger sons, Joseph and William, fourteen and eighteen. Her elder sons, John and Thomas, had reached maturity, Thomas was twenty-one and John, twenty-three. Fanny was buried in the churchyard in Longford and her tombstone reads as follows.

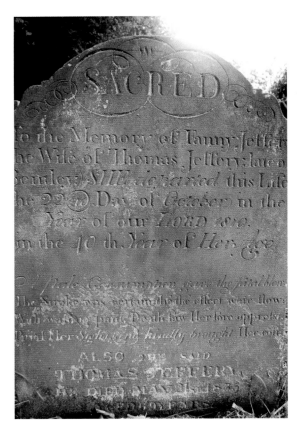

Sacred

To the memory of Fanny Jeffery

The wife of Thomas Jeffery

Of Bentley she departed this life

The twenty second day of October

In the year of our Lord 1810

In the Fortieth year of her age

A pale consumption gave the fatal blow

The stroke was certain tho' the effect were slow

With waning pain death saw her sore opprest

Pities her sighs and kindly gave her rest

Also the said Thomas Jeffery

He died the 31st of May 1835

LEFT *The tombstone of Fanny Jeffery 1786–1810 and Thomas Jeffery 1765-1835, Longford Church*

It is during the nineteenth century that we begin to find significant written records of Hungry Bentley in the form of county histories and local directories. In Glover's *History of the County of Derby, 1829*, Hungry Bentley was described as:

A small village, township and constabulary in the parish of Longford and hundred of Appletree ('hundred' being one of the administrative divisions of the county of Derby), *four miles south-west of Ashbourne and eleven miles northwest of Derby. The village contains thirteen houses, thirteen families and eighty-eight inhabitants who are chiefly employed in agriculture. Although here is no place of worship in the village, the remains of a church can be seen. The township contains about 1050 acres of 'middling' land and the average rental is about 32s. per acre. The estimated annual value of the buildings and land is about £1268. 1s. The average parochial expenses are about the same as Alkmonton. The vicar of Longford holds the great tithes and Sir Robert Wilmot of Chaddesdon, Bart. is proprietor and lord of the manor.*

In 1829 at least nine of the recorded inhabitants of Hungry Bentley were Jefferys. At *Bentley Cottage* were William and Elizabeth Jeffery with their fourteen-year-old son William and eleven-year-old daughter Fanny. The *Riddings* at this time was the home of Thomas and Margaret Jeffery with their twelve-year-old daughter Fanny and their six-year-old son Thomas together with widower, sixty-four-year-old Thomas Jeffery.

Thomas died twenty-five years after Fanny. His death was reported in the *DERBY MERCURY* 27 May 1835:

DEATHS
On the 20th instant, at Hungry Bentley in this County, Mr. Thomas Jeffery in the 71st. year of his age.

In the light of the monumental inscription above, indicating that Fanny and Thomas were 'of Bentley', it is possible to speculate that they farmed at the *Riddings* after Thomas's sister, Elizabeth, was there with her husband Joseph Smith and family. Alternatively, it might be inferred that the Bentley refers to *Bentley Fields* or *Bentley Cottage Farm*. It is difficult to confirm either case. However, it does seem to be a high probability that Thomas and Fanny Jeffery were the first to farm at the *Riddings*. What is certain is that Thomas and Fanny's son, Thomas, farmed at the *Riddings* in the next generation.

The Early Bentley Jefferys

Descendants of Sixth Generation John Jeffery of Bentley Cottage Farm, Eldest Son of Thomas and Fanny Jeffery

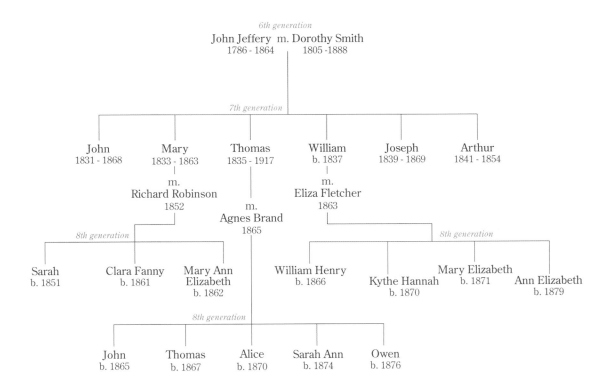

The story becomes more detailed in these years as more information is available via the official registration of births, marriages and deaths, tombstones and the census.

The next two generations take the Jefferys through the nineteenth century. The SIXTH generation continued the family story, primarily through Thomas and Fanny's three eldest sons: John, Thomas and William. It was THOMAS who carried the direct line and became the grandfather of the fifteen children of the *Riddings*. His story will be told later.

The story of this SIXTH generation opens with the eldest son, John, who was baptised at Longford Church on 3 January 1786. Forty-four years later he married Dorothy Smith on 14 October 1830 and his marriage

also was celebrated at St Chad's, Longford. John's bride was born in 1805, the year of Nelson's victory at Trafalgar. She was nineteen years younger than her bridegroom. Dorothy was from Yeaveley, the village next to Alkmonton, and had been baptised at the adjacent village church of Shirley on 16 June 1805. John and Dorothy, who now farmed at *Bentley Cottage Farm*, had five sons and a daughter during the first twenty years of their marriage. Their first son, John, was baptised on 27 February 1831, the year before the Great Reform Act. Two years later, their only daughter, Mary, was baptised on 28 July 1833. Their second son, Thomas, was born on 2 May 1835 and baptised on the 31 May 1836. Their son, William, was baptised on 14 May 1837, the year of the death of William IV and accession of Queen Victoria. Their last two sons were Joseph, born in 1839, and Arthur in 1841.

Bentley Cottage Farm

In the spring of 1841 John and Dorothy were farming at *Bentley Cottage Farm* with five of their children: John was now aged ten, Mary eight and the three younger boys, Thomas aged six, William four and Joseph two. Dorothy gave birth to their last child, Arthur, later that year. Also living and working on the farm was John's fifteen-year-old nephew William (his younger brother William's son) together with a farm labourer eighteen-year-old Charles Fritterton. In addition, Hannah Millington (eighteen) and Sarah Wardle (thirteen) were living in as house servants.

During the summer of 1850, John and Dorothy's daughter, Mary, now seventeen, came to know eighteen-year-old Richard Robinson from neighbouring *Stydd Hall*. Romance clearly blossomed for the two young people and one can imagine them meeting in the fields between *Stydd* and *Bentley Cottage Farm*. The outcome of their trysts was made evident in February 1851 as,

on the 30 March 1851 census, John and Dorothy's one month-old granddaughter, Sarah Jeffery, appeared, in addition to their own six children. Sarah was to become the great grandmother of Margaret Walker (*see* acknowledgements). Sarah's father and Mary's lover, Richard Robinson, was recorded at his home at *Stydd* at this time. It was not until a year later, on 10 March 1852, that Richard Robinson and Mary Jeffery were married, perhaps discreetly, at All Saint's Church, Derby. Richard then moved into *Bentley Cottage Farm* to be with Mary and their year-old daughter, Sarah.

1854 was the year when Britain was at war in the Crimea. It was also a year marred by tragedy for the family at *Bentley Cottage Farm*. Christmas this year was sad for all the family for, on 15 December, thirteen-year-old Arthur, John and Dorothy's youngest son, died. His funeral took place just one week before Christmas and he was buried in Longford Churchyard.

In
Memory of
Arthur, son of
John and Dorothy Jeffery
of Hungry Bentley
Who died December 15th 1854
Aged 13 years

Ye who with youthful steps lightly
tread o'er these green hillocks of the
unconscious dead pause a few
moments at this lowly tomb and
learn an early death may be thy
doom

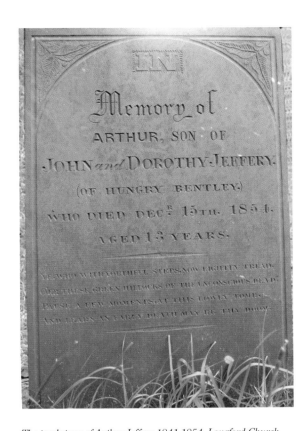

The tombstone of Arthur Jeffery 1841-1854, Longford Church

MARRIAGES
On Thursday the 19th inst. at the Parish Church, Longford, by the Rev. T. A. Anson, Mr. William Jeffery of Hungry Bentley, to Miss Eliza Fletcher of Rodsley.

Six years later, by the spring of 1861, the picture of the Jeffery family at *Bentley Cottage Farm* had changed from that of ten years earlier. By 1861, the year when Queen Victoria's consort, Prince Albert died, John was seventy-three and Dorothy, fifty-eight. Their eldest son, John, had left home and the household now comprised their sons Thomas, William and Joseph together with their daughter Mary and son-in-law Richard Robinson. Mary and Richard now had a second daughter, five-month-old baby Clara Fanny, a sister for ten-year-old Sarah. At some time after April 1861 Richard and Mary, with their daughters, moved out of *Bentley Cottage Farm* and went to live in Sheffield where their third daughter, Mary Ann Elizabeth, was born in 1862. Clara Fanny was only a year old when her sister was born.

In 1863, John and Dorothy's third son, William, married Eliza Fletcher on the 19 November and the event was reported in the *DERBY MERCURY* 25 November 1863:

However, the end of the year was yet again overshadowed by death, when their daughter Mary died on 2 December, aged only thirty. In Yorkshire Mary's health had declined seriously after the births of her two youngest daughters Clara Fanny and Mary Ann Elizabeth. Her death certificate stated that she had suffered from 'ulceration of the bowel' for two years. Her death, from 'stricture of the bowel', must have been a painful one. Her two young daughters were left motherless. This inevitably meant that twelve-year-old Sarah needed to grow up very quickly when she became 'mother' to her young sisters, Clara Fanny and Mary Ann Elizabeth. Mary was brought back to Derbyshire and was buried at Edlaston. Surprisingly, Mary Ann Elizabeth was nearly

LEFT *Sarah, daughter of Mary Jeffery and Richard Robinson who married William Saunders*

BELOW *Sarah with her husband William Saunders and family*

two years old when she was baptised in Yeaveley, on 4 September 1864. Later, Richard married again, this time to Elizabeth Doxey, from Osmaston, and continued living in Sheffield.

By this time, however, father John's health was failing and in the summer of 1864 he died aged seventy-six. He was saved from having to witness the death of his eldest son, thirty-seven-year-old John, who succumbed to typhoid fever and died in the Derby Infirmary on 25 February 1868. His younger brother, Thomas, was present at his death. John's death was reported in the *DERBY MERCURY* 11 March 1868:

DEATHS
On the 25th ult. John, the eldest son of Mr. John Jeffery late of Hungry Bentley, in the 37th year of his age

Dorothy's second son, Thomas, and fourth son, Joseph, had moved to Leeds some time before 1865. In 1865, Thomas married Agnes Brand from Scotland, in Leeds. His younger brother, Joseph, died, aged only thirty, in 1869, also in Leeds. The Jeffery connection with this Yorkshire city is intriguing as, in the next generation, two sons of Thomas and Mary Jeffery of the *Riddings*, also spent some years working in Leeds in the 1870s. The link, as yet, remains unexplained.

For Dorothy, the years between 1854 and 1869, had been marred by tragedy and loss with the deaths of four of her

children, Arthur, Mary, John and Joseph and also of her husband John. In 1871, she was with her son William and daughter-in law Eliza. They were now living in Alfreton in north Derbyshire, where William kept the Three Horseshoes Inn. In 1881, she was living on her own at 56 Bridge Gate, Derby. Seven years later, she died aged eighty-three, in 1888. Her death was registered in Belper, Derbyshire. The registering of the death in Belper, the registration district for Denby may suggest that she returned to live with her son William and family, who were now farming in Denby.

Dorothy's son, Thomas, was working at neighbouring *Bentley Hall Farm* in 1861. By 1865 he had married Agnes Brand in Leeds and their first son, John, was born on 22 July 1865. Their second son, Thomas, was born on 27 April 1867 and two more children had followed by the summer of 1872. By this time, however, Thomas and Agnes had decided to emigrate to Canada. On 18 July 1872 the family sailed from Liverpool on the *SS Hibernian* arriving in Quebec ten days later. Thomas was now thirty-seven and Agnes was thirty-three. Their two young sons, John and Thomas, were six and four, their daughter, Alice, was two and the baby only a month old. It would have been a sad day for Thomas's mother, Dorothy, when she bade farewell to her son Thomas and four of her grandchildren.

Thomas was not the first Jeffery to settle in the New World. (Thomas and Joseph Jeffery, from the *Riddings*,

BELOW LEFT *William Frederick Jeffery, third son of John and Dorothy Jeffery*

BELOW RIGHT *William Henry Jeffery, son of William Frederick of Denby*

had already left in the mid 1860s. Their brother George emigrated to Canada in the 1880s). For Thomas and Agnes, their early years in Canada, were challenging. Their two-year-old daughter Alice and the baby did not survive the family's difficult early years. They had two more children, Sarah born on 29 April 1874 and Owen born on 26 July 1876. Both of these youngest children were born in Ontario. (*See* PART THREE: THE PIONEERS)

Dorothy's son William and his family were at the Three Horseshoes Inn in Alfreton between 1867 and 1871. Prior to moving to Alfreton, William and Eliza's son, William Henry, was born in 1866 in Mansfield, Nottinghamshire. Their daughters Kythe Hannah and Mary Elizabeth were born in Alfreton in 1870 and 1871. Following the births of their daughters, William left the Three Horseshoes and returned to farming. The family settled at *High Park Farm*, Denby, Derbyshire, where their youngest daughter, Ann Eliza, was born in 1879. William's son, William Henry, continued farming there and *High Park Farm* remained in the family for over a hundred years.

William and his son, William Henry, and his great grandson, John, became prominent figures in the local community. I am indebted to his great grandson, John Jeffery, for the photographs and information about his grandfather and great-grandfather.

The photograph of the older man, the one with the shaggy beard, is my Great Grandfather, William Frederick Jeffery, of High Park Farm, Denby. He was Surveyor of Highways from 1896 – 1891 and Chairman of the Vestry Committee in 1880. The Vestry Committee was superseded by Parish Councils in 1894.

The younger is my Grandfather, William Henry Jeffery, also of High Park Farm who was on the Parish Council 1897 – 1911 and on the Belper Rural District Council.

The story of the sixth generation also includes Thomas and Fanny's third son, William who was born in 1792. William married Elizabeth Allen of Measham, Leicestershire, on 9 December 1817, in Derby.

JEFFERYS: The Early Bentley Jefferys

Descendants of Sixth Generation William Jeffery of Bentley Cottage, Third Son of Thomas and Fanny Jeffery

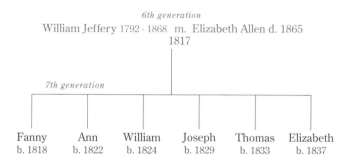

6th generation
William Jeffery 1792 - 1868 m. Elizabeth Allen d. 1865
1817

7th generation

Fanny	Ann	William	Joseph	Thomas	Elizabeth
b. 1818	b. 1822	b. 1824	b. 1829	b. 1833	b. 1837

William and Elizabeth lived at *Bentley Cottage* and their six children, Fanny, Ann, William, Joseph, Thomas and Elizabeth, born between 1818 and 1837 were to grow up close by their cousins at the *Riddings* and *Bentley Cottage Farm*. The youngest daughter, Elizabeth, married Charles Outram when she was nineteen in July 1856. The marriage was reported in the *DERBY MERCURY* 9 July 1856:

MARRIAGES
On Monday, July 7th, at St John's Church, Alkmonton, by the Rev. A. Slight M.A., Charles Outram, to Elizabeth Jeffery, both of Hungry Bentley.

Elizabeth's mother, Elizabeth, died nine years later, on 29 May 1865 and her death was reported in the *DERBY MERCURY* 7 June 1865:

DEATH
On the 29th. ult. Elizabeth, wife of Mr. William Jeffery of Hungry Bentley, aged 70.

William died three years later on 31 March 1868 and his death was also recorded as follows in the *DERBY MERCURY* 15 April 1868:

DEATHS
On the 31st. ult., at Hungry Bentley, Mr William Jeffery, aged 76.

There is an intriguing story relating to this William Jeffery and his family of *Bentley Cottage*. The day before he died, he signed his will. It was a will in which he left everything to just one of his sons, disinheriting all of his other five children. It was his youngest son Thomas who was his sole beneficiary. The will was signed both by himself and his youngest son. It was witnessed, with a signature, by his neighbour, Thomas Coxon.

This is the last will and testament of me, William Jeffery. I give and bequeath to my son Thomas Jeffery all my goods and chattels in my home situate (sic) at Hungry Bentley in the County of Derby be the same more or less and also what money I may have after all my debts and funeral expenses so and that my other children shall not have anything belonging to me in my said House in aforesaid situate at Hungry Bentley in the said County of Derby and that my said son Thomas Jeffery shall have the same said goods and chattels at my decease to have and to do with them as he thinks fit all whatever and whatsoever in both my House and Garden, out premises and we all witness in his presence and at the request of the same William Jeffery be witness to the above the thirtieth day of March 1868 – William Jeffery - signed and sealed by us – Thomas Jeffery – Thomas Coxon.

William and Elizabeth were both buried at St Chad's, Longford.

The Riddings Jefferys

Thomas and Margaret (nee Coxon) Jeffery of the Riddings, and their Children

The SIXTH generation story continues with the direct line of Thomas and Fanny's second son, THOMAS, who was baptised on 9 September 1789. Thomas farmed at the *Riddings* at the same time as his elder brother John was farming across the fields at *Bentley Cottage Farm* and his younger brother William was at *Bentley Cottage*. It was this Thomas who was destined to become the grandfather of the fifteen children who become central to the Jeffery story from the mid-nineteenth century. This Thomas poses something of a mystery. The question as to how he came to warrant a remarkable and terrible epitaph on his tombstone in Longford churchyard must so far remain unanswered.

Thomas married Margaret Coxon on 12 February 1817, at St Oswald's Church, Ashbourne. They had three children all born at the *Riddings*. Their only daughter, Fanny, born on 6 August 1817, was baptised at Nethergreen Independent Chapel, Yeaveley, on 17 August. Almost six years later their son, Thomas, was born on 8 April 1823. He was baptised, at the Lady Huntingdon Chapel in Ashbourne. It was another seven years before their younger son, John, was born on 1 March 1830 and he too was baptised at the Huntingdon Zion Chapel on 22 September 1830. The baptisms in nonconformist chapels suggests that a religious schism divided the family from their Anglican background

Thomas and Margaret's family was complete by 1830 but Margaret did not live to see her youngest son's tenth birthday. Her health had begun to fail sometime after John's birth and her decline may well have accelerated when her only daughter married young and against the wishes of her father, Thomas. Eighteen-year-old Fanny married Thomas Hunt, in 1835. Margaret, however, lived to see only two of her grandchildren, John and Thomas Hunt, before her early death.

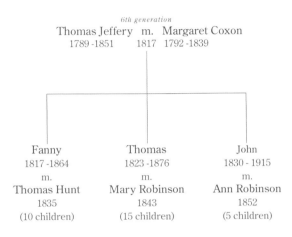

6th generation
Thomas Jeffery m. Margaret Coxon
1789 -1851   1817   1792 -1839

Fanny	Thomas	John
1817 -1864	1823 -1876	1830 - 1915
m.	m.	m.
Thomas Hunt	Mary Robinson	Ann Robinson
1835	1843	1852
(10 children)	(15 children)	(5 children)

When Margaret died, on 16 November 1839, she was only forty-seven. She was survived by her widower Thomas, her sons, John and Thomas, aged nine and sixteen respectively, and her twenty-year-old married daughter, Fanny, together with her two young grandsons, John

RIGHT *The Riddings Farm*

and Thomas, aged three and one. Her death was reported in the *DERBY MERCURY* of 30 November 1839:

*On the 16th inst., after a long illness, Margaret, wife of Thomas
Jeffery of the Riddings, Hungry Bentley, deservedly respected and
much lamented by a numerous circle of friends and relatives.*

Margaret was buried at Longford and the epitaph on her
tombstone reads:

Sacred

*To the memory of Margaret
Wife of Thomas Jeffery
Of Hungry Bentley
Who died November 16th 1839
Aged 47 years*

*Afflictions sore long time I bore
Physicians all in vain
Till God till please to give me ease
And keep me from my pain*

After Margaret's death, Thomas continued farming at the
Riddings with his two young sons, sixteen-year-old
Thomas and nine-year-old John. The year of Margaret's
death was a year when government legislation was to
have a major impact on all landholders and farmers across
the land. In 1839 the Commutation of Tithes Act was
passed. Until this time, farmers had followed the feudal
system whereby they were required to pay annual tithes
to the Church. The new legislation required apportion-
ment of a Rent Charge in lieu of a Tithe. Hungry Bentley covered an area of 1074 acres, I rood and 28 perches
of which 642 acres 1 rood 25 perches was subject to
tithe. The *Riddings* comprised 110 acres 3 roods 36
perches, approximately a sixth of the total.

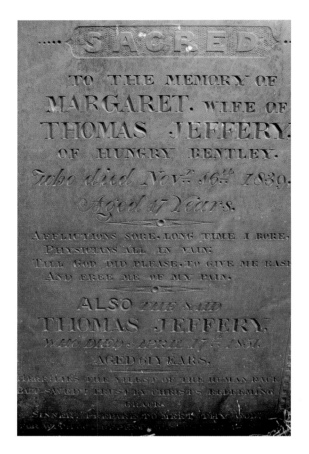

The following is a record of the agreement:

*ARTICLES OF AGREEMENT for the commutation of the
Tithes of the township of Bentley in the parish of Longford in the
county of Derby in pursuance of the Act for the commutation of
Tithes in England and Wales made at a meeting on the twenty
ninth day of June in the year of Our Lord One thousand Eight
hundred and thirty nine and between Sir Robert Wilmot
Baronet and Frances Buckston Widow, owner of all the lands
within the said Township* (Hungry Bentley) *of the one part and
the Reverend Frederick Anson, Doctor of Divinity, of the said
parish and owner of all the tithes.*

*It is hereby agreed that the annual sum of Sixty Seven Pounds
and ten Shillings by way of Rent Charge shall be paid to the said
Frederick Anson as Vicar of the said Parish and owner of all the
tithes of the said Township.*

The new Act required a full and detailed analysis providing names of the fields and description of the premises,
condition of the land, its acreage and production in order
to determine the equivalent rent to be apportioned to the
Vicar of Longford. This analysis needed to be produced

by each individual farm and small holding in Hungry Bentley. Compiling the return for the *Riddings Farm* would have exercised Thomas Jeffery greatly, particularly as he was required to complete the return at the same time as his wife Margaret's serious illness and subsequent death. The total amount which was due from Thomas Jeffery of the *Riddings* was £13 8s. 10d. (That would have the equivalent purchasing power of around £1,000 today).

Three years later, on 7 June 1841, fifty-year-old widower Thomas was shown on the census, with his sons Thomas aged fifteen and John aged eleven. The given age of his eldest son Thomas was, in fact, inaccurate. Thomas was born on 8 April 1823 and so he would be eighteen at the time when the census was taken. There were two female servants living-in at the *Riddings* at this time, Ann Bold (thirty-five) and Harriet Leason (twenty).

Thomas and Margaret's son, Thomas, married Mary Robinson of neighbouring *Stydd Hall*, four years after his mother's death. Thomas and Mary married on 14 December 1843. He was twenty years old at the time although on his marriage certificate, he is shown as aged twenty-two. This was over seven years before his father, Thomas, died at the *Riddings* on 17 April 1851. Thomas brought his bride, Mary, home to the *Riddings*. The early years of their marriage from mid-December 1843 to mid-April 1851 could not have been easy for them. They had six children at a time when Grandfather Thomas still exercised control at the *Riddings*. How difficult it was can only be imagined but, the epitaph on Thomas the elder's tombstone, may give some indication. It reads:

Here! lies the vilest of the human race
But saved I trust by Christ's redeeming grace.
Sinner! Prepare to meet thy God.
For without repentance there is no salvation

Kathryn O'Malley, the great, great, great-granddaughter of Thomas and Margaret's only daughter Fanny, has posited an interesting theory, which may help to explain this extraordinary and shocking tombstone inscription. She reminds us firstly that, although Thomas and Margaret's daughter Fanny was baptised at Nethergreen

Independent Chapel in Yeaveley, their sons Thomas and John, were baptised at the Lady Huntingdon Zion Chapel in Ashbourne. She points out that:

The family were Methodists but perhaps not in the mainstream ………. The Zion Chapel was a product of the Methodist revival of the eighteenth century. That movement split on the doctrinal question of Calvinism or Arminianism. John Wesley and his followers chose Arminianism – a belief that all could be saved: Lady Huntingdon and others were Calvinists – believing that only those chosen could be saved. Such strong beliefs may account for Fanny's (and Thomas and John's) *father Thomas' tomb inscription.*

However, it is difficult to see how this accounts for the vehemence of feeling which occasioned describing a father as 'the vilest of the human race'. We may never know the answer as to why his children thought this was warranted. It is a secret which his daughter Fanny, and sons John and Thomas, have taken to their graves.

This Thomas Jeffery, born in the year of the French Revolution, was my great, great- grandfather. At the time of his death, he was survived by two brothers, John and William, two sisters, Mary and Fanny, three children Fanny, Thomas and John and twelve grandchildren.

❦

The SEVENTH generation story continues with the three children of Thomas the 'Vile'. His only daughter, Fanny, and his younger son, John, moved away from the *Riddings* when they married. His eldest son, Thomas, remained to farm the *Riddings* and his story is told in the 'Patriarch and Matriarch' pages following.

Thomas and Margaret's only daughter, Fanny, had been married to Thomas Hunt for nearly sixteen years when her father died in 1851. Their marriage was announced in the *DERBY MERCURY* July 1835:

MARRIAGES
July 15th, Mr. Thomas Hunt of Hungry Bentley to Miss Fanny Jeffery, eldest daughter of Mr. Thomas Jeffery of the same place.

They had married in Longford Church and Thomas Hunt's cousin, George and his wife Elizabeth Hunt, were witnesses to the marriage.

Children of Fanny Hunt (nee Jeffery) and Thomas Hunt

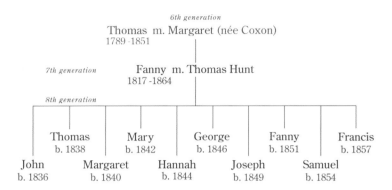

6th generation
Thomas m. Margaret (née Coxon)
1789 -1851

7th generation
Fanny m. Thomas Hunt
1817 -1864

8th generation

| Thomas | Mary | George | Fanny | Francis |
| b. 1838 | b. 1842 | b. 1846 | b. 1851 | b. 1857 |

John Margaret Hannah Joseph Samuel
b. 1836 b. 1840 b. 1844 b. 1849 b. 1854

Thomas Hunt was seven years older than his new young wife, Fanny. He was the son of Thomas and Hannah (nee Woodhouse) Hunt and was baptised on 20 May 1810. His father was the local blacksmith and the smithy was located close to the farm at *Bentley Fields*. It is not clear whether Fanny and Thomas spent the early years of their marriage at Thomas's home at the smithy or else-where in Hungry Bentley. It is unlikely that they would have been living at the *Riddings* as Thomas is reputed to have disowned his daughter on her marriage. They had ten children, born between 1836 and 1857. Their first seven children were born in Hungry Bentley and their last three, in Derby.

At the time of the 1841 census, Fanny and Thomas Hunt and their one-year-old daughter, Margaret, were living with Thomas Hunt's married sister, Fanny Aves and her children, in Mansfield, Nottinghamshire. Their older children, five-year-old John and three-year-old Thomas, were living with their grandparents, Thomas and Hannah Hunt at the Bentley Smithy. The following year, on 15 April 1842, Fanny and Thomas Hunt's fourth child, Mary was born. They had six more children between 1844 and 1857.

At the time of the 1851 census, Fanny's husband and their first six children, John aged fifteen, Thomas thirteen,

Margaret eleven, Mary nine, George seven and Joseph three, were living in Measham, Leicestershire. They had moved to be next door to Thomas's cousin, George Hunt, who had also been a blacksmith. George, however, was now a successful mill owner and textile manufacturer employing 140 workers in Measham plus 80 in Derby in addition to farming fourteen acres of land. However, Thomas Hunt and the children only stayed there for a short time before settling in Derby where Fanny and Thomas's last three children, Fanny, Samuel and Francis were born.

Fanny was only forty-six when she died of consumption in Derby on 23 March 1864. At the time of her death, five of her children had yet to reach their majority. She was just one year younger than her mother, Margaret (Coxon) Jeffery, had been when she had died at the *Riddings*, twenty-five years earlier. Fanny's death was announced in the *DERBY MERCURY*:

DEATHS
On Monday week, Fanny, wife of Mr. Thomas Hunt, Brook St. Derby, and daughter of the late Mr. Thomas Jeffery, Hungry Bentley, aged 46.

Fanny was not forgotten by the Jeffery family at the time of her death which, like that of her younger brother, Thomas, is recorded in the family bible at the *Riddings*.

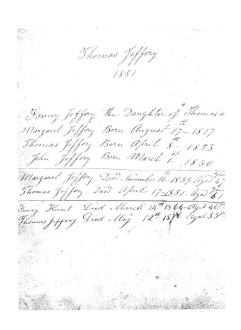

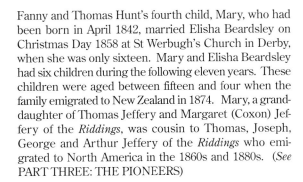

ABOVE *From the Riddings Bible – the births and deaths of Thomas and Margaret Jeffery and their family*

RIGHT *Mary Hunt, second daughter of Thomas and Fanny (nee Jeffery) Hunt with her husband Elisha Beardsley*

Fanny and Thomas Hunt's fourth child, Mary, who had been born in April 1842, married Elisha Beardsley on Christmas Day 1858 at St Werbugh's Church in Derby, when she was only sixteen. Mary and Elisha Beardsley had six children during the following eleven years. These children were aged between fifteen and four when the family emigrated to New Zealand in 1874. Mary, a grand-daughter of Thomas Jeffery and Margaret (Coxon) Jeffery of the *Riddings*, was cousin to Thomas, Joseph, George and Arthur Jeffery of the *Riddings* who emigrated to North America in the 1860s and 1880s. (*See* PART THREE: THE PIONEERS)

I am indebted to Fanny (Jeffery) Hunt's great, great-granddaughter, Kathryn O'Malley, for stories of Fanny Jeffery. I quote direct from this oral history which has been passed down through the generations in New Zealand.

Fanny Jeffery has been part of my life from my very earliest childhood even though I never knew her name, she was just known as Mary Beardsley's mother. My mother, Elaine Richards, told me the same stories she had heard from her mother, Myrtle Hiddlestone, who had been told them by her mother, Ada Mary Beardsley and before that, Ada Mary had heard them from Mary Hunt, Fanny's daughter. Women in each generation of our family have passed down the oral history to each other and finally to me, and I have been the one to sift the truth from fantasy, courtesy of the computer age.

But first the myth about Fanny which is always best. Fanny, according to family legend, was a lady (whether that was with a capital or lower case letter has been debated endlessly between my aunt and myself). She fell in love with the local blacksmith and against her family's wishes married him, and for that was disowned by her family. The blacksmith's name was Thomas Hunt and he was also a Sunday school teacher. The story is that he managed to drink his way through three of her small fortunes. Fanny and Thomas had twelve children and they were so beautiful, that people would stop her in the street to ask if they belonged to the gentry, and was she their nanny?

There only appear to be records for ten children but it is possible that the additional two were still births or infant deaths which were not registered.

The truth, as always, is not far away. Fanny's father would have been quite a substantial landowner (a farmer) *in the area and, as the only daughter she would perhaps have been rather spoilt and used to getting her own way. Thomas Hunt's mother came from a similar farming background, but with smaller acreages, and the Hunt family seem to have been blacksmiths in the area for a number of generations. I like to think that Fanny, perhaps, met Thomas when taking her horse to be shod at the smithy in Hungry Bentley. She was almost eighteen when they married, and not pregnant, as their first son was born ten months later in Hungry Bentley. Whether the family disapproved of the marriage is hard to prove, but it is perhaps telling that the two witnesses to their marriage* (at Longford) *were from the Hunt family.*

Kathryn O'Malley points out that Fanny is visiting the *Riddings*, without her husband and children, at the time of the 1851 census. This, which was taken shortly before Thomas Jeffery's death, suggests:

Fanny is not with them (her husband and children) *as she is at the Riddings. Her father died a couple of weeks later. I like to think it was deathbed reconciliation.*

Perhaps the tombstone epitaph suggests otherwise or maybe the strength of her brother Thomas's feeling prevailed. Again, we shall never know.

There is another strange twist to the oral history that came to New Zealand. Thomas Hunt's mother, Hannah, had a brother, Thomas Woodhouse, and his will recently shed light on the story about Fanny's husband drinking away the family fortunes. In the will, Thomas Hunt received money, and his parents received both money and land. Perhaps that is the origin of the family story of Thomas drinking his way through several small fortunes. They may not have been Fanny's but actually his to do with as he wished.

Fanny Jeffery (Hunt) was nearly thirteen when her youngest brother, John, was born at the *Riddings* in 1830. John, like his sister Fanny and elder brother, Thomas,

She was almost eighteen when they married, and not pregnant, as their first son was born ten months later in Hungry Bentley. Whether the family disapproved of the marriage is hard to prove, but it is perhaps telling that the two witnesses to their marriage were from the Hunt family.

married young. He was only five years old when his sister married Thomas Hunt and only nine when his mother died in 1839. John, therefore, grew up in an all male household where the only 'mothering' he might receive would be from the female house servants. At the time of the 1841 census, when he was eleven, twenty-year-old Harriet Leason was the 'living-in' maid. When he was thirteen, his brother married Mary Robinson and brought her to live at the *Riddings*. John was to become an uncle to six young nephews and two nieces, before he left to marry Mary Robinson's youngest sister, Ann.

Eighteen months after the death of his father, Thomas, John married Ann Robinson on 21 October 1852 in Ashbourne. He was twenty-two years old. Ann, who was born on 17 September 1831, was just twenty-one. Ann was fourteen years younger than her sister Mary, who had married John's elder brother, Thomas, eight years earlier. These Robinson sisters, of neighbouring *Stydd Hall*, would have known the Jeffery brothers at the *Riddings* for most of their lives.

......and his will recently shed light on the story about Fanny's husband drinking away the family fortunes.

Children of John Jeffery and Ann (nee Robinson)

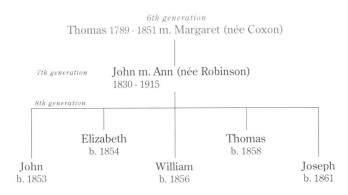

6th generation
Thomas 1789 - 1851 m. Margaret (née Coxon)

7th generation   John m. Ann (née Robinson)
                         1830 - 1915

8th generation

John   Elizabeth   Thomas   Joseph
b. 1853   b. 1854   b. 1858   b. 1861
                        William
                        b. 1856

LEFT *John and Ann (nee Robinson) Jeffery*

RIGHT *John, eldest son of John and Ann Jeffery, Poynton, Cheshire*

John did not continue in farming. He trained as a joiner and his skills were much in demand in the local area. After his marriage he and Ann set up home at *Malt House* farm cottage, Yeaveley where their five children, four sons and a daughter, were born: John on 4 April 1853: Elizabeth, 11 November 1854; William, 29 March 1856; Thomas, in 1858 and Joseph, 6 July 1861. The 1871 census recorded that the family was living at Aston, Sudbury, Derbyshire on Vernon land, but at some time after this date and certainly by 1873, the family moved to Poynton where John worked as a joiner on the Vernon Estate in Cheshire.

John and Ann's younger children went to school in Poynton and the four oldest made their lives in Cheshire. Their eldest son, John, married Mary Hall in September 1880 and they had two daughters, Ethel Mary born in 1883 and Dora in 1887.

The year following their eldest son's marriage, their third son, Thomas, died aged only twenty-two, on 28 March 1881 and is buried in the churchyard of St George's Church, Poynton, where his tombstone reads:

William, second son of John and Ann Jeffery with his wife Phoebe

Thomas
The beloved son of John and Ann
Who died March 28th 1881
Aged 22 years
Blessed are the dead that died with the Lord

The following year their second son, William, married Phoebe Hall on Christmas Day, 1883. William and Phoebe had two daughters Nellie, born in 1885 and Mabel, born in 1897. Their son Thomas William, born on 8 April 1891, was to lose his life in World War 1. He died on 22 April 1917 and is commemorated on the Loos Memorial in France.

RIGHT AND FAR RIGHT *'Schoolmaster' Joseph Jeffery, c.1890, youngest son of John and Ann Jeffery, in Newark, Nottinghamshire*

OPPOSITE RIGHT *John Jeffery 1830-1915*

The career of their youngest son, Joseph, followed a different path. He became one of the first of the many Jefferys, English and American, to be teachers.

I first learnt of 'Schoolmaster Joseph Jeffery', first cousin of the fifteen children of Thomas and Mary of the *Riddings*, from a conversation with Margaret Jeffery at the *Riddings* some years ago. Margaret's sister, Dorothy, had 'discovered' him in her early research many years ago. This was followed up by a letter which I received, again some years ago, from a Marjorie Pirie in California. Marjorie, who died in San Marino, Los Angeles in 1988, was English 'schoolmaster' Joseph Jeffery's granddaughter and she sent me some wonderful photographs of her grandfather, together with some interesting information:

At 12 years of age, in May 1873, Joseph entered Lord Nelson's Church of England Boys School, Poynton, Cheshire. Either his home was in Poynton (which it was) or he boarded there for the headmaster noted in the Log Book of the school on January 23 1877:

J. Jeffery, Pupil Teacher, was so wet this morning as to feel obliged to return home for a change of clothing'.

'A very wet and stormy morning. Attendance small. J. Jeffery, Pupil Teacher, was so wet this morning as to feel obliged to return home for a change of clothing'.

'He progressed creditably in grammar' but 'needed to attend to Euclid (Geometry) and Algebra.'

He became a Pupil Teacher of writing, composition and geography, and in 1880 he qualified as an Assistant Teacher. In November 1878 he received: 'two valuable books as a prize shown at the scripture examination'.

In 1881, he entered St. Peter's College, Peterborough, graduating in 1883 and later became Schoolmaster of the Parish Boys School in Rosherne, Cheshire.

Joseph married Zillah Louisa Tomlinson in September 1888 in Newark, Nottinghamshire. In 1891, Joseph and Zillah were living in Rosherne, Cheshire, and his occupation is described as 'Certificated Schoolmaster'. Their daughter, Zillah Margaret was born on 2 April 1892 in Rostherne and their son, John Gordon, was born on 3 January 1896 in Altringham, Cheshire. Zillah Margaret married George Pirie and it was their daughter, Zillah Marjorie Pirie, born in 1911, who contacted me in 1987.

John and Ann Jeffery's son, 'Schoolmaster Joseph' died young. He was only thirty-nine when he died in January 1901 in Newark, Nottinghamshire. His widow, Zillah, who was the daughter of James H. Tomlinson and Louisa Rookes, was born on 4 March 1863 in Minto, Ontario, Canada. After Joseph's death, she and her children, Zillah Margaret and John Gordon, left for Canada. They went to Calgary, Alberta, where Zillah's father was in the publishing business.

Seven years after the death of John's youngest son 'Schoolmaster Joseph', John's wife Ann died on 23 February 1908. Almost eleven months later, their only daughter, Elizabeth, died on 17 November 1908. They too are buried at St George's Church, Poynton where the tombstone inscription continues under that of their son Thomas, who had died in 1881:

Also Ann the beloved wife of John Jeffery

who died 23rd February 1908

Aged 76 years

Also, Elizabeth, daughter of the above

John and Ann Jeffery

who died November 17th 1908

John *(photo left)* was eighty-five when he died on 19 May 1915. He also was buried at St George's Church, Poynton and the tombstone continues:

Also John Jeffery who died

May 19th 1915

Aged 85 years

'Patriarch and Matriarch' of the Riddings

Thomas Jeffery 1823-1876 and Mary (nee Robinson) Jeffery 1817-1906. From my sister's locket. Given by Ellen (nee Jeffery) Hellaby to her eldest granddaughter

The SEVENTH generation story continues with the eldest son of Thomas the 'Vile' who died in 1851. It was this eldest son, THOMAS, who carried the direct line forward and who, over seven years before his father's death, had married Mary Robinson of *Stydd Hall*, in December 1843.

The Jefferys of the *Riddings* and the Robinsons of *Stydd Hall* were neighbouring farmers. Thomas Jeffery of the *Riddings* would have known the children of William and Elizabeth Robinson of *Stydd* for most of his life.

Mary was the second daughter of William Robinson and Elizabeth Oakden. (Elizabeth had been born at neighbouring *Bentley Hall*). A separate note in a *Bentley Fields* Bible, in the possession of Stella Spencer, informs us that Mary was born on 26 October 1817 at 2 o'clock in the morning. William and Elizabeth had ten children between 1814 and 1832. The time of birth for all of them is noted, apart from the two youngest. Their second and third sons, Thomas and William, were closest in age to Thomas Jeffery at the *Riddings*. Their youngest daughter, Ann, was to marry Thomas Jeffery's younger brother, John, and their youngest son, Richard, was to marry Mary Jeffery of *Bentley Cottage Farm*.

Mary Robinson was almost five years older than Thomas Jeffery. Thomas and Mary married on 12 December 1843, at Shirley Parish Church. The witnesses to the

marriage were Mary's oldest brother, twenty-eight-year-old Joseph Robinson and a younger sister, seventeen-year-old Elizabeth Robinson. Thomas, aged twenty, was under-age although, as we have seen, on his marriage certificate, his age is given as twenty-two. He may have been marrying without his father's consent. However, his father could not risk alienating his son and losing him from the farm. Whatever the position was, Thomas brought his bride home to the *Riddings* where they were to spend the rest of their lives.

From the Bentley Fields Family Bible

Children of Thomas Jeffery and Mary (nee Robinson) of the Riddings

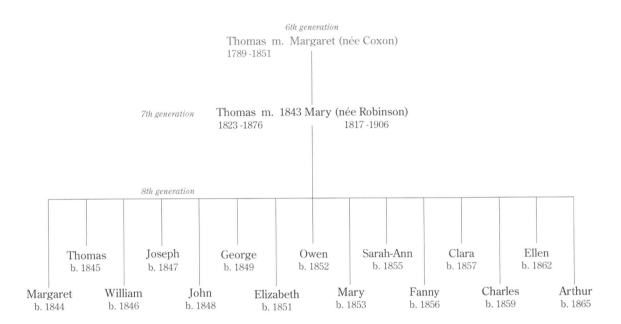

6th generation
Thomas m. Margaret (née Coxon)
1789 -1851

7th generation Thomas m. 1843 Mary (née Robinson)
1823 -1876   1817 -1906

8th generation

| Thomas b. 1845 | Joseph b. 1847 | George b. 1849 | Owen b. 1852 | Sarah-Ann b. 1855 | Clara b. 1857 | Ellen b. 1862 |

| Margaret b. 1844 | William b. 1846 | John b. 1848 | Elizabeth b. 1851 | Mary b. 1853 | Fanny b. 1856 | Charles b. 1859 | Arthur b. 1865 |

Thomas and Mary's first six children were born before Grandfather Thomas died in 1851. On the census, recorded on 30 March 1851, Grandfather Thomas was still shown as the head of the household at the *Riddings* with twenty-seven-year-old son, Thomas, and thirty-four-year-old daughter-in-law, Mary and their children. Grandfather Thomas's younger son John was still at home. Visiting at this time, was Ann Robinson, Mary's sister, who was to marry John the following year. Also visiting at this time was Thomas's married daughter Fanny, who, we have seen, was there without either her husband, Thomas Hunt, or her children.

Thomas and Mary had fifteen children between 1844 and 1865. Thus, they became the 'Patriarch and Matriarch' of the *Riddings* Jefferys. They and their children are the key 'gateway' family. It is through Thomas and Mary and their fifteen children that access is gained to the succeeding and current generations of Jefferys. Thomas and Mary's family was essentially Victorian. All of their

children were born and brought up during Queen Victoria's reign. For the Jeffery family at the *Riddings*, family life was not untypical of that of middle class yeoman farming families throughout Victorian rural England.

It is interesting to note that there are curious parallels, in size and structure, with the family of their 'Dear Queen'. Victoria and her consort Albert had nine children born between 1840 and 1857. Mary, born fifteen months before Victoria, died five years after her and both Mary and Queen Victoria outlived their husbands by over three decades. In both families, some of their members and their descendants made their lives abroad and both may be said to have had their 'black sheep'. Victoria became the 'Grandmother of Europe' and Mary the 'Grandmother of Jefferyland', Derbyshire and, indeed, lands further afield. Mary was to become '*Grandma Riddings*' to Adelaide, (daughter of her eldest son, Thomas) and the only one of her American granddaughters that she was to meet.

The Bentley Fields Family Bible – Births of Children

Thomas and Mary's first child, Margaret, was born on the 9 October 1844. By the time she was five years old, Margaret had five younger brothers: Thomas, born on the 16 September 1845; William, on 5 August 1846; Joseph, on 24 July 1847; John, on 23 August 1848 and George, on 22 November 1849. Shortly after Grandfather Thomas's death, Elizabeth was born on 25 April 1851. The year following the elder Thomas's death was marked by the birth of their eighth child, Owen, born on the 27 May 1852. Five more children were born during the 1850s: Mary on 18 September 1853; Sarah-Ann on 25 March 1855; Fanny on 10 May 1856; Clara on the 20 September 1857 and, on 5 June 1859, their thirteenth child, Charles. (*See* family tree.)

The census of 1861 was the first to show Thomas as the head of his own household at the *Riddings*. He was now thirty-eight and Mary was forty-three. All of their thirteen children were there, from sixteen-year-old Margaret to

the baby Charles. In addition to the family, there were three servants, Ann Morley (twenty-nine) as housemaid and nursemaid, together with John Yeomans (eighteen) and John Smith (thirteen) who were farm labourers.

The 1860s were to prove a decade of change for the family at the *Riddings*. It would be a decade of both joy and pride; of sorrow, loss and justifiable concern. The family was not yet complete and on 6 January 1862, Mary, aged forty-four, gave birth to her fourteenth child, Ellen. Ellen was the seventh daughter and would become my grandmother. The family now comprised seven daughters and seven sons with Ellen's eldest sister, Margaret, now seventeen and her eldest brother, Thomas, sixteen. Sadly the balance was short lived. Ellen was only two years old

Thomas Jeffery, father of fifteen children

when one of her elder sisters, nine-year-old Sarah Ann, died on 15 June 1864. Her death certificate recorded that the cause of death was cephalitis (a form of meningitis) which she had suffered for thirteen days.

It was on 3 October 1865 when Mary gave birth to her fifteenth child, Arthur. This was two weeks before she reached her forty-eighth birthday. Shortly afterwards, Thomas and Mary would bid farewell to their first-born son Thomas. He had just turned twenty when he sailed for America. A year later, their third son, nineteen-year-old Joseph followed his brother across the Atlantic. Although both Thomas and Joseph would return home for visits, both of these sons were to make their lives in America. They established the trans-Atlantic family links in both directions that would continue into the twenty-first century. As this decade of change was drawing to its close, their eldest son, Thomas, was the first of their children to marry, although neither of his parents could attend his wedding. Thomas married Maria Hague, who was from Derbyshire, in New York City, on 2 November 1869.

The decade of the 1870s continued as one of significant changes at the *Riddings* as more of Thomas and Mary's children left home. Their sons, John and George, obtained work in Leeds and three more of their children married. On 28 March 1871 their eldest daughter, Margaret, married John Poyser, at St John's Church, Alkmonton. Nearly seven months later, their fifth son George married Sarah O'Brien in Leeds. On 3 April 1873 William, the eldest of their sons remaining at home, married Hannah Wood at St John's Church, Alkmonton.

By early 1874 Thomas and Mary had their first four grandchildren. Their first two were George and Sarah's children, Mary Ellen born in 1872 and William born in 1874. Margaret and John Poyser's first son, Owen John, also arrived in 1874 as did William and Hannah's first daughter, Sarah Ann. The following year, 1875, Thomas and Mary's first American grandchild, John Arthur, Thomas and Maria's son, was born in New York City.

Meanwhile, Thomas's health had started to fail. He developed the heart disease which would lead to his death. On 10 May 1876 he signed his will, in the presence of his solicitor, Samuel Coleman of Ashbourne and also, his friend, William Ratcliffe of Cubley. He died two days later on 12 May. He was only fifty-three years old. His

Alkmonton Church

death certificate stated that the cause of death was: *Disease of the heart (valvular)* which had been present for three years. It was signed by Robert D. Goodwin, who was a Fellow of the Royal College of Surgeons, which seems to suggest that it was signed in hospital. His son William was present at his death.

Thomas's will appointed his wife Mary and sons William and John as his executors and trustees. William and John were also appointed as guardians of his '*infant*' children (Fanny, Clara, Charles, Ellen and Arthur had not yet reached their majority) after the death of his wife. After Mary's death, his estate was to be divided equally between all of:

..such of my children who shall be living at the death of my said wife as being sons shall attain the age of twenty-one years or being daughters shall attain that age or marry ....

The will also declared that:

... my Son Owen Jeffery shall have the option of carrying on the farm now in my occupation after the decease of my said wife upon taking the live and dead farming stock and other effects at a valuation thereof to be made by two valuers or their umpire in the usual way and the amount of such valuation to be paid by my said Trustee within twelve calendar months from the decease of my said wife.

ABOVE *The tombstone of Thomas Jeffery 1823-1876*

BELOW *Mary Jeffery with thirteen of her children at the Riddings 1882*
Seated l. to r.: William, Margaret, Arthur, Mother Mary, Ellen, Thomas, Elizabeth
Standing l. to r.: Mary, John, Fanny, George, Joseph, Clara, Owen

A year later, the will was proved at Derby on 17 December 1877:

… by the oaths of William Jeffery, sons and two of the Executors, to whom administration was granted. Power was reserved to Mary Jeffery, Widow the Relict and the other Executor.

And:

The testator Thomas Jeffery was late of Hungry Bentley in the County of Derby and died on the 12th of May 1876. His personal estate was recorded as under £800 which was extracted by Samuel Coleman, Solicitor, Ashbourne.

Thomas was buried at St Chad's Church, Longford and his epitaph reads as follows:

Affectionate remembrance
The late
Thomas Jeffery
Of the Riddings
Who died May 12th 1876
Aged 53 years

Who is he that liveth
And shall not see death? Shall he
Deliver his soul from the hand
Of the grave?

Thomas was survived by his wife Mary, fourteen of his children and seven grandchildren. Six years after Thomas's death, their son Charles died suddenly of a heart attack.

Mary remained at the heart of the family at the *Riddings*, outliving Thomas by almost three decades, when she died on 17 February 1906. Her death was reported in two items in the local Ashbourne press as follows:

HUNGRY BENTLEY

****

Death of an Old Inhabitant

By the death of Mrs. Jeffery, widow of the late Mr. Thomas Jeffery, the district of Hungry Bentley has lost one of its oldest and most highly respected inhabitants. The deceased lady had reached the advanced age of 89 (89th year) ere she was called to her well earned rest. She was of a quiet and unassuming disposition, a devoted wife and a model mother. During her long life she ever evinced her kind and charitable nature which was well worthy of emulation. The funeral took place yesterday (Thursday) at Alkmonton.

And:

ALKMONTON, February 27, 1906

On Thursday last, 22nd ult. The remains of Mrs. Jeffery, widow of the late Mr. Thomas Jeffery of the Riddings farm, Hungry Bentley, were laid to rest in the quiet Churchyard at Alkmonton. The deceased was a member of a highly respected family who have occupied the Riddings as farmers for over half a century and was the mother of a numerous family.

She was the oldest resident in the Parish and was very highly respected by all who knew her. She was of a very retiring nature, had been a tireless worker in the affairs of her home and had also a very devout and spiritual disposition.

Her family (with the exception of her four sons in America) and children and other relations and friends attended the funeral. Beautiful wreaths were sent, in token of love and regard by the following:- John, Margaret and children of Shardlow House (Poysers); Owen and Hetty of Bentley Fields (Jefferys); Lizzie and John of Burton (Holbrooks); Polly, Fanny and Percy of the Riddings (Fanny Jeffery and Spencers); Arthur, Clara and children of Donington Park (Cooks); William and Ellen of Bentley Hall (Hellabys); Mary Ellen and Charlie (Balls); Owen, Robert, Hannah and Polly (Poysers and Hidderleys); Tom and Nellie (Poysers); Dolly and Tom (Jefferys); Sister Marie (nurse); Mrs Jeffery of Bentley Cottage; Rev. W.D. Dearden, (Vicar); Captain and Mrs. Clews of Norbury Hall (Owners of Bentley estate); Mr and Mrs. Reid of Norbury.

The funeral rites were conducted by the Vicar – The Rev. W.D. Dearden. The hymn, 'Safe in the arms of Jesus' led by Dearden was sung.

On Sunday at the morning service at Alkmonton Church the Vicar made touching allusions to the deceased and appropriate hymns were sung. A large congregation of mourners and friends were present.

The named mourners at the funeral anticipate a number of the descendants who figure significantly in PART FOUR: THE PEOPLE WHO STAYED.

Mary is buried at Alkmonton Church. Her memorial reads:

*In loving memory
Of Mary Jeffery,
Riddings Farm
Who died February 17th, 1906
Aged 88 years
Peace, Perfect Peace*

East window in Alkmonton Church. The right-hand panel has a dedication in memory of Thomas and Mary Jeffery and was donated by their children

A side panel of the East Window at Alkmonton Church was donated by the Jeffery family after Mary's death in 1906. It reads:

To the Glory of God in memory of the late Thomas and Mary Jeffery by their children 1907.

Mary was survived by thirteen children, forty-two grand-children and a number of great grandchildren. One of her American granddaughters, Adelaide Jeffery, who was the daughter of her eldest son Thomas, always knew Mary as *'Grandma Riddings'*. Mary was very fondly remembered by my father, Jeffery Hellaby, who, at the time of her death, was one of her youngest grandsons. Six days before his own death, my father recalled his childhood memory of attending his grandmother's funeral when he was four years old.

The Eighth, Ninth and Later generations are descended from twelve of the children of Thomas and Mary of the *Riddings*. Thomas and Mary fully deserve to be called the Patriarch and Matriarch of the Jefferys.

ABOVE Mary Jeffery at the Riddings with her children, their spouses and her grandchildren in 1882

Standing l. to r.: John, Fanny, Arthur, Ellen, Joseph, Mary, George, Thomas, George's second wife Mary, Elizabeth, Owen, John Poyser (Margaret's husband), Clara, William

Seated back row adults l. to r.: Maria (John's wife) with their daughter Mary (aka May) on knee, John (younger brother of Father Thomas who had died in 1876), Mother Mary, Maria (Thomas's wife), Margaret, Hannah (William's wife) with their son William Charles on knee

Front row children l. to r.: Sarah Ann (William and Hannah's daughter), Owen Poyser (Margaret and John's son), John Arthur (Thomas and Maria's son), Elizabeth Annie (William and Hannah's daughter).
Two children in front middle: George's two children by his first wife Sarah – William and Mary Ellen

Four of Thomas and Mary's sons emigrated to the New World. Their lives, and those of their descendants, are covered in PART THREE: THE PIONEERS. Three of their sons, William, John and Owen remained to farm in Derbyshire. Four of their daughters also remained in farming as the Poysers, Spencers, Cooks and Hellabys. Their lives, and those of their descendants, are considered in PART FOUR: THE PEOPLE WHO STAYED.

PART THREE

THE
PIONEERS

THE PIONEERS: INTRODUCTION

Whilst Hungry Bentley with the *Riddings* is the heart-land of the Jeffery family, the mid-nineteenth century witnessed the beginnings of a family dispersal which has had international, national and local dimensions across the reigns of two Queens, Victoria and Elizabeth.

It is the sons of Thomas and Mary Jeffery of the *Riddings*, who emigrated to North America in the 1860s and 1880s, who form the focus of the story of the pioneers to the New World. However, it should be recognised that they had cousins from Hungry Bentley, who, during the nine-teenth century, also emigrated abroad.

The first of these cousins was another Thomas Jeffery, second son of John and Dorothy Jeffery of *Bentley Cottage Farm*, who emigrated to Canada in 1872. The second was Mary Beardsley (nee Hunt), who emigrated to New Zealand in 1874. Mary was a daughter of Thomas and Fanny (nee Jeffery) Hunt. Her mother, Fanny Jeffery, born at the *Riddings* in 1817, was Aunt Fanny to the four Jeffery pioneer brothers whose stories are told in the following pages.

The Thomas and Agnes Jeffery family in Canada from 1872

Thomas Jeffery, the second son of John and Dorothy of *Bentley Cottage Farm*, married Agnes Brand in Leeds in 1865. In 1872, he emigrated with his family to Canada.

On 18 July 1872, Thomas and Agnes Jeffery with their young family sailed from Liverpool on the *SS Hibernian*. They arrived in Quebec ten days later. They were trav-elling with a one-month-old baby and three young chil-dren, two-year-old Alice, four-year-old Thomas and six-year-old John. Their two youngest children were not to survive the hard early years in Canada. The family settled in Ontario where, on 29 April 1974, their daugh-ter Sarah was born. Two years later, on 26 July 1876, their third son, Owen, completed their family.

In 1879 the family travelled in a one-horse wagon into the largely unsettled Parry Sound District on Georgian Bay, Lake Huron. They set up home at Spence, a small town-ship at the cross roads of the Nipissing Colonisation Road and the Ryson Road. It was a very different land from the family's Derbyshire homeland. These boreal forests were a demanding area in which to farm. Thomas, however, succeeded and when he died, aged eighty-one in 1917, he was described as 'one of the pioneers'.

Today Spence is a ghost town. In its prime, the popula-tion was between 100 and 150 residents. When Thomas arrived with his young family, there was a store, a post office (opened in 1872), a blacksmiths shop, two saw-mills, a church, a school (opened in 1875) and an inn. Hamilton Brown, the schoolmaster who taught their younger children, was also the innkeeper.

The Nipissing Road, which runs through the centre of the Parry Sound District, is today the Ontario Ghost Trail. It was once home to many settlements of hopeful pioneers. Today all that remains are their abandoned log cabins and weathered barns. Although these lands were touted as a Utopia for land-hungry immigrants, the colonisation roads were built mainly to help the great lumber compa-nies gain access to their distant lands.

However, the descendants of Thomas and Agnes Jeffery have thrived in Canada. During the 1980s, John Jeffery from Denby, grandson of Thomas's brother William Jeffery (See PART TWO: THE PREDECESSORS), traced the family. A reunion was organised and three of Thomas and Agnes Jeffery's granddaughters met with their Derbyshire relatives.

The Mary and Elisha Beardsley family in New Zealand from 1874

Emigrant Ship, Eastern Monarch bound for New Zealand with emigrants aboard 1874
From the Illustrated London News, with acknowledgements to the Mary Evans Picture Library

The third daughter of Fanny (nee Jeffery) Hunt, sixteen-year-old Mary, married Elisha Beardsley on Christmas Day 1858. Sixteen years later, the family emigrated to New Zealand.

On 17 April 1874 Mary and Elisha Beardsley and their six children, sailed from Gravesend on the *SS Hereford* bound for New Zealand. Their children were Margaret aged fifteen, Alfred thirteen, Millicent ten, Henry eight, Ada six and Annie aged four. It was three months later, on 14 July, when they arrived at Lyttleton. There is a family story, told to me by Kathryn O'Malley, whose ancestors these were, that when they arrived at Christchurch they

……..took one look at the snow-covered Southern Alps and experienced the freezing cold weather, they wished desperately that they had the money to turn round and go back to England.

The family, however, thrived and there are many descendants in New Zealand to this day. Kathryn herself, although currently living with her family in America, considers herself a 'Kiwi'.

But, it is to the four *Riddings* sons that we now turn.

THOMAS JEFFERY
1845 – 1927

ENTREPRENEUR ON THE FRONTIER
Man of Business and Property

Thomas Jeffery, the eldest son of Thomas and Mary Jeffery of the Riddings, was born on 16 September 1845. He was the first of their sons, aged twenty, to emigrate to America, in 1865, six months after the ending of the American Civil War. He became a successful man of business and prominent citizen in the city of Minneapolis, Minnesota and retired to an orange grove in Redlands, California, where he died on 11 May 1927.

Descendants of Thomas Jeffery 1845 – 1927
(Four Generations)

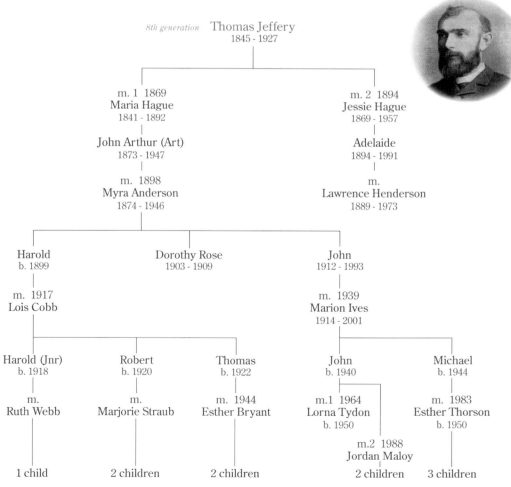

8th generation Thomas Jeffery
1845 - 1927

m. 1 1869
Maria Hague
1841 - 1892

m. 2 1894
Jessie Hague
1869 - 1957

John Arthur (Art)
1873 - 1947

Adelaide
1894 - 1991

m. 1898
Myra Anderson
1874 - 1946

m.
Lawrence Henderson
1889 - 1973

Harold
b. 1899

Dorothy Rose
1903 - 1909

John
1912 - 1993

m. 1917
Lois Cobb

m. 1939
Marion Ives
1914 - 2001

Harold (Jnr)
b. 1918

Robert
b. 1920

Thomas
b. 1922

John
b. 1940

Michael
b. 1944

m.
Ruth Webb

m.
Marjorie Straub

m. 1944
Esther Bryant

m.1 1964
Lorna Tydon
b. 1950

m. 1983
Esther Thorson
b. 1950

m.2 1988
Jordan Maloy

1 child

2 children

2 children

2 children

3 children

Thomas Jeffery 1845-1927

Entrepreneur on the Frontier

My first night in America I slept on the floor of Castle Gardens with my blanket for my pillow. On Saturday I secured a room at a low price having less than ten dollars in my pocket. On Sunday morning I went to Trinity Church and in the evening to Plymouth Church to hear Henry Ward Beecher. On Monday I went to the Y. M. C. A New York where Mr. Lee, the President, gave me introductory letters to several firms. I did not find a position but continued through the week going up one side of Broadway and down the other, very discouraged.

Thomas Jeffery on landing in America, November 1865

We went down town and sat in Uncle Tom's building ......
I remember Uncle Tom's house with its lovely flower beds.....
Shopping at the 'Glass Block' Store ...... Driving around with
Uncle Tom in his fine horse and carriage.

Joseph Jeffery's daughter Florence on a visit to Minneapolis c. 1895

Thomas Jeffery: Owner of Jeffery Furniture Company,
Minneapolis 1880s – 1890s

Thomas, the first of Thomas and Mary's eight sons, was born on 16 September 1845. His elder sister Margaret had yet to reach her first birthday and his widowed grandfather, Thomas, only just turned fifty-six, was still the head of the household at the *Riddings*.

By the New Year of 1851, he had four younger brothers: four-year-old William, three year-old Joseph, two-year-old John and one-year-old George. By the end of April that year his sister Elizabeth had joined the rapidly growing family.

Almost eleven years later, sixteen-year-old Thomas was one of a family of fourteen children. He and his seventeen-year-old sister Margaret now had six younger brothers and five younger sisters. In addition to younger brothers William, Joseph, John and George, nine-year-old Owen and two-year-old Charles had joined the family. Also, there were now six younger sisters, Elizabeth aged ten, Mary seven, Sarah Ann six, Fanny four, Clara three and the newly arrived baby, Ellen.

In the spring of 1865, nineteen-year-old Thomas was working on the farm. He realised that he would have yet another brother or sister before the year was out. His father, aged only forty-one, with a large family to support, was in no position to retire from the farm in the foreseeable future. For a young man, who's energy, determination, ideas and entrepreneurial flair would be so ably demonstrated in the years ahead, this was very frustrating.

Thomas decided to seek his fortune in the New World. During the spring and summer of 1865 he made his travel plans. Many years later, Florence, daughter of his younger brother Joseph, wrote:

Of the four boys who came to America, Tom came first because he wanted to make his fortune. Years later he sent for his youngest brother Arthur. They settled in Minneapolis.

Oh my America, my new found land.

John Donne

The nineteenth century witnessed an increasing flow of emigration from Europe to America. Further settlement from Europe was encouraged when President Abraham Lincoln signed into law the Homestead Act of 1862 which authorised any citizen, or immigrant who intended to become a citizen, to select any surveyed unclaimed parcel of land up to 160 acres, settle it, improve it and by living on it for five years, gain title to it. In the midst of Civil War, President Lincoln was hoping to strengthen the Union by creating an unbroken link between the East and the West. Additionally, he hoped to encourage orderly settlement by families and discourage abusive exploitation by cattle ranchers and land speculators. Learning of this legislation doubtless made some impact on Thomas's thoughts about his own future.

Thomas did have some contacts in America. His mother's youngest brother, John Robinson (born 7 December 1828) had emigrated earlier and was farming in Connecticut. His friend and 'cousin' Thomas Hague had emigrated in 1864 and was living in Brooklyn. Thomas's niece, Florence (daughter of his brother, Joseph), when writing of the time when her father went to America, described the Hagues as cousins:

He went to the Hagues in Brooklyn (cousins of his mother).

Florence also wrote:

Thomas Jeffery, the first of the family to come to America, spent some time in New York with Thomas Hague, an English friend.

Even though he had these contacts, it was still a courageous step that Thomas took in the autumn of 1865. For a young man, living on an isolated farm in Derbyshire, setting out for the New World was a venture into the unknown.

In the early spring of 1851, seven-year-old Thomas Hague was living with his parents, Samuel and Charlotte, and his three brothers and three sisters in Newbold, near Chesterfield, Derbyshire, where his father was described as a manorial agent. Eighteen years later, one of his sisters, Maria, would become Thomas Jeffery's first wife.

Emigrant Ship leaving for the USA alongside the quay prior to departure 1869.

From the Illustrated London News with acknowledgements to the Mary Evans Picture Library

The year before Thomas Jeffery left for America, his friend and 'cousin' Thomas Hague, aged twenty, had already emigrated. He had embarked on the *Limerick* from Liverpool and arrived in New York on 22 August 1864. By 1870 he was a 'commission dealer' and living with his wife Ann and baby daughter Victoria, in Hempstead, Queens, in the city of New York. They were still there in 1880, by which time his family had grown to include five children. Three years later, Rosamond Jeffery, the new bride of Thomas's brother Joseph, was met by the Hagues when she arrived in New York in November 1883.

In the 1860s America was still a land of 'Cowboys and Indians'. The West was still occupied by the Plains Indians, the Lakota and Sioux. It would be eleven years after Thomas Jeffery's arrival in America that the massacre of Custer's command at the Little Big Horn occurred. The decade of the 1860s included four years of bloodshed and bitterness in a nation divided by the Civil War. The 'War between the States' ended in April 1865 and was followed by John Wilkes Booth's assassination of Abraham Lincoln. This momentous event occurred just six months before Thomas left for his new life in America.

In May 1865, the *DERBY MERCURY* printed in full the official report from Washington DC. The report was dated 15 April, following the assassination on the 14th, and in its final paragraph concluded:

It is needless for me to say anything in regard of the influence which this atrocious murder of the President may exercise upon the affairs of this country, but only add that horrible as the atrocities that have been resorted to by the enemies of this country, they are not likely in any degree to impair the public spirit or postpone the complete final overthrow of the rebellion.

The *DERBY MERCURY*, which was the sole Derbyshire countywide local newspaper, had a regular column where it reported *News from America*. Following the arrival of the ship *SS City of Washington* into Liverpool from New York, in September 1865, their edition of 27 September included the following under a heading of:

The Value of Human Life in America

———

The New York correspondent of the Times writes:

———

According to returns given by the *New York Tribune*, there have been 67 disasters on American railroads during the past 12 months, in which 300 persons were killed and more than 600 injured. The New York Tribune, however, gives fuller returns, from which it appears that no less than 45 railway accidents have taken place since last April and that the total number of killed and wounded is 1,500. ....
........Nearly the whole of these disasters were caused by sheer undeniable and almost wilful neglect. Yet, within the last two days, when an unusually horrible accident has happened in New York, scarcely any attention has been paid to these events, the coroner's inquest being solely a matter of form and ending as soon as it is begun. The disregard of human life shown since the War is certainly extraordinary.

———

Railroad building was proceeding rapidly but it was not until May 1869 that the first transcontinental link was achieved. The rails had been laid though desert and mountains, over rivers and lands where hostile Indians viewed the 'Iron Horse' with suspicion. By the time the link had been achieved, Thomas had been in New York for nearly four years.

The newspaper reports in the *DERBY MERCURY* would doubtless have caused his parents much unease but by this time Thomas's emigration plans were well advanced. He had already confirmed his passage to America and ensured that he would sail at some time following the birth of his mother's last child.

On 16 September 1865, Thomas celebrated his twentieth birthday. His plans were now finalised and his steerage passage booked on the *SS Etna* sailing from Liverpool for New York in early October. He arrived in New York on the 10 November. The journey time would probably have been about four weeks depending on weather conditions. He left shortly after his youngest brother, Arthur, was born on 3 October 1865. His mother Mary welcomed her last son shortly before she was to bid farewell to her first-born son.

When Thomas sailed into New York, the entrance to the harbour and the Manhattan sky-line would have looked vastly different from the sight which impacted so vividly on me when I arrived on the *Queen Elizabeth* just over one hundred years later, on 15 August 1967. Arriving in 1865, Thomas would have been over a decade too early to be greeted by the Statue of Liberty and many decades too early for the Manhattan skyscrapers of today.

Thomas recalled his early days following his arrival in America, in a letter to his wife, son and daughter. This letter was written on 5 March 1927, two months before he died on his orange grove in California, on 11 May 1927.

I was born in England, September 16th, 1845. I left home in October 1865, arrived in New York, November 1865, having borrowed a small sum of money to help me pay my steerage passage as an emigrant. This was all paid back later. My first night in America I slept on the floor of Castle Gardens (immigrant reception centre before the opening of Ellis Island in 1892) *with my blanket for a pillow. Saturday I secured a room at a low price – having less than 10 dollars in my pocket. ($10 is worth less than £100 in today's money). On Sunday morning*

I went to Trinity Church, in the afternoon to Sunday School – Plymouth, Class 99, in the evening to Plymouth Church to hear Henry Ward Beecher.

It is very interesting to note that, not only did Thomas go to church three times on his first Sunday, two days following his arrival in America, but also that he elected to go to Plymouth Church in Brooklyn to hear this particular prominent clergyman speak. Henry Ward Beecher was a famous preacher, social reformer and abolitionist who had acquired a national reputation for his skill as an orator. He was the favourite brother of Harriet Beecher Stowe, famed as the author of *Uncle Tom's Cabin*. His father was the Rev. Lyman Beecher, a Yale graduate and respected revivalist pastor in the Presbyterian Church in Connecticut, who had been a significant figure in the American Bible Society, The Sunday School Union and the board of Foreign Missions, and who had proclaimed:

A Bible for every family, a school for every district and a pastor for every thousand souls must be our motto and our religious institutions must be invigorated or we are undone. They must move onward with our flowing emigration to the Mississippi – must pass the Rocky Mountains; and pour their waters of life into the oceans beyond; and from the north to the south must bear salvation on their waves.

Heckt Bros., wholesale china etc., kindly gave me a letter to Ovington Bros., Brooklyn, who said they would need someone later for the holidays. I begged them to give me work now. I would do anything, scrub floors, sweep etc. as my money was nearly all gone. Mr Ovington said 'you appear an honest young man' and asked what I did last Sunday.

After Beecher's death in 1897, statues were erected in his honour in the gardens of Plymouth Church, Brooklyn Heights and in Columbia Park in front of the Brooklyn Borough Hall. He had visited England during the American Civil War to promote the cause of the Unionists against the Confederates.

Four years after listening to Henry Ward Beecher, on his first Sunday in New York City, Thomas was to marry in Plymouth Church, Brooklyn and eight years later, in 1873, his son was baptised there by Henry Ward Beecher.

Thomas's letter continued:

Monday I went to the Y.M.C.A. New York. Mr Lee, the President, gave me letters to several firms. Did not find position but continued through the week going up one side of Broadway and down the other until Saturday – very much discouraged. Heckt Bros., wholesale china etc., kindly gave me a letter to Ovington Bros., Brooklyn, who said they would need someone later for the holidays. I begged them to give me work now. I would do anything, scrub floors, sweep etc. as my money was nearly all gone. Mr Ovington said 'you appear an honest young man' and asked what I did last Sunday. He (Mr. Ovington) replied 'I belong to Plymouth and know Class 99.' They found me a boarding place at the home of a shipping clerk at five dollars per week. My work was dusting, keeping stock, carrying out fine china, clocks etc. Near closing time I was given the car-fare to deliver heavy packages. I began my first savings by carrying the goods on my shoulder and saving the five cents car-fare. I worked on my Uncle John Robinson's farm the first summer, saved my wages, came back to New York and obtained a position as salesman in a fancy goods store. Next I became a travelling salesman for a white goods house.

Mr Hill, Class 99 teacher, wanted me to take a position with him as shipping clerk, then as bookkeeper. (I took a Commercial College course in the evenings) and then travelled for them selling oil-cloths etc., always saving something out of my salary.

These early years in New York were very demanding. Thomas was working exceedingly hard, putting in long hours and saving his earnings. His commitment and determination to succeed is crystal clear. By the time he married in November 1869, four years after arriving in New York and tramping up and down Broadway with less than ten dollars in his pocket, his salary was one thousand dollars a year. This was a quite remarkable achievement in the space of only four years.

Photos of Thomas and Maria (nee Hague) Jeffery in a gold locket I have inherited from my grandmother, Ellen (nee Jeffery) Hellaby

Thomas married Maria B. Hague on 2 November 1869, in the Church where he had joined the Sunday School, Class 99, on his first Sunday in New York. None of his family could be present at the wedding but his parents arranged for the following notice to appear in the *DERBY MERCURY* of 8 December 1869:

MARRIAGES
****

On the 2nd. instant, at Plymouth Church, Brooklyn, New York, U.S. by the Rev, HM Gallaher, Thomas, eldest son of Mr Thomas Jeffery, Riddings Farm, Hungry Bentley, to Maria B. Hague, second daughter of Mr Samuel Hague, Whittington, Derbyshire.

Maria Hague was an older sister of the Thomas Hague who Thomas Jeffery had met with in New York in 1865. Maria was born in 1841 in Greasborough, Yorkshire, but by 1850, the family were in Derbyshire.

Maria was a clever girl and trained as a teacher. In 1861, at twenty-one, she was in her final year of training and one of only forty-seven women trainee teachers resident at St Werburgh's Diocesan Teacher Training College on New Uttoxeter Road, Derby.

Having trained in Derby and, with her home in Derbyshire, Maria probably embarked on her teaching career in a local school. She may have taught at Longford

School or Alkmonton School. The latter was newly built in 1856, and either school would have been attended by some of Thomas Jeffery's younger brothers and sisters. If so, then maybe this is how she met the man she would marry. However, in the absence of firm evidence, this has to remain as speculation. It could just as easily have resulted from family links between the Jefferys and Hagues.

Maria sailed from Liverpool for America almost exactly one year after Thomas had arrived. She arrived in New York on 7 November 1866. She probably came to house-keep for her younger brother Thomas Hague who had emigrated in 1864 and who, like Thomas Jeffery, also married in 1869.

As a married man, Thomas Jeffery now made his firm commitment as an American citizen: his naturalisation was confirmed in King's County, New York on 25 October 1870.

Thomas became increasingly successful, working extraordinarily hard and spending long hours travelling. He was clearly very well regarded by his firm. In his letter he recorded that:

In 1871, Mr Hill sent me to England for my health, paying me my wages, during three months absence.

Maria doubtless returned with him and three months rest and recuperation at the *Riddings* would have been very well earned. During his few months at the *Riddings* in 1871, Thomas came to know his two youngest siblings, nine-year-old Ellen who had only been three when he left and six-year-old Arthur who had only just been born.

Two years later, twin sons were born to Thomas and Maria, on 29 April 1873, in New York. Sadly one of them died. The other was John Arthur. Thomas records that Henry Ward Beecher baptised John Arthur. Thomas and Maria had two more children during the following seven years but John Arthur was the only one who survived. He was always known as Art.

In 1874 Thomas wrote that he was travelling for oil cloth manufacturers, Alden, Sampson and Sons and his salary was now twenty-five hundred dollars plus expenses. This was a far cry from the young man who had tramped the streets on arrival in New York, homeless and without work, less than a decade previously.

His work with Alden, Sampson and Sons entailed travelling long distances out into the rapidly expanding Midwest. On one of his trips he visited Minneapolis, Minnesota and was obviously very taken with this frontier city. Early in 1875 he and Maria with young John Arthur, who had yet to reach his second birthday, moved to Minneapolis to set up on his own in business. They settled in Hennepin County, and initially lived in an apartment.

Thomas wrote of how he opened a small carpet store in March 1875 in Minneapolis next to the National Hotel. He and Maria shared all of the work. Maria sold goods in the store when he was out laying carpets during the day and linoleum in banks and public buildings at night. He continued recording how, later, they made an unfortunate move taking over what he describes as '*McConnell's second floor*'. He described how McConnell violated his agreements, which caused them significant losses and failure in business. They therefore chose to move their business to a new site at 225, Nicollet Avenue where they prospered. Thomas wrote how each year's business increased and how they saved enough money

…. to pay every dollar to all creditors in full who had compromised us at the time of failure.

Only five years after his arrival in Minneapolis, Thomas, in spite of his set back, was a highly successful man of

business with his carpet store: an entrepreneur of considerable merit. His achievement was remarkable and he featured in the history of Minneapolis.

In 1880 Edward D. Neill and J. Fletcher Williams wrote *A History of Hennepin County and the City of Minneapolis*, which was published by the North Star Publishing Company in 1881. This history, which included biographical sketches of significant figures who had contributed to the growth and prosperity of the fast growing Midwestern City records that:

Thomas Jeffery, a native of England, was born September 16th, 1845, in Derbyshire. In October 1865, he came to the United States and lived in New York City until 1875, when he removed to Minneapolis and started in the carpet business; first alone and then as Keynon and Jeffery, and now the firm's name is T. Jeffery and Company. Their place of business is No. 225, Nicollet Avenue. He married in 1869, to Miss M. B. Hague of England; the fruits of this union were four children, only one of whom survives: John Arthur, aged seven years.

What was the nature of this North Midwestern city on the west bank of the Mississippi where, in the latter half of the nineteenth century, Thomas was one of its foremost citizens? Although Minnesota, as a state, had not been admitted to the Union until 1859, St Anthony and Minneapolis cities had been incorporated in 1855 and 1856. St Anthony Falls, where the first early settlers arrived in 1848, is where the Mississippi's one and only naturally occurring waterfall occurs. Early settlers harnessed the force of this water to power the lumber and flour milling industries.

By the 1880s, the flour milling industry had really taken off with the expansion of wheat production on the plains of Minnesota, Iowa and the Dakotas. The first significant wave of settlers reached Minneapolis in the 1850s and 1860s. Many of these, from New York and New England, came in as town site developers, timber speculators and small businessmen, together with a sizeable migration from Scandinavia from the mid-1860s onwards.

In 1875, when Thomas and Maria with young John Arthur travelled from New York, Minneapolis was a frontier town of immigrant, largely Scandinavian people. With the development of the railroads, the Midwest was rapidly being opened up and developed. In the decade from 1880 to 1890 the population of Minneapolis almost

quadrupled from 46,887 to 164,738. Thomas arrived shortly before this rapid growth, in the early spring of 1875, just when the harsh Midwestern winter was starting to lose its grip. He would have been well placed to fulfil the requirements of the expanding populace who needed to furnish their new homes. He also recognised the urgent need for rented accommodation to serve the rapidly growing population. He invested in property in this increasingly prosperous, thriving and expanding city.

Minneapolis remained as America's leading saw milling and flour milling centre until well into the twentieth century. The city, which developed its own horse-drawn streetcar system from 1875, before electrification began in 1889, had many fine public buildings in its wide-open streets by the time Thomas and Maria with young John Arthur arrived. This was the city where Thomas made his mark as a highly successful man of business and of property.

Thomas's obvious business acumen, entrepreneurial flair and prodigiously hard work resulted in significant success and his business continued to prosper. He wrote:

We earned enough above our business requirements to build our home on Third Avenue South, to build an apartment block on 16th Street and our store on Sixth Street. We worked almost night and day.

Within five years of moving to Minneapolis Thomas was renting out homes in the apartment block that he had built on Sixteenth Street. Their new home, which he built in the south of this city of lakes, was located on a prime site near the shores of Diamond Lake and lay between Taft Park and Pearl Park.

Thomas and Maria, with ten-year-old John Arthur, returned for a visit to England in 1882-83. This visit followed the sudden death of his younger brother, Charles, who had collapsed with a heart attack and died, aged twenty-two, in 1881. It was also the time when Thomas's brother, Joseph, had been granted a year's sabbatical leave from his work as a minister in Iowa. Thomas and Joseph must have shared many of their experiences of their lives in America with the family during this time. Doubtless, this was also when their brother George, who had by now been widowed for nine

NORTHWESTERN FURNITURE MANUFACTURERS.

Thomas's nieces Ethel and Florence, Joseph and Rosamond's elder daughters, recalled being entranced by their Uncle Tom's home and Florence recorded:

Thomas Jeffery, the first of the family to come to America, spent time in New York before moving to Minneapolis where he established his own store and prospered in business. He bought a fine house and invested in other property – owned 'Flatts' (sic) which he rented – a good business man.

Thomas's intensely hard work and impressive achievement had, however, taken its toll on his health. He recorded that:

My health failed. Sold store and stock to W. L. Harris. My health improved. Returned to business.

His return to business was marked by expansion into furniture manufacture in addition to the ownership and management of what was now a major carpet and furniture store. By 1892 he was one of fifteen major North Western furniture manufacturers and owner of the Jeffery Parlor Furniture Company, manufacturers and wholesale dealers in upholstered furniture. It was based at numbers 525 to 531 Central Avenue in the heart of Minneapolis. A Sale Catalogue, dating from 1892, reveals an extensive building on Central Avenue producing a vast range of high quality furniture and household goods.

Central Minneapolis location of Jeffery Furniture Company

years and whose young children were being brought up at the *Riddings*, gave serious consideration to emigrating himself. The youngest brother, Arthur, was now approaching eighteen: he had been only a baby when his elder brothers left home and only six years old when Thomas had returned for a brief visit. He was most particularly enthralled as he learned first-hand of Thomas's life in America.

At some time before November 1883, Thomas and Maria and family returned to Minneapolis. They were certainly there to meet Rosamond, brother Joseph's new bride, off the train, on her journey westwards from New York. Arthur also came out to America at this time, returning with Thomas and family. When Arthur left, only Thomas's brother, twenty-seven-year-old Owen, remained at home to farm the *Riddings*.

By 1885 Thomas, Maria and twelve-year-old John Arthur were well established in their new home, with a German-born house servant, eighteen-year-old Miriam Seims. Thomas's young brother Arthur, aged nineteen was also living with them and working in the business.

Sadly however, serious tragedy struck the family in 1892 when Maria died, aged only fifty-two. Thomas had previously seen the death, as infants, of three of his children. Now, after twenty-two years of marriage, he had lost his much loved wife. She had given him invaluable support through the demanding early years as he was establishing their new life together. Thomas was left with their nineteen-year-old son John Arthur. Maria was described by Florence as:

… our generous Aunt Maria who sent us very nice Christmas presents when we were children. I remember little muffs and neck pieces of grey fur.

Florence recorded that when Maria died, Tom grieved for her and erected a large monument at her grave. When, thirty-five years later, Thomas died, he was taken and buried in Minneapolis next to Maria in the Jeffery plot in Lakewood Cemetery by Lake Calhoun, Minneapolis. It was quite close to where they had lived in Minneapolis.

It may well have been after Maria's death that Thomas had his significant sale of goods manufactured from his Jeffery Parlor Furniture Company. The sale catalogue is illustrative of the very high quality of furniture and household furnishings produced. This major sale occurred before America was to descend into the worst depression it had yet experienced. The late 1890s marked a period when economic conditions for both industrialists and farmers were poor.

After Maria died, Thomas's youngest sister, thirty-year-old Ellen (my grandmother), travelled out to America to keep house for him. According to Joseph and Rosamond's daughter Florence, she stayed for nearly a year. Thomas himself returned to visit the *Riddings* after Maria's death. He arrived in Liverpool from New York on the *Majestic* of the White Star Line on 26 April 1893. Only his unmarried brother Owen and unmarried sisters Fanny and Ellen remained at home with their mother Mary. Ellen may well have travelled with Thomas when he returned home to Minneapolis later that year. It may have been at this time that Thomas gave his mother a beautiful gold locket on which there is the delicate engraving '*Mother*' and which encloses pictures of Maria and himself. His mother Mary subsequently left it to her youngest daughter Ellen and I have now inherited it from her. It is today, one of my most treasured possessions and was worn by our own daughter on her wedding day a hundred years later.

In March 1927, two months before he died, Thomas wrote that the value of their estate at the time of Maria's death in 1892,

…. including Lodge Insurance, real estate, loans and mercantile business was much higher than at present.

It was doubtless during the time when he was in England in 1893 that he renewed his contact with Maria's twenty-four-year-old niece Jessie Hague. He asked her

The 'Teutonic' which brought Jessie Hague to New York in December 1893

to marry him and she agreed. Jessie spent the next few months preparing for her marriage and emigration. She departed from Liverpool in November on the *Teutonic* and arrived in New York on 15 December. It is likely that she was met by the Hagues of New York prior to travelling on to Minneapolis. Thomas and Jessie were married on 10 January 1894.

Jessie, Maria's niece, like her aunt, had trained as teacher. She was born on 17 June 1869 at Mansion Cottage, Whittington in Derbyshire. She was not yet six months old when Thomas had married Maria, over twenty-three years earlier, in November 1869. Her father, William B. Hague, a surveyor and mining engineer, was one of Maria's younger brothers and her mother was Lydia, nee Balmforth. Jessie was the second of five children and by 1891 the family were living at North Wingfield. The Derbyshire census of 1891 records that twenty-one-year-old Jessie was an assistant school-mistress.

On 11 November 1894 Jessie gave birth to twins, Adelaide and Charles. On the 1895 Minnesota State census, Thomas and Jessie are shown with their six-month-old twins, twenty-two-year-old John Arthur, seventeen-year-old Amelia Munroe and twenty-seven year-old Lily Fisher, domestic servants from Germany. There is no record of Charles after this date and it appears that, like John Arthur's twin brother, he must have died as a very young child.

There was some sort of celebration in Minneapolis. We went down town and sat in a window of Uncle Tom's building – there were bright lights and street cars – some horse drawn - the policemen on horse back. Some of the lights seemed to be floating in the sky.

It was around 1895 to '96, when Thomas's brother, Joseph, with his wife Rosamond and their five young children, who at the time were living in Sioux Rapids, Iowa, stayed with Thomas and Jessie in Minneapolis. Their elder daughters Florence and Ethel recall the visit:

Florence recalled:

I remember a visit to Minneapolis when we were living in Sioux Rapids. It was very wonderful to us five children. There was some sort of celebration in Minneapolis. We went down town and sat in a window of Uncle Tom's building – there were bright lights and street cars – some horse drawn - the policemen on horse-back. Some of the lights seemed to be floating in the sky. I remember Uncle Tom's house with its lovely flower beds. Shopping at the 'Glass Block Store' - Driving around with Uncle Tom – his fine horse and carriage – the paved streets – wood paving in places. I remember that Dad took us for walks so that we would be out of the way. We resented that. No doubt they, especially Aunt Jessie, were glad to see us leave. I even heard some remark she made to a neighbour that it was usually the relatives you knew least who visited you most. Another wonderful thing – there was a bedroom with running water and a light always on. We must have been pests with that. We five had our pictures taken.

I even heard some remark she made to a neighbour that it was usually the relatives you knew least who visited you most.

In May 1897 Thomas, Jessie and two-and-a-half year-old Adelaide returned for another visit to the *Riddings*. Having embarked from Portland, Maine on the *Laurentian* of the Allen Line of Royal Mail Steamers, they landed at Liverpool in May. This would be Adelaide's first visit to her grandmother's home and Mary's first sight of the fifth of her eight American granddaughters. Jessie, writing many years later, recalled her vivid memories and the kindness of her mother-in-law, Mary and all the family.

Thomas's children, grandchildren and great grandchildren and his retirement to grow oranges in California

Thomas and Jessie, with their young daughter Adelaide, were building a new life together. At the same time Thomas and Maria's son, twenty-five-year-old John Arthur, (Art), was preparing to embark on his own married life. Art married Myra May Anderson, on 19 November 1898. They settled in Hennepin, Minneapolis at 2643 Irving Avenue South.

Myra nee Anderson Jeffery around the turn of the century

Myra came from a family which would bring an extraordinarily interesting heritage to Thomas and Maria's grandchildren. Her direct ancestors, originating from north Yorkshire and Scotland, were from Virginia and amongst some of the earliest Colonial settlers. At some time before Myra's birth, her forebears had moved from the ordered life of Old Virginia society to the raw frontier lands of the Midwest.

Myra Anderson, born in Minneapolis on 22 May 1874, was the daughter of Richard Whiting Anderson from

Dubuque, Iowa and Adeline Amelia Ham of Cedar Falls, Iowa. Myra's paternal grandfather had married Frances Ann Whiting. It was these Anderson-Whiting forebears who provided Thomas and Maria's grandchildren, and their descendants, with their remarkable ancestral heritage.

Frances Ann Whiting was born in a lovely old family plantation home, built in 1800, near Marshall, Virginia. It nestled in the valley between the Wildcat and Blue Ridge Mountains and was appropriately named Mountain View. Her paternal grandfather, Lieutenant Henry Whiting, Commissioner of Berkeley County and Justice of Frederick County, Virginia, served with the Fourth Virginia Regiment during the Revolutionary War. Both Colonel Henry Whiting and his father Major Henry Whiting served under the British Crown during the Colonial Wars.

In fact, it is possible to trace this heritage back even earlier in the life of the American Colonies when, Colonel Henry Whiting, the great, great-grandfather of Frances Ann Whiting, married Anne Beverley, granddaughter of Major Robert Beverley. Robert Beverley, from Beverley, Yorkshire came to Virginia and settled near Jamestown, in 1663. He became a prominent figure in the Colony and

From the year 1668 to the year 1676, I served His Majesty in military and civil offices of trust with fidelity and approbation. [1]

In addition to his military and political activities, Major Beverley was a plantation owner of considerable standing.

Frances Ann Whiting's maternal grandfather, Dr Gustavus Brown, served as assistant Surgeon General in the Army during the Revolutionary War. Mustered out in 1783, he later practiced medicine in Warrington, Virginia.

[1] Virginia Historical Magazine Volume 2 page 405

ABOVE *Myra Anderson in her twenties around the time of her marriage to John Arthur (Art) Jeffery*

RIGHT *Myra with her youngest sister Fay*

Myra nee Anderson Jeffery in the San Bernadino mountains when staying with Thomas and Jessie at Redlands, California

This ancestral heritage, and that of their Jeffery grandfather, with his roots in the farmland of Derbyshire for over 400 years, provided a proud inheritance for Thomas and Maria's descendants.

Art and Myra's three children were all born in Minneapolis. Harold Whiting arrived on 2 September 1899 and was followed four years later by Dorothy Rose who sadly died in 1909. Their last child, another John Arthur, was born on 7 December 1912.

Around the time that Art and Myra were embarking on their own family life, in the final years of the nineteenth century, Art's father, Thomas, recorded that he met with several misfortunes and losses from fires.

He wrote that

I finally retired from mercantile business and came to California on account of my health.

He invested funds from the sale of the Minneapolis business in orange groves and a home in Redlands, between Los Angeles and San Bernardino.

The land was in his blood although the dairy farm in Derbyshire, which he had left over thirty years before, was a far cry from his orange grove in California where he spent the rest of his days.

Thomas's new home in Redlands with its beautiful views of the San Bernadino Mountains was located at 405 West Palm Avenue, Redlands. The house was usually simply referred to by the family as *Redlands*.

BELOW *Art and Myra Jeffery with their first two children, Harold Whiting and Dorothy Rose circa 1905*

ABOVE TOP *Thomas's first grandchild, Harold Whiting Jeffery with his nurse in 1899*

ABOVE *Thomas, Jessie and Adelaide visiting Art and Myra and grandchildren in Minneapolis circa 1903. L. to r. Myra holding baby Dorothy, Harold, Art, Jessie, Adelaide, Thomas*

They bought a house and an orange grove in Redlands, California at a time when oranges were a profitable crop. It was a pleasant hobby for him and kept him out of doors.

Florence wrote of her memories of her Uncle Thomas at this time.

After Tom retired, he and Aunt Jessie and Adelaide moved to California. Tom had worked hard and his health needed a warmer climate. They bought a house and an orange grove in Redlands, California at a time when oranges were a profitable crop. It was a pleasant hobby for him and kept him out of doors. He liked gardening and when he came back to California after one of his many trips to England, he brought two fuchsia plants from the Riddings garden. To his surprise they grew and became giants and were a great curiosity.

Art and Myra and their young family would regularly escape the bitter cold of the Minnesota winters and stay with Thomas, Jessie and young Adelaide in their large home in Redlands, California where, some years later, Jessie, in a letter before Christmas, to her sister-in-law Ellen, wrote:

Today is another warm day – temperature about 80 which we would gladly exchange for a drenching shower of rain, not having had any rain, except for a little shower, since last April. Everything is very dry outside of the gardens and the orange groves, which are thoroughly irrigated twice a month – running water for four or five nights to keep the fruit growing.

LEFT *Art and Myra Jeffery with Harold, Minneapolis circa 1909*

ABOVE *Art and Myra Jeffery at home in Minneapolis*

ABOVE *Thomas in his orange groves with Mexican workers, Redlands*

LEFT *Thomas riding on his Redlands property, California*

BELOW *At Redlands circa 1902. L. to r. Thomas, Jessie, Adelaide, Myra, Art*

In the summer of 1905, Thomas, Jessie and ten-year-old Adelaide, returned to visit the *Riddings*. Departing from New York on the Cunard liner *Campania*, the three of them arrived in Liverpool on 10 June. Thomas's mother, Mary, was now aged eighty-seven. She had remained at the *Riddings*, with her unmarried daughter Fanny, together with her widowed daughter Mary and fifteen-year-old grandson Percy Spencer. Owen, who had married Hester Bannister in 1895, now farmed both the *Riddings* and *Bentley Fields* farms. They were living at *Bentley Fields* with their children Dorothy (Dolly) and Thomas (Tom).

Adelaide remembered this visit vividly and recalled not only her grandmother, uncles and aunts, but particularly her young cousins. Fifteen-year-old Percy Spencer, eight-year-old Dolly and six-year-old Tom were her particularly close companions during that Edwardian summer of 1905.

When I visited Adelaide in Santa Barbara in 1968, I recall being shown photographs taken by her parents during this visit of 1905, and the warmth with which she recalled her cousins Percy, Dolly and Tom.

ABOVE TOP *Leaving from Redlands on a hunting expedition circa 1903. Thomas and Art in the front of the carriage with Jessie and Myra in the back. Adelaide rides her pony*

ABOVE *On the beach, Californian coast, circa 1903, l. to r. Myra, Thomas, Jessie, Art, Adelaide*

Thomas's youngest sister, Ellen, had married William Hellaby in 1897. By the end of 1902 they were farming at nearby *Bentley Hall* with their first-born son, three and a half year-old William Jeffery, always known as Jeff, my father. Adelaide, with her parents, visited her Aunt Nellie and Uncle Will and so met another young cousin. This would be the first occasion when my father met with his American cousin Adelaide. It would be fifty-three years before they met again.

In a Christmas note written seventy years later, Adelaide recalled her memories:

I treasure a wonderful picture of 'Grandma Riddings' in my room. It was probably given to my parents in 1905 when we were there and I could ride on Percy Spencer's horse.

Below *Thomas, Jessie and Adelaide circa 1902*

The family's memorable visit to the *Riddings* in the summer of 1905, would be the last time Thomas would see his mother. He had maintained regular contact over the forty years since sailing to America and visited on numerous occasions. That same summer was also one when lasting warm and vivid memories of her *Grandma Riddings* were indelibly imprinted on Adelaide's mind and in her heart. Mary died on 17 February 1906. Thomas's son Art and his daughter Adelaide were the only two of her eleven American grandchildren that she would ever see.

The last three decades of Thomas's long and fulfilling life were spent with Jessie on his orange groves at Redlands. It was at their Redlands home on West Palm Avenue that Adelaide grew up and Art and his family would regularly visit. After his successful but stressful life in business and as a prominent citizen of Minneapolis, his time at Redlands may well have been some of his happiest years.

Redlands in Southern California, around fifty miles from the Pacific coast is situated in a beautiful area near the

foothills of the San Bernadino Mountains. Until the 1880s, when it was connected by rail to San Francisco and Salt Lake City, it was frontier territory. The railroad connection triggered a land boom and the area, with its

Above *Thomas with his daughter Adelaide circa 1901*

Above *Thomas and Jessie's daughter Adelaide circa 1905*

hot dry climate and ready access to water, was recognised as an ideal centre for the growth of oranges. By the late 1880s citrus production had taken off and Redlands has been described as the only known 'Agricultural Boom Town' in America.

In the mid 1890s Thomas established his orange groves at Redlands. Pioneering Thomas from the *Riddings* farm in Derbyshire had landed in New York in 1865. (Strangely, it was the same year that a sheep herder is recorded as being the first settler on the present day site of Redlands.) In 1875 Thomas's pioneering spirit had taken him to the developing frontier city of Minneapolis: he had indeed responded to the mantra of 'Go West Young Man' which had been popularised by Horace Greeley in the mid-nineteenth century. Twenty years on he was part of the booming Redlands orange industry and enjoying family life in an area which today continues to attract visitors for its majestic scenery and favourable climate. Indeed, he may well be said to have fulfilled the American dream.

The San Bernadino Mountains provide a magnificent backdrop to the Redlands region and in the early years of the twentieth century it was a land which Thomas's family grew to love. It is the area where my husband, daughter and I first met Thomas's younger grandson John and his wife Marion when we stayed with them in their log cabin at Big Bear Lake in 1968. The Southern Californian coast

ABOVE LEFT *Adelaide with Jessie at Redlands, California circa 1906*

ABOVE RIGHT *Adelaide at Redlands circa 1907*

is also where I met his daughter Adelaide again and, in the summer of 1992, his great grandsons, John and Michael.

In the foothills of the San Bernadino Mountains there is a large and intriguing rock carving which can be seen for

ABOVE *Thomas with his family on the beach, Pacific coast circa 1910. L. to r. Myra, Jessie, Thomas, Adelaide, Harold, Art*

many miles around. A significant landmark, which has for centuries been a symbol of the San Bernadino Valley, firstly to the indigenous Indians and then to the pioneers and settlers who followed, it was a site which Thomas and family would frequently visit.

Although a regular visitor with his family to his father's home in California, Art remained in Minneapolis where, as president of the Menzel and Jeffery Iron Foundry, he had become a prominent man of business like his father before him.

ABOVE LEFT *Thomas with family at Arrowhead in the San Bernadino Mountains circa 1909. L. to r. Art, Harold, Adelaide, Jessie, Thomas*

ABOVE RIGHT *Jessie nee Hague at Ocean Point, Santa Monica, California in the early twentieth century*

LEFT *Menzel and Jeffery Iron Foundry, Minneapolis*

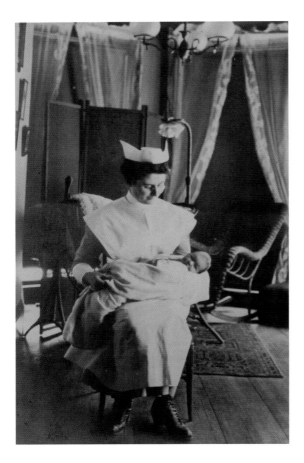

Thomas's younger grandson John Arthur the second with his nurse in his grandfather's old home at 2000, Third Avenue South, Minneapolis

On 7 December 1912 Art and Myra's second son was born in Minneapolis. They had tragically lost their six-year-old daughter Dorothy three years previously and their son Harold was now thirteen years old. This second grandson for Thomas was christened John Arthur after his father. He was always known as John.

Art and Myra eventually retired to Southern California but those days were far ahead at the time of their younger son's birth in 1912. However, John Arthur was very young when he was first introduced to the land of the San Bernadinos and his Grandfather Thomas's home in Redlands.

ABOVE TOP *A journey to Arrowhead in the San Bernadino mountains. L. to r. Harold, Thomas, Art with young John in front, Jessie*

ABOVE CENTRE *L. to r. Myra, Thomas, Jessie, John on his brother Harold's knee*

ABOVE *Thomas's grandsons Harold and John at Devil's Lake in the San Bernadinos*

The family at Redlands circa 1914, l. to r. Myra, John, Harold, Thomas, Jessie

Art, Myra and Harold's visit to Arthur Jeffery's family in Seattle. L. to r. Alex, Myra, Charles, mother Margaret, daughter Margaret, Arthur, Harold

Thomas maintained contact with his youngest brother Arthur, who had joined him in Minneapolis in 1883, throughout his life. Arthur and his family had also moved out West but in their case it was to the state of Washington. Around 1914, when Arthur and his family were living in Seattle, Art and Myra visited them and their son Harold met his cousins Charles Arthur, Alexander and Margaret Jeffery.

On 22 November 1917, Thomas, Jessie and Adelaide, attended the wedding of Art and Myra's elder son, Harold Whiting Jeffery, when he married Lois Steel Cobb. Later the following year, on 17 April, Thomas was presented with his first great grandson, Harold Whiting Junior, born in Preoria, Illinois.

Harold and Lois gave Thomas two further great-grand-sons: Robert Frederick, born 21 September 1920 in Preoria, Illinois and Thomas Arthur, born 16 June 1922 in Chicago, Illinois.

RIGHT *Harold Whiting Jeffery with his sons, l. to r. Harold, Thomas, Harold Jr., Robert*

ABOVE *Adelaide Jeffery's husband, Professor Lawrence Henderson*

LEFT *Adelaide at Smith College, University of Massachusetts– fourth from the left*

Meanwhile, Adelaide had moved East for her Higher Education. She entered the prestigious highly elite Smith College of the University of Massachusetts in 1911 and graduated in 1915.

In 1920 she was living with her half-brother, Art and his wife, Myra, in Minneapolis and it was here that she met her future husband – Lawrence Henderson. Lawrence was a student at St Olaf College, Northfield, Minnesota between 1911 and 1915. He studied for both his Masters Degree and Doctorate in Chemistry at the University of Chicago. He and Adelaide lived in Winnetka, Chicago until they retired to Santa Barbara, California. Lawrence had a brilliant career as a scientist and, in addition to working as a research chemist with Atlantic Refineries in the late 1920s and early 1930s he became Professor of Chemistry at the Universities of Minnesota and North Western University, Chicago.

Thomas and Jessie maintained very close contact with Adelaide and Lawrence across the two thousand miles which now separated them and this was continued after Thomas's death. Jessie, who was a regular correspondent of her sister-in-law, my grandmother, wrote that Adelaide and Lawrence:

...... have a lovely home and though over two thousand miles distant we have constant communication by long distance telephone and they sometimes make the long journey and come and visit .... This continent is so vast in size and methods of travel are so comfortable and so easy that a journey of two or three thousand miles either by plane or bus or motor car is considered nothing at all.

.... a lovely place, situated in beautiful forest land and on the borders of mighty Lake Michigan.

In another letter, Jessie wrote of Adelaide and Lawrence's lives in Chicago:

The great city of Chicago of world-wide fame, or should I say notoriety?

And subsequently she went on to say that Winnetka, where they live, is

.... a lovely place, situated in beautiful forest land and on the borders of mighty Lake Michigan.

Thomas continued to enjoy his orange groves in Redlands but, at some time during the 1920s, there was a year when serious and unusually late frosts killed off the orange blossom and so wrecked the harvest. Thomas described it as the 'big freeze' which

.... reduced the value of our orange groves.

After the freeze, when the value of orange groves depreciated significantly, and with America moving into recession, he went on to record that:

Lodge Insurance values decreased, Knights of Honour failed and the Remington addition had also depreciated.

Clearly, recession was having a serious effect on Thomas's investments at this time.

Thomas and Jessie did make a further visit to the *Riddings* after his mother had died. It is reasonable to suggest that this may well have been in the early summer of 1925, before Thomas's own health started to fail. Jessie recalled that she first met Dorothy Jeffery, the daughter of Thomas's brother Owen, when Dorothy, who was born in 1923, was

…. just a little girl at the Riddings.

Thomas was approaching eighty-two when he died on 11 May 1927. The letter which he wrote to his wife Jessie, son John Arthur and daughter Adelaide, which outlined the key events of his life and finally told of the depreciation in value of the orange groves, was dated 5 March 1927. It concluded:

It became necessary to change my will.
All household goods belong to my wife except a few requests:

REQUESTS:
To my wife, Jessie H. Jeffery,
To my son, John Arthur Jeffery,
To my daughter, Adelaide J. Henderson

The automobile we use is exclusively the property of my wife.
I request all of any interest I may have in the household goods become the property of my wife, except items mentioned below.
I request that my daughter, Adelaide Jeffery Henderson, shall have my writing desk and gold pen. I request that my son, John Arthur Jeffery, shall have my gold watch and chain, picture of Henry Ward Beecher who baptised him, picture of Christ at the well (his mother wished that he should inherit the same).
My mother gave him the English brass candlesticks at my death.

Additional Statement: October 7, 1919, I made a will giving to my wife the home place in Redlands, after that my wife, son and daughter to have share and share alike in my estate. March 5, 1927, I made a codicil to my will providing additional income from my estate of $20,000.00 to my wife to which my son and daughter were pleased to consent and appreciate the care and nursing during my long illness and since.

All I possess is absolutely my own. I never received one dollar from my first wife or my second. From my father's estate I received about $300 00.

Thomas Jeffery   March 5, 1927

Thomas Jeffery Memorial, Lakewood cemetery, Hennepin, Minneapolis

Thomas was buried with his first wife Maria at Lakewood cemetery, Minneapolis, bordering Lake Calhoun.

Two of Thomas and Maria's great grandsons, Harold Whiting Jr. and Thomas Arthur, also went on to have sons who were christened Thomas, born in 1946 and 1948 respectively. It is interesting to note that great-grandson Thomas Arthur, who later married Esther Lois Bryant on 27 July 1944, in Augusta, Georgia, went on to have a son Thomas Arthur who was born on 16 June 1946 in Chicago, Illinois. This, great, great-grandson Thomas was born just over one hundred years after Thomas Jeffery was born at the *Riddings*, Derbyshire on 16 September 1845.

Roots and Links through time and space

The year following his father's death, Art, with Myra and their younger son, fifteen-year-old John Arthur Junior (always known as John), visited the family in England on a couple of occasions. Art, at fifty-five, had now retired from his work as president of a foundry company. On 21 April 1928 the three of them arrived in Cardiff on the ship *Mui* of the Harri Steamship Company shipping line. It was a long voyage as they had departed from Vancouver. They stayed initially at the Hotel Cecil in London. Later the same year, they returned on the *SS Scythia* of the Cunard line, leaving from New York, calling in at Boston, and arrived in Cardiff on 31 July. On this second trip, they also visited Europe. They sailed from Cherbourg on the *Montrose* on 14 September and arrived at Quebec on the 21st before proceeding back home to Minneapolis.

Mary Jeffery of the *Home Farm, West Broughton*, who would have been ten years old at the time, remembers their visit well. She particularly recalled her young cousin John.

I remember when they visited here. I particularly remember their good-looking young son.

BELOW *R.M.S. Scythia on which Art, Myra and their son John Arthur Jeffery sailed on 20 July 1928*

Eighty years later, John's son Michael Jeffery and his family from Alaska, were to meet Mary at the *Home Farm, West Broughton*, at the time of the Jeffery Reunion of 2008.

When Art and Myra with fifteen-year-old John sailed for England on the Scythia on 20 July 1928 they were to be away from home two months. They spent a few days in London visiting the sights before travelling to Derbyshire where they stayed with Art's Aunt Nellie and Uncle Will (Ellen and William Hellaby) at *Bentley Hall*. In the photograph album recording their visit they wrote:

Bentley Hall August 5 1928 where we stayed – now owned by the Hellabys (Nellie Jeffery). Supposed to be haunted.

They visited many of the family including those at the *Riddings*, *Bentley Fields*, *Home Farm West Broughton*, *Aston House* and *Fauld House* before spending five weeks touring in Europe. On 6 August they took a small Fokker plane from Croydon to Amsterdam and on a photograph taken from the air Myra recorded:

I was the only woman on this plane with fifteen men. We rode for three hours. Landed at Amsterdam starting at Croydon Fields, England.

BELOW *Passport photograph John Arthur, Myra and John Arthur Jr. Jeffery 1928*

LEFT *Art with his son John at Croydon Airport at 10 am on 6 August 1928*

BELOW LEFT *John Jeffery in his study at the University of Pennsylvania 1931*

BELOW RIGHT *John Jeffery with his car at University*

Art and Myra maintained contact with his father Thomas's family in Derbyshire as did their youngest son John Arthur. He, in addition to visiting with his parents in 1928, visited on his own when he was twenty-three, returning to New York on the *Queen Mary* on 1 June 1936. Later, John also returned with his wife Marion when they stayed at *Bentley Fields* farm in the early 1960s.

John's return visit to England in 1936 followed his graduation. In October 1931 John started at the University of Pennsylvania. It was here where later he entered the Wharton School of Finance and Commerce.

After Art retired, in addition to visiting relatives in England, he and Myra took a number of trips to states

in the east, particularly Virginia. Here they explored the land of Myra's seventeenth-century Colonial ancestors. Myra was particularly interested to discover her roots via her paternal grandmother, Frances Ann Whiting. She recorded the following in a letter from Madison, Wisconsin, to her sister Fay, dated 18 October 1932.

We are on the last leg of our trip and are staying overnight here, after doing over 300 miles today. Have stayed here before so feel at home .... We went to Washington D.C. and as we were going south the next morning, called the Atkesons and they came down to our hotel. She was Helen Whiting. She was from Marshall, Virginia where our branch came from. .... She is very pretty and her accent is so southern that you have to listen hard. .... Well, we got information from her regarding the location of old 'Mountain View'. It is about 45 miles from

Washington D.C.. Helen told us of a Mrs Cooper Dawson who lives just outside of Alexandria, and who was a Homer before her marriage, who is the present owner …………….. . She cannot keep it up, or rather restore it as she is not financially able. It goes to her brother when she dies so it 'goes down the family' this way. Consequently, I guess the old place is doomed. What a shame as it was once a lovely place, mountains around it, the Blue Ridge on one side and the Wild Cat at the back – the latter almost part of the farm. ……… I imagine 'Mountain View' must have had about 15 rooms. We went through it. I gathered some black walnuts which abound on the place and will send you and Rose some as a souvenir from the old place – our grand-mother's old home.

The following are also excerpts from letters to her sister Fay during this search for the ancestors of Thomas and Maria's grandchildren.

At Highgate, Gloucester County, Virginia is the tomb of Catherine Beverley Whiting, daughter of Colonel (later Major) Whiting and Elizabeth Sewell, his wife. On the tomb are the Whiting Arms.

Major Henry Whiting's daughter Catherine married John Washington of Highgate who was the uncle of General George Washington.

From what I can make out, our Whiting family seem to have been mostly lawyers. You know Uncle George and Uncle Henry Anderson were lawyers too.

The memorial window of the Whitings is in Berryville, Virginia, one mile from Summit Point, Virginia.

We went through it. I gathered some black walnuts which abound on the place and will send you and Rose some as a souvenir from the old place – our grandmother's old home.

This particular letter contains a wealth of information of meetings with Whiting cousins and former homes in Virginia, of which the following is an excerpt.

It is pure Colonial inside, with a staircase and delicate rail going to the third floor – exquisite taste.

…………... . As it was late in the after noon when we arrived at Gloucester, Virginia, we decided to look up 'Elmington', the old home of the Whitings, about four miles out. …………… The present beautiful place isn't the original house built by our ancestor, Major Henry Whiting. That burned down, as so many of the wonderful old homes did in those times. Only five acres remains of the original three thousand. ……….. . 'Elmington' is a gorgeous old place, in the midst of a high plantation, located on the North River. It is pure Colonial inside, with a staircase and delicate rail going to the third floor – exquisite taste. It occurred to me to ask 'which is the worse – to own 'Elmington' and not to belong or to belong and not to own it?'

Old *Elmington*, the family home of the Whitings of Gloucester County, Virginia was built in the mid-seventeenth century. Living there in 1674 was Major Henry Whiting, Warden of Ware Church. In 1775 it was the home of Colonel Thomas Whiting, King's Attorney. No Whiting has lived there since 1803 when Peter Beverley Whiting sold it to a Mr Thomas Dabney, who lived there for some time before selling it on to a Mr John Tabb of Whitemarsh, Virginia. When the original old house burned down, somewhere between 1842 and 1844, Mr Tabb built the present house and in 1848 presented it to his son Professor Tabb as a wedding gift. Professor Tabb sold *Elmington* during the Civil War and it has since changed hands many times. A colonnade has been added, at both the front and the back since the original construction. It was described by Myra in the 1930s as a beautiful old building.

Their Whiting-Anderson heritage provided the descendants of Thomas and Maria with a fascinating inheritance in which both the military and the legal professions are prominent. It is interesting to note that their first great grandson, born in 1918, became Lieutenant Commander Harold Whiting Jeffery during World War II and that their last great grandson, born in 1944, has become Superior Court Judge Michael Jeffery in Barrow, Alaska.

Return to California

In their later years, Art and Myra followed Thomas and Jessie and moved from Minneapolis to California. Their home was in Los Angeles, on South Beverley Glen Boulevard. This enabled them to see more of their married sons and their families, who were also living in California. Additionally, they could see more of Art's stepmother, Jessie, who continued to live on in the family home in Redlands. Myra died in Los Angeles on 10 March 1946 and Art died the following year on 13 November 1947.

Thomas and Jessie's home, at 405 West Palm Avenue, Redlands, was beautiful and clearly much loved by all the family. Jessie continued to live there for thirty years after Thomas's death. Writing to her sister-in-law Ellen, Jessie painted a vivid picture of her life in California. On 30 November 1949 she wrote:

Jessie Jeffery in her later years at Redlands, California

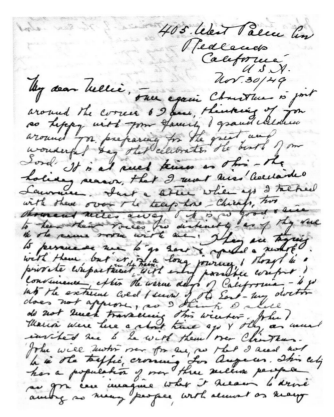

Letter from Thomas Jeffery's widow, Jessie to my grandmother, Ellen

My Dear Nellie,

Once again, Christmas is around the corner and I am thinking of you with your family and grandchildren around preparing for the great and wonderful Day that celebrates the birth of our Lord.

It is at such times as this, that I most miss Adelaide and Lawrence. Just a little while ago, I talked with them over the telephone – Chicago, two thousand miles away and it was so good and nice to hear their voices as distinctly as if they were in the same room with me.

They are trying to persuade me to go East and spend a month with them, but it is a long journey and, though in a private compartment on the train with every possible comfort and convenience, after the warm days of California, to go into the extreme cold and snow of the East, my doctor does not approve, so I think I shall not do much travelling this winter.

John and Marion were here a short time ago and they, as usual, invited me to be with them over Christmas. John will motor over for me, so that I need not be in the traffic crossing Los Angeles. This city has a population of over three million people so that you can imagine what it means to drive among so many people with so many cars. I think I wrote to you in one of my

letters that John's home is at Santa Monica – about 120 miles from Redlands. I do always so enjoy being with them and their two young boys. (John and Michael). *After the holidays, John and Marion will drive me home and stay a few days. The weekend after next, they and the boys are coming to spend the weekend with me.*

Art and Myra's younger son, John, had married Marion Ives on 2 March 1939 in California. John and Marion's elder son, John Arthur, born on 17 January 1940, continues to live in California and their younger son, Michael Ives, born on 29 December 1944, now lives in Alaska with his wife Esther and their three children, Christina, Nicole and Jordan.

LEFT *John and Marion Jeffery in 1939*

BELOW *Wedding of Thomas and Maria's younger grandson John Arthur the second to Marion Ives 1939*

John A. Jeffery, Jr., Southern California Branch, who came with Nylic August 22, 1940, qualified for Club membership his first year in the business and is doing a fine job of clientele building. He has been on the $20,000-a-Month

John A. Jeffery, Jr.

Honor Roll consecutively since his first month. A graduate of the Wharton School of Finance and Commerce at the University of Pennsylvania, Mr. Jeffery had three years' sales experience with an advertising agency before joining Nylic. His goal for 1942 is Top Club membership.

LEFT *Thomas and Maria's son, grandson and great grandson – John Arthurs One, Two and Three, 1941*

ABOVE RIGHT *John Arthur Two – news item – 1941*

Jessie's letter to my grandmother continued.

The last three weeks we have been surrounded by carpenters and painters. The terrific and continued snowstorms, the first in the history of California, caused the floor on the front veranda to warp and that meant taking down the rail and canopy and taking up the floor – a space of 31ft x 10ft and relaying an entire new floor with all its underpinning. It was quite a job but it does look really beautiful now it is finished with all the new white paint. Tom was always so proud of his home that I try to keep it just as he would have if he were here. I often wish that you and Clara could come over for a six months visit. We could all be so happy together. The house is large with six bedrooms and three bathrooms etc. Years ago, when Art and Myra and their children used to come and spend the winters with me, the bedrooms were all used but now the family is more or less scattered it is very seldom that all the bedrooms are occupied and I realise that this is a house that needs a family and the sound of many voices to keep it cheerful. Fortunately I have many friends so that I never feel lonely and though I have a very good gardener I like to work among the flowers and the shrubs. I enjoy reading very much and Lawrence frequently sends me interesting books but since the serious operation on my eyes I am not allowed to read for too long at a time.

I do not wear glasses, except for reading and distance glasses when driving, though I do not drive my own car anymore, but have a chauffeur, driving conditions being what they are in heavy traffic, it is safer that I should not drive. I feel the loss very much having driven a car for 38 years. When I wished to do anything or do an errand or go to the Post Office it was easy to hop into the car and drive away – but now I have to wait to be driven. The years as we grow older do make a difference to our lives.

I suppose you will be seeing sister Clara – please do give her my most affectionate remembrances, and to all your family and the best of good wishes.

ABOVE *Thomas and Maria's grandson, John, with his wife Marion at Big Bear Lake in the San Bernadino Mountains, California*

Adelaide and Lawrence are well and happy and the busiest of busy people. Last week, the college at which Adelaide won her B.A .degree was conducting a campaign in the Chicago area to raise the sum of $ 7,000 000 – and she is taking her part in the many meetings, banquets and luncheons. Tom was always so proud of his daughter and Art was proud of his sister.

The years bring many changes and the children grow up and take their places in the world and its activities. I realise what a joy and comfort it is to you to see your sons and grandchildren doing so well in school – preparing for what life may hold for them.

Again a Merry Christmas and a most Happy New Year – keeping in the best of health and my love from

Jessie

John Arthur the Second with Jessie at the family home at Redlands, California

My grandmother was an assiduous correspondent and maintained close links with her emigrant brothers and their families. After her death in 1950 these links were continued initially via my cousin Dorothy Jeffery of the *Riddings* and then followed up by myself.

During the year 1951-52, my cousin Dorothy visited America on a teaching exchange and during that year met many of the descendants of the three brothers – Thomas, Joseph and Arthur – who all made their lives in America. I followed this up some years later when my husband was also on a teaching exchange. We too met up with many of our American cousins spread across the continent and my own parents also came out to see us during our year when my father experienced the delight of meeting the American descendants of his mother's brothers.

Many letters have crossed the Atlantic between the American and English Jefferys and, in addition to providing a wealth of interesting vignettes of family lives, all are indicative of the warmth and strength of the family bonds across the many years and thousands of miles.

In one of Jessie's New Year letters from *Redlands* in 1953, she revealed that that they had had a warm winter to date and although there was much snow on the mountain peaks, the temperature in the valley had been around 70 to 75 degrees. The peach trees were a mass of pink flowers and the orange groves were laden with colourful fruit. The garden was looking very colourful with roses and many other flowers, especially daffodils, narcissus and purple and white iris, and soon the white lilac would be in bloom.

She wrote that Lawrence took a three weeks vacation from the laboratories and he and Adelaide drove down from Chicago to spend Christmas with her. They motored for Christmas week to Ranch Santa Fe, a beautiful resort about 160 miles from Redlands where they were able to enjoy the pleasures of La Jolla Beach and Tennis Club for a couple of days. En route to San Diego, they also visited John and Marion and their boys, John and Michael, in Los Angeles.

Jessie also maintained close contact with Thomas's brother Arthur's family in Washington. She recounts that Aunt Maggie (Arthur's widow) would be coming to stay with her and, that Arthur's son, Alex and his wife Frieda, together with Arthur's daughter, Margaret and husband Jack would also be visiting. (See chapter on Arthur.)

This letter also spoke of the recent election of President Eisenhower and that newspapers reported the preparations in England for the coronation festivities. Several of her Redlands friends, who would be sailing for Southampton in March and April in order to be in London in June, wished her to go with them. They hoped that after the coronation, they could motor in England and that she would be able to advise them on places to visit. Jessie, however, indicated that she would prefer not to be in England in what she felt would inevitably be such a crowded season as Coronation Year.

The two of Thomas's sisters in Derbyshire, who were closest to Jessie, were Ellen and Clara. Ellen passed away as the New Year opened in 1950 and Clara died the following year. Jessie's letter expressed how good they

Adelaide and Lawrence and their
Santa Barbara home, California

were about telling her news of the family and how very much she missed them. They had been the last remaining link with Thomas's generation.

Jessie's letter finished with fondest regards to family and most particularly to Percy Spencer (Thomas's nephew) who she remembered so well when visiting *Bentley Fields* and the *Riddings*.

In 1955 Adelaide and Lawrence moved from Winnetka, Chicago to Santa Barbara, California, where they could be significantly closer to Jessie in Redlands and also to John and Marion and their two boys in Westwood, Los Angeles. Their home, which they had built in Santa Barbara, was delightful and my family and I had the great pleasure of visiting Adelaide there during the summer of 1968.

Adelaide described their hillside house as being quite different from their old home in Winnetka. She described the view of the mountains as superb and enthused that there was much to do in the community and, although people were friendly, she still missed her incomparable friends of Winnetka days. When we visited her, she showed us photographs taken of family members living at the *Riddings* and *Bentley Fields* and I recall a particular one of her cousin Percy Spencer of whom she had clearly been very fond. She was wonderfully hospitable and most particularly kind to our young daughter Clare, when she arranged for us to visit Disneyland. Following our visit with Adelaide, we also experienced the delight of visiting with John and Marion, in their summer home of a log cabin by Big Bear Lake in the San Bernadino Mountains behind

Los Angeles. Here we discovered that John made powerful martinis and cooked a mean steak!

In the early summer of 1955, before Adelaide and Lawrence had completed their move into their new home, Jessie suffered a heart attack and spent five weeks in hospital. During this time they took care of her Redlands home. Jessie made a good recovery and eventually spent three weeks recuperating with Adelaide and Lawrence in Santa Barbara. Jessie herself described how, following her recovery, Adelaide and Lawrence, took her for a while to their new home in Santa Barbara. She described it as a beautiful house with a lovely garden which they enjoyed very much. When she had fully recovered, Jessie returned to her Redlands home but was not allowed to be alone in the big house any longer.

Jessie, now in her eighties, described the many changes which had taken place in Redlands over recent years. Many orange groves had been rooted out and over 2000 new homes built and the streets downtown were *simply packed with motor cars*. She pointed out that those who had lived there for so many years did not like the crowds, preferring the quiet residential resort Redlands was in former years but that time *brought many changes which it was necessary to accept*.

By the end of the year of 1955 she had recovered and stayed at *Redlands* for Christmas where Adelaide described her mother as:

Looking very well, very pretty and very much in command of her ship!

Following that Christmas, Jessie wrote to family in England saying how very enjoyable it had been to have the house filled with happy people making the most of a joyous Christmas season. She also described the midnight service on Christmas Eve at Trinity Church which had been most enjoyable with a full choral service and three choirs. The floral decorations had been beautiful and there had been a very full congregation.

Christmas 1956 would be Jessie's last. She suffered a further heart attack and died at *Redlands* at 5.15 a.m. on Sunday 26 May 1957. She had managed to telephone her doctor on the Saturday night and he, together with a nurse, stayed with her through the night. It was almost thirty years to the day from the date of Thomas's death on 27 May 1927. In three weeks time, on 17 June, she would have reached her eighty-eighth birthday. Born in Derbyshire, where she had worked as a teacher in the early 1890s, she lived sixty-three years of her long and full life in America – in Minnesota and California. The funeral was held in the beautiful little Trinity Church in Redlands where she had worshipped for many years.

In the following year, Adelaide and Lawrence came to England. They embarked on the *Queen Mary*, arriving in Southampton 25 August and in early September spent time at the *Riddings*. It was almost fifty-three years since Adelaide had visited the *Riddings* with Thomas and Jessie, when, as a ten-year old, she had spent most of her time with her cousins Dolly and Tom – the children of her Uncle Owen and Aunt Hester and also with Percy Spencer, the son of her Aunt Polly (Mary). This was also the occasion when she first met her young three-year-old cousin Jeffery Hellaby at *Bentley Hall*, but doubtless found him rather too young to become a playmate. I do know, however, that my father very much enjoyed meeting Adelaide again during their 1958 visit.

Adelaide and Lawrence met up with many of their Jeffery relatives and it was during this visit that I first met Adelaide – my father's first cousin – at a family party thrown by William Offley Jeffery at the *Home Farm, West Broughton*. It would be ten years later, in the summer of 1968, when I returned to see Adelaide again, at her home in Santa Barbara, California.

In June 1964, writing from California, Adelaide warmly recalled her memories of meeting family in England and how very happy she and Lawrence were that they did

Adelaide and Lawrence's First Class passage to England on the Queen Mary

go to England in 1958 and had the pleasure of seeing so many of her cousins and visiting the *Riddings* together with other family homes. These others included the *Home Farm,* West Broughton, where Adelaide's cousin Offley Jeffery farmed and it was where I first met Adelaide.

The decade of the 1960s saw Adelaide and Lawrence well into their seventies and although, sadly, Lawrence's health started to fail, Adelaide continued to inform the family of news of John and Marion and their two boys John and Michael. She told of how:

When May arrives I always have a great desire to take off for other parts, to see England in the spring, then to the Loire valley in France and then to the Philadelphia area with its lovely gardens and the flowering dogwood. Come June, however, I am happy to relax and am quite content to settle for the comforts of home and the Santa Barbara climate.

BELOW Family party at the Riddings, 1958. Photo taken by Dorothy Jeffery
l. to r.: Thomas and Louie Jeffery, Lawrence and Adelaide, Ernest and Dolly
Hand, Jeffery Hellaby, Margaret Jeffery, William Jeffery, Percy Spencer,
Fred. Jeffery, Mabel Spencer, Ernest Hellaby, Thomas Jeffery, Ida Hellaby.

John's wife Marion was very active at this time, working at Resthaven, a small psychiatric hospital in Los Angeles. Originally she was on the board of trustees and made a contribution by organizing a volunteer group for service in the hospital. Then, as she did such a good job in personnel and public relations, she was asked to become a paid member of staff. Adelaide was left wondering how she managed to achieve so much as both she and John led an active social life and the drive from Westwood to down town Los Angeles was a good fourteen miles and always through heavy traffic. However, she observed that Marion loved this activity and its contacts and was much happier working than just being at home.

John and Marion's sons meanwhile were embarking on Higher Education and travelling. Adelaide, obviously very fond of them both, emphasised how very different they were in temperament.

During the late 1960s Lawrence's health declined further and his memory failed to the extent where Adelaide was advised he needed the regular care of a nursing home. Adelaide herself remained in good health in Santa

ABOVE John and Marion Jeffery with their sons, John and Michael

Barbara until shortly before Christmas, 1973, when she fell and broke her hip. On the very same day, 17 December, Lawrence, now aged 84, died. His death had been expected for some time and Adelaide expressed her profound gratitude that Lawrence never knew of her accident. John and Marion joined her in her hospital

LEFT *John and Marion sailing to the Virgin Isles*

ABOVE *Thomas Jeffery's descendants circa 1963: his younger grandson John Arthur the Second and his daughter Adelaide are on the left and his great grandsons Michael (left) and John Arthur the Third stand behind their mother Marion*

room for the funeral service. He was buried in the Jeffery plot in Minneapolis. Adelaide recovered well from her accident and in November 1974 she was writing to say that she was very well and that it didn't seem possible that she was about to be eighty years old. Her doctors had expressed their amazement and gratitude at her recovery and healing properties. She herself expressed her sincere gratitude and appreciation for her ancestry and put her recovery down to

…..her good Jeffery blood.

Shortly before Christmas 1975, Adelaide was still actively enjoying life in her Santa Barbara home where

….. with temperatures in the '70s, the roses, azaleas and poinsettias were in bloom.

John and Marion, who had recently visited Michael in India, drove up to spend time with her at least once a month. As always, her letters recalled her wealth of memories of time spent at the *Riddings*.

John and Marion's elder son – John Arthur the third, known to Adelaide as Johnny, studied at Yale and then at University in California. On 30 May 1964 he married Lorna Jane Tydon in Los Angeles. Later they were divorced and John married again. He had two children

but that marriage also ended in divorce. He lives at Manhattan Beach where we shared a beer with him in 1992. He was also very kind to our daughter and son-in-law when they visited briefly in February 1993.

John and Marion's younger son, Michael, graduated from both Stanford and Yale Universities. He graduated from Yale University Law School and, on graduation, Adelaide went to New Haven to visit him. During this time she was delighted to have the opportunity to learn about his interest in the programme to protect the rights of the Eskimos in Alaska. Earlier in the 1970s he had spent an extended period staying at an ashram in India, before practicing Law. In the vacations he also worked on behalf of the migrant farm workers in California. Michael moved as a law attorney, to Barrow, Alaska in January 1977. In 1978, on a business trip to London, he took the opportunity of visiting his roots and returned to visit family at the *Riddings*.

In 1978, aged eighty-three, Adelaide moved into a retirement home where she had her own apartment set in beautiful gardens and where there were many other retired professional people and where she was able to enjoy many interesting lectures. John and Marion continued to visit regularly and she enjoyed retirement living, including driving although, at eighty-four, she did not go down to Los Angeles any more with herself at the

Adelaide at her home in Santa Barbara, July 1980

wheel! The following Christmas of 1979 she spent with John and Marion and both their sons, as Michael would be coming south from Alaska.

In the summer of 1981, the strong trans-Atlantic links between the English and American Jefferys were reinforced when Jonathon Spencer, grandson of Adelaide's cousin Percy Spencer of *Bentley Fields* farm, visited Adelaide and managed to speak with Michael in Alaska, on the telelephone.

Adelaide continued to be active, enjoying her retirement for almost a further decade. She did, however, gradually slow down, becoming increasingly frail as she approached her mid-nineties, and thus it was John and Marion who continued the links with Jefferys in England.

Meanwhile, their younger son, Michael, was establishing himself in Alaska. On 20 December 1981, four years after moving to Barrow, Alaska, he wrote to his many friends and family across the world:

It seems like a good idea to share some of the things that have been happening to me this year. As usual, the time does not seem to arrive to me too often to write letters. As I write these words, the winter solstice is coming tomorrow and it is dark almost all day. In Barrow, the sun is gone from November 18th to January 24th. But at noon we have some light and pink glows on the southern horizon. The rest of the day we see the stars, the Northern lights rippling in the sky, and feel the wind that blows across the flatness of the tundra or the ice pack. Warm clothes, fur-lined parkas with wolf-trimmed hoods, make a lot of difference to keep everyone comfortable.

The hard climate brings the people together, and the Eskimos are a constant joy to be with. This year, for the first time since I've been in Barrow, I am staying here for the Christmas season. Occasions like this are a community event with church services, communal sharing feasts and native dances that everyone goes

to. After Christmas, there are native athletic games every night until New Year. On New Year's Eve there are church services until midnight, then native games all night until the night of January 1st, then a big Eskimo dance that finishes off this beautiful week of community activities.

At work, the high point this year was when the Supreme Court of the State of Alaska travelled to Barrow to hear the attorneys argue the law suit about the oil lease sale, that happened in 1979, for half a million acres in the Arctic Ocean. I have helped to represent the Eskimo people who have been telling the government that it should slow down. Such oil leases should be done later, but people are afraid right now that if there were an accident and an oil spill in the ocean, no-one could clean it up. Right now, we still do not have a decision from the Supreme Court – but it was an historic event for the highest court in the land to travel to a remote place like Barrow to hear these legal arguments.

Now we have space that is big enough for our legal services, and there are two more attorneys besides me. That is making it easier for me to do the travel that is necessary as part of the work that I do. It is also easier now to think about time to travel to other places.

I have continued to practice with the group of people who are doing the Eskimo dancing and singing. After being with them for over three years, I am now a regular member of the group. We have made several trips in Alaska, and we also perform during the major community events in Barrow. It is a joy to me to be a part of the group, and to be learning this absolutely key part of current Eskimo culture. I have also shared the bowhead whale hunting that is done in the spring of each year. This spring, I was part of one of the whaling crews, living with crew for about ten days in a tent on the ice pack, helping to watch for the whales. That is also a precious experience to share with people here.

In September it was possible to travel Outside (to the lower 48) to attend the board meeting for the SEVA Foundation in Chelsea, Michigan, and then to share the Varanda and gathering of the many friends from India. That happened in Northern California on the anniversary of Maharaj-Ji's Samadhi. The highlight of the gathering was Dada Mukerjee's presence. It was good to see him after the five years since leaving India, and we all shared many stories about Maharaj-Ji's satsang during those few days. The ties of love remain, even if time and distance separate us so often.

In 1982, if it is the Lord's will, it will be possible for me to spend a few weeks working full time at the SEVA offices in Chelsea.

John and Marion in Los Angeles in 1992

Perhaps that will happen in January and February. Later in the year, I am hoping to spend more than ten days as a full-time member of a whaling crew. Then, I hope, it will be possible to return to India and visit Nepal later in the year. Perhaps it will be in the summer, or in the fall. It would be for 4-6 weeks, but it remains to be seen exactly when it will be open for me to do this. In the meantime, so many of all the brothers and sisters are in my thoughts.

Almost two years after this letter was written, on 3 December 1982, Michael was installed as Judge of the Superior Court of Alaska presiding over the northernmost court in America.

One year following his appointment, Michael married Esther Virginia Thorson, who originates from Norway, on 30 December 1983 at Utkeaqvik Presbyterian Church, Barrow, Alaska. The wedding reception was followed by an Eskimo Dance to which guests were invited from around the world.

In the early 1980s Michael's parents, John and Marion visited England, staying at *Bentley Fields* and visiting many family members. They continued to visit Adelaide regularly who, by the mid-1980s, had become increasingly frail.

In January 1990 John and Marion moved from their home south of Los Angeles, where they had lived for forty-seven years and brought up their family, to a more central apartment in the city.

In 1991 Adelaide, at ninety-six, was no longer in a position to write. She died on 30 August 1991, two months short of what would have been her ninety-seventh birthday.

When visiting John and Marion in California, during the summer of 1992, our family met their elder son John, with his second wife, and Michael and Esther with their three young children - Christina, Nicole and Jordan. This included a visit to Sea World in San Diego. Michael and Esther and family joined our Family Reunion, of over a hundred Jefferys from around the world, which took place in the land of our roots – Derbyshire - in August 2008.

On 20 May 2008, shortly before our family reunion, Michael was re-appointed to the post of Superior Court Judge when the Governor of Alaska, Sarah Palin, although a Republican, stated that:

Michael brings a wealth of academic and professional experience to the bench. The people of Barrow and Alaska will be well served by his expertise and passion for the law.

JOSEPH JEFFERY
1847 – 1933

Pastor on the Prairie

Joseph Jeffery, the third son of Thomas and Mary Jeffery of the Riddings, was born on 24 July 1847. He was their second son to emigrate to America, aged only nineteen, in 1866. He became the Reverend Joseph Jeffery and spent fifty-four years as a minister in North West Iowa. He died on 25 April 1933 in Sioux Rapids, Iowa, USA.

Descendants of Joseph Jeffery - Four Generations

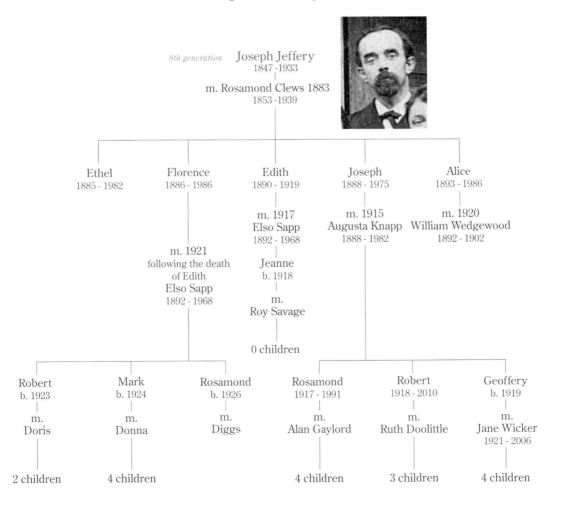

8th generation   Joseph Jeffery
1847 -1933

m. Rosamond Clews 1883
1853 -1939

Ethel	Florence	Edith	Joseph	Alice
1885 - 1982	1886 - 1986	1890 - 1919	1888 - 1975	1893 - 1986

Edith — m. 1917 Elso Sapp 1892 - 1968

Joseph — m. 1915 Augusta Knapp 1888 - 1982

Alice — m. 1920 William Wedgewood 1892 - 1902

Florence — m. 1921 following the death of Edith Elso Sapp 1892 - 1968

Jeanne b. 1918
m. Roy Savage

0 children

Robert	Mark	Rosamond	Rosamond	Robert	Geoffery
b. 1923	b. 1924	b. 1926	1917 - 1991	1918 - 2010	b. 1919
m. Doris	m. Donna	m. Diggs	m. Alan Gaylord	m. Ruth Doolittle	m. Jane Wicker 1921 - 2006
2 children	4 children		4 children	3 children	4 children

Joseph Jeffery 1847-1933

Pastor on the Prairie

One winter day, Dad and I were riding in the sleigh over the hard snow and the sleigh tipped over, but the little horse waited till we tipped the sleigh back again. Dad was wearing a brown fur coat which had been given to him by one of his parishioners and we had a buffalo robe.

Joseph's daughter Florence. Iowa, USA c. 1896

The Reverend Joseph Jeffery became one of the early Pioneer Ministers of the American Midwest. His parishioners were the pioneers who, in their Covered Wagons, had pushed westwards in the mid-nineteenth century, to farm and settle the frontier prairie lands west of the Mississippi.

Joseph made an indelible impression on the minds and hearts of his parishioners. They told of their memories of him for many years after his death. His last Church was in Sioux Rapids, Iowa. Over twenty years after his death, the *SIOUX RAPIDS BULLETIN PRESS*, in a centennial edition (1855–1955), recorded people's memories of his early ministry:

Florence and Elso (his daughter and son-in-law) *have met people – grandchildren perhaps who had known him. Florence met a woman years ago at a convention. She told her of the time when her little sister had died of diphtheria and no-one dared come to the house, but he came and held prayers with them. She said that they would never forget him.*

Joseph, born at the *Riddings*, on 24 July 1847, was the fourth of Thomas and Mary's fifteen children and their third son. Their second son, William, had yet to reach his first birthday and their first son, Thomas, was not quite two years old. These three eldest sons, with the same heritage, would lead vastly different lives. By the time, Joseph reached school age, three younger brothers John, George and Owen and younger sister Elizabeth had joined the family.

As there was no school at Alkmonton until 1856, Joseph walked a mile across the fields and a further four miles along the lanes with his brothers, to the church school at Longford. Here the vicar taught the boys English, English History, Church History and a little music. This was thought to be enough for farm boys but additionally, for those who showed a strong aptitude for learning, the

Joseph Jeffery 1847-1933

idea was to raise priests for the Church. Young Joseph proved an able scholar and many years later, his elder daughters Ethel and Florence recorded that their father wanted to take his education further than just the village school:

......perhaps because he loved learning and did not like the farm.

By the early 1860s Joseph had outgrown the village school and his dreams and determination to broaden his horizons were becoming more focused. He would have recognised that his father, who was keen to expand his farming locally, would be anticipating that the future of all of his sons would lie in farming.

By January 1862 Joseph already had six brothers and seven sisters, although shortly before his seventeenth birthday, his nine-year-old sister, Sarah Ann, had died. In his mid-teens, the conflict between his father's expectation that Joseph would work on the farm and his own wishes to escape were resolved by a decision to run away from home. He went to live with an uncle, a relative of his mother, who lived in the East Riding of Yorkshire. He found a job in Hull and according to Florence, worked for:

...... the man who sold wine, I think.

However, although his father succeeded in getting him back home on this occasion, Joseph's determination to get away became even stronger. It was not long before he was making plans to leave home again.

By the time that he had returned home from Yorkshire, his elder brother, Thomas, had already made firm plans to leave for America. In addition, his mother would soon give birth to his youngest brother Arthur – her fifteenth child. Joseph concluded that his prospects within such a large family were going to be very slender indeed. Certainly, opportunities to pursue the higher education he craved were highly unlikely to present themselves. Like his brother Thomas, Joseph determined to seek his fortune in America.

From the middle of the nineteenth century, with the development of steamship travel across the Atlantic, the flow of European immigrants to America was increasing. It was also the time when the United States was offering both low cost passage and land to immigrants in order to encourage orderly settlement as the Union pushed west-

Passengers on Emigrant Ship, Britain*, 1869, as the Ship is loaded prior to its departure to the USA, 1869.*
From the Illustrated London News with ackn. to the Mary Evans Picture Library

wards. However, transatlantic travel in the early days of the steamship era was long and often hazardous with shipwrecks common and even occasional fatal fires on board. Travel in steerage, as Thomas had experienced in October/November 1865, was cramped, ill lit and badly ventilated. It also involved living in close proximity to people suffering both from sea sickness and the effects of tainted water and poor sanitation.

Joseph was only nineteen in 1866 when he left home for America, following his elder brother Thomas, who had blazed a trail the previous year. However, on this occasion, his mother helped to pay for his passage, knowing of the hardships which her eldest son had experienced when travelling steerage. When he arrived in New York, Joseph, as Thomas had done the previous year, contacted their mother's cousins, the Hagues. However, from that point onwards, he embarked on a very different career path from the one followed by his brother.

Initially he obtained work in New York but, within three years, he was living in the township of New Providence, New Jersey. Whilst there, he learnt of the recently established Theological Seminary of Drew at Madison, New Jersey and it was here that he enrolled as one of their first students. Drew was to become a highly regarded and prestigious theological college which produced many eminent professors.

Joseph was about to embark on the first stage of fulfilling his determination to pursue higher education and become a minister of the church. It was a determination which had initially been inspired, directed and nurtured by the teaching he had received, and to which he had so eagerly responded, at Longford church school, over a decade earlier.

However, life was far from easy as he needed to support himself whilst studying. His mother did, from time to time, send him small sums of money but he needed to find work and take extended time off in order to support his studies. He did this by working as a teacher in New Jersey and Connecticut In addition, during the summers, as had his brother Thomas, he worked on his Uncle John Robinson's farm in Connecticut

He was thirty-two before he finally achieved his ambition. It was thirteen years after he had disembarked in the USA before he graduated from the Seminary of Drew

Iowa, the Tall Corn Country

the open prairie lands of the Great Plains beyond the Mississippi earlier in the century. His work and family life, for over half a century, would be in North Western Iowa. The Indian language meaning of Iowa is 'beautiful land' and today it forms a richly productive part of America's agricultural heartland, the 'Corn Belt'.

University in 1879. He was among the first of Drew's graduates and ready to embark on his new life as one of the early Methodist 'ministers' of the Midwest of America. Many of his parishioners would be those pioneers who had pushed westwards to settle and farm

In the early years of the nineteenth century it was the older, traditionalist, hierarchical Anglican and Catholic churches which had held sway, particularly in the earlier settled lands of the east of America. By the middle of the century, the nonconformist religions had taken hold. In the America of the 1860s, it was the Methodists, with their expanding network of itinerant preachers, who became particularly strong and influential. This mirrored the appeal of Methodism in the burgeoning industrial towns of Victorian England and Wales. At the time of the American Revolution of 1776, there were virtually no Methodist Churches in the USA but by the 1860s, there were around 20,000, which was about as many as there were Post Offices at the time. At the end of the following decade, Joseph would be part of that Methodist Church Ministry.

Northern Iowa USA Joseph Jeffery's Pastoral Centres

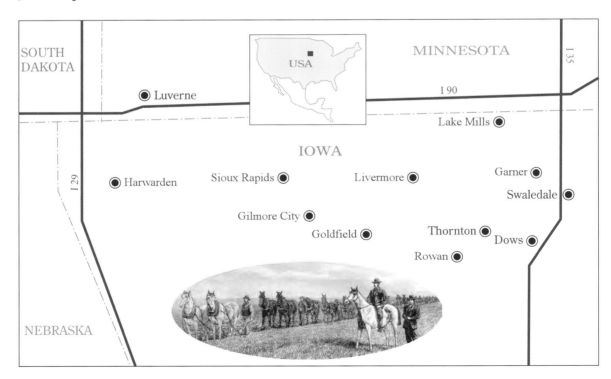

Following his graduation from Drew, the New York State Methodist Conference appointed him to the newly formed Northwest Iowa Conference, which at that time, included a part of the Territory of South Dakota, which was not yet a state. Joseph was to serve for fifty-four years as a minister in the Methodist Episcopal Church and his entire ministry was spent with the Northwest Iowa Conference. The Methodist Church had been incorporated in the Buena Vista Court House, Iowa in 1876, but meetings (services) had been held in homes as far back as 1864. The Methodist 'circuit riders' were the first Christians to cater to Iowa's Pioneers.

North West Iowa was a bleak and desolate region almost devoid of trees, where the early settlers were forced to construct 'sod' houses (from the turf of the prairie). It remained a frontier area until well into the 1860s.

It was usual to serve two to three-year terms of office in different locations in the North Western Conference region. Joseph spent his probationary year as a pastor serving the small settlements of Garner and Britt, Iowa. In 1880 he received Deacon's Orders and was directed further west to the prairie settlement of Brookings in the valley of the Big Sioux River, South Dakota and it was here that he spent the second year of his ministry. These early days of his ministry largely involved him in 'circuit-riding' visiting the widespread farms and homesteads of the early settlers. In 1881 he was back in Iowa, east of Sioux City, at Estherville and it was while he was here that he was instrumental in the building of the town's first church. In 1931, two years before his death, he was invited back to celebrate its fiftieth anniversary. It must have been a very moving occasion for him.

The early years of his ministry were very hard. Midwestern winters are harsh and the farms and small town communities widely scattered. Joseph rode on horseback through the snows, a travelling minister and circuit rider, preaching in country schools and visiting his parishioners across the prairie in South Dakota and Iowa. Conditions in summer could be just as extreme with soaring temperatures and excessively uncomfortable humidity. Tornadoes were not uncommon and deadly prairie fires could be devastating.

Towards the end of 1882, as he was completing his year at Estherville, he obtained leave of absence from his ministry for the year 1882-1883 and returned to England. On his return in 1883, the Iowa Conference appointed him to Lake Mills lying to the east of Estherville.

Joseph's request for leave of absence followed the recent death of one of his younger brothers, Charles, who had been only seven years old when Joseph had left home in 1866. Joseph was concerned for his widowed mother who now had only two of her original eight sons remaining at home – Owen who was running the farm and sixteen-year-old Arthur. His elder brother, Thomas, with Maria and their young son John Arthur (Art) also returned to visit to the *Riddings* at this time. At the time of Charles's death, Charles was engaged to be married to Rosamond Clews. She was for many years a close friend of his elder sister Mary (Polly).

When Joseph had left for America fifteen years earlier, thirteen of his siblings remained at home with both his parents. By the time he returned to the *Riddings*, his father had been dead for five years and only seven of his siblings remained at home. Shortly there would only be six as his sister, Clara, was about to leave to be married in the spring of 1882.

It was probably over the Christmas 1882 and New Year 1883 period, with her two sons home from America, that their mother Mary organised the iconic family photographs of the thirteen children taken outside the *Riddings*. It was a golden opportunity which would never be repeated as, by the end of 1883, not only were Thomas and Joseph back in America but George and Arthur had followed and by 1884, the futures of four of the original fifteen would be on North American soil.

Whilst on this visit to England, Joseph, who had known Rosamond Clews from the many times when she had visited the *Riddings* as a young girl, came to know her more closely and asked her to marry him. Rosamond was living at the *Old Hall*, Littleover, just south of Derby, at the time. The two farming families had known each other for many years from the time when the Clews had lived in the neighbouring village of Yeaveley. Yeavely was where Rosamond's father John and her grandfather James had been born. When Rosamond was visiting her grandparents in Yeaveley she could walk across the fields to the *Riddings* and meet with her friend Polly. Rosamond's mother had died when she was very young and her Aunt Emily had kept house at the *Old Hall* for her widower father as well as caring for the children.

Rosamond kept house for her father, John Clews, up to the time of her own marriage after her Aunt Emily and her elder sisters, Fannie and Annie, together with her younger brother Sam, had all married and left home.

Joseph and Rosamond married on 10 August 1883, in the Wesleyan Chapel in Borrowash, Derbyshire. Rosamond's brother Samuel and his wife Florence were witnesses at the marriage. A few weeks later, in September, Joseph returned alone to Iowa to rejoin the North Western Conference and settle into his new responsibilities at Lake Mills. Rosamond spent the next few weeks making all her necessary and exciting travel preparations for her new life in America as a minister's wife. She arrived in New York in November 1883.

Over fifty years later, Joseph and Rosamond's elder daughters, Ethel and Florence, recorded some of their memories of the stories which their mother told them of her early life and experiences.

Florence's recollections of what her mother told her of her family and early life in Derbyshire paint the following picture of Rosamond's childhood.

In 1865, Rozzie Clews, about ten years old, went down the Hollow and past the Old Cottage, on her two mile walk from her home at the Old Hall in Littleover, to Miss Merwood's School for Young Ladies in Derby. At times she bowled her hoop down Old Hollow Lane.

The Hollow, Littleover, was at one time the main road into Littleover from the south and in the Hollow is Littleover's oldest building. The *Old Cottage* is one of the last remaining thatched cottages in this part of Derbyshire and along the road are the village stocks located under a large walnut tree and an ancient stone trough, probably the last survivor of the many such troughs which would have been found around the village and a reminder of the former times when the horse played a key part in farming and travel.

Paintings of The Hollow (LEFT) and The Cottage, The Hollow, Littleover (RIGHT) by Raymond Dearn, signed and dated 1888, hanging in the dining room at Bentley Fields

At times she bowled her hoop down Old Hollow Lane

She went past the ancient Church where her ancestors were buried. Sometimes she went through the church yard and saw the Sexton dig up old bones when a new grave was being made.

Florence continued her recollection's of her mother Rosamond's stories of her childhood.

She went past the ancient Church where her ancestors were buried. Sometimes she went through the church yard and saw the Sexton dig up old bones when a new grave was being made. These ancestors in Littleover churchyard were her mother's people – they were Church of England people – the Lowes. The Clews family – John Clews – were Chapel people or Dissenters (Nonconformists). John Clews read to his children – John Bunyan and Milton, Shakespeare and the Bible.

With this background, Rosamond was prepared for marriage to a nonconformist minister.

Joseph and Rosamond's life in late-nineteenth and early twentieth-century America is faithfully and vividly recorded by these two elder daughters. Florence writes initially of her mother's journey as she left home in November 1883 to travel alone to her new life with Joseph in America.

Mother came alone to America on the 'Queen'. She had very many lovely clothes to wear in her new home as a minister's wife. I remember her fur-lined Dalman which she kept for many years. She also had a seal jacket and cap. She had a wonderful time on the ship coming over and was royally treated and given a place on the Captain's table for meals.

When she landed in New York the Thomas Hagues met her and she visited them for a while. She saw the sights of New York and drove across Brooklyn Bridge which was new and wonderful then. From there, she went by train to Minneapolis, to Tom and Maria's home. They were all there to meet the train and when Rosamond arrived, Aunt Maria said: 'there she is, the girl with the rosy cheeks.' Joseph joined her in Minneapolis where they stayed until after Christmas.

Early In the New Year of 1884, Joseph and Rosamond set off across the snow-covered, windswept prairie, for the small town of Lake Mills, Iowa, over 150 miles south of Tom and Maria's home in Minneapolis. The new home, that Rosamond found in Lake Mills, was a far cry from her old home of *Littleover Old Hall* and indeed, from Tom and Maria's now well established home, where she had spent her first Christmas in America. Rosamond's new life was about to begin and Joseph's parishioners would be eagerly anticipating their minister's new bride.

Florence continued:

The trip by train to Lake Mills, Iowa, was another new experience. It was winter time and very cold in this little north Iowan town. The house did not have much of a foundation and the floors were cold. It was small, but had an upstairs and was clean and new. With the help of some carpet and gifts from Uncle Tom it was soon furnished adequately. The people of the church came with food and supplies which were always part of the minister's salary. Everyone wanted to see the minister's new English wife. They were made welcome and Mother started a new life. The house is still in Lake Mills with a few improvements. We took pictures of it recently. Lake Mills was in a beautiful wooded area of oak trees and the wild flowers in the spring were beautiful.

However, when Rosamond arrived in Lake Mills in early January 1884, Iowa was still in the grip of a harsh Midwestern winter. The temperatures outside were in sharp contrast to the warmth of the welcome which she received from Joseph's parishioners. Soon after her arrival she wrote to her family back home. Her letter is addressed to her brother Sam and his wife. Rosamond was always particularly close to her brother and she maintained close contact with him throughout her life. The letter tells of her experiences since leaving the family when they parted at Liverpool and she is obviously beginning to feel a little homesick. It provides an interesting contrast between farming and life generally between America and England.

The house did not have much of a foundation and the floors were cold. It was small, but had an upstairs and was clean and new. With the help of some carpet and gifts from Uncle Tom it was soon furnished adequately.

Lake Mills,
Winnebago County,
Iowa, America.

January 7, 1884

(Note – I began this letter a week ago. Be sure to write to me soon and will you please send me an almanac for 1884. Leave it open at the end.)

My dear Sam and Florrie,
I was pleased to have your letter on Saturday. I am beginning to feel that I should like to see you very much. Now that my journey is over and I am getting settled, I want you to come and see me. But you are too far away for that, although it does not seem far to me now.

I want to tell you a little about my journey. I felt very lonely after you and Aunt left me at Liverpool. I shall always remember how you looked as you went away on the boat. I wondered how I could let you go.

I went down to the cabin when your boat was out of sight. I was sick the first two days although not very badly compared to others. Some were sick all the way. After that I enjoyed the voyage very much. We had such splendid weather. I stayed on deck nearly all day. I also spent time on deck in the evening in the moonlight. We stayed an hour or two at Queenstown and then after that we lost sight of land. We saw no more land until we got to New York. Nothing but water, a few seagulls that kept up with us all the way and a few steamboats bound for Liverpool. We had a good captain. I liked him very much. He said he had not had such a good voyage for years.

Mr Hague was at the landing stage to meet me. I knew him immediately – he looked an Englishman. I stayed at his house till Tuesday morning – we landed on Sunday. And then he started me off to Chicago. I got there about eight o'clock on Wednesday night. Then I had to drive through the city to another station. I was frightened about that. I thought I would be sure to lose my luggage or get lost myself, but I got there alright. A gentleman who had travelled some distance with me was very kind. He helped me to get my ticket and put me in the right carriage. I left Chicago for Minneapolis at nine o'clock and I got there at half past three on Thursday afternoon. I was tired of sitting still. I had been travelling since Tuesday morning at eight o'clock and changed only once in 1500 miles. I had a sleeping car and everything was very comfortable, but I did not like it half as much as sailing.

Mr and Mrs T. Jeffery and Arthur met me at the station. It was nice to see a familiar face. My Mr Jeffery (Joseph) was not there. He did not come till the Monday after. We stayed for Christmas in Minneapolis. I think they make more of Christmas than we do in England, only they don't make "POSSET". I thought of you all at Christmas and wondered if you were all having posset and mince pies.

We came here the Friday after Christmas Day. The house was empty. We brought most of our things from Minneapolis. So, I have been very busy since we came, putting things straight. The first Sunday I was here it was given out in church that there would be a 'pound sociable' at the parsonage on Wednesday evening. And, true enough, on Wednesday evening they came, quite a crowd of people (members of the church and others), each bringing something for us towards housekeeping. We shall not be short of something to eat for a long time. I will send you a list of what they brought. It is a queer way to do but I suppose it is the custom. I like the people very well – they are very kind to me. Everybody seems alike – no rich or poor – no masters or servants. They don't work as hard as we do in England. They can live easier. The women don't do much but cook. There is no scrubbing every day. I think they are very lazy but they would be right for you wouldn't they?

In the large towns and cities, men are busy and active – more so than in England. The shops and businesses are open early – particularly in New York and Brooklyn. And I was sorry to see there was almost as much traffic on Sundays as weekdays. But out here, in Lake Mills, they take things easy. They have no rents and taxes to pay and provisions are cheap. I suppose they work hard in summer and take it easy in winter.

It is terribly cold here now. Last week the thermometer stood at 35 degrees below zero. It is a little warmer now but not much. We should be frozen if we stayed out of doors. I have not seen a bit of green grass since I left Ireland. There are very few evergreens and no holly or ivy. And there are no big trees like we have in England. I suppose the winters are too cold for them to grow. Nevertheless, the people are happy enough. They dash about in their sleighs over the snow and have bells on the horses that make a merry jingle. I like to hear them. On the whole they seem to live much easier than we do in England. No rent days to worry them I guess.

We have a nice church here. It is attended very well. We had a meeting every night last week and shall have this week, I expect. Our house is built all of wood, the roof and everything. It is not very large but comfortable. I think it will look very pretty in the summer. There are plenty of trees around.

Now I must conclude. Give my love to Aunt and Uncle, Fanny and Maude, Mrs Blood, Fanny and to all enquiring friends. And Florrie, please give my love to Edith, Arthur and Hannah when you write.

Mr Jeffery sends his love to you both. He says I must tell you that he is very good to me, fetching all the water and wood that I want and "he behaves pretty well generally".

I hope you had a happy Christmas and I wish you a happy New Year. I had a letter from Father and from Annie this morning. Father says he has only Eva with him now.

Your loving sister,

Rosa.

Florence, writing about her Uncle Sam, recorded the following about how family money financed the purchase of an organ for Joseph's Midwest mission.

Samuel Clews, a brother whom mother adored, married a distant cousin, Florence Clews (Aunt Florrie). He was a highly regarded man and a successful farmer and office holder in his area during his lifetime. He inherited some money from a maiden lady – the eccentric Miss Peach of Mother's tales. She had lived with the family and she must have been wealthy. Sam was her favourite child and she left all of her money to him. The nephews and nieces of Sam and Florrie's side received the inheritance. There were many of them and we were among them so it was not a large amount but very welcome. I remember very well when my Dad (Joseph) received this legacy. I recall that Uncle Sam always sent money at Christmas. (A note from Ethel: Mother bought an organ with Uncle Sam's Christmas money. It was a large blond oak affair with a mirror at the top and below that a shelf on which the family pictures were kept. It was a Methodist organ from some Methodist Company. We all took lessons.)

Mother bought an organ with Uncle Sam's Christmas money. It was a large blond oak affair with a mirror at the top and below that a shelf on which the family pictures were kept.

Samuel and Florence Clews, who had married shortly before Rosamond and Joseph left for their new life in America, celebrated their Golden Wedding in December 1932. A report in a local newspaper told how the Derbyshire Royal Infirmary had received an unusual Christmas gift from Mr and Mrs Samuel Lowe Clews. It was a cheque for £50 as '*A thank-offering for 50 years of good health*'. The news report also told of his farming at the *Elms* and *Hall Farms*, Littleover and his public service as a Local District Councillor.
Florence remembered:

Uncle Sam died when Mother was living with me. It was an overwhelming grief to her. Her father, who had married for a second time, died while she was living in Sioux Rapids. I remember the day the news came. She did not realise when she left England that she would not see him again.

Florence's record of life as a minister's wife in Iowa continued as follows.

Mother had the English complexion with rosy cheeks. At one meeting, a woman rubbed her finger across Mother's cheek to see if the colour was natural.

Mother found that her clothes were almost too dressed up for the people of the church. At one time, her husband asked her if she did not have something not quite so good to wear. Mother often told us of an amusing incident of the Lake Mills time: the people had 'pound socials' for the minister and brought food and garden produce and pork when they butchered. Once there was a bag of beans. Mother had never baked beans in England and did not know what to do with them, so she took them with us when we moved until we came to Dows where she threw them out to the chickens in the yard. The chickens would not eat them so they began to grow. Later mother learned how to bake beans in a crock with a piece of bacon or pork and molasses. They were the most delicious I have tasted and so good in winter when we came home from school.

'...we had snowdrops in January. I have sent Rosa half a dozen just to remind her of her old home.'

Snowdrops from home

A year after arriving in Lake Mills, on 21 January 1885, Rosamond gave birth to her first child, Ethel. It was bitterly cold but their home was heated by wood-burning stoves.

The following letter was written by Rosamond's father, John Clews, to his son-in-law, Joseph Jeffery, upon receipt of his letter telling of the birth of Ethel Mary Jeffery at Lake Mills, Iowa.

Littleover Old Hall
February 10, 1885

Dear Joseph,

Your letter of the 22nd came duly to hand. It did me a great deal of good for I feel very lonely at times. It was like a gleam of sunshine on a cloudy day. I feel very much pleased to hear of the birth of your little daughter and that Rosa has born up so well. I hope she will be a great comfort to you both. I should like you to name her Mary after both her grandmothers.

We are having a mild winter here again – we had snowdrops in January. I have sent Rosa half a dozen just to remind her of her old home. I don't know that I have much news to send that will interest you. We are going on much as usual. Mr. Penny is giving up his farm in Draycott and Sam has taken it. He is tired of so much plough farming. Tom Penny and his wife are returning to England. Polly Haywood's brother George and his wife sailed for America last August and they have returned. He called last week. Tell Rosa that I have a letter from Mr Booth in New Zealand. He says how very prosperous he has been. His wife's health is completely restored. He says he is now able to repay the money I lent him and he has promised to do this shortly.

Miss Peach is at Draycott this week. She has been there a good deal lately. Excuse me for not writing oftener. It is not because I forget you. I miss Rosa more than all the rest. She was the last I had left.

With kind love and best wishes, I remain your affectionate father

John Clews.

The following year, Joseph was posted to Luverne and, in the depths of winter - January 1886 - the little family moved 150 miles west. As at Estherville, Joseph was instrumental in the building of a new church. They moved initially into accommodation which was far too cold, particularly for baby Ethel, but eventually, Florence recorded:

After living in a cold house awhile, they moved to some good warm rooms over a creamery and I, Florence Annie, was born at 4 p.m. on November 4th, 1886. Mother was always afraid of fire in that house and used to plan how she would get out with the two babies in case of fire.

Many years later, Ethel wrote.

The citizens of Luverne gave Dad a big silver watch, inscribed with his name and 'for the service to the town and the building of the church'. Years later, he gave it to someone who didn't have a watch and needed one.

Two years later, the family were on the move again when Joseph was directed to the little Iowan town of Dows. There was no parsonage here but the house which they rented was the best accommodation they had had since coming to America. It was at Dows that both Joseph and Edith were born and it was a home which Ethel remembered well. She wrote:

The next move was to Dows, Iowa, where Joseph Ewart was born on March 16, 1888. Two years later, Edith Clews was born on March 15, 1890. There was no parsonage so they had to rent a house and it was the best they had since coming to America. It is the first place that I remember. There were big shade trees – a neighbour – Miss Graves – a hammock and a swing and a green lawn – and pasture for the horse that was young and skittish and not easy for Dad to manage at times. Mother had a Swedish girl named Elda when the babies came; also there was a hired girl named Mary Knox. Dad had been away holding protracted meetings in Rowan where he had a church. When he returned, Joseph Ewart had arrived. Some church members greeted him with news, 'You have a son and heir'. Dad, of course, was elated and excited after having had two girls and said 'Is it a boy?' which amused everybody."

Ethel continued:

Three years later and another move, this time to Goldfield, another small town: I started school here. My teacher was Miss

Phoebe Morgan. I remember how easily I learned to read with her good teaching. Years later, when Dad retired she wrote him a letter telling her memories of him and our family. Then we moved to Hawarden where Alice was born. I remember the morning of her birth, July 7, 1893. We children were taken over to a neighbour's and sat on her porch. We did not know why, but when we returned home, we found that there was a new baby – a dear little dark haired, dark eyed baby who, some have said, resembles her grandmother, Mary Robinson Jeffery of the Riddings.

The church in Hawarden was large and difficult. The former minister, H. W. L. Mahood, had gone leaving debts everywhere. I remember the Christmas at the church that year – a big tree, candle-lit with gifts which everyone brought for their families. There was a beautiful doll at the top of the tree which I imagined was for me and wept with disappointment when it was not.

Joseph and Rosamond's next move, with their five young children, was to Sioux Rapids. This would be Joseph's sixth appointment as a minister in northern Iowa. He served three years in the Sioux Rapids church. The church made '*quiet but substantial growth*' during his years there and he was spoken of very highly.

Florence continued:

From there it was Sioux Rapids, a very pretty town surrounded by hills and through which the Little Sioux River runs. We spent three years there. We liked the town and friends so much that we returned there after Dad retired, bought a house and forty acres on a hillside. There were some people in Sioux Rapids who were Free Methodists, who came to church and at many meetings their 'Amens' and shouts could be heard all over the neighbourhood. Then we went to Swaledale which was a flat, swampy location and when the snow melted there were big ponds. It was a good place to float boats and get our feet wet.

Dad often had three churches to serve. It was called a 'charge'. There was Swaledale, Thornton and a school house appointment called Mackenzie where he preached on Sunday afternoons. I remember going with him in the horse and buggy to the meetings. These were very nice friendly farm people and as Mother would call them 'God fearing people'. I remember one Thanksgiving when people from a country church brought a turkey, pumpkins, a squash and everything needed for Thanksgiving. How we all feasted. There was no lack of food.

Dad had many long rides in the winter to his churches and to sick members and to bury the dead. Riding in horse and buggy and in cutter and sleigh was rough in winter. Bob sleds were used by farmers. One winter day, Dad and I were riding in the sleigh over the hard snow and the sleigh tipped over, but the little horse waited till we tipped the sleigh back again. Dad was wearing a brown fur coat, which had been given to him by one of his parishioners, and we had a buffalo robe.

We get some insight into Joseph and Rosamond's family home life from the words of their son, Joseph Ewart, who was to become Superintendant of Schools for Bridgeport, Connecticut. On his appointment, in 1945, the local press reported:

FATHER MINISTER

You could almost guess it that Jeffery is the son of a Methodist Minister.

The Rev. Joseph Jeffery, graduate of Drew, had gone to Sioux Rapids, Iowa, in the 70s when Horace Greeley was telling young men to go west.

Their home, the son says today, ran on the 'plain living and high thinking plan.'

Joseph, as the minister for the three churches of Swaledale, Thornton and Mackenzie, found this appointment particularly demanding. Ever conscientious and concerned to do a good job for his parishioners, spread across the wide open prairie farmland, committed him to very long hours of travelling in particularly difficult conditions during the severe winters. The hard work told on his health and, consequently, he opted to take a sabbatical year.

Florence continued:

After living in Swaledale for a year or two, Dad's health was poor and he gave up preaching for a year. We moved out of the parsonage and rented another place in town. I remember we

liked this house very well. Dad sold religious books there and in other towns. There had been a Baptist Church across the corner from the Methodist Church. Jessie Bryant, the minister's daughter was Ethel's friend and her age. She was so very good – a real preacher's daughter and sometimes Ethel and another friend, Blanche Schaffer, made her life miserable. Dad sold books in Mason City also and helped at some special meetings with his prayers and testimony and 'saving souls' which made him feel in his right element.

Next came Gilmore City and Livermore. In Gilmore City there were some 'worldly members' who liked horse racing. Dad preached too hard for their comfort and they resented it. Even we children felt the coldness. But we always had some good friends. Livermore was another town that we liked as children because of the nearby woods and footbridge over Letts Creek and the Des Moines River. We had some good friends there, in and out of church. Jessie Leighton was a long time friend of Ethel. There were also the Sandersons and the Hunts. The Hunts came from New York State in a covered wagon in the early days and Mr Sanderson had fought in the Civil War and was full of stories about that.

Then we moved back to Sioux Rapids to live in our house on the hill which we had purchased long before. Mother loved this place. Dad did supply preaching in the surrounding towns – sometimes Milford which was near Spirit Lake.

In the summer of the first year of the new century, Joseph returned alone to England for a visit. He sailed from New York, on the *SS Luciana* of the Cunard Line and arrived in Liverpool on 4 August 1900. His mother, Mary, was approaching her eighty-third birthday. His unmarried sister, Fanny, was still at home and his widowed sister, Mary (Polly) was back at the *Riddings* with her young son Percy. His brother Owen was now farming both the *Riddings* and *Bentley Fields* farms and living with his wife Hester and young family, Tom and Dolly, at *Bentley Fields*. As far as I am aware, this was to be the last occasion on which Joseph would return to the home of his youth. It would be the last time he saw his mother, who died five and a half years later.

In 1905 Joseph took what was described as a superannuated relationship with the Church, undertaking to take services on request. Having bought a house and land in Sioux Rapids, it was there he would spend the rest of his life. The United States Federal census for 1910 recorded that he owned his own farm. He still felt very strongly the pull of the land and his Derbyshire farming heritage.

Joseph's Children and Grandchildren:

From Eastern Seaboard to Pacific Coast and the un-severed link with Derbyshire

Meanwhile, Joseph and Rosamond's family of four daughters and one son were growing up. All went on to Higher Education and then into teaching. By 1910, twenty-five-year-old Ethel was teaching away from home. Florence, Joseph Ewart, Edith and Alice were still living at home and Florence and Edith were also teaching in the local country schools.

From 1915 onwards their family started to disperse. Joseph E., known as Joe to his family, married Augusta Knapp in 1915 and they moved to Connecticut. Augusta was a 'Daughter of the American Revolution' (which meant that she could claim lineal bloodline descent from an ancestor who aided in achieving American independence). Her own ancestry went back to some of the earliest settlers on the Eastern Seaboard. Her grandmother's great, great-grandfather, was among a group of explorers who set out from Connecticut, in 1789, to settle in what was then the 'wilderness territory' of the Finger Lakes area of upstate New York State.

During the four years following their marriage, Joe and Augusta presented Joseph and Rosamond with three grandchildren: Rosamond in 1917, Robert in 1918 and Geoffrey (always known as Geoff), in 1919.

In 1917 Edith married Elso Sapp and they had a daughter Jeanne. Tragically, Edith died during the 1919 influenza epidemic. In 1920 her younger sister, Alice, married William Wedgewood and their early-married life was spent farming in Missouri.

Two years after the death of her sister Edith, Florence married the widower, Elso Sapp, on 30 July 1921 and over the following five years, Florence and Elso gave Joseph and Rosamond three more grandchildren: Robert in 1923, Mark in 1924 and Rosamond in 1926.

Their eldest daughter, Ethel, never married. She did, however, play a great part in the lives of her nephews and nieces and was a regular correspondent of my grandmother's.

Joseph and Rosamond remained on their much loved farm on the edge of Sioux Rapids for some time, before buying another house in the town and renting out the farm. They continued as highly respected figures in the local community. By 1920, Joseph, at seventy-two, described himself on the census as a retired minister. Their grandson, Geoff, son of Joe and Augusta, recalls visiting his grandparents in Sioux Rapids when he was aged ten in 1930. He stayed with them in their home in town but also visited their old farm on the hill.

Joseph and Rosamond endeavoured to maintain close contact with their family during their retirement in Sioux Rapids. Florence and Elso, with their own growing family in Buffalo City, were the only ones to remain in Iowa. By the end of 1920, Ethel, Joe and Alice had all moved away. Maintaining contact, therefore, involved long journeys. Ethel was teaching in Hartford, Connecticut, Joe was married with a young family and teaching in Milford, Connecticut, and Alice had recently married and moved to Missouri.

Joe and Augusta's home in Milford, Connecticut

In May 1920, when his son Geoff had just reached his first birthday, Joe wrote to his sister Ethel. Ethel, at this time, was visiting their parents in Sioux Rapids before moving to her new teaching post in Hartford, Connecticut. The 'trip east' mentioned in the letter did take place and did include his parents, Joseph and Rosamond. 'Gussie' is, of course, Joe's wife Augusta. In the letter, he calls attention to the use of his name 'Joe' as he was always called 'Jeff' by Gussie and his friends. His parents and sisters continued to call him 'Joe'. He also refers to his son as 'Geoff Marron' and this became Geoff's household name. Apparently the 'Marron' came from Joe's life-long friend of graduate schooldays at Washington University in St Louis.

Milford, Connecticut
May 14, 1920

Dear Ethel,
Your letter to Gussie reached here yesterday, Geoff Marron's birthday. We were so glad to hear from you and to know that you are planning to come to us this summer. I hope that more of you can come if possible.

We expect to be in Milford all summer. My own plans for summer work are indefinite yet. The school year does not end until June 18. There is a possibility that I may take some courses in Columbia in the summer season but if I do I shall go back and forth to Milford on the train daily. I may feel, however, that it is necessary to work at something.

I have wondered how you are all getting along constantly and how Mother (Rosamond) *and Dad* (Joseph) *stood this last hard cold winter. We have all been more or less miserable at times and I was 'laid up' for some time which is quite unusual for me. It has required some time to return to my normal condition. We are all better now.*

I have recently given up my Red Cross work and realise that I have been attempting too much, sort of case of burning the candle at both ends. We shall miss the money, over one hundred dollars a month, but I feel that I must give more time to my school work and that it was wise to forestall the possibility of becoming a nervous wreck by being so rushed. I didn't have a minute to myself, but now it seems like loafing to be through work at 12 30 every day and have all afternoon free. After a time I expect to find some other work for my afternoons which will be less exacting. Just now, I'm painting, whenever a clear day comes, a new screened porch we have built this spring and

I have built a yard for ten hens that we keep and am working around the house and garden.

Geoff Marron had a wonderful birthday yesterday. His mother (Gussie) *made him a cake with one candle and we had dinner at five o'clock so that he could enjoy the festivities before he became too tired. You should have seen him when the candle was brought in lighted! He gazed in wonder for five minutes straight. He was allowed to eat a little of the 'frosting' and some milk chocolate I bought him. I bought him a red ball and Gussie had balloons for each of the youngsters so it was a gala occasion all round. Rosamond* (Joe's daughter) *is planning already for her birthday and her cake with four candles. Bob* (Joe's eldest son) *will be on hand too with his usual large appetite.*

Geoff Marron has walked for some time. He took his first steps when he was ten months old and now he is everywhere and in everything. He is such a big boy for his age. He sleeps in a bed right close to his Dad and around five o'clock he awakens and immediately tumbles over into my bed. In about ten minutes he insists on getting up so we are early risers. He comes over to my chair at the breakfast table every morning and scolds me until I give him part of my toast.

I would relate more about this wonderful boy and his older brother and sister but I fear that you only think it is only the same kind of glowing description in which any doting dad might indulge.

You did not say what your plans are for next year or Florence's. I am glad that you are going to summer school but don't overwork. You will need energy left to enjoy your trip East. We will meet you in New York and possibly Albany if it is an appropriate time for a boat trip up the Hudson.

I hope that teachers' salaries are raised in Iowa. My salary was raised to $2,250 for this year and $2,700 for next year. That isn't much for these days, but during the last two years, with only a half day session I have been able to supplement my salary to the extent of $1,000 to $1,500 a year by outside work. I hope to do the same next year and it is quite likely that my $2,700 for next year will be increased before the year is far gone.

Gussie will probably write to you soon. We are looking ahead to your visit. Write to us soon. I would like to hear from all of you.

Love to Mother and Dad and all.
Joe
P.S. I feel like as if I were signing an assumed name when I sign myself Joe. I never hear it.

LEFT *Milford, Connecticut, 1930s*
L. to r.: Joseph E. Jeffery; Jeanne Sapp
(Edith Jeffery's daughter); Geoffrey M.
Jeffery; Ethel Jeffery; Alice Wedgewood
(nee Jeffery); Myrtle Ellis Knapp
(Augusta's mother); Robert K. Jeffery;
Rosamond Jeffery; Augusta Knapp
Jeffery

BELOW LEFT *The family home of The*
Farm at Dundee, upstate New York
where Joseph and Augusta retired in
1965

BELOW RIGHT *Alice and Bill Wedg-*
wood's home, Cooperstown, Finger
Lakes area upstate New York

Joe visited his parents in Sioux Rapids, Iowa in July 1927. At that time, his father, Joseph, gave him the names and ages of all his brothers and sisters and their children, both in America and England. Joseph's brothers Thomas, William, George and Owen had already died as had his sisters Elizabeth and Fanny. These family details were passed on to Joe's son Geoff.

During the year 1967 to '68, when, with my young daughter and husband, I lived in the United States, we met many of Joseph and Rosamond's children, grandchildren and great-grandchildren. We visited their son Joe with Augusta, on their wonderful old farm, where they had retired, in Dundee, in the beautiful Finger Lakes area of upstate New York. This was the home which had been in Augusta's family from the days of her ancestors' settlement in the area in the eighteenth century.

Additionally, we visited their youngest daughter Alice, and her husband Bill Wedgewood, in nearby Cooperstown. Later that year, my own parents visited the area and my father, another Jeff, experienced the delight of meeting his first cousins Ethel, Florence, Joe and Alice for the very first time. It was, I know, a moving occasion for him.

We also visited Joe and Augusta's son, Geoff and his wife Jane and family, in Maryland, in August 1967, whilst my husband, Colin, was being 'orientated' in Washington DC, prior to his teaching exchange to Indiana. Geoff at this time was working at the medical research institute in Bethesda, Washington DC. Likewise, my parents were welcomed by Geoff and Jane in June of the following year.

Additionally, we visited many others of their grandchildren and great-grandchildren including Edith and Elso Sapp's daughter Jeanne and her husband Roy Savage in Wheaton, Illinois and, Florence and Elso Sapp's sons, Mark and Robert. We stayed with Mark and his wife Donna and their family in Flagstaff, Arizona and with Bob and his wife Doris and family in Piedmont, Oakland, California.

Sixteen years earlier, during the year 1951-52, my cousin Dorothy Jeffery of the *Riddings* had also visited these descendants of Joseph and Rosamond. Indeed, it was Dorothy who gave me all of the contact details of these many descendants who are scattered across the continent.

Joseph and Rosamond's grandson Geoff (Joe and Augusta's son) who now lives in Atlanta, Georgia, has been very generous in telling me of his family memories and I am recording them in his own words.

BELOW *Alice and Bill Wedgwood's home, Cooperstown, Finger Lakes area upstate New York*

I had very little contact with my father's family during the years I was growing up. The distance between Iowa and Connecticut was too great to encourage much visiting in those days. In the early 1920s, my Aunt Ethel came East and took a job teaching in the High School in Hartford, Connecticut. I think she taught English. She came to our house in Milford for many weekends and most holidays. We were all very fond of her - she always brought us interesting books and other goodies when she came to visit. We always looked forward to her coming. She never married. Occasionally we would visit her in her apartment in Hartford or at her school. Almost every year she went out to Iowa to spend the holidays with her mother or sisters out there. In the mid twenties she took my sister Rosamond with her. They took the train to Buffalo and then a boat through the Great Lakes to Chicago, then the train the rest of the way. A year or so later, she took my brother Bob on the same trip. It was a great adventure for them and I recall being very envious. I never got to go, probably because I had been ill and my aunt understandably didn't want the responsibility. At Christmas time in either 1929 or 1930 or thereabouts, my father took me on the train to Iowa for about a week's visit. We took a sleeper out of New York for Chicago the 'Wolverine Limited'. We had to change in Chicago and then in Storm Lake, Iowa, where we got on a single car 'toonerville' type of conveyance to Sioux Rapids.

Joseph and Rosamond's daughter Ethel Mary Jeffery at The Farm, Dundee, NY

My father's sister, my Aunt Florence was also there and I recall that we went up to Buffalo Center to visit the rest of her family – my Uncle Elso Sapp and cousins Jeanne, Robert, Mark and Rosamond. Uncle Elso was the local banker in Buffalo Centre. (It might be remembered that he had married Edith Jeffery and they had one child Jeanne before Edith died. He then married Florence Jeffery and they had three children.) Whilst we were with Aunt Florence and family, my father's youngest sister, my Aunt Alice with Uncle Bill Wedgewood also came down for a short visit from their farm in Minnesota.

Over fifty years later, in the mid 1970s, I dropped in to see Florence's youngest daughter Rosamond, in Missoula, Montana. Her husband is a thriving orthodontist. My brother Bob has contacted one or both of the boys in California or elsewhere in the west during his travels.

I wish I had been a little older when I visited Iowa. I didn't absorb much family background on that occasion. Jeanne Sapp came east and I think worked in New York for a while. She married Roy Savage and they lived in New Hampshire. She and her husband were quite close to my Aunt Ethel in her later years. He was extremely kind to her, even after Jeanne's early death. In her later years, my folks arranged for Aunt Ethel to move to an apartment in Dundee, New York State where they and my sister Rosamond could be of help in caring for her. She stayed independent in her own apartment until way into her 90s.

My father's youngest sister, my Aunt Alice, and her husband Bill Wedgewood had a big farming operation, I think near Fargo, North Dakota, but it might have been somewhere in Minnesota. When the depression struck in the 1930s they lost the whole thing – probably too much debt land and machinery etc. So, knowing that they were in deep trouble, my parents offered to let them come to the farm up in New York State, where they would at least have a house, some farm machinery, some livestock, and could start over again without any investment. So, they seemed to jump at the chance and during the summer of 1932 (give or take a year) they packed all of their worldly goods in a big trailer, hauled by a farm truck (also loaded) and a car, and they and a hired man headed east. They arrived at the farm in good shape but after that things didn't go too well. Bill Wedgewood had farmed in flat, fertile, stone-less terrain and was absolutely aghast at the hills and rocks one finds in the so-called arable lands of western New York. I don't think it took him very long to decide that this wasn't for him. He and my Aunt Alice left all their stuff in the barn at the farm and drove down to meet an old army buddy who was in business in Scarsdale, Westchester County. They were apparently very good friends and had been in

Joseph and Rosamond's daughter Florence Jeffery Sapp (June 1951)

the First World War overseas together. Bill was offered a job in this man's wholesale business. He accepted it, found a place to live and came back to the farm for his things. I recall that they unpacked everything, re-packed the things they would need and sold the rest, including his trailer. We saw them occasionally over the years and apparently everything worked out very nicely for them. Much later on they retired and bought a beautiful old house in Cooperstown, New York. Mother and I, along with Jane's parents, dropped in to see them on one occasion. Aunt Ethel spent quite a bit of time with them in later years. The Wedgewoods had no children. He had a couple of sisters who we had met several times. The family was reputed to have descended from a common ancestor of the Wedgewoods of china fame and fortune.

LEFT *Joseph and Rosamond's son Joe Jeffery, Superintendant of Schools, Connecticut*

ABOVE *Joseph and Rosamond's daughter Alice with her husband Bill Wedgewood, Cooperstown*

Prior to my own meeting with Alice and Bill in Cooperstown in the 1960s, Alice confirmed in one of her letters, that her husband Bill was a descendant of the English Wedgewoods. The same letter also noted with interest, the number of teachers among the Jefferys as '*our family all are or have been teachers*'.

Whilst their children Ethel, Joe and Gussie, Alice and Bill, were establishing their own professional and family lives in Connecticut and Minnesota, during the 1930s, only Florence, with her husband Elso, remained in Iowa. Joseph and Rosamond, still in Sioux Rapids, were now into their eighties and although Joseph remained active in the church community until shortly before his death, his health had started to fail. By 1933 they had seven grandchildren aged between sixteen and seven.

Joseph was eighty-five, just three months short of his eighty-sixth birthday, when he died on 25 April 1933. The local newspaper of 4 May 1933 provided the following obituary.

Sioux Rapids Mourns Pastor
Pioneer Minister Answers Final Summons

****

In the death of Rev. Joseph Jeffery, who passed away at his home in Sioux Rapids at about 6 o-clock on Tuesday evening last week, this community mourns the loss of one of its beloved residents. For years, Rev. Jeffery has been in poor health but had been active up to the day of his last sickness. Unless physically unable, he was always to be found in his accustomed place at all services of the Methodist church and often attended other religious and worthwhile gatherings, taking an active part in such meetings whenever opportunity was given for him to do so. He had a very retentive mind, being able to quote Scripture freely, giving chapter and verse. Many times in his talks and prayers he would recite from memory many of the old hymns of the church. He will always be remembered by those who knew him for his genuine Christian refinement and his firm faith in his Saviour, Jesus Christ, and his Heavenly Father. He was taken seriously ill on Monday evening. His soul answered the final summons twenty four hour later.

Very impressive and beautiful rites were conducted at the Methodist church in Sioux Rapids on Friday afternoon at 2 o'clock. This was especially fitting as Brother Jeffery dearly loved his church. In the absence of the pastor, Rev. J. D. Wilcock, the service was in the charge of Rev. J. H. Edge of Spencer, who read the Scripture and offered prayer. Rev. W. E. Brew of Eagle Grove spoke briefly of his personal relations of his five years as Rev. Jeffery's pastor. The Rev. H. E. Hutchinson of Spence, who has known Rev. Jeffery for 37 years, brought a fine tribute and message. The following ministers acted as pall bearers: Rev. Arrowsmith of Cherokee, Rev. Praul of Rembrant; Rev. Schneider of Marathon; Rev. Seward of Laurands; Rev. Day of Havleuk; Rev. Barkley of Newall. Five other ministers attended the funeral.

************************ ## Native of England ************************

Joseph Jeffery was born on July 24th, 1847 at Riddings Farm, near Longford, Derbyshire, England. He came to the United States when he was nineteen years of age. He attended Drew Theological Seminary at Mission, New Jersey graduating in 1879 and returned to England for a short time in 1882. On August 10, 1883, at Borrowash Wesleyan church he was married to Miss Rosamond Clews of Littleover and returned to the United States in September 1883.

To them were born one son, Joseph E. Jeffery and four daughters, Ethel M. Jeffery of Hartford, Connecticut, Mrs. E. Sapp of Buffalo Centre, Mrs. A. Wedgewood of Felton, Minnesota and Edith who predeceased her father in May 1919. There are also seven grandchildren

Rev. Jeffery was one of a family of eight brothers and seven sisters and was the last surviving of four brothers who came to the United States. One brother and three sisters are still living in England. (John, Clara and Ellen).

Brother Jeffery's entire ministry has been in the Northwest Iowa Conference. He received Deacon's orders in 1880 and Elder's Orders in 1886. He served at Gardner, Britt, Brookings, Estherville, Lake Mills, Luverne, Dows, Goldfield, Hawarden and Sioux Rapids.

The burial was at Lone Tree Cemetery. Thus we come to the end of the earthly ministry of this faithful soldier of the Cross and in a special manner the text of Dr. Hutchinson was true: Well done thou good and faithful servant, enter thou into the joys of the Lord. Thou hast been faithful over a few things. I shall make you ruler over many things.

Relatives here from a distance to attend the services were Mr. and Mrs. E. Sapp and family, Buffalo Centre; Mr. and Mrs. W. A. Wedgewood of Felton, Minnesota and Miss Helen and Albert Wedgewood.

At Church in Bridgeport, Connecticut, flowers for the altar were given by Rosamond, Robert and Geoffrey Jeffery in memory of their grandfather, the Reverend Joseph Jeffery, for fifty-four years minister in the Methodist Episcopal Church.

Rosamond lived with Florence and family after her husband's death. She survived Joseph by six years and died on 25 July 1939. She was also buried in Lone Pine Cemetery, Sioux Rapids, Iowa.

In June 1968, my husband, young daughter Clare and I, drove to Iowa, staying overnight at Sioux Falls, before travelling on westwards. Sadly, I did not know at that time, how very close we were to the land of my Great Uncle Joseph Jeffery.

Thirty years later in the 1990s, Joseph's grandson Geoff, together with his wife Jane, traced the locations of his grandfather's pioneering ministry across Iowa. Geoff recalled visiting Lake Mills, Luverne, Livermore, Hawarden, Gilmore City Goldfields, Rowan, Dows and Sioux Rapids. This land of northern Iowa today remains predominantly rural. Some of the towns are thriving but many are more aptly described as 'ghost towns'. Geoff kept a diary of his and Jane's trip to Iowa during the first week in May, 1996:

. . . . . nearly every town has what they call 'River Boat Gambling Casinos'. Sioux City seems to lead all the rest. I guess the Indians are making a killing in other ways than Little Big Horn these days.

Day 3: Continued north past Omaha into Sioux City, Iowa. Spent a little time in Sioux City, mostly having a look at Morningside College, where Dad (Joe) did his undergraduate work, and also received an honorary doctorate in later years I believe. It's a very pretty college – still quite small. I'm sure that some of the very old looking buildings were there in the early 1900s. It's of interest that all along the Missouri River, from Kansas City on through Sioux City, nearly every town has what they call 'River Boat Gambling Casinos'. Sioux City seems to lead all the rest. I guess the Indians are making a killing in other ways than Little Big Horn these days. We went north a little way out of Sioux City and then turned east to Hawarden (pronounced "Hey warden"). This was the fifth post where Grandfather Jeffery served and is the town where Aunt Alice was born on June 7, 1893. We found the Methodist Church, but thought it was unlikely that it was the one which existed in 1892. The parish was founded in 1881, and we found Joseph Jeffery's name in the roll of pastors (1892). The adjacent ones listed were Mahoud (1891) and Morrow (1893), so it was a short assignment.

After Hawarden we drove east to Storm Lake, a town a few miles south of Sioux Rapids, where we spent the night. I remember quite well being in Storm Lake when I visited out there at about the age of ten.

Day 4: Drove the short distance north to Sioux Rapids where we spent about half a day. Sioux Rapids was Grandfather Jeffery's sixth post – I think it was in 1893. We found the Methodist Church. It was built in 1913, and I have a faint recollection of going to church there when I visited at the age of ten. We visited the town library and found the staff most helpful and friendly. Had a chance to look through several volumes of local history, and they made me a copy of a couple of pages describing the

LEFT *The graves of Joseph and Rosamond,*
Lone Pine Cemetery, Sioux Rapids

history of the Methodist Church. Grandfather Jeffery was listed as one of the former ministers. We spent quite a lot of time in the Lone Tree Cemetery looking for the Jeffery plots. Surprisingly we did find them. They are at the back end of the cemetery, so it took a lot of looking. I was quite surprised to find the Sapp plot is right next to the Jeffery plot. I guess I thought this would be in Buffalo Center. The Jeffery plot has three graves: Rosamond C. Jeffery, Joseph Jeffery and Ethel Jeffery. In the Sapp plot is Edith Jeffery Sapp, Florence Jeffery Sapp and Elso Sapp. It's a beautiful cemetery with beautiful large pines in the older areas. ……….. After three more posts they (my grandparents and family) returned to Sioux Rapids in semi-retirement.

Geoff and Jane drove on to Lake Mills and found the Methodist Church which they suspected was the same one as had been there in the 1880s.

Day 5: From Forest City we headed south, then east and then south again to Luverne. This was the second post for Grandfather Jeffery and must have been in early 1886. ………….. We found the church and it seems pretty certain that it was the same one that was constructed, during Grandfather's tenure. It would have been difficult to get further information, since it was Sunday morning and services were in progress. The town was typical of the semi 'ghost town' appearance. ………….. From Livermore we drove south and west to Gilmore City. This was Grandfather's eighth assignment. It was another rather typical small town which had seen better days. ……………… From Gilmore City we went east about thirty miles to Goldfields, the Jeffery's fourth post, (between Dows and Hawarden time-wise) – 1891 or 1892………………..

Geoff and Jane's trip took them on to Dows where his father (Joe) and Aunt Edith were born. They didn't

visit the towns in Iowa which were included in Grandfather's earlier 'circuit-riding' days, although we drove through some of them.

Commenting on the value of his trip, Geoff observed that he felt a little bit better connected to a part of the family history.

Although Geoff's father, Joe, never visited the *Riddings*, Geoff himself has returned on a number of occasions to explore the land of his grandfather's birth. His first memorable visit was in the summer of 1939 just before the start of World War II. In August 2007, in an e-mail to me, he wrote:

A college friend of mine and I decided that year that we wanted to see the British Isles before the inevitable war came along so we spent almost three months cycling virtually from John o'Groats to Land's End — including a side venture to Ireland.

One of my very favourite memories is of my visit to the Riddings in the summer of 1939. A college friend of mine and I decided that year that we wanted to see the British Isles before the inevitable war came along so we spent almost three months cycling virtually from John o'Groats to Land's End – including a side venture to Ireland. In about the middle of the trip we spent about five days at the Riddings. The hospitality we received was really wonderful, and through the efforts of your grandmother (Ellen Jeffery Hellaby) and transportation provided by Percy Spencer and others we met a lot of relatives.

During this memorable visit of 1939, Geoff, met a large number of his Jeffery family in Derbyshire, including his grandfather's brother John and sister Ellen. Additionally he was welcomed into the homes of many of the children of his grandfather's brothers William, John and Owen and his grandfather's sisters Margaret, Mary and Ellen. He also met many of his own generation: the grandchildren of his great aunts and uncles including Dorothy, Tom, Margaret and Fred at the *Riddings*; Harold and Jeffery Spencer at *Bentley Fields Farm*; Lillian Poyser at *Oaklea Farm*, Somersal; John and Mary Jeffery at the *Home Farm, West Broughton*; Christopher and Robert Jeffery (aged three and one) at *Aston House*, Sudbury; and five young Hellabys, Barbara, Bill and Sheila at *Fullwood Farm*, Hulland, and Marjorie and Valerie at *Fauld House Farm*, Fauld. One of these younger Hellaby grandchildren was me but sadly, at the age of three, I have no memory of this first meeting with Geoff. It would be twenty-eight years before I met him again, on the other side of the Atlantic, in Washington DC.

Geoff's travel notes of his 1939 visit, which follow, introduce a number of the Derbyshire Jefferys who will be described in more detail later. The family is indebted to Geoff for the graphic record of his visit. Perhaps even more significantly, he is a lynch pin in the family's transatlantic relations. Prior to his visit, there had been family exchanges but they were essentially between siblings. Geoff was the first member of the family to cross the generations and in doing so, demonstrated the importance of family roots. He set an example to be followed after World War II, by Dorothy Jeffery and others. Both inspired my own determination, in 1967-8, to seek out the descendants of the Jeffery pioneers.

Friday, July 14: ………… We stayed on the back roads and went through Ilkeston over to Derby. We both got some mail at the post office and inquired there about where the Riddings is. I didn't have the right address but they told me to go out to Brailsford, a town about six miles north-west of Derby, where we asked again. From there we were directed to Longford where we asked again. The one we asked at Hungry Bentley turned out to be the 'son of one of Dad's cousins' so he directed us to the Riddings. Of course, we got lost again so we had to enquire at a house. It turned out to be the house of a hired man of a cousin's and he directed us across the fields to the Riddings. He took us part way there and we walked about a mile and a half through cow pastures etc. We got to the Riddings about nine o'clock. Thomas Jeffery is very nice and has a very nice wife and family. There are four children: Dorothy 16; Tom 14; Margaret 8 and Fred 6; all very nice looking and quiet children. The Riddings is a quite large house and very pleasant inside. It's built of brick like most of the farm houses in the district. We talked until quite late and didn't get to bed until 12:30. We slept in a room in the south-east corner, upstairs. It had a thick feather bed which was very comfortable.

Saturday July 15: Got up about ten and had breakfast about 11 o'clock. Had mushrooms for breakfast which is something I've never had before. Didn't do anything else in the morning and had dinner about 12:30. After dinner, Mr. and Mrs. and the two little Jefferys walked up across the fields with us to Stydd Hall. Stydd Hall is the farm that the elder Mrs. Jeffery owns and is rented at present. (That's Mrs. Owen Jeffery – Thomas's mother). The house itself is built on the foundations of an old monastery that at one time stood there. The lower part of the house is the original and about 50 feet from the house stands one wall of the abbey which was connected to the other building. There are several graves scattered around the yard, reckoned to reach back to the time of the Crusades. The ruins are being preserved by some society, but nobody seems to pay much attention to them ……….

After returning to the Riddings we had tea, about 5:30. Then Lin (Geoff's college friend) *and young Tom and I walked to the Percy Spencer farm, which connects with the Riddings. Harold Spencer was going to take us to Derby to get our bag from the station. We didn't get off until about 7:30 because they insisted on giving us another tea, of the higher variety, before we left. Finally got to Derby where we got the bag and did a few other small things. Got back to the Riddings a little after ten and had a big supper. We sat up until about one talking.*

Sunday, July 16: Got up about ten and had breakfast with part of the family for a change. Right after breakfast Mr. and Mrs. Jeffery, Lin and I walked across the fields to a road where Mr. Hand, Thomas Jeffery's sister's husband, picked us up in a car and took us to his home at Shirley Mill. (This was Dorothy Jeffery Hand). *We had dinner there and after dinner Mr. Hand and Mr. Jeffery took us for a long ride through Ashbourne into Dovedale and to Ilam Hall and Church. Ilam Hall is a huge mansion and is now a Youth Hostel, being on Nat. Trust Property. We looked through the church which is very old – Norman, I guess. On the way back we stopped in Ashbourne to see the Cathedral* (St Oswalds's Church) *there. Had tea when we got back to Shirley Mill and shortly afterwards everyone piled in the car, six together, and we drove to the home of Ernest Hellaby* (actually John Ernest) *where Mrs. Hellaby* (Ellen Jeffery Hellaby), *Grandfather's sister lives. Ernest, her son, is married and has three children. Mrs. Hellaby, the elder, is very nice and seemed quite glad to see me. She has a good memory and told me a lot of things about the family. I guess she was the youngest of the family and lived by herself until a short time ago. We had supper at this place* (Fullwood Farm, Hulland) *and talked quite late. We got home about twelve. Had to walk across the fields again, a distance of a mile and a half. It was a beautiful night and the mist hung low in the valley with the tops of trees just sticking through, looking like huge thunder heads. Nearly stumbled over a few cows. They said that in winter, when it got dark earlier, that it wasn't uncommon to walk into a cow. Had a snack before bed and got there about one.*

Monday, July 17: …………… Mr. Jeffery, Lin and I walked up to the Spencer farm. Percy Spencer (Mary Jeffery Spencer's son) was going to take all of us to meet as many relatives as possible. Mrs. Hellaby arrived shortly … to go with us. We had dinner at Spencer's before we left, and got off about one. Firstly, we went to see Owen Poyser, son of Margaret Jeffery Poyser, Dad's Aunt. He's a retired farmer and has built himself a house on part of his old farm. (Oaklea). *His wife is crippled with rheumatism and doesn't leave the house much. An unmarried daughter lives with them* (Lillian) *and another daughter* (Margaret) *is a missionary somewhere. He has a beautiful rock garden built in an old gravel pit ...... a pool at the bottom and flowers all around the banks etc. The second place we visited was the home of the daughter of William Jeffery (name ?).* (This was probably Elizabeth Annie Jeffery Hidderley at *Palmer Moor Farm.*)

Next stop: the farm of (William) Offley Jeffery at West Broughton. Offley is the son of John Jeffery (grandfather's brother) who lives with his son and is 91 years old. We talked with him for quite a while. He was in bed and pretty feeble. His memory was excellent – much better than his hearing. He and Mrs. Hellaby tried to make me look like a Jeffery but couldn't find any typical features. There were a boy and girl there, about my age and they were very nice to talk to. (These would be John and Mary Jeffery, who were close in age to Geoff. Mary has spoken to me of her memories of meeting Geoff when he visited in 1939). *Left the house and saw Offley, who was working in the fields. He was very glad to see us and very nice to talk to.*

The fourth place we went was the farm of William Jeffery (William Charles Jeffery, son of William Jeffery, who was a brother of my grandfather). (This would be *Aston House*). *Mr. Jeffery was busy with the milking when we got there so we inspected the farm while we waited. It's supposed to be one of the best farms in the district and it was a very good one. Had tea about 6: 30 and talked with Mr. Jeffery for some time afterwards. He had a beautiful garden and a holly hedge about 10 ft. high and 4 ft. thick, perfectly trained, across one side of the garden.*

The next call was at the home of Owen Poyser's youngest sister who is married and on a farm. (This would be Fanny. Owen and Fanny were two of the children of Geoff's grandfather's oldest sister, Margaret.) *She was very nice but we didn't stay long as it was getting late. The sixth and last call was at the home of Jeffery Hellaby, Mrs. Hellaby's other son. He is married and has two children, one six and the other a year old.* (Geoff gave the wrong ages for my sister and me as we were eight and three respectively.) *We had supper there and talked till about 11 o'clock. Left and went back to the Spencer farm (Bentley Fields). Walked back to the Riddings and went to bed after eating and talking some more. I did a little writing after everyone else had retired.*

My grandmother Ellen, with her nephew Percy Spencer as chauffeur, organised a truly formidable number of family visits for this grandson of her brother Joseph. Geoff's mind must have been buzzing as he wrote up the above diary during the early hours of 18 July 1939.

Tuesday July 18: Got up rather late to find it raining a little harder than usual. Decided not to do much in the rain so we stayed around the house until after dinner when we walked up to Cubley to the Post Office and store. It continued to rain most of the day so we stayed close to the Riddings, helping the kids feed the turkeys etc. Took a walk after tea, getting back just in time for supper. Talked with the family all evening and retired rather early.

Wednesday July 19: Arose early and decided to start on our way again. Shipped our bag to Uttoxeter by bus and said goodbye to the Riddings. Rode past the Longford Church and saw the memorial window and graves of a good many Jefferys. (There is a little confusion here as the memorial window is in Alkmonton Church although there are many Jeffery graves at both Longford and Alkmonton.). *Next went past a Methodist Chapel near Cubley where Grandfather preached a sermon when he came back to England before he was married. Then we went on into Uttoxeter where we picked up the bag and sent it onto London by train. It was market day in Uttoxeter, a very interesting sight ....*

Geoff was to make a number of return visits to the land of his roots. In an e-mail letter to me in September 2007 he wrote:

Of course we have been back there a number of times since – for very brief visits, and three of our children have also had the opportunity of seeing the old family home. Your grandmother was a very delightful person and I have always been glad that I had a chance to meet her. I remember her so well. I can't be altogether sure but I think your father was the only first cousin that my father ever met. We were always trying to get him to visit England, but he just didn't like to travel, and after he retired his health was something of a problem.

Your grandmother was a very delightful person and I have always been glad that I had a chance to meet her. I remember her so well.

Joseph and Rosamond's only son, Joe (Geoff's father) had a very successful career in Education. By the 1920s he had become a High School Principal and in 1945 was appointed Superintendant of Schools (Director of Education) for Bridgeport, Connecticut. The newspaper report of his success provides an interesting pen picture of his career and family.

MEET OUR NEW SCHOOL SUPER

****

Those Who Know Him Enthusiastically Approve Selection Of Joseph Jeffery

You can call him Joe – but not too often.

This is one way of tagging the heir apparent to the superintendancy of Bridgeport's public schools.

For Joseph Ewart Jeffery has that kind of balance. He is a Yankee 101%, but not the hard-bitten species. He is conservative in education but he reads. He keeps an open mind. He is precise, teacherish but good for a laugh. He will resort to higher math to get all of his rights in a bridge or bowling score. But he lets his hair down during the game.

He doesn't smoke, but will hustle around you to get an ash tray for the repugnant individual who uses the weed.

The best advice is to call the coming super, now Bassilick High principal for the 11th year, Mr Jeffery, until your acquaintance is ripe.

Boss of some 900 teachers when he reaches the top next August as Supt. Mary A. Sullivan retires, Jeffery is in many respects a younger version of the late Supt. John A. Young. They were close friends in fact. They bowled once a week, punctually, for many years. One of the first to phone the new appointee with best wishes was Mr. Young's widow.

Like Young's, Jeffery's face has firm structure. It is Puritan with modern improvement, and in it, the first thing you read is man of principle. It would be hard to imagine Jeffery countenancing a lack of honour, or lack of dignity.

The Puritan has been melted down. He knows his literature and he reads a great deal. Asked what he read last. Jeffery said yesterday: 'Well, last night, I read Richard Wright's Black Boy'.

You could almost guess it that Jeffery is the son of a Methodist minister. The Rev. Joseph Jeffery, graduate of Drew, had gone to Sioux rapids, Iowa, in the 70's, when Horace Greeley was telling young men to go west. He had married Rosamond Clews. Their home, the son says today, ran on the 'plain living and high thinking plan'.

Joseph was able to go to Morningside College because he won a scholarship. Later he took a master's at Washington University, St. Louis.

His father's passion for setting the world to rights, took the shape of social welfare with Joseph. Little known in Bridgeport, where he has been for 28 years, is the fact that he is a graduate of the St. Louis School of Social Work. For two years he was in charge of the People's Institute and associated Charities at Mount Vernon, New York State.

But he was in the groove as a schoolman. His first principalship was in Keithsburg, Illinois. Others were at Birmingham, Alabama and at Dundee, New York State.

He was also a summer teacher at the universities of Louisiana and New Hampshire and took post graduate courses at Yale and New York University.

Joe – just for once – came to Bridgeport as a civics teacher during the last war (World War I). Within a few years he had headed Congress High.

Like Young's, Jeffery's face has firm structure. It is Puritan with modern improvement, and in it, the first thing you read is man of principle. It would be hard to imagine Jeffery countenancing a lack of honour, or lack of dignity.

NOW THEY ARE SIX

The Jefferys have a happy house at Milford. Garden and things, antique furniture, a well used volume on genealogy – that sort of house.

The co-principal over there is Augusta Knapp, music teacher whom Jeffery married in New York State at the Little Church around the Corner.

Here's another thing kids. The future super knows all about children. He has half a dozen grandchildren.

Daughter Rosamond Gaylord with her three lives at the Jeffery house while her husband Pfc. Alan Gaylord is with the First Army in Europe.

Pfc. Robert, older of the two young Jefferys, is at the Army war College, in Washington. He is married to Ruth Dolittle of Milford. Like his sister, he attended Hobart College.

Baby of the Jefferys is Dr. Geoff M. Jeffery. That's right – he took his name from way back in the family in Derbyshire, England. Geoff, or Jeff, is a graduate of John Hopkins and today he is doing a grand job – research in malaria control for the TVA's (*Tennessee Valley Authority*) public health service. He is married to Jane Wicker, a Syracuse girl.

In the 1950s, Joe faced many challenges in his work as Superintendant of Schools in Bridgeport, Connecticut. Education was facing serious financial constraints and schools were only able to open part-time. *THE BRIDGEPORT POST* reported the position on 25 January and 6 February 1952.

Jeffery Outlines Operations

Sharing the speaking platform with Mr. Benson, President of the Board of Education, was Supt. of Schools, Joseph E. Jeffery, who outlined the scope of operations of the public schools.

Discussing the needs of the schools, Mr. Jeffery pointed out that at the present time there were 1,900 high school students and 600 elementary pupils on part-time. He termed this an 'unfortunate' situation which can only be corrected by a building programme. Part-time education, he said, is not a normal or desirable condition.

In presenting the case for the urgent need for increased funding for new schools, he went on to say that:

While modern schools should be safe and sanitary and should have pleasant surroundings adaptable to study, he deplored recent trends, in some communities, towards a 'country club' atmosphere.

Discussing the School Board's budget request this year, he said that increases in costs of materials, salaries and wages, enrolment and equipment resulted in the Board's requesting $4, 666. 707, compared with the current apportionment of $3, 913, 730

Joe had reached the top of his profession. At the time when he was grappling with these serious financial constraints in education, he was already in his mid-sixties. All of his children were now married and he and Augusta had eleven grandchildren.

Some years after his retirement, they left Connecticut and moved back to Augusta's old home of *The Farm*, Log City Road, Dundee in upstate New York. Their daughter Rosamond with her husband Alan Gaylord and their family had renovated this wonderful old house and made it their home after their marriage.

Joseph and Rosamond's elder daughters, Ethel and Florence, maintained regular contact with their Aunt Nellie, my grandmother Ellen. My inheritance of some of these letters, via my father's papers, has been invaluable in piecing together some of the story of Joseph and Rosamond's children and grandchildren. Ethel's letters tell of the lives of her nephews and nieces – particularly Florence and Elso Sapp's children, Mark and Rosamond, who she visited in Arizona and Montana, and also of Joe and Augusta's family in Connecticut. Her letters also refer to the families of Joseph's brothers, Thomas and Arthur, then in California and the state of Washington. During the year before my grandmother died, Ethel wrote:

14 May, 1949

Dear Aunt Nellie,

I hope you have received my last letter when I thanked you for the pictures of Alkmonton Church. Florence told me that you had sent her one too.

Dorothy Jeffery at the Riddings, who writes to my sister-in-law, Augusta Jeffery, in Milford, said that you had been ill but were better. I do hope that you are well now and enjoying this spring. I know that the spring in England is beautiful. It has been especially lovely here this year.

Next week I'm going down to Milford to see the family there but I won't see Geoff and his family this time.

With lots of love and hoping that you are well again.

Ethel

Letter from Ethel to my Grandmother telling of their visits to see Mark and Rosamond and their families in Arizona and Montana

Ethel had a rewarding career teaching English at a High School in Hartford, Connecticut and became a much loved aunt to her nephews and nieces. She spent much of her retirement in Hartford before, in her later years, moving to be closer to her brother and family, Joe and Augusta and her sister Alice and husband Bill, in upstate New York. She died in Dundee, New York State, in November 1982, two months short of her ninety-eighth birthday.

Her younger sister Florence, who had also been a teacher, lived with her husband, Elso Sapp, in Buffalo Center, Winnebago County, Iowa where Elso was a successful local banker. Florence and Elso spent their whole lives in Iowa but regularly visited their married children and families after they moved away to California, Arizona and Montana respectively. In a letter to my grandmother, in the late 1940s, Ethel spoke of travelling by road with Florence and Elso, to visit Mark and family in Arizona and Rosamond and family in Montana. Another letter from Florence spoke of flying out to California to see son Bob and family.

*Banker Elso Sapp died
January 1968*

Florence survived her husband by eighteen years. Elso Sapp died on 6 January 1968. After his funeral service in Buffalo Center, he was buried in the Jeffery plot at Lone Pine Cemetery, Sioux Rapids, Iowa. His obituary was recorded in the *BUFFALO CENTER TRIBUNE* of 11 January 1968.

BANKER ELSO E. SAPP DIED SATURDAY

52 years in Farmer's Trust & Savings Bank

Funeral Services for E. E. Sapp, prominent Buffalo Center banker and business figure, were held in the First Congregational Church here Tuesday, January 9 at 10 00 a.m. Mr. Sapp had passed away Saturday, January 6, in a Rochester, Minnesota hospital after being taken there that morning by ambulance. He was 75 years, eight months and 27 days old at the time of his death.

In January 1967, Mr. Sapp had retired from an active part in the affairs of the Farmers Trust & Savings Bank after some 52 years association with the firm. Upon sale of his interest to W. D. Ley of Lakota, Mr. Sapp maintained office quarters in an advisory capacity but continued as chairman of the board.

At that time he was quoted as saying ill health was the prime factor in his decision involving the transfer of stock along with his confidence in the future of the bank being placed with Mr. Ley. During the last year, his brown automobile parked at the southeast corner of the bank was a familiar sight to local residents.

In his 52 years of banking endeavours he saw the firm move from a modest beginning to listed resources of $5,914,260.00 shortly before his retirement. An ascetic man, yet possessing a keen sense of humour, Mr. Sapp was always ready to serve his community to the best of his ability when called upon and occupied the President's chair of Buffalo Center School Board, along with several successful terms on the Town Council.

The son of Ham and Elizabeth Sapp, Elso Edward was born on April 9, 1892, on a farm near Parkersburg, Iowa where he attended country schools for several years. In the spring of 1901, the family moved to a farm two and a half miles north of Buffalo Center where they lived until 1912 when they moved to Buffalo Center.

He attended local schools until 1908 when he entered Hope College Preparatory department and graduated from there in 1910. From 1912 until 1915 he was in the employ of the McQuire Lumber Company and in the spring of 1915 he entered the Farmers Trust & Savings Bank which was also owned by the McQuires.

His association with the bank had continued uninterrupted until 1967 in an active capacity, and since that time until his death in an inactive role as chairman of the board.

Mr. Sapp was one of seven children, all of who preceded him in death except two: Mrs. John H. Winter (Elizabeth) of Buffalo Center and Herman R. Sapp of Nevada, Iowa.

On October 15, 1915, he was united in marriage to Edith Jeffery, daughter of Rev. and Mrs. Joseph Jeffery of Sioux Rapids, Iowa. To this union one daughter was born, Jeanne, Mrs. L. E. Savage of Wheaton, Illinois. Edith was a victim of the flu epidemic in March, 1919.

On July 30, 1921, he was united in marriage to Florence Jeffery, sister of Edith. To this union three children were born: Robert J. Sapp of Piedmont, California; Mark Alan Sapp of Flagstaff, Arizona and Rosamond, Mrs. Dr. D. Diggs of Missoula, Montana, all of whom survive to mourn his death with eleven grandchildren. Surviving also are nieces, nephews, cousins and a host of friends.

New Crocker Bank Opens

Crocker Bank's new Oakland main office opened for business on Monday morning, with clients and guests enjoying refreshments, music, free gifts and a drawing for four colour television sets.

Former Piedmonter Robert J. Sapp, senior vice president will manage the branch, which covers the entire first floor of the new 24 storey Clorox Building at Oakland City Centre.

Consolidated in the move were two nearby Crocker branches at 13th and Franklin and 1450 Broadway.

Mr. Sapp, who had been associated with Crocker Bank for 12 years currently resides in Moraga with his wife Doris. Two daughters, Anne and Katie, graduated from Piedmont High School, and are currently attending college. Daughter Mary is a student at Miramonte High.

In the summer following Elso Sapp's death we visited their two sons, Bob and Mark, with their families, in California and Arizona.

Robert Sapp, like his father, had a very successful career in banking. The newspaper cutting right, dated May 1977, provides a snapshot.

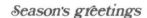

Florence and Elso's younger son, Mark, became a teacher and an insurance dealer and settled on a wonderful ranch near Flagstaff in Arizona. He and Donna had four children, Colleen, Jeffery, Steven and Kelly.

Florence continued active for many years following her husband Elso's death. In January 1986 she moved into the Timely Mission Nursing Home in Buffalo Center where, on 27 April she was written up as the resident of the month.

1968 - Joseph Jeffery's Great Granddaughter Kelly Sapp meets with his Sister Ellen's Great Granddaughter Clare Hardy

ABOVE *Mark and Donna's daughter Kelly (left) with our daughter Clare*

LEFT *Clare on Mark's horse held by Donna, Flagstaff, Arizona, summer 1968*

Resident of the Month

Florence Sapp
January 19, 1986

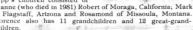

Florence Jeffery Sapp – Resident of the Month

April's resident of the month at TMNH is Florence Sapp. Florence Jeffery was born on November 4, 1886, in Luverne, Iowa to Rev. Joseph and Rosamond Clews Jeffery. Her parents came from Derbyshire, England to northwest Iowa and South Dakota where he was a pioneer Methodist minister.

On July 30, 1921, she was married to Elso Sapp. They lived in Buffalo Center all their married life. Mr. Sapp passed away in 1968. The Sapp's children consisted of Jeanne (who died in 1981); Robert of Moraga, California; Mark of Flagstaff, Arizona and Rosamond of Missoula, Montana. Florence has 11 grandchildren and 12 great grandchildren.

She has been an active member of the Buffalo Center Methodist Church for many years. Florence was also active in the order of the Eastern Star (of which she is a past Worthy Matron) and the Buffalo Center Literary Circle. She has written a number of poems and has unique memory retention. She can recite many epic poems in their entirety as well as long passages from the Bible.

Florence came to TMNH on January 19, 1986 and keeps active in the nursing home activities. Our congratulations go to Florence Sapp, April's Resident of the Month.

Three months later, on 24 July 1986, Florence died. She was aged ninety-nine and only three months short of her one-hundredth birthday. Her funeral and memorial service was held on 28 July and she too was buried at Lone Tree Cemetery, Sioux Rapids, Iowa.

Joe and Augusta's children were establishing their own lives and careers as they married and moved away. Rosamond had married Alan Gaylord and they made their home in Dundee. Robert married Ruth Dolittle and Geoff married Jane Wicker.

Although I didn't meet Joe and Gussie's daughter, Rosamond (Gaylord), I did meet her daughter Robin (another Rosamond), who was staying with her grandparents when we visited in 1968. I also met Robin's elder sister,

L. to r.: Geoff, Jane, Ruth and Robert at The Farm, Dundee

LEFT *Joe and Augusta with children and grand-children at The Farm, Dundee 1951*

BELOW *Joe with granddaughters Sally and Beth at Columba, South Carolina, Christmas, 1960*

BOTTOM LEFT *Joe and Augusta, Columba, South Carolina, Christmas 1960*

Betsy (Barker) when I was working in Cumbria in 1982. Betsy had, in her Uncle Geoff's words, 'emigrated back to England'. She is now living in Scotland and joined the Jeffery family reunion of 2008.

In September 1947 Ethel wrote to my grandmother and, in addition to giving family news, she included a news-paper cutting about her nephew, Joe's son Geoff, who had recently returned from a research project in Puerto Rico. Geoff, who had visited Derbyshire in 1939, had a distinguished academic career and the cutting (right) provides a thumbnail sketch of his career to date.

G. M. JEFFERY NAMED TO UNIVERSITY STAFF

Direct from service on a research project for the United States Public Health Service in the School of Tropical Medicine, Dr. Geoffrey M. Jeffery, has accepted ap-pointment as a member of the faculty, University of Bridgeport, President James H. Halsey announced last night.

Dr. Jeffery, who is a son of Superintendant of Schools and Mrs. Joseph E. Jeffery, will be a member of the Depart-ment of Biology at the University of Bridgeport. He is married and has two children and will return with his fam-ily to his home town of Bridgeport some time in August in preparation for the Fall term of the University year.

Dr. Jeffery holds a B. A. degree from Hobart College; an M. A. degree from Syracuse University; and a ScD. from John Hopkins University.

He was a student assistant in Parasitology at John Hop-kins University and a special instructor in courses in Clinical Laboratory, a biological aide at the Tennessee Valley Health Authority Health and Safety Department; and has been commissioned as first lieutenant in the United States Public Health services.

LEFT *Joe and Augusta's son, Geoff Jeffery, in the 1930s*

BELOW LEFT *Geoff and Jane with Thomas, Janet, Sally and Beth*

RIGHT *Geoff, third from the left with Jane and their daughters far right, visiting the Riddings in the 1950s*

Geoff and Jane's eldest children were Janet, born in 1943 and Thomas, born in 1944. They went on to have two more daughters – Sally in 1949 and Beth in 1950. When we met the family in Bethesda, Washington DC in 1967, Sally and Beth were still at home. Geoff was the Director of the Laboratory of Parasitic Chemotherapy in the National Institute of Allergy and Infectious Disease, Bethesda.

In August 2008, Geoff, with two of his daughters, Janet and Sally, and their husbands and one of his grandsons, David Houghton, and his wife together with one of his great-grandsons, Henry, travelled from America to attend our Jeffery family reunion. Afterwards Geoff wrote to me:

… My delay in writing is not indicative of my enjoyment of the wonderful reunion in Ashbourne. All of us here are immensely grateful to you and Irene and all the others who did so much in arranging and managing the whole weekend of events. I was somewhat amazed at the number of Jeffery descendants who were able to attend. For me it was a real privilege to renew acquaintance with those who I had been fortunate to meet previously, and

to meet so many others who I had known only as names on a genealogic chart. It was such a pleasure to see you and Colin and Clare again, and to meet Clare's delightful family. I often think of the privilege it was for us to have visits from your family and from your mother and father. I think that would be about 40 years ago but it is still one of my nicest memories. I was very pleased that it was possible for some of my immediate family to be part of the reunion and wish that the others could have been there. All of those who were there enjoyed it immensely. Even little Henry enjoyed all the attention he had from some of the young ladies who were there, two of whom, I think were your grand-daughters. It occurred to me that I was there celebrating the descendants of my great grandfather and that Henry is my great grandson – which covers a fair number of generations.

Geoff Jeffery now has fourteen American great grand-children. Geoff's daughter Sally later wrote:

Ken and I enjoyed the reunion so much. I think my favourite part was just meeting so many interesting Jefferys from all over the world. I particularly loved watching my father interact with relatives that he had never met or hadn't seen in more than 40 years. And of course, the fact that our baby grandson, Henry Houghton, was there meant so much to me.

Joseph and Rosamond's family story has covered 150 years on both sides of the Atlantic. Today, their many descendants are spread across the continent many thousand miles from where their story began.

RIGHT *Joseph's grandson Geoff Jeffery with his great grandson James Thomas Coleman, January 2009*

GEORGE JEFFERY
1849 – 1922

'Black Sheep' or Man of Fortitude?

George Jeffery, the fifth son of Thomas and Mary Jeffery of the Riddings, was born on 22 November 1849. The third son to emigrate to North America, in 1883, he became one of the earliest pioneer farmers in Manitoba on the Canadian prairie. He died in Spokane in the state of Washington, USA on 17 January 1922.

Descendants of George Jeffery

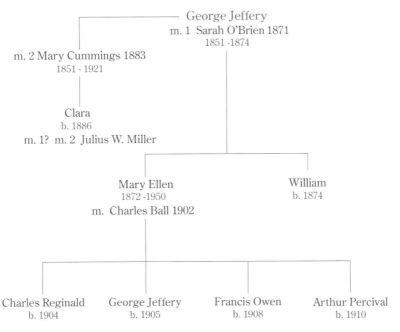

George Jeffery
m. 1 Sarah O'Brien 1871
1851 -1874

m. 2 Mary Cummings 1883
1851 - 1921

Clara
b. 1886
m. 1? m. 2 Julius W. Miller

Mary Ellen
1872 -1950
m. Charles Ball 1902

William
b. 1874

Charles Reginald
b. 1904

George Jeffery
b. 1905

Francis Owen
b. 1908

Arthur Percival
b. 1910

George Jeffery 1849-1922
'Black Sheep' or Man of Fortitude?

George poses something of an enigma. Tradition has it that he was the 'black sheep' of the Jeffery family. After all, he did abandon the children of his first marriage and took to 'the demon drink'. An explanation might lie in the tragic loss of his first wife Sarah when he was only twenty-four leaving him with two very young children. His jobs as a hotel waiter and later a cellar-man gave him access to alcohol and there was no family around to support him at this time. However, he later demonstrated very considerable fortitude, resilience and courage as one of the early pioneer farmers who settled in the Canadian prairies. The black sheep soubriquet is just one illustration of the many mysteries surrounding George's story.

From my earliest days, when listening to stories of my grandmother's family at the *Riddings*, the tag 'black sheep' and drunkard was how I heard family members describe George. Later I learnt that, like his two elder brothers, Thomas and Joseph and his youngest brother Arthur, he emigrated to North America. Further, it also seemed that no-one had any clear idea of what happened to him in the early years following his departure from Liverpool. He appears to have been 'lost'.

George's black sheep image followed him in the stories which were also told of him in America. His niece Florence, daughter of his brother Joseph, recorded the following in her memoirs:

George Jeffery who also came to America was at one time considered the black sheep of the family, so I have heard. He left his children at the Riddings to be cared for and went to Canada. I do not know much about his life there. He was buried in Spokane, near where Uncle Arthur and Aunt Margaret and little Ethel were buried. Our cousin Margaret (Arthur and Margaret's eldest daughter) *didn't know it and when she was told she said – 'Just think of that man being buried near to my father who was a most exemplary and religious man.' Her father was the Sunday School Superintendant in the large church they attended in Seattle when they had the two little boys.*

George was born on 22 November 1849, shortly before the sixth anniversary of his parents' marriage. He replaced his fourteen-month-old brother John in the cradle. His sister Margaret had just turned five years old and, in addition to one-year-old John, his other elder brothers, Thomas, William and Joseph were all under five. His birth may have been something of a disappointment as,

George Jeffery as bridegroom at his wedding in Leeds
19 November 1871

after four sons, his parents and sister may well have been hoping that the new baby would be a daughter.

Before George reached his eighth birthday his brother Owen had joined the family together with five younger sisters, Elizabeth, Mary, Sarah Ann, Fanny and Clara. He was sixteen by the time Charles, Ellen and the last baby, Arthur, had completed the family.

It is interesting to speculate on the extent to which George's position in the family as a middle son, with four older and three much younger brothers influenced his character development. Was he constantly striving to emulate his four older brothers and to secure his own place within the family? Growing up in the rough and tumble of a large family, he would, as a five-year-old have joined his elder brothers in their walk to school at Longford, although, by the time he was seven he may have transferred to Alkmonton where the school had been opened in 1856. He was only fourteen when his nine-year-old sister, Sarah Ann, died but by this time he had left school and joined his four older brothers working on the farm. By the time he reached his seventeenth birthday, his elder brother William was providing major support for his father on the farm whilst his elder brothers Thomas and Joseph had already left for America.

George's elder brother John was only a year older and the two brothers appear to have been close. On the occasion of John's twenty-first birthday, George gave his brother a beautiful leather-bound photograph album in which he inscribed:

Many Happy Returns to John Jeffery, August 23rd. 1869 from his affectionate brother George Jeffery.

John was to fill the album with many family photographs including a number of George, both of his wives and son William. The album includes one of George with a fur hat – a hat that was probably Canadian. The existence of this particular photograph may suggest that, although there are no surviving letters from Canada, George did not entirely cut himself off from family and that the closeness between the brothers was maintained.

In his late teens, George seems to have been determined to make his own way in the world and by the time he had turned twenty, he had left the *Riddings* and was living in Leeds. In 1871, he was working as a waiter at the Albion Hotel in Leeds. His brother John had also left home and he too was working in Leeds at this time. However, John's sojourn away from the farming life was quite brief as, by the time of their father's death in 1876, he had returned home. It would be over a decade later before George returned to a life in farming when he left for Canada in 1883.

At the same time that George was working at the Albion Hotel in Leeds, the attractive young Sarah O'Brien was also employed there. Sarah, born on 18 May 1851,

in Leeds, was the daughter of Ellen and James O'Brien. Her father was a linen weaver. On 19 November 1871, twenty-one-year-old George married twenty-year-old Sarah in the Parish Church in Leeds. The marriage was witnessed by Ann Davies, who worked at the Albion Hotel with George and Sarah, and a Charles Wathall. There were no family witnesses at the wedding.

Two years earlier, in November 1869, George's elder brother Thomas had married Maria Hague in New York and his parents had proudly placed an announcement of the marriage in the *DERBY MERCURY*. There was no such announcement for the marriage of the young George and Sarah. His parents no doubt considered that their fifth son, in addition to being very young and barely able to support a wife, was marrying beneath himself socially. He was exhibiting a rebellious streak, having left the farm and married out of his class.

George Jeffery, farmer on Canadian prairie

George's first wife Sarah at the time of her marriage.
November 1871

George and Sarah were never to share their third wedding anniversary. The years following their marriage were turbulent ones with more than their fair share of both happiness and tragedy. On 15 August 1872 Sarah gave birth to a daughter. She was christened Mary Ellen after two of George's sisters. By the beginning of 1874 the family had moved to Wakefield and on 1 February 1874 their son William was born. It seems likely that Sarah's recovery from her son's birth did not go smoothly and just a few months later tragedy struck the little family in Wakefield. On 10 August 1874 Sarah died aged only twenty-three. Her death certificate recorded that the cause of death was acute rheumatism and pericorditis.

George was distraught, a widower at twenty-four and left with two very young children. His baby son William was just six months old and his daughter Mary Ellen had yet to reach her second birthday. He decided to bring the children home to his mother where they were brought up at the *Riddings* by their grandmother and young aunts. The children were not to remember their grandfather, who died less than two years later. For Mary Ellen and her brother William growing up at the *Riddings*, their Uncle Owen would become a father figure and their young Aunt Ellen and Uncle Arthur would be more like older siblings to them. William, always known as 'Little Willie' died quite young and was thought to be handicapped in some way. The handicap may have been a physical one as a photograph taken in 1882 seems to indicate callipers on his legs. Other photographs taken when he was a child do not appear to indicate any other handicap.

A photo of the extended family outside the Riddings in 1882.
Mary Ellen and William are seated in the middle at the front.
George and his second wife Mary in the back row

George's son William
with toy trumpet

FAR LEFT *George's daughter Mary Ellen, at Weymouth*

LEFT *George's son William aged about 16*

BELOW *George's second wife Mary*

Although family folklore has always described George as the 'black sheep' of the family and maybe something of an alcoholic, the traumatic loss of his young wife Sarah, leaving him with two young motherless children may help to explain why he gained this reputation. By the spring of 1881, he had left Yorkshire and was working at the Royal Hotel in Leyton with Warbeck, Lancashire, as a cellar-man.

By 1882 George had met Mary Cummings, who was born on 17 March 1851 in Thurso, Caithness, Scotland. Mary's father was James Cummings and her mother Christina MacLeod. It maybe that George met Mary whilst he was working at the Royal Hotel in Leyton with Warbeck but this has to be purely speculative. Wherever they met, Mary was the woman with whom he would share the rest of his life. Meanwhile, all of his older siblings, apart from his brother Joseph in Iowa, had married and started to establish their own families.

1882 was the year when, following the death of his twenty-two-year-old brother Charles, his elder brothers Thomas and Joseph returned from America for a visit. George also returned home from Lancashire, in order to see his children and to introduce his fiancée, Mary, to the family. It would be the last time that all of the *Riddings*

George's second wife Mary Cummings

family would be together and was therefore the opportunity to take the memorable photographs of the remaining thirteen children with their mother and also, with husbands, wives and grandchildren. Studying the 1882 photograph of the extended family, it is interesting to note that Mary, although standing next to him in the doorway, is somewhat removed from him in her pose reflecting their current status.

At the time of this visit when the family were together, it was inevitable that George would be interested in hearing of the experiences of his pioneering brothers, Thomas in Minnesota and Joseph in Iowa. Doubtless by this time, he was beginning to look forward, after the traumas of the previous decade, and seriously considering what life might hold for him if he followed in their footsteps.

Life in the New World beckoned. It was in the spring of 1883 that George Jeffery and Mary Cummings sailed

from Liverpool on the *SS Sarmation*. They arrived in Quebec on 28 May 1883. The passenger manifest shows that they were still unmarried. The eventual date of their marriage is not known although Mary is recorded as George's second wife in the *Bentley Fields* Bible.

George and Mary were about to embark on their new life together in the Dominion of Canada. They travelled westwards into the prairies of Manitoba. The Canadian prairies of Manitoba, Saskatchewan and Alberta, which were to become one of the world's great wheat producers, were only just starting to be developed and settled by the early 1880s. Thus George and Mary were among the earliest pioneers in Manitoba.

It is interesting to wonder why George decided to build his new life in Canada rather than in the USA. However, it is also interesting to note that, in opting to settle in Manitoba, he was choosing the Canadian province bordered in the south by the state of Minnesota, where Thomas was prospering in Minneapolis and that Minnesota, in turn, borders Iowa, where Joseph was established as a minister. A great swathe of middle North America had become home to three Jeffery pioneer brothers and their families during the last decades of the nineteenth century.

By the time that thirty-three-year-old George left Liverpool in 1883, his first wife Sarah had been dead for almost nine years and the only life their children Mary Ellen and William had ever known had been spent at the *Riddings*. George appeared determined to make a new life for himself and Mary in Canada. There are records of him crossing the border, probably to visit his brothers, including Arthur, in America, but I have not discovered any records of him returning home to visit family in England. In fact, he appears to have been 'lost' to the family back home. His siblings, particularly Ellen, my grandmother, communicated regularly with her other pioneering brothers, Thomas, Joseph and Arthur and their families but no-one appeared to have been sure of what had become of George.

However, there does appear to be evidence that he did not cut himself off entirely from his family. Although no letters survive, there are clues suggesting that communications were not entirely broken. Firstly, the presence of the photograph of George, wearing a fur hat which looks Canadian, in his brother John's photograph album. This photograph was taken in Manchester and George appears to be in his late forties. It was first shown to me by Mary Jeffery at *Home Farm*, West Broughton. Secondly, the two newspaper reports – of the fire on George's farm in Canada in 1915 and the obituary of his wife Mary's death in 1921 which were sent to the *Riddings*. These were first shown to me by Margaret, Owen's granddaughter, at the *Riddings*.

Research in the 1980s, by my cousin Dorothy Jeffery (1923-1991) of the *Riddings*, revealed that George had purchased land and farmed in Manitoba. I followed this up in the 1990s, whilst undertaking research in Sarasota, USA. This gave me access to Canadian censuses before they became more readily available on the internet. It was a 'eureka' moment when I 'found' George after a century of mystery!

Returning to George's story in the Canada of 1883, the scene that would have met him was one of vast open prairie grasslands in the very early stages of transformation into the 'world's bread basket'. Prairie land was divided up into Quarter Sections and homesteaders were encouraged to farm the land for a minimum of three years and erect a home. Livestock could be substituted for cultivation under certain conditions. The claimant for a homestead had to be the head of a family or an unmarried man and a British subject by birth or naturalisation. The claimant had to pay a registration fee of ten dollars and live on the homestead for at least six months each year for five years and fulfil certain other requirements.

George purchased 160 acres of land at the equivalent price of six old pence per acre (about two-and-a-half pence in present currency) near Elkhorn, Manitoba. Elkhorn lies 189 miles due west of Winnipeg and quite close to the border with Saskatchewan. Lying on what is now the Trans Canada Highway, its population today is still only around 500. It was established in 1882 when it was reached by the mainline of the Canadian Pacific Railway.

George went to Canada. He became a sheep owner. . . Aunt Jessie said he was a real patriarch with a long beard and had this great ranch.

The engineers named it for the large rack of elk horns found on the line of survey. Elkhorn lay 64 miles west of Brandon, a somewhat larger settlement, where telegraph PO communication was established on 1 December 1883. This was true pioneer territory and a very challenging environment in which to make a new start. The prairie lands were still being settled in the same manner nearly thirty years later, as a synopsis of Canadian Land Regulations described in the *ELKHORN MERCURY* of 1915 indicated, although by that time the price had increased to three Canadian dollars an acre.

Life as a pioneer rancher on the Manitoba prairie lands in the late nineteenth and early twentieth centuries was vastly different from life on the Derbyshire farmland where George had grown up. However, the land was in his blood and he clearly made a success of his new life as later evidence was to reveal. He maintained contact with his brothers in America and his niece Florence (Joseph and Rosamond's daughter), when recording her memories, wrote:

George went to Canada. He became a sheep owner. I think not much is known of him but one time Aunt Jessie and Uncle Tom went to see him. Aunt Jessie said he was a real patriarch with a long beard and had this great ranch.

George and Mary established their ranch and homestead at Archie in the Marquette District ten miles north of the small town of Elkhorn. Archie is a rural municipality in the Province of Manitoba and even today its population amounts to less than 400. Farming life for these early pioneers on the wide open, windswept, treeless Canadian prairie, where they encountered many physical difficulties and where the winters were severe and the summers could be excessively hot, was extremely challenging. It certainly required commitment and determination to succeed and George exhibited the very same commitment, determination and hard work that his brothers, Thomas and Joseph, were revealing in their very different spheres, south of the border, in Minnesota and Iowa.

George and Mary, early pioneers of the prairie lands, rose to challenges which defeated others with less inner strength and enterprise. The Canadian Pacific Railway, built between 1881 and 1885, was instrumental in the settlement and development of Western Canada and for decades was the only practical means of passenger transport in most regions of Canada. The railway had only just reached Winnipeg when George and Mary emigrated in 1883.

Life was exceedingly hard for these earliest of pioneers who succeeded through sheer grit and determination. Land, in the very early days, was cheap but purchase of land was only the first step. The new owners were required to build the house and barns, dig a well, fence the land and break up the soil for cultivation. It would be 1888, five years after George had established his ranch in the Marquette District, that Manitoba amended its land regulations and the Canadian Pacific Railway commenced an intense campaign to bring immigrants to Canada. CP agents operated in many overseas locations and immigrants would often be sold a package, which included passage on a CP ship, travel on a CP train and land, at the increased price of $2.50 per acre and above, sold by the Canadian Pacific Railway. By the end of the first decade of the twentieth century, when George had been farming on the Canadian prairie for nearly forty years, life was a great deal easier for the new settler, as immigrants were offered farms which had been fully prepared by the Canadian Pacific Railway Company and they were allowed to fund their purchases by way of easy instalments.

It was in 1888 that the branch line opened between Sudbury and Saulte Ste Marie where the Canadian Pacific Railway connected with the American railway system and its own steamships on the Great Lakes. Sudbury was the junction for the CPR line to Saulte Ste Marie where the Soo line would eventually make connection with the Duluth, Minneapolis and St Paul Railway and so facilitate easier communication between George and his eldest brother Thomas.

Although there are no letters from George and Mary, recording life on a farm on the Canadian prairie in the late nineteenth century, their neighbour, Arthur Sherwood, was a wonderful letter writer. His letters provide a graphic picture of the experiences of a young immigrant who farmed in the region of Wellington, Elkhorn and Kola in the Marquette District between 1882 and 1892. Extracts from these letters were published by the Manitoba Historical Society in their journal *Manitoba Pageant*, Winter 1971 and taken from Professor Jackman's publication.[1]

[1] The Letters of Arthur Sherwood. Preface by S. W. Jackman. Extracts taken from Manitoba Pageant, Winter 1971, Volume 16, Number 2.

These letters were written during his first early years when George also was beginning to establish himself in the area. The first two letters are from Wellington, near Portage, which lies to the east of Elkhorn. The following ones, from Elkhorn and Kola, would have been written when Arthur Sherwood would have been farming land quite close by George's farm at Archie.

❦

Wellington Post Office
December 16, 1882

Dear Mother,
You ask me about life, neighbours etc. Manitoban life is nothing like Australian. It is more like a farmer's in the Old Country except that you have not the luxuries, the friends or the rents and have to rough it a good deal and go long distances for anything purchasable.

And now the neighbours, well a good many Englishmen come out here but when they get to Winnipeg, they either don't like the place and go home or to the States and knock about the towns and speculate in town lots or anything else with money or loss of money in it. Again, some take to farming, but there are so few that they get lost in this big country and you run across them every now and then and they seem as glad to see you as if you were an old friend.

The house we live in is a frame one made of lumber and put up by ourselves with help from our next door neighbour, a carpenter. It has two rooms on the ground floor and two upstairs.

We had to sleigh down to Portage, our nearest town, about twenty-five miles distant to get groceries etc. We also had to get our winter outfit, namely mitts which are fingerless gloves, as any other kind are too cold. Even my fur ones do not keep my fingers from freezing, and moccasins, which you could not get out here. They are made of rawhide, either buffalo or moose and are much warmer than tanned leather, besides which, they are shapeless things which allow room for three or four pairs of socks and allow circulation of the blood besides.

❦

Wellington Post Office
February 11, 1883

My Dear Girls,
You must excuse my putting in a great deal about the weather,
but as that is about the only thing of interest at present in the
country, and as one is always being most painfully reminded of
the fact that it is winter, it is not surprising that it should be more
a subject of conversation than at home.

Our thermometer is a mercury one which freezes at 42 degrees
below freezing so does not register the very cold days, but it has
been as cold as 50 degrees below I believe and in the province
west of here it fell as low as 56 degrees, 88 degrees of frost. Try
and imagine it if you can.

All of my fingers, both of my ears, my face, and last but not least,
my nose have all been frozen times innumerable. They first lose
all feeling, then on snow or very cold water being applied, they
come to life and hurt fearfully.

It was kind of you to think about the mince pies but I ate more
than was good for me this Christmas in the way of mincemeat
and plum pudding so you see we are not so uncivilised out here
as you think.

Elkhorn
August 13, 1884

Dear Mother,
You can't tell how glad I am that you are all pleased with my
venture and I think myself that on the whole it is the best thing
I could have done.

We are in our house at last and pretty well settled. We got
drowned out in the shanty and most of our things were pretty
near spoiled. It rained twenty six hours without stopping and the
heaviest rain I ever saw in the country.

We have had the most fearful storms this summer. One man
about five miles away was killed by lightning and others stunned,
numerous horses, oxen and buildings struck. This summer has
also been hot. Last Sunday the thermometer was 120 in the
shade and it has often been up to 110.

We have thirty tons of hay stacked and are going to stack twenty
more. Hay is very scarce this year. After haying we are going to
put up a lumber stable 20 x 30 and then we shall have nothing of
importance but (indecipherable) to do. The cows are all doing
well but there is not a very good sale for butter at present so we
are packing. We hope it will go up in price next month. We still
get rid of a good deal among the neighbours.

We found the pony and since then have got two more. They draw
the mower and hay rake just as well as heavy horses, are tougher,
cost less to feed and are procurable at half the price.

Elkhorn
September 28, 1884

Dear Tom,
I got your letter last night and was awfully glad to hear that you
are thinking of coming out here. I think that the sooner you come
out the better. If you could get out here by the end of November or
beginning of December you will get here nicely before the really
cold weather sets in and you will be able to stand the winter all
the better for having some good Old Country blood in you and
you will be better prepared for work next year.

You will want a pretty good stock of strong flannel shirts, under-
shorts, drawers etc. socks and stockings. Get them all as strong as
you can. Bring a good many pairs of service boots as you cannot
get a good boot out here. Those K boots are the very thing for this
country. Don't get any lined as I did. You will find them useless
as they are too cold for winter wear. Don't have the soles nailed
as the soles always last longer than the uppers.

Bring all your old clothes and invest in as many cord trousers or
britches as you like. Blankets, towels, pillow –slips etc. all come
in handy, especially the blankets. Sheets are not necessary.

We are getting on pretty well now. Have started a small store and
are doing a pretty good business considering we are in an out of
the way place. I don't know whether I mentioned about the store
and the post office but we have applied for the latter and have a
pretty good chance of getting it.

Kola
May 5, 1886

My Dear Father,

We have had a grand spring this year. I am cropping fifteen acres, ten of which I am sowing with barley. There was a great demand for barley last year at fair prices and there promises to be an even greater demand this year.

I should like to be able to get a good bull by next year. I have a good grade now which I shall kill in the fall as this is his second year. I want to get a thoroughbred as most of my cows are poor though the young stock are not so bad but they are nearly all steers.

⚜

These letters to family back home paint a vivid and personal description of some of Arthur Sheldon's experiences in the Marquette District in Manitoba in the 1880s. No doubt George and Mary would have experienced comparable challenges.

It was at the end of their third summer, when the harvest would have been safely gathered, that Mary gave birth to their daughter on 18 September 1886. They called her Clara, after another of George's sisters. Her childhood on the Canadian prairie would have been vastly different from that of her half sister and brother, Mary Ellen and William, growing up at the *Riddings*.

⚜

At the time of Clara's birth in Canada, George's first daughter, Mary Ellen, was thirteen and his son William was eleven. Their grandmother, Mary, had been widowed for ten years and only their Uncle Owen, who now farmed both the *Riddings* and *Bentley Fields*, and their Aunts Mary, Fanny and Ellen remained at home. In the early summer of 1888, George's brother Joseph and his wife Rosamond from Iowa visited the *Riddings* and when they left, they took fifteen-year-old Mary Ellen back home with them for a visit. The three of them sailed from Liverpool on the *SS City of Rome*, arriving in New York on 7 June 1888. The family hoped that Mary Ellen would be able to contact her father. There is no record known that she achieved this before she returned to England.

The year 1891 found eighteen-year-old Mary Ellen and sixteen-year-old William, still at the *Riddings* with their grandmother together with their Uncle Owen and Aunt Nellie (Ellen) whilst George and Mary, with three-year-old Clara, were by now well established on their ranch in Manitoba.

Mary Ellen's marriage to Charles Ball at Snitterton Hall

LEFT *Full family group*

RIGHT *Far left of the bridal group is Owen Jeffery who was a father figure to Mary Ellen.*
The bridesmaid on her right is Mary Ellen's cousin Gertrude, daughter of Aunt Clara and Uncle Arthur Cook

As the new century opened, whilst George, Mary and thirteen-year-old Clara were farming on their ranch near Elkhorn, Mary Ellen increasingly spent time in the homes of some of her married aunts. In 1901 she stayed with her Aunt Margaret (Poyser) and family at *Shardlow House Farm* and in 1902 she was living with her Aunt Clara (Cook) and family at *Snitterton Hall*. It was at Snitterton that she came to know Charles Ball from Cumber Hills, Duffield, Derbyshire.

On 30 October 1902 Mary Ellen married Charles Ball in the Congregational Church, Matlock Bank, Matlock. The reception was held at the home of her Aunt Clara and Uncle Arthur at *Snitterton Hall*, which had been her home at the time of her marriage. Her cousins, Gertrude and Jeffery Cook were bridesmaid and pageboy. Her cousin Mary Mabel Jeffery, aka May, daughter of her Uncle John of *West Broughton* was a witness to her marriage and she was given away by her Uncle Owen. Both her father, George Jeffery, in Canada, and Charles' father, Charles Ball, were recorded as farmers on the marriage certificate. Although her father did not attend, all of her aunts and many of her cousins were present at her wedding. Mary Ellen's Aunt Nellie (Ellen) had married five years earlier and the group wedding photograph shows her holding her ten-month-old son Jeffery Hellaby (my father). Mary Ellen's brother William was not present: his death may have occurred prior to November 1902.

A mystery surrounds what happened to George's son William who was brought up at the *Riddings*. There is a small table remaining there which is still referred to as 'Little Willie's table'. As there are no records of him after the 1891 census, it has been suggested that he died young but, despite persistent searching, I have yet to discover either any record of his death or the location of his grave. It remains a mystery and raises the question of whether he endeavoured to join his father in Canada.

...They told me they did not think I would live and that I was baptised at home. I seem to have proven them wrong.

George's daughter Mary Ellen and her husband Charles Ball started their married life farming at the *Cottage Farm*, a neighbouring farm to the *Riddings*. They moved in there as Ellen and William Hellaby moved out prior to their move to *Bentley Hall*. Mary Ellen and Charles Ball had four sons between 1904 and 1910. Charles Reginald was born in 1904; George Jeffery, named after his grandfather, on 21 February 1905; Francis Owen in 1908 and Arthur Percival in 1910. Their third son, named after Mary Ellen's Uncle Owen, who had been a father to her while she was growing up at the *Riddings*, was always known as Owen. He moved to Scotland to be near his solicitor son and family but maintained close links with his Jeffery family throughout his life. He recalled some of his early memories in his last letter, in December 1995:

It's a long time since I first saw the light of day at Cubley Cottage Farm. I don't know much about it! They told me they did not think I would live and that I was baptised at home. I seem to have proven them wrong.

Back in Canada, by 1911, George and Mary's daughter, Clara, now twenty-four years old, had left home. George was now sixty-one and in need of additional hired help on the farm. On the 1911 census for Manitoba, another mystery is indicated, as an additional member of the household, twenty-year-old Jarden Browne, who was born in Ireland, was resident. Jarden is recorded as the son of George and Mary. However, the question must remain as to whether he was officially adopted by them after Clara had left home. It seems doubtful as, four years later, George still referred to a hired man who lived on the farm.

In 1915 tragedy struck on the ranch when George suffered heavy losses by fire. The *ELKHORN MERCURY* of Thursday, 4 November 1915 had the following report on its front page. The newspaper was sent home to the *Riddings*.

This devastating fire, with its serious loss of most of the summer's harvest and all of his valuable horses, seemed like a case of arson. It happened shortly before George reached his sixty-sixth birthday. It would be a long time before he recovered from such a disaster.

Meanwhile, life for their daughter Clara, who had married and moved away, had not been without its problems. In 1920, thirty-three-year-old Clara appeared on the United States Federal census. She was divorced and living as a lodger in the home of Paul and Eleanor Wymond and their twenty-five-year-old son Hawley in Great Falls Ward, Cascade, Montana. By the following April, 1921, she had married Julius W. Miller and was living in San Francisco. A Directory for San Francisco of this time showed Clara Julius Miller at Route 487, 23rd Avenue, San Francisco.

It is possible that Clara met her second husband in Canada as a J. W. Miller is recorded as being born in Canada in 1885. Additionally, it is interesting to note that, in the *ELKHORN MERCURY* of 4 November 1915, a J. Harvey Miller advertised his services as a 'Dealer in agricultural implements, Auctioneer and Real Estate Agent.' This could be the same family but further research would need to be done to verify this.

It does appear that Clara and her husband lived and eventually farmed in California as J. W. Miller is listed in a 1938 Directory for the Ojai Valley, California: his occupation

FARMER'S HEAVY LOSS

****

Fire destroys barn and horses belonging to Mr. G. Jeffery

Another blaze of mysterious origin started in the early hours of Monday last and wiped out valuable property

Fire destroyed the stable, seven valuable horses, all the harness and a large quantity of hay and oat sheaves in the loft, on the farm of Mr. George Jeffery, north of the town in the early hours of Monday morning. The cause of the fire is so far a mystery. Mr Jeffery, whose bedroom window faces the stable, was up at about 2 a.m. and at that time there was no appearance of fire. He awakened again about 4 a.m. and immediately noticed a bright reflection in the direction of the cow stable. He called his man who, partly dressed, rushed out to return immediately with the news that the stable was burnt to the ground. Neighbours were quickly on the spot once the alarm was phoned, and the ashes raked over and put out to prevent further damage should the wind arise. It is impossible to understand what could have caused the fire. No lantern had been used in the building since Saturday evening. The hired man does not smoke and Mr. Jeffery himself had not been to the stable at all during the previous evening. The night was perfectly calm, so calm in fact that the heat and blaze must have gone straight up as not even the grass was burnt outside of a small circle close around the building. The roof of the cowshed was blistered by the heat but fortunately there was no wind and that building escaped destruction. Insurance only amounts to about $500.

Newspaper report of fire

was recorded as a farmer and his address is stated as being two miles North West of Ojai on Maricopa highway. J. W. Miller's death was recorded in California in 1961 but I have not found a record of Clara's death or, whether they had children.

During the early summer of 1920, Clara's father, George was travelling, probably to visit Clara and his brothers in America. Border Crossings from Canada to the USA show him in Vancouver on 23 May 1920 and interestingly, arriving in Buffalo four days later on 27 May. He was travelling on his own as, for some years, Mary's health had been failing. At the time of her death, in 1921, she was described as an invalid.

As Mary's health declined, Clara returned home to spend time with and care for her mother who died on 12 April

Newspaper version of
OBITUARY

OBITUARY
Mary Jeffery

Old timers, of this district especially, will learn with regret of the passing away of Mrs. Geo. Jeffery in her 71st year, at the homestead, N.W. 22-13-28 ten miles north of Elkhorn, on Tuesday, April 12th, 1921. The news will not be altogether unexpected as for several years Mrs. Jeffery has been an invalid and gradually growing weaker. The deceased was one of the earliest settlers in the north district coming to this country with her husband in 1883. She was of a reserved but most kindly disposition, a real neighbour of the old fashioned type and one who made the home the centre of her activities, whose greatest pleasure lay in extending a warm welcome to her friends there. Those who knew her intimately will best be able to recognise the great loss that Mr. Jeffery has been called upon to bear and they will extend their deep sympathy to him and the bereaved daughter, Mrs J. W. Miller of San Francisco who was present at the time of the death of her mother.

The funeral takes place today, April 14th. Service being held at the residence and Elkhorn Presbyterian Church with the Rev. F. C. Pecover officiating. The remains will find a resting place in Elkhorn cemetery.

Card of Thanks

Mr. George Jeffery and daughter Mrs. J. W. Miller desire to express their heartfelt thanks for condolence and help extended to them at the time of their bereavement.

1921. A copy of her obituary as reported in the *ELKHORN MERCURY* of 14 April 1921 was also sent to the *Riddings*.

At the time of Mary's death, George was aged seventy-one. Some time later, he sold the ranch, left Canada and moved to Spokane, Washington, to be close to his brother Arthur. He died nine months later, on 17 January 1922 and is buried in the Jeffery family plot in Spokane. His brother Arthur, who died seven years later, is also buried there.

George and Sarah's daughter Mary Ellen, and her husband Charles Ball, retired to Weston Coyney on the Leek Road, North Staffordshire. They called their home Cumber Hills recalling the home of Charlie's youth. It was here, on 17 June 1950, that Mary Ellen died of a cerebral haemorrhage and arterial sclerosis, in her seventy-eighth year. My sister, Marjorie, can remember visiting Mary Ellen and assures me that I too visited as a little girl but sadly I cannot recall the occasions. Mary Ellen and Charles Ball's son, Owen, who moved to Aberdeenshire, maintained contact with his cousins at the *Riddings*, until his death in the 1990s. There are other descendants from Mary Ellen and Charles Ball's four sons.

The mystery of what happened to George and Sarah's son William remains for others to solve.

Our story of Clara (Miller) ends after discovering her in San Francisco in 1921 and in Ojai Valley in 1938. We do not know whether she had children. However, any descendents of George and Mary, through Clara in the USA, have step relatives in the UK, from his first marriage to Sarah through Mary Ellen (Ball).

ARTHUR JEFFERY
1865 – 1929

Come West Faithful Little Brother

Arthur Jeffery, the youngest son of Thomas and Mary Jeffery of the Riddings, was born on 3 October 1865. He emigrated to America in 1883 and joined his eldest brother Thomas in business in Minneapolis, Minnesota. He moved out west to Seattle in the state of Washington and died there, on his ranch in Spokane, Washington, USA, in 1927.

Descendants of Arthur Jeffery

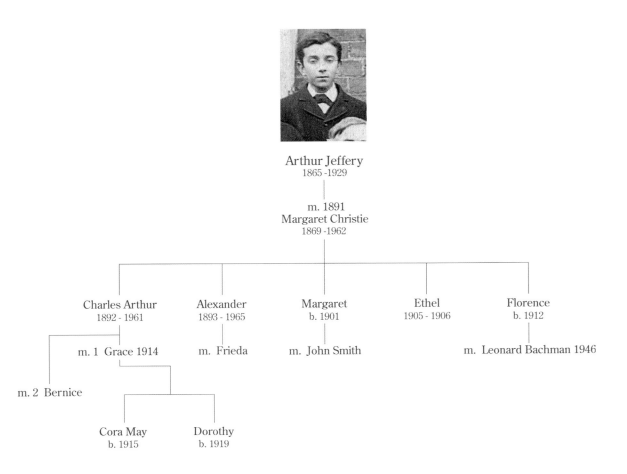

Arthur Jeffery
1865 -1929

m. 1891
Margaret Christie
1869 -1962

Charles Arthur	Alexander	Margaret	Ethel	Florence
1892 - 1961	1893 - 1965	b. 1901	1905 - 1906	b. 1912
m. 1 Grace 1914	m. Frieda	m. John Smith		m. Leonard Bachman 1946
m. 2 Bernice				

Cora May
b. 1915

Dorothy
b. 1919

Arthur Jeffery 1865-1929
Come West Faithful Little Brother

Autumn 1865 heralded a bitter sweet time for the family at the *Riddings*. Thomas and Mary's first–born son, Thomas, prepared to leave for America while their last-born son, Arthur, was welcomed into the family.

Shortly after Arthur's birth, on 3 October 1865, twenty-year-old Thomas left for America. The destinies of these first and last born sons were to become very closely linked as both lived the greater parts of their lives far from the land of their birth. Before Arthur reached his twentieth birthday, he had joined his eldest brother Thomas in Minnesota and so became the fourth pioneer son of the Patriarch and Matriarch to spend most of his life in the New World.

Just over a century later, during the summer of 1968, I met Arthur's daughter Margaret, together with her husband Jack, in Fresno, California. Margaret was born in Minnesota although Arthur and his family later lived much of their lives in the state of Washington whilst Thomas's family spent much of their later lives in California.

For Arthur, growing up as the 'baby' of the family it was a very different experience from that of his older siblings in the previous two decades. He was the youngest of a family whose members were already spreading their wings. By the time he had achieved his first birthday, another of his elder brothers, Joseph, had also left for America. These brothers were to become fabled figures in Arthur's early childhood and he was into his teens before he came to know them.

By the time he was going to school, his elder brothers, John and George, as we have seen, had also left home and both were working in Leeds. By 1871 his only brothers at home were twenty-four-year-old William, eighteen-year-old Owen and eleven-year-old Charles. There were also his sisters, Mary, Fanny and Clara who were in their teens and nine-year-old Ellen. Like his siblings before him, he attended Longford School, where he was recorded on the school register for 1874, together with his sister Ellen.

Arthur was only ten years old when his father died and five years later he was to lose his elder brother Charles. By the time he was seventeen, his closest brother, Owen, was running the farm and only his sister Ellen was still at home helping to care for their young niece and nephew, George's abandoned children, Mary Ellen and William.

Arthur aged about ten years old

Arthur aged about sixteen

During the year 1882 to 1883 both of Arthur's elder brothers, Thomas and Joseph, returned to visit the *Riddings*. For seventeen-year-old Arthur, their visit would be life changing. His eldest brother Thomas, with his wife Maria and young son, John Arthur, was now a well established man of business and property in Minneapolis. Arthur realised that it was Owen who was destined to take over the farm at the *Riddings*. As an aspiring young man, Arthur was now considering what his own future might hold. He was clearly inspired by his eldest brother, Thomas, who was old enough to be his father. Listening to his brothers talking of their lives in America must have been spellbinding, full of promise and limitless possibilities. It was clearly the life which Thomas had made for himself, rather than that of his other brother, the Reverend Joseph, which most particularly enthused and appealed to Arthur.

As a consequence, when Thomas and his family returned to America in 1883, Arthur accompanied them. Understandably, their mother Mary was very saddened at the loss of another son, her youngest. Joseph's daughter, Florence, later wrote in her memoirs:

Arthur, the youngest son of the Jefferys, followed his brother Tom to America. His mother did not want her youngest to leave.

When, some months later, Joseph's new wife Rosamond arrived in Minneapolis in December 1883, on her way to join her husband, Arthur was already there. Together with Thomas, Maria and young John Arthur, he met her off the train. Joseph and Rosamond were to spend Christmas with Arthur and Thomas and family, before they travelled south to Iowa in the New Year. On the United States census for Minnesota of 1885, nineteen-year-old Arthur is shown living with Thomas and Maria and their twelve year-old son John Arthur. Thomas had taken Arthur into his business.

Arthur settled quickly into his new and very different life. He met his future wife, Margaret Christie, in Minnesota and they married on 5 March 1891. She was always known to him as Maggie. Following their marriage, they moved initially, into one of the apartments in the city, owned by Thomas.

Margaret (Maggie) Christie, a farmer's daughter, born in Minnesota in 1869, was of Scottish descent. Her parents, Alex and Henrietta Christie, with their two elder daughters, had left from Glasgow on the *Brittania*, arriving in New York on 29 June 1868.

Almost one year following Arthur and Maggie's marriage, their first son, Charles Arthur, was born in Chicago, Illinois on 9 February 1892. Arthur was still in the furniture and carpet business with his brother Thomas but had now moved to Chicago as a salesman. Their second son, Alexander Christie (usually known as Alex) was born on 9 December 1893, also in Chicago.

The 1900 United States Federal census showed Arthur and Maggie living on Wilton Avenue in the township of Lake View in the city of Chicago with their young sons, eight-year-old Charles Arthur and six-year-old Alexander. In 1901, their daughter Margaret Robinson was born. At the time of her birth, the family had returned to Minnesota. It is interesting to note that their daughter, not only took her mother's name but also her paternal grandmother's surname of Robinson. It is also interesting to note that Arthur was in touch with his elder brother George in Canada at this time. The Canadian census for the Province of Manitoba revealed that he visited George in Canada in the spring of 1901.

Early in the new century, Arthur and Maggie with their young family did that very American thing and moved out West. In their case, almost as far west as they could go, to the Pacific coast state of Washington where they set up home in Spokane County. Arthur was still in the carpet business. However, whilst in Spokane, he invested in land and bought a ranch. This proved to be a good investment as it significantly increased in value. Like his other pioneering brothers he was proving that although you may take the farmer's sons out of the Derbyshire farmland, you cannot take the land out of the farmer's sons!

She was a lovely child and they grieved her loss.

On Christmas Day 1905 Arthur and Maggie's fourth child, Ethel, was born. Sadly, this last granddaughter of Mary of the *Riddings* died young. Arthur's niece, Joseph's daughter Florence, was nine years older than her cousin Ethel and remembered her well. Many years later, in her memoirs she wrote that:

She was a lovely child and they grieved her loss.

LEFT *Arthur and Maggie with Alexander, Margaret and Florence, Jan 1914, 4703, Densmore Ave, Seattle, Washington*

BELOW *Florence Elizabeth Jeffery, Arthur and Maggie's youngest daughter*

In a letter written by Maggie, shortly before Christmas in 1948, to her sister-in-law Ellen, my grandmother, she wrote:

……….. As you know, we have had five children. The little girl who passed away many years ago would have been forty-three years old this Christmas, being born on Christmas Day…….

Arthur and Maggie with their family made their home on the ranch in Spokane for some years while Arthur continued in business as a carpet buyer. The 1910 United States census for Spokane County, Washington, records forty-four-year-old Arthur and forty-one-year-old Margaret (Maggie) with Charles Arthur (eighteen), Alexander (sixteen) and Margaret (nine). In 1912, their last child, Florence Elizabeth, was born. By 1914 the family had moved to King County, Seattle where they lived at 4430, Densmore Avenue. They continued to own the ranch in Spokane. A photograph of the family of six, at their new home in Seattle, was sent home to the *Riddings* at this time. It reached there before Owen, Arthur's brother, died in December 1919.

Shortly after these photographs were taken, their eldest son, Charles Arthur, married Grace. They went on to have two daughters, Cora May born in 1915 and Dorothy born in 1919. Sadly Dorothy died as a young child. Four years after Arthur's granddaughter Dorothy was born, another Dorothy Jeffery, granddaughter of Arthur's brother Owen, was born at the at the *Riddings*.

For some years before Arthur emigrated, his brother Owen, who was thirteen years his senior, was the only one of his elder brothers still at home at the *Riddings*. Arthur had become particularly close to him. He always maintained regular contact with his brother Owen and sister Ellen. A letter written by him at Christmas 1916 records:

Enclosed are our photographs. We pray that 1917 may bring you happiness not known this year. Please write to us soon, we are anxious to hear about those dear to us.

With love and best wishes,
Arthur and Maggie.

The reference to 1917 may be a reference to the fact that Owen's son Thomas was in the Royal Navy during the World War I.

Ellen maintained regular contact with Arthur and Maggie, giving them family news. In the late summer of 1919, she wrote to Arthur alerting him to the fact that Owen was seriously failing in health. Arthur replied directly to Owen on 19 September.

My Dear Owen,

I have received a letter from Nellie which convinces me that you are quite ill. There is just one thing that we need in time of trouble and that is love. True love brings help, comfort and sympathy and I know that you have many that love you and will do all that they can for you in every way. About all that I can do is to write to you and pray for you, as I did this morning, using your name, when we as a family had our family altar, all kneeling down and talking to Our Heavenly Father, after reading his word in the Holy Bible. What comforting words these are. .... I have a little book given me by the Rev. Slight – 'The Gate and the Glory' but best of all is the old Bible mother gave me on my eleventh birthday. Yes, that will guide us through. ....Maggie writes with me in prayer, love and best wishes for you.

Your loving brother,
Arthur.

Ten days later, on 29 September 1919, Arthur wrote again now clearly even more anxious about the state of his brother's health.

My Dear Owen,

*You realise how impossible it is to call personally to see you, which I would do if I were in England, so take this manner, that I may in some way help to give you some sympathy and consolation during your illness. So whenever you receive a letter from me, it represents me the best I can with a brother's love, and prayers that you may be able to bear your illness and, if it is the Lord's will that you be healed, though disease may weaken the physical, by God's help, it cannot touch the soul. ....
...............Maggie and I send our very best love and most sincere wishes to you.*

Your loving brother,
Arthur

An indication of the close affection between the two brothers was demonstrated two months later. Probably in November 1919, Arthur and Maggie re-crossed the Atlantic to visit the *Riddings* and see Owen before his death in the following December. A *Mr. and Mrs. A. Jeffery* are listed in a local newspaper report as being present at Owen's funeral. In a letter written by Arthur's daughter, Margaret, in 1951, she refers to the visit made by her parents to the *Riddings* '*many years ago*'.

Owen died on 14 December 1919. Arthur maintained contact with family members in Derbyshire throughout the rest of his life and his widow, Maggie, continued the contact, with my grandmother, up to her death.

In 1920 Arthur and Maggie, together with Alexander (twenty-six), Margaret (nineteen) and Florence (nine), were still in King County, Seattle whilst still continuing to own the ranch in Spokane County. Arthur also remained in the carpet and furniture business. Their second son, Alexander, having gained his dental qualifications, was now a practising dentist. His sister Margaret was working as his receptionist in the practice. In 1920 their eldest son, Charles Arthur, was also living in King County, Seattle with his wife Grace, four-year-old daughter Cora May and four-month-old baby daughter Dorothy.

In a letter to Owen's widow, on 26 June 1926, Arthur wrote:

Probably you have expected a letter nearer the birthday of dear Owen. So many things seemed to prevent my writing, principally on account of our Florence having scarlet fever for several weeks. She is now well.

Whenever I write, I naturally have in my mind Owen, and of course I think of the old home, the place of my birth and Father, Mother and others of the family. Yes, we are scattered on this earth, with almost half of the family gone to the home above, and my prayer is that everyone who is any way related to our family may all accept Jesus Christ as our personal saviour, then we shall know each other and live together forever.

Our newspapers tell us about the labour troubles in England, which are serious and not at an end. Although I do not as a rule admire the leaders of the Labour party and much less the agitators, who seem to like to make trouble, I sympathise greatly with those who work and do not get paid enough to live. Real Christianity would probably solve most of our troubles.

We are all well. Remember us to all our relatives. Be sure and write all about your children and grandchildren. Margaret and I write in sending our love and best wishes,

Your loving brother,
Arthur.

Arthur and Maggie spent his retirement on the ranch near Spokane. As we have already seen, they were joined by Arthur's brother George, who had sold his ranch near Elkhorn, Manitoba following the death of his wife Mary.

Grave of Arthur Jeffery 1865-1929

When Arthur died in 1929 he was only sixty-four, which was relatively young in comparison to many of his siblings. He was buried in the Jeffery plot in Greenwood cemetery, Spokane, Washington, where his little daughter Ethel had been buried over twenty years before and, his brother George, seven years previously.

Joseph's daughter, Florence, wrote of Arthur:

Arthur worked with Tom in Minneapolis. He married Margaret Christie, a very pretty woman of Scottish descent. They were living in one of Tom's flats when we visited them there. They moved to Chicago, then to Spokane and later to Seattle until Uncle Arthur died. He was always in the carpet business. He did not do as well as Tom but he did well enough. He bought some land near Spokane which increased in value and was a good investment. Their children were Arthur, Alex, Margaret and Florence and Ethel who died young. She was a lovely child and they grieved her loss. Arthur (his son Charles Arthur) married twice or more and may have been divorced. Alex had no children. Arthur had one daughter Cora May. (She does not refer to Charles Arthur and Grace's daughter Dorothy who died young.). Alex was a very successful dentist. Margaret and Florence both married and live in California. Neither have children. Margaret visited us in Iowa. She was a pretty girl and an attractive woman – also quite a talker.

*She was a pretty girl and an
attractive woman — also quite a talker.*

In 1930 Arthur's widow, Maggie, moved back to their home in Seattle and continued living with her family at Densmore Avenue. The household was a large one at this time. Her unmarried son, Alexander, continued with his own dental practice and remained at home together with her youngest daughter, nineteen-year-old Florence. Her eldest son Charles Arthur, now divorced from Grace, was also living at home with his fifteen-year-old daughter, Cora May. Maggie's daughter, Margaret, had married John Calvin Smith (always known as Jack) who was in the lumber business. They also were part of the household at this time. Charles Arthur later moved with Cora May to live in Los Angeles. Margaret and Jack Calvin Smith later moved east, to Wilmington, Delaware, then back

west again to Fresno, California. They finally settled in Claremont, California. Alexander, who later married Frieda, remained in Seattle where he became a highly successful dentist. He and Frieda, who remained childless, eventually retired to Sun City, California.

On 15 December 1948 Maggie wrote to her sister-in-law Ellen. Later in her letter, she refers to her eldest son, Charles Arthur, as Arthur.

My Dear Nellie

I truly am ashamed when I realise the months which have passed since I received your nice letter. Just hearing from you is so wonderful and I know it is my own fault. We have thought of Arthur's family in England and the condition the world is in and still we have not written to see how you are all getting along. But all this is no help to you now. All I can say is that I am sorry. ………………………… It is almost twenty years since Arthur passed away. Our children are now, Arthur 57, Alex 55, Margaret 48, Florence, 36. Florence and I lived in our home, at 4403, Densmore Ave, until 1941. When I sold the home, she and I went to Los Angeles to live where Arthur and his daughter then lived. Florence and I lived in an apartment for about seven years. Florence and her husband (Leonard Bachman) are now living in the same apartment They will have been married for two years on December 21st, '48. I have had quite a spell of arthritis and went to Alex in Seattle where his Doctor did wonders for me in several months. Then Margaret wanted me to come here. I am now making my home with Margaret and Jack.

Margaret and Jack were then living at 1508, Pennsylvania Avenue, Wilmington 6, Delaware and Maggie had

Maggie Christie Jeffery in mid 1950s in Los Angeles

We have thought of Arthur's family in England and the condition the world is in and still we have not written to see how you are all getting along. But all this is no help to you now. All I can say is that I am sorry. ....

LEFT *Letter from Margaret Jeffery to her sister-in-law Ellen*

RIGHT *Maggie with daughter Margaret Calvin Smith and daughter and son-in-law Florence and Leonard Bachman, 13 May 1956*

FAR RIGHT *Margaret and Jack Calvin Smith in California*

RIGHT BELOW *Florence and Leonard Bachman on a cruise in 1986*

lived with them since August 1947. Margaret described her mother as '*quite a gal*' explaining that at aged 83 (letter of 1951) she thought nothing of flying across the country to see family, indeed, she loved it.

Arthur's widow, Maggie, continued her letter to her sister-in law Ellen:

When your letter came, I was visiting my family in Los Angeles. I went by air plane – both ways – and stayed there three months. I had a good visit and am now here where I call my home. One never knows what life has in store for us do we? What a blessing a family is and I have four wonderful children. Arthur and

I had a wonderful happy life together and, as I say, he is still taking care of me – I still have the ranch (in Spokane) and live on the income of it so I am independent of my children. They will not let me live alone and now that I am getting along in years, 80 this past August, I am sure I do not want to live alone. The Lord has given me a wonderful life and I do thank him for it. Life is sweet, but when it is his will to call me, I am ready to go and be with those who are gone, and waiting for me. What a grand reunion it will be when the Jeffery family get together with our Lord.

Write to me and tell me how you are getting along.
Much love, Margaret Jeffery.

The Lord has given me a wonderful life and I do thank him for it. Life is sweet, but when it is his will to call me, I am ready to go and be with those who are gone, and waiting for me.

This was one of the last letters which my grandmother received from Arthur's widow, Maggie. However, in a letter which his daughter Margaret wrote in 1955, to the family in England, it was clear that her mother was then living in an apartment in Los Angeles where her son Charles Arthur and daughter Florence were close by. Florence and Leonard Bachman both became Deacons in the Church. Their mother Maggie also continued to fly up to Seattle to visit her son Alex and his wife Frieda.

After Maggie's death, in September 1962 aged ninety-three, she was also buried in the family plot with Arthur, in Spokane, Washington

———◦———

Arthur and Maggie's eldest son Charles Arthur was sixty-nine when he died in San Bernadino, California in May, 1961. Always known as Arthur, he had married again and his second wife Bernice remained active until well into her late eighties.

Arthur and Maggie's second son Alex died aged seventy-one, on 11 November 1965. Alex's death, which was sudden and dramatic, occurred only three years before I met his younger sister Margaret, in California, in 1968. Margaret had continued in contact with her father's family. Indeed, it was through meeting with the grand-daughters of her father's brother and sister, Owen and Ellen, that this was maintained. Margaret had always been close to her brother Alex. In a letter to family in England she described the circumstances of his death.

The owner said to me 'you should be very proud of your brother, he must have been a very beloved man. A fine gentleman and highly respected man to receive such an outpouring of expressions of love as these flowers portray'.

We lost our beloved Alex, November 11th. As you know, Alex has been a very big man in Dentistry, all over the country, even in Hawaii and he was attending a meeting in Los Angeles when this happened. Some years ago, Alex was the one who started an exclusive Dental group called the Academy of Gold Foil Operators, to which only the finest dentists could belong. When he started it he made the plans for it and they, of course, wanted him to be their President but he was still practicing then and also teaching three Study Groups in Oregon so felt could not take on anything else. Since retiring three years ago, they have been after

him to take the Presidency, so a year ago in November he became the President Elect. In this office he had to prepare all programs, clinics etc. for four meetings a year and he had arranged this one in Los Angeles. It was on Thursday night, November 4th. that he was stricken, while getting dressed to go downstairs in the hotel to attend a cocktail party at which he and Frieda were to be the honoured guests. Instead, he was taken in a screaming ambulance to the hospital. You can well imagine what this did to the party – AND – the very next night he was due to be installed as President. They DID install him and even read his acceptance speech. I was told that there was not a dry eye in the room when it was read for Alex was a very much loved man. We had a hard vigil at the hospital for a week and he finally left us on Thursday night, November 11th. We are still all in a daze – it seems so unreal – they had such wonderful plans for all of this coming year. They were going to be travelling most of the time and had many reservations made including three weeks in Honolulu in January. If he could only have lived for just one more year to complete all his plans. He had reached the top in his profession.

This was certainly evidenced in his funeral which was in Seattle. We drove up with Frieda to it and returned a few days ago. .….. ………………….. The flowers were absolutely unbelievable. The owner (of the mortuary) *told us that maybe once a year they have so many flowers and as many in attendance. ……………. Everyone attending commented on them and that there were so many present – surely a wonderful tribute to him – many men came from all over Washington, Oregon and Canada and one flew up from L.A. to attend. The owner said to me 'you should be very proud of your brother, he must have been a very beloved man. A fine gentleman and highly respected man to receive such an outpouring of expressions of love as these flowers portray'.*

Arthur and Maggie's four surviving adult children all married but it was only their eldest son, Charles Arthur who provided them with grandchildren. As one of these granddaughters died in infancy and their sole surviving granddaughter, Cora May, did not marry, there are no direct descendants of the Arthur Jeffery line.

———◦———

PART FOUR

THE PEOPLE
WHO STAYED

THE PEOPLE WHO STAYED: INTRODUCTION

There are a great many descendants of ten of the fifteen children of Thomas and Mary Jeffery of the *Riddings*. These ten are Margaret, Thomas, William, Joseph, John, George, Owen, Mary, Clara and Ellen. Thomas and Mary had nearly a hundred great grandchildren of whom ten are still alive at the time of writing.

As we have seen, the four sons who emigrated gave them sixteen great grandchildren. The descendants of two of these sons, Thomas and Joseph are now spread across North America. It has yet to be determined whether there are American descendants from George through his daughter Clara.

We now pick up the story of the eleven children who remained on this side of the Atlantic. Almost all of these children continued in farming in Derbyshire and Staffordshire. The sons usually married farmer's daughters and the daughters married the sons of farmers: the Poysers, Spencers, Cooks and Hellabys. However, only eight of the eleven had children of whom seven gave Thomas and Mary over eighty great grandchildren between them.

Four of the children had no descendants. Sarah Ann and Charles died relatively young. Fanny did not marry. Although Elizabeth married and had a son, he remained single.

A significant number of this generation of Jefferys became yeoman farmers. In the early decades of the twentieth century many took advantage of the sale of farms on the Bentley (Clews) and Vernon estates to buy the land where formerly they and their ancestors had been tenants.

Marriages of Thomas and Mary Jeffery's children as recorded in the Bentley Fields Family Bible

MARGARET JEFFERY
1844 – 1937

A Poyser and Hidderley Matriarch

Margaret Jeffery, the first of Thomas and Mary's fifteen children was born at the Riddings on 9 October 1844. She married John Poyser on 28 March 1871. The first of her eleven children were twins who died in infancy. Margaret and John farmed at Parkside Farm, Ramshorn in the Staffordshire Moorlands district, Somersal Mill and Shardlow House, Derbyshire. At the time of her death on 24 February 1937 she had twenty-five grandchildren. Descendants of her eldest son Owen John Poyser remain at Somersal Mill to this day and others are twentieth-century emigrants to Canada.

Descendants of Margaret Jeffery

8th generation

Margaret Jeffery m. John Poyser 1871
1884 -1937   1846 - 1920

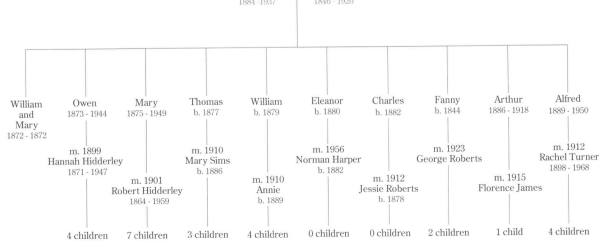

William and Mary 1872 - 1872	Owen 1873 - 1944	Mary 1875 - 1949	Thomas b. 1877	William b. 1879	Eleanor b. 1880	Charles b. 1882	Fanny b. 1844	Arthur 1886 - 1918	Alfred 1889 - 1950
	m. 1899 Hannah Hidderley 1871 - 1947		m. 1910 Mary Sims b. 1886		m. 1956 Norman Harper b. 1882		m. 1923 George Roberts		m. 1912 Rachel Turner 1898 - 1968
		m. 1901 Robert Hidderley 1864 - 1959		m. 1910 Annie b. 1889		m. 1912 Jessie Roberts b. 1878		m. 1915 Florence James	
	4 children	7 children	3 children	4 children	0 children	0 children	2 children	1 child	4 children

Margaret Jeffery 1844-1937
A Poyser and Hidderley Matriarch

Margaret was the eldest of Thomas and Mary's fifteen children. She was born on 9 October 1844. Before she had reached her fourth birthday she had four younger brothers. By the age of seventeen, she was the eldest sister to seven brothers and six sisters. She was less than a week away from her twenty-first birthday when her youngest brother, Arthur, was born and her eldest brother, Thomas, was about to leave for America.

As the eldest child growing up in a large family, Margaret doubtless became something of a second mother to her younger brothers and sisters. She was twenty-six when she married and left home. Over the next eighteen years she became the mother to eleven of her own children. A farmer's daughter, she married a farmer: all of her sons continued in farming and two of her three daughters also married into farming.

On 28 March 1871, Margaret married John Poyser at St John's Church, Alkmonton with her sisters Elizabeth and Mary as her bridesmaids. Her brother, William, and John Poyser's brother William, were witnesses to the marriage.

Margaret's husband, John Poyser, was born in 1845 at Foxt, a remote hamlet in the Staffordshire Moorlands lying just south east of Ipstones and about ten miles west of Ashbourne. John's father, William, is reputed to have managed the estate of *Calwich Abbey* lying five miles south east of Foxt, near Ellastone, on the western bank of the Dove valley.

Margaret (nee Jeffery) Poyser 1844-1937

John Poyser 1845-1920

John Poyser may have learnt his farming from his father on the Calwich estate. In 1861, when he was fifteen, he was living and working on the seventy-nine acre *Calwich Common Farm* with Jeremiah Cope and his young family. By the time he married Margaret Jeffery, he was farming *Parkside Farm*, Ramshorn.

In the spring of 1871, when John Poyser brought his bride Margaret to *Parkside Farm. Parkside* was as remote and isolated as the *Riddings* and, like her old home, only accessed along an unfenced lane. Although similar in its isolation its setting was vastly different. This upland farm, on the western edge of Wooton Park in the Staffordshire Moorlands, with unimproved moorland pasture to the north and the Weaver Hills to the northeast, presented a much wilder setting than that of the *Riddings*.

Parkside Farm, Ramshorn today

Parkside Farm was where Margaret and John spent their first eighteen years together. It was here that all of their eleven children were born. They started their family with twins, Thomas William and Mary Ellen, born on 7 April 1872. Sadly, these two first-born children did not survive their first month: Mary Ellen died on 28 April and her brother, Thomas William, four days later on 2 May 1872.

In May the following year, Margaret gave birth to a healthy son, Owen John, named after one of her siblings. He was baptised at St Peter's Church, Ellastone on 18 May 1873. Over the next sixteen years, Margaret went on to have eight more healthy children at *Parkside*. Mary was baptised on 21 March 1875; Thomas Jeffery on 13 May 1877; William on 13 April 1879 and Eleanor in 1880. Charles Jeffery was baptised on 15 October 1882; Fanny on 7 September 1884; Arthur on 12 December 1886 and lastly, Alfred Joseph, on 23 April 1889. It is interesting to note that most of Margaret's children were named after her siblings and she also included the name Jeffery for two of her sons.

Their first six children went to the village school in Ellastone. It was a long walk, for young children, across the fields and along the country lanes, a distance of around three miles.

Shortly after the birth of their youngest son Alfred, in the spring of 1889, Margaret and John with their nine children moved from the small upland farm at Ramshorn

They started their family with twins, Thomas William and Mary Ellen, born on 7 April 1872. Sadly, these two first-born children did not survive their first month: Mary Ellen died on 28 April and her brother, Thomas William, four days later on 2 May 1872.

Pollard Graham

LEFT *Fanny, youngest daughter of Margaret and John Poyser*

to the Mill Farm at Somersal. *Somersal Mill* was at this time part of the Vernon estate and the Poysers moved in as Margaret's brother and sister-in-law, John and Maria Jeffery, moved with their three children, to the neighbouring *Home Farm*, West Broughton. Also close by were *Northfields* and *Somersal House* farms where Margaret's brother and sister-in-law, William and Hannah Jeffery farmed. Thus the children were to grow up close to their nine Jeffery cousins at *Northfields* and *Somersal House* and their three Jeffery cousins at the *Home Farm*, West Broughton, so establishing the Somersal cluster of Jeffery farms in this part of Jefferyland.

Margaret's husband, John Poyser, together with their eldest son, Owen, eventually purchased *Somersal Mill Farm* from Lord Vernon before Owen married Hannah Hidderley in 1899. Owen and Hannah continued to farm

there and it remains as a family farm, inherited by their grandson Colin Poyser, to this day.

When their eldest son Owen took over at *Somersal Mill*, Margaret and John moved across the fields to *Somersal Heath Farm* on Flacketts Lane. They spent a very short time there before moving back to Margaret's former home area, Longford Woodhouse, where their son Thomas Jeffery was later to farm. Margaret and John then moved beyond Longford to Sutton on the Hill, where their son Charles was to farm.

By 1901 Margaret and John were farming at *Shardlow Home Farm*, south of Derby, with their five younger children. Also at this time, Margaret's niece, twenty-seven-year-old Mary Ellen Jeffery, daughter of her brother George, who had been brought up at the *Riddings*, was making her home with them.

Descendants of Margaret (Jeffery) and John Poyser

The end of the nineteenth and early twentieth century saw Margaret and John's children establishing their own lives. Their eldest son, Owen, married in 1899 and their eldest daughter, Mary, in 1901. Also in 1901 their second son, Thomas, was farming at the *Barn Farm*, Drakelow, in South Derbyshire. His younger sister Eleanor (Nellie) was with him as his housekeeper. Drakelow was close to his parents' farm at Shardlow.

It was at the turn of the century that *Bentley Hall* started to feature again in the Jeffery family story. *Bentley Hall* had been the home of Margaret's grandmother, Elizabeth Robinson (nee Oakden). (See PART ONE: PLACES). In the 1880s and early 1890s it was the home of Samuel and Sarah Hidderley and their family. Margaret's eldest son, Owen, and her eldest daughter, Mary, were to marry two of Samuel and Sarah Hidderley's children, Hannah and Robert.

Robert and Hannah's father, Samuel Hidderley, had met with an untimely death a few years before these marriages. On Christmas Eve, 1892, Samuel had driven

with his horse and trap from *Bentley Hall* to Ashbourne where he had visited the *Green Man Hotel*. It was here that he was involved in an accident with his horse when the wheels of the trap ran over him causing serious internal injuries. He died a week later on New Year's Eve, aged only fifty-five, leaving a widow, Sarah, and six children. An inquest into his death was held on 2 January 1893. Samuel's twenty-seven-year-old eldest son, William, took over farming at *Bentley Hall*.

In 1899 Margaret's oldest son, Owen, married Hannah Hidderley. Owen's sister Mary, always known as Polly, continued to live at *Somersal Mill Farm* until, on 19 March 1901, she married Hannah's older brother, Robert Hidderley. They farmed at *Aston Bank Farm*, Stafford. One of their sons, Cyril, became the heir to his uncle, Charles Poyser.

Somersal Mill Farm was where the four children of Owen Poyser and Hannah (nee Hidderley) were born. Their first daughter, Lilian Sarah, was born on 15 September 1900 and their second, Edith Margaret (always known as

LEFT *Hannah (nee Hidderley) Poyser*

BOTTOM LEFT *Robert Hidderley*

BELOW *Owen John and Hannah Poyser on their marriage*

ABOVE *Wedding of Mary Poyser and Robert Hidderley. The bride's grandmother, Mary Jeffery of the Riddings and mother, Margaret Poyser, are seated on her left*

Margaret) on 15 July 1903. Their son, Arthur Owen, arrived three years later on 17 October 1906. Eight and a half years after Arthur's birth, their second son, Charles John, was born on 20 March 1915. Sadly, Charles lived for only just over two weeks. He was baptised on 3 April and died on 5 April 1915.

Ley Hill Farm (LEFT), *farmed by Owen Poyser's son Arthur Owen and his grandson Godfrey and* (BELOW) *The rear of Ley Hill Farm*

In addition to farming at *Somersal Mill*, Owen Poyser purchased a number of other farms in the Somersal area. These included *Ley Hill Farm*, where both his son Arthur and his grandson Godfrey were to farm; *Palmer Moor Farm*, where Elizabeth Annie (nee Jeffery) Hidderley (Margaret's niece) and three of her children, Jeffery, Eric and Elsie, lived for some time following the death of her husband, William Hidderley, in 1938; *Cottage Farm*; *Mill Cottage* and a number of other cottages, which were rented to people who worked for him. He also built *Oaklea Farm* for his retirement. Also, following the death of his Uncle William Jeffery in 1916, Owen purchased *Somersal House* from Lord Vernon. His cousin, Owen Jeffery, continued farming there. *Somersal House* remained as a home of Jefferys and their descendants, owned by the Poysers until 1975.

(See map in PART ONE: PLACES for the location and photos of a number of these farms).

It was Owen and Hannah's son, Arthur Owen, who married Mary Smith, who provided them with their first grandchildren. Their eldest granddaughter, Margaret (nee Poyser), always known as Peggy, has been very generous in sharing with me many of her family memories, together with family photographs of her father, Arthur Owen and Aunts Lilian and Margaret and others of the family.

BELOW LEFT *Lilian Poyser in 1901*
BELOW CENTRE *Lilian, Margaret and Arthur Owen Poyser, 1907*
BELOW RIGHT *Arthur Owen Poyser*

W.H.HORNE   69. DERBY STRE
LEEK

FAR LEFT *Arthur Owen Poyser aged three*

LEFT *Arthur Owen Poyser in his twenties.*

BELOW *Margaret Jeffery's grand-daughter, Margaret Poyser in her early teens*

a year. Joseph died on 22 April 1944, aged seventy. Lilian survived him by forty-six years when she died on 23 February 1990, aged eighty-nine. They are buried together at Somersal.

Peggy continued:

Edith Margaret became a deaconess and worked for fifty-three years in the Derbyshire Village Mission, which was registered with the London Bible College. It's now part of the University of London.

Peggy told me:

The Poyser family at Mill Farm numbered three. My father, Arthur Owen, was the youngest. His older sisters were Lilian Sarah, who married at forty-five (sic, she was forty-three) *years to Joseph Frederick Gamble, a musician and first violinist* (sic). *He was a farmer's son who ran away to study music and Auntie Lil was his second wife.*

Lilian's husband, Joseph Gamble, was sixty-nine when she married him. Their married life was to last for only

He was a farmer's son who ran away to study music and Auntie Lil was his second wife.

Margaret Poyser in her late teens

Peggy has vivid memories of her Aunts Lilian and Margaret. She was clearly particularly fond of her Aunt Margaret who never married and was ninety when she died, three years after her sister Lilian, in 1993. She recalled:

Auntie Margaret was a woman of immense charm and a great sense of humour. She had that ladylike charm which made her acceptable. She had wit and humour and a tenacity which I shall never forget. She could 'crank-up' her Austin 7 and lived in a caravan visiting different villages and preached in churches and chapels. She could really speak – I mean in volume! She was known as Sister Margaret throughout the County. She did a year in a Mission Hospital – the Mild Mary Memorial Hospital. She wasn't as clever as Auntie Lilian, who went to Ashbourne Grammar School, but more determined. She went to Uttoxeter Manor School under Miss Beck before it became the Girls' High School. She did just as well in her Cambridge Local Examinations as Auntie Lil. She was determined with her music – she could play that silly little pedal-organ in the caravan brilliantly. She had such charm. She just made things funny. She was a sport. Auntie Lil was much more prim and proper. Auntie Margaret was more accepting. She used to say: 'Acceptance is Peace.' She was that sort of character.

She had wit and humour and a tenacity which I shall never forget. She could 'crank-up' her Austin 7 and lived in a caravan visiting different villages and preached in churches and chapels. She could really speak – I mean in volume!

Auntie Lil was somewhat timid – a bag of nerves but she was so brainy and a wonderful pianist. She could hold children spellbound when she told stories. She told gentle little jokes which suited children very well.

Peggy's grandparents, Owen and Hannah Poyser, who farmed at *Somersal Mill*, also bought the *Mill Cottage* where they lived for short time before retiring to *Oaklea* in 1934. Peggy's parents, Arthur and Mary Poyser, farmed at *Ley Hill* when her brother Colin took over at *Somersal Mill*. When her younger brother, Godfrey, married, he farmed at *Ley Hill* and lived with his family in half of the house before going to Canada.

Owen John Poyser was Margaret and John Poyser's eldest son. The early years of the twentieth century also saw their other eight children establishing their own lives. Their second child, Margaret's eldest daughter Mary, who had married Robert Hidderley in 1901, had seven children, Oswald, Cyril, Walter, Gerald, Mildred, Muriel and Myra.

Auntie Lil was somewhat timid – a bag of nerves but she was so brainy and a wonderful pianist. She could hold children spellbound when she told stories.

She was lovely to look at and had auburn/golden hair. She was charming and came with 'Devonshire Cream'!

Great niece Peggy has a fund of stories relating to her Great Uncles and Aunts. Of William she recalled:

William Poyser married Auntie Annie and they had one son and three daughters. They lived at Hemmington Fields Farm where the gravel pits made the family wealthy. They had a daughter called Refua and one of their daughters, Eileen, trained at Leicester Royal Infirmary and was awarded their gold medal. The son, Harold, failed in medicine and went into the army.

Margaret's second daughter, Eleanor, married seventy-four-year-old Norman Harper in 1956. Peggy recalled:

Auntie Nellie lived with her mother at Shardlow and then Aston-on-Trent. She eventually came to live in a cottage in Marchington. She was engaged three times in her youth. She eventually went secretly to Somersal Chapel at the age of seventy-six and married Norman Harper. I understand he was very stingy and she was not too happy.

Margaret's fourth son, Charles, married Jessie Roberts on 11 December 1912 in Shardlow. Jessie was a school teacher and after their marriage they farmed at Sutton on the Hill. They retired to live at *Elm Tree House*, Flaxholme, Duffield, near Derby. Peggy recalled visiting there with her grandparents, Owen and Hannah. She recalled it was:

The house with the monkey puzzle tree, a rather austere looking building.

Margaret's second son, Thomas Jeffery, married Mary Louisa Sims, on 2 February 1910 in Holbrook, Derbyshire. Their three children were Gwendoline, Harold and Arthur. After their marriage, they farmed at Longford Woodhouse.

Mary Louisa, nine years younger than her husband, was always known as Lulie and her great niece, Peggy, remembers:

She was lovely to look at and had auburn/golden hair. She was charming and came with 'Devonshire Cream'! It was before the War and I was four and a half. They had three children. Their daughter Gwen married farmer Frank Morley and lived at Bath Farm, Kedleston, Derby. It's now the Kedleston Hotel.

Margaret's third son, William, farmed at *Hemington Fields Farm* in the Trent valley close by his parents at the *Shardlow Home Farm*, whilst her daughter, Eleanor, continued living with her parents.

She was engaged three times in her youth. She eventually went secretly to Somersal Chapel at the age of seventy-six and married Norman Harper. I understand he was very stingy and she was not too happy.

Charles and Jessie did not have children and their nephew, Cyril Charles Hidderley (second son of Mary and Robert Hidderley) was to inherit after their deaths.

The fifth son, Arthur, died young. He was only thirty-two when he contracted Wiles disease (from rats) and died on 26 September 1918. He was buried at Shardlow. Arthur had married Florence James in 1915 and their daughter Margaret was born in 1917. Florence and Margaret emigrated to Canada shortly after Arthur's death.

Peggy recalled:

They wrote to Auntie Lil from Canada but she must have destroyed the letters. It seems we have no trace of these cousins.

Two years after Arthur's death, his mother Margaret lost her husband of nearly fifty years. John Poyser died at *Shardlow Home Farm* on 20 December 1920. He too was buried at Shardlow. Margaret spent her later years living at Weston upon Trent near Shardlow.

ABOVE LEFT *Tombstone of Margaret and John's youngest son, Arthur 1886-1918 at Shardlow*

ABOVE RIGHT *Margaret (nee Jeffery) Poyser's home in her later years, Horton Villa at Weston upon Trent*

Three years after her father's death, Margaret's third daughter, Fanny, married George Roberts on 4 April 1923 in Shardlow. They had a daughter Margaret and a son Owen and farmed at Aston Lane, Sudbury.

Margaret's last son, Alfred, farmed in Hemmington, in the Trent valley, close by his brother William. He married Rachel Turner and their four children were John, Joan, Ruth and Arthur.

Margaret had twenty-five grandchildren. She outlived her husband by nearly sixteen years and at the time of her death had a number of great grandchildren. She was buried at Shardlow on 24 February 1937. Her funeral was reported in the *DERBY EVENING TELEGRAPH*.

FUNERAL OF MRS. M. POYSER

WESTON ON TRENT TRIBUTES

The funeral of Mrs. Margaret Poyser, who died at Horton Villa, Weston on Trent at the age of 92, took place at Shardlow Church-yard yesterday.

The service at Shardlow Church was conducted by the Rev. P.F. Robinson, Rector of Weston on Trent, assisted by Mr. A.E. Goodall. The committal service was read by Canon B. Lethbridge Farmer.

The mourners were Owen Poyser, William Poyser, T.J. Poyser (Thomas Jeffery) and J. Poyser (Alfred Joseph) (sons) Miss Poyser (Eleanor), Mrs. Hidderley (Mary) and Mrs. Roberts (Fanny) (daughters), Mrs. Hellaby (Ellen) (sister), Mr. R. Hidderley (Robert) and Mr. G. Roberts (George) (sons in law), Mrs. O. J. Poyser (Hannah), Mrs. T. J. Poyser (Lulie), Mrs. W. Poyser (Annie) and Mrs. A. J. Poyser (Rachel) daughters in law, Mrs. Owen Jeffery (sister in law), Mr. W. Jeffery, Mr. O. Jeffery (of the Home Farm West Broughton), Mr. J. Archer, Mr. J. Cook, Mr. J. Hellaby and Mr. Ernest Hellaby (nephews), Miss K. Jeffery and Mrs Walton (nieces), Mr. and Mrs. P. Spencer (nephew and niece), Mr. and Mrs. F. Archer (nephew and niece), Miss L. Poyser, Miss M. Poyser, Miss M. Hidderley, Miss Gwen Poyser, Miss A. E. Poyser and Miss N. W. Poyser (granddaughters), and Mr. Arthur Poyser (grandson).

The bearers were Messrs. O. J. Hidderley, C. Hidderley, Harold Poyser and Arthur Poyser (grandsons).

The Derbyshire Village Mission was represented by Sister Catherine and Sister Margaret (granddaughter).

CHAPEL TRIBUTES

Wreaths were from: Owen and Hannah and family, all at Hemmington Fields (William and Annie and family), Charles and Jessie, Tom and Luly, Fred and Rachel, Nellie, Offley and family (West Broughton), Dolly and Ernest, Arthur, Clara and family, Frank and Muriel, Brother John (West Broughton), Mr. Mrs. and Miss Roberts, Refra and Neville, Cyril, Walter, Gerald, Oswald and Edie, Percy and Mabel (Bentley Fields), Gwen, Harold and Arthur, John, May, Joan and Ruth ...... and many more.

ABOVE *Grave of John and Margaret Poyser, Shardlow*

Margaret's eldest son, Owen John, died seven years after his mother on 12 February 1944. The *UTTOXETER AND ASHBOURNE ADVERTISER* reported:

SOMERSAL HERBERT

Death of Mr. O. J. Poyser – the death occurred at the Queen Mary Nursing Home, Derby, on Saturday, at the age of 70, of Mr. Owen J. Poyser of Oaklea, Somersal, a well-known farmer of the Uttoxeter district. His health had been failing since September last and he had been at Derby for about five weeks. He leaves a widow, son and two daughters. Mr. Poyser went to the Somersal Mill Farm from Ramsor 64 years ago and retired to Oaklea ten years ago. He was Chairman of Somersal Parish Council up to the time of his death and had been society steward of Somersal Wesley Chapel for 36 years and for a period was churchwarden. The funeral took place at Somersal Chapel yesterday (Tuesday).

Owen's wife Hannah died three years later on 14 July 1947 and they are both buried at Somersal.

The little Dove Evangelical Church in Somersal is the last resting place of a great many of Margaret's children and grandchildren – Poysers and Hidderleys. It is also where her brothers William and John Jeffery and many of their children and grandchildren are buried.

Postscript to the story of Margaret nee Jeffery Poyser

A number of Jefferys may recognise the name 'Mary Ann Evans'. Many more will know her by the pen name 'George Eliot'. There is an intriguing suggestion that this well-known nineteenth-century author was associated with Margaret's mother's family, the Robinsons of *Stydd Hall* and also with her husband John's family, the Poysers of Ellastone. It has to be acknowledged that the only evidence is oral history.

My own father told me when I was a child, who always had her nose in a book and was discovering the classics, that there was a family link with George Eliot. I didn't pursue the matter with him at the time. However, Peggy

George Eliot

........that George Eliot, Mary Ann Evans, visited Stydd Hall and that the Mrs Robinson she visited was a Miss Poyser........

Adam Bede Place

Halton (nee Poyser), Margaret Jeffery Poyser's great granddaughter, added substance to the story indicating that her Aunt Lilian Poyser also told her of the connection. Additionally, Peggy had information in the form of a letter which supported the idea of the link. Unfortunately the letter has been lost.

Peggy related that her Aunt Lilian had told her:

There are some interesting family connections......... including that George Eliot, Mary Ann Evans, visited Stydd Hall and that the Mrs Robinson she visited was a Miss Poyser who had been head-mistress at Yeaveley School.

In 1861 twenty-three year-old Ellen Poyser, who was born in Ellastone, was living at the School House in Yeaveley. In 1864 Ellen married Samuel Robinson of Stydd Hall. Samuel was related to Mary Robinson who had married Thomas Jeffery in 1843 – our matriarch and patriarch. Samuel and Ellen Robinson, with their children Frederick 13, Samuel 10 and five-year-old Estella were at Stydd Hall in 1881. Ellen was described as a farmer's wife and schoolmistress. In 1882 their youngest son Alfred was born. They lived at Stydd until Samuel's death in 1912 and Ellen's in 1913 and they are both buried at Yeaveley. Their daughter Estella was known to Peggy as her Auntie Stella.

It is very interesting to note that in 1851, Ellen Robinson's elder sister, Lydia Poyser, was living and working in the household of George Eliot's Uncle William Evans in

Ellastone. William Evans was a brother of George Eliot's father Robert Evans and he had followed his carpenter father in the family business. By 1881 he was a prominent builder and employer living in the house in Ellastone which today is known as *Adam Bede's Cottage*.

Peggy continued:

It is quite likely that the reason my Grandfather (Owen John Poyser) met the Robinsons and called them cousins was two-fold as there may have been a Poyser as well as a Jeffery connection.

Peggy went on to tell me of what she had learnt following her move to Roston, Derbyshire. Roston was where Robert Evans, George Eliot's father, was born and is on the Derbyshire side of the River Dove adjacent to Ellastone in Staffordshire. In her new home in Roston Peggy explained that she had been visited by a Mrs Orme who said:

I am related to you. I was a Robinson from Stydd Hall. She started telling me the details of how we are related to Mary Ann Evans. She wrote to me telling me of all the details of this relationship and sadly I have managed to lose the letter. It all came through the Miss Poyser who was the schoolmistress at Yeaveley and who had married Samuel Robinson. She (Mrs Orme, a Robinson of Stydd Hall) described the family likeness to the Poysers which George Eliot spoke of when she was describing Hetty in Adam Bede......... the dark eyes etc...... she thought she was describing the Poyser family.

She (Mrs Orme, a Robinson of Stydd Hall) described the family likeness to the Poysers which George Eliot spoke of when she was describing Hetty in Adam Bede . . . . . the dark eyes etc . . . . . . she thought she was describing the Poyser family.

Ellastone (Hayslope) from across the Dove in Derbyshire (Stonyshire) to Staffordshire (Loamshire) with the Weaver (Binton) Hills rising in the background

It is of course very sad that the letter giving a written record of the details of the link has been lost but the fact that it did exist does add substance to the story.

What is extraordinarily interesting is that the Derbyshire/Staffordshire borderland area is the setting for George Eliot's Adam Bede and that it is possible to trace the originals of the characters and places which feature in this novel. In 1876, Guy Roslyn in his book George Eliot in Derbyshire asserted that:

The dramatis personae of many of her (Eliot's) *novels have had a flesh and blood existence in the heart of England.*

To support the assertion that George Eliot is closely linked with Derbyshire, we get our strongest evidence from *Adam Bede*. The character Adam Bede is thought to have been based on George Eliot's Uncle William Evans, the builder and joiner. The village of Ellastone, birthplace of generations of Poysers, is the 'Hayslope' of *Adam Bede*. Her 'Loamshire' is Staffordshire and her 'Stonyshire' is Derbyshire. 'Eagledale' is Dovedale and the 'Binton Hills' are the Weavers. Ashbourne is disguised as 'Oakbourne' and Wirksworth as 'Snowfield'. Either Wotton Hall or Calwich Abbey may have served as 'Donnithorne Chase' and 'Donnithorne Hall Farm' was the home of the inimitable Mrs Poyser.

An article in *The Bookman* Vol. XX11 no. 131 of August 1902 by Esther Wood incorporates a photograph of what is suggested as Mrs Poyser's Farm, Ellastone with a caption quoting from *Adam Bede*.

It was once the residence of a country squire, whose family probably dwindling down to mere spinsterhood, got merged in the more territorial name of Donnithorne. It was once the Hall; it is now the Hall Farm.

William Mottram, a grandson of George Eliot's Aunt Anne Evans, the author of *The True Story of George Eliot*, published by Griffiths in 1905, wrote:

Even as a child of seven she (George Eliot) *had been driven by her father over the whole region covered by the fiction* (Adam Bede) *and this experience was repeated later on. The bleak hills were familiar to her own eyes. Ellastone and Ashbourne were well known to her.*

Many of the landscape descriptions in *Adam Bede* are most certainly evocative of the Derbyshire/Staffordshire borderlands of this western edge of Jefferyland. Indeed, there are some views which can be quite specifically identified.

It has not been possible to determine exactly in what way the Jeffery family had any link with the family of George Eliot. However, the intriguing possibility exists.

WILLIAM JEFFERY
1846 – 1916

Crossing the Turnpike

William Jeffery, the third of Thomas and Mary's fifteen children was born at the Riddings on 5 August 1846. He married Hannah Wood on 3 April 1873 and they had nine children and twenty-seven grandchildren. William and Hannah farmed at Northfields and Somersal House, Derbyshire and their sons and daughters – Jefferys, Princes, Hidderleys and Tippers – continued in farming during the twentieth century. William died on 16 May 1916. A significant number of William's descendants remain in the Derbyshire and Staffordshire borderlands area to this day although the number in farming has declined. Descendants of his youngest son Owen have settled in South Africa.

Descendants of William Jeffery

8th generation

William Jeffery m. Hannah Wood 1873
1846 –1916   1849 - 1930

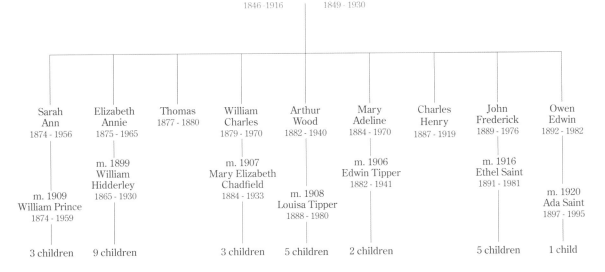

Sarah Ann	Elizabeth Annie	Thomas	William Charles	Arthur Wood	Mary Adeline	Charles Henry	John Frederick	Owen Edwin
1874 - 1956	1875 - 1965	1877 - 1880	1879 - 1970	1882 - 1940	1884 - 1970	1887 - 1919	1889 - 1976	1892 - 1982
	m. 1899 William Hidderley 1865 - 1930		m. 1907 Mary Elizabeth Chadfield 1884 - 1933		m. 1906 Edwin Tipper 1882 - 1941		m. 1916 Ethel Saint 1891 - 1981	
m. 1909 William Prince 1874 - 1959				m. 1908 Louisa Tipper 1888 - 1980				m. 1920 Ada Saint 1897 - 1995
3 children	9 children		3 children	5 children	2 children		5 children	1 child

William Jeffery 1846-1916

Crossing the Turnpike

A well known and most successful agriculturalist.

Obituary of William Jeffery 1916

Thomas and Mary's third child, William, has a special place in the Jeffery story. While his elder brother, Thomas, initiated the process of scattering the family around the globe, William was less adventurous. It was he who first left the family nucleus of Hungry Bentley and crossed the Ashbourne Turnpike. In crossing the old turnpike road, now the A515 bisecting Jefferyland, William established a second cluster of Jeffery farms. His brother John, sister Margaret and her husband, his own sons and nephews, were also to farm in the area of Somersal. *Somersal House* at Somersal Herbert became a second heartland to the *Riddings* at Hungry Bentley. Uttoxeter became to the Jeffery farmers of Somersal what Ashbourne was to those of Hungry Bentley. (See map in PART ONE: THE PLACES). Their grandchildren moved even further afield, crossing the River Dove into Staffordshire.

When William, was born at the *Riddings* on 5 August 1846, his brother Thomas had yet to achieve his first birthday and his sister Margaret was not yet two years old. His younger brother Joseph arrived before he had reached his own first birthday and by the time he was seven, with four younger brothers and two younger sisters, he was one of a family of nine children under the age of ten.

By the autumn of 1865, when he had just turned nineteen, his youngest brother Arthur was born, his oldest brother Thomas left for America and he was his father's right-hand man on the farm. William and his younger brothers John and Owen were destined to continue the family farming tradition and a number of their descendants continue that tradition within Jefferyland to this day.

William was twenty-seven when he married in 1873, crossed the Turnpike and started farming on his own at Somersal Herbert. On 3 April 1873 he married Hannah Wood at St John's Church, Alkmonton. They first farmed at *Northfields Farm*, Somersal and later moved on to *Somersal House Farm*, leaving their eldest son, William Charles, to continue farming at *Northfields*.

William Jeffery 1846-1916

William and Hannah Jeffery

BELOW *William and Hannah's youngest son, Owen, aged about four*

ABOVE *William and Hannah Jeffery with eight of their nine children at Northfields Farm c. 1890. William Charles stands left by his father, Sarah Ann and Elizabeth Annie stand with Arthur far right. The smaller children are l. to r. Charles, John Frederick (on Hannah's knee) and Mary Adeline with Owen in the pram*

William and Hannah had nine children over the eighteen years between 1874 and 1892: six sons and three daughters. Their first child, Sarah Ann, was born on 11 February 1874 and her sister, Elizabeth Annie, arrived nearly two years later on 11 November 1875. Their first son, Thomas, was born on 2 September 1877 but sadly died, just prior to reaching his third birthday, on 12 October 1880. Their next two sons were William Charles, born on 18 November 1879 and Arthur Wood, born on 8 June 1882. Their youngest daughter, Mary Adeline, born on 18 October 1884 was followed by three younger sons, Charles Henry, born 3 April 1887, John Frederick, born 3 June 1889 and Owen Edwin who arrived on 24 April 1892.

Around the turn of the century, William, in addition to farming *Northfields*, farmed the land at *Somersal House*. By 1901, William and Hannah, together with four of their children, Arthur, Adeline, Charles and Owen, were living at *Somersal House*. Their eldest son, William Charles, remained to farm at *Northfields* with his older sister Sarah and younger brother Frederick.

William and Hannah's grandson, Arthur Jeffery, explained to me how this came about. Arthur was the only son of William and Hannah's second son, Arthur Wood Jeffery. I first met ninety-seven-year-old Arthur in the early summer of 2008 and he later joined us for our Jeffery family reunion of 2008. He was ninety-eight years old when we met again and he maintained vivid recollections of his early life. I visited him at his home in Roston, Derbyshire where he had farmed all of his life.

He recalled:

My grandparents, William and Hannah, farmed at Northfields Farm, Somersal. The fella who lived at Somersal House was a gentleman farmer and all he wanted was a croft and stabling for his horses. His name was Bott. The agent (for the Vernon estate) *asked grandfather to take over the land and use the house. So, they moved in, leaving young William* (eldest son, William Charles) *to farm Northfields.*

The last year of the nineteenth century and the first decade of the twentieth saw the marriages of five of

Somersal House

SOMERSAL HERBERT

We regret to record the death of Mr William Jeffery, of Somersal House, Somersal, which occurred on Tuesday night in last week after a short illness at the age of 69 years. The deceased was a well known and most successful agriculturalist and was the oldest tenant on the Sudbury estate. He was a prominent member of the Wesleyan denomination, to which he rendered great service. The funeral took place on Saturday afternoon at Somersal, when members of the Uttoxeter Wesleyan Church were among those present. The wreaths included one from the teachers and scholars of the Uttoxeter Wesleyan Sunday School. A memorial service was held at the Wesleyan Chapel, Somersal, on Sunday evening, conducted by the Rev. T. S. Berry, superintendant minister of the Uttoxeter Circuit, who made sympathetic references to the deceased's life.

William was buried in the quiet little churchyard at Somersal where there are very many Jeffery, Poyser and Hidderley graves and where, as a former lay preacher at the church, his name is carved on a corner stone of the church wall. His wife Hannah survived him by nearly fourteen years. Their memorial reads:

In

Dear and Loving Memory of

WILLIAM JEFFERY OF SOMERSAL HOUSE

Who passed away May 17, 1916

In his 70th year

Thy Will be done

Also of Hannah

Wife of the above

Who died February 4, 1930

Aged 81 years

Peace Perfect Peace

William and Hannah's nine children. The weddings of their three daughters, Elizabeth Annie (Lizzie) in 1899, Sarah Ann (Sally) in 1902, and Adeline in 1906 were followed by those of their two eldest sons: William Charles married in 1907 and Arthur Wood in 1908. It was also the decade when they became grandparents to their first eleven grandchildren.

William and Hannah's two youngest sons, John Frederick and Owen Edwin, were the last to leave the family home. These two Jeffery brothers of *Somersal House* were to marry sisters, the daughters of John and Celia Saint of *Alkmonton House*, Alkmonton.

Only Hannah lived to celebrate the marriage of her youngest son Owen to Ada Saint. William had died, less than three months after the marriage of his son Frederick to Ethel Saint. William was sixty-nine when he died on 17 May 1916 at *Somersal House*. His death was reported in the *UTTOXETER ADVERTISER* of 24 May 1916.

Mrs. Jeffery, who had resided at Somersal House nearly all her life, was a regular visitor to Uttoxeter market up to within the past few months, and had only been confined to her bed for about a month.

William and Hannah's Tombstone at Somersal

The year following the birth of her last grandchild at the end of January, Hannah died on 14 February 1930. She had continued living at *Somersal House*, with her youngest son, Owen, following her husband William's death. At the time of her death she was living with her daughter Elizabeth and son-in-law William Hidderley at *Palmer Moor*, Doveridge. Her funeral, where the family were very well represented, was reported in the *UTTOXETER ADVERTISER*, of 19 February 1930.

SOMERSAL HERBERT

We regret to record the death of Mrs. Hannah Jeffery (widow of Mr. William Jeffery of Somersal House) who passed away at Palmer Moor on Friday at the age of 81. The late Mr. Jeffery – a well known agriculturalist who died about fourteen years ago – and his wife were prominent members of the Wesleyan Methodist connection. Mrs. Jeffery, who had resided at Somersal House nearly all her life, was a regular visitor to Uttoxeter market up to within the past few months, and had only been confined to her bed for about a month. She leaves a family of four sons and three daughters. The funeral took place on Monday, the Rev. R. J. Russell of Uttoxeter being the officiating minister The mourners were Mr. and Mrs. W. Jeffery (son and daughter-in-law) (William and May), Mr. and Mrs. A. Jeffery (son and daughter-in-law) (Arthur and Louisa), Mr. and Mrs. O. Jeffery (son and daughter-in-law) (Owen and Ada), Mr. and Mrs. W. Prince (Sarah Ann and William), Mrs. W. Hidderley (Elizabeth Annie), Mrs. Tipper (Adeline), Mr. J. Hidderley, Mrs. Spencer (sister-in law Mary of Bentley Fields), Mr. E. Tipper, Mr. and Mrs. Hellaby (my grandparents, William and Ellen), Mr. and Mrs. Cook, (sister-in-law Clara and Arthur), Mrs. O. Jeffery (sister-in-law Hester), Mrs. Poyser (sister-in-law Margaret), and Mr. and Mrs. Hand (niece Dollie and Ernest). The coffin was borne by Messrs. T. Poyser, O. Jeffery, J. Wood, T. Jeffery, P. Spencer and J. Hellaby (nephews).

The floral tributes included those sent by the following: Sarah Ann and Will; Lizzie and Will; William and May; Sister Margaret and May; Fred and Ethel; Connie; Willie; Ida and May Prince; all at the Mill; all at West Broughton; Mesdames Wadham and Barker; Mrs. Saint and Jack; Elsie, Marjorie, Edith and Winnie; Jeffery and Ida; Fred, John, Dorothy, Vera and Freda; J. M.Bloor; Will, Nellie and Ernest; Sister Polly, Percy, Mabel and the boys; Arthur, Clara and family; Arthur and Louie; Dollie and Ernest; Owen and Ada; Hester, Tom and Louie.

Descendants of William and Hannah

William and Hannah's eldest daughter, Sarah Ann, usually known as Sally, acted as housekeeper for her brother William Charles at *Northfields Farm* until she married William Prince, a farmer from Denstone, on 18 March 1902 in Sudbury Church, Derbyshire. Sarah Ann and William Prince farmed at the *Home Farm*, Crakemarsh, near Uttoxeter and they provided William and Hannah with three grandchildren: William Henry, born on 8 August 1904; Ida Mary on 27 January 1908 and Dorothy May on 4 May 1911.

Sarah and William Prince's three children who were all born at the *Home Farm*, Crakemarsh, married during the decade of the 1930s. All continued the tradition in the farming world of farmer's sons marrying farmer's daughters.

Their son, William, farmed at the neighbouring *Longacre Farm*, Crakemarsh after he married Kathleen Halden, on 25 April 1935. The *UTTOXETER ADVERTISER* of the first of May reported:

Two well-known farming families of the Uttoxeter District were united by marriage on Thursday when Mr. William Henry Prince was married by the Reverend W. E. Drinkwater (Rector) at Checkley Parish Church to Miss Kathleen Mary Halden, fourth daughter of Mr. and Mrs. John Halden of the Rectory Farm, Checkley

Later in the year, when, on 30 November, Sarah and William's daughter, Ida, married Ernest Hall at the Uttoxeter Wesley Church, the *UTTOXETER ADVERTISER* again reported

Both the bride and groom are members of well-known farming families

The Halls farmed at *The Lount*, Anslow, near Burton on Trent.

Three years later, on 6 October 1938, the Prince's, younger daughter, Dorothy May, married Henry Langridge. They too were to farm locally, at *Fole Hall*, Uttoxeter and the *UTTOXETER ADVERTISER* reported:

A wedding of much interest in agricultural circles over a wide area was solemnised at St Michael's Church, Stramshall, on Thursday, the Vicar of Stramshall, (the Rev. E. Wells) officiating.

The bridegroom, Mr. Henry William Langridge, is a popular member of the Young Farmers' branch of the National Farmers' Union in Uttoxeter. He is the only son of Mrs. and the late Mr. H. W. Langridge, of Fole Hall, Uttoxeter, and when his father died, he continued the farm.

His bride, Miss Dorothy May Prince, younger daughter of Mr. and Mrs. W. Prince also comes of a well respected farming family in the Uttoxeter District as her parents farmed for many years at the Home Farm, Crakemarsh.

William and Hannah's two eldest daughters, Sarah Ann (Sally) Prince and Elizabeth Annie (Lizzie) Hidderley lived all of their lives within the farming world. Sarah died before her husband, on 17 June 1956. The *UTTOXETER ADVERTISER* reported:

FUNERAL AT STRAMSHALL

The funeral of Mrs. S. A. Prince (82) of West View, New Road, Uttoxeter, took place on Tuesday last at Stramshall Parish Church.

Mr. and Mrs. Prince had farmed for many years at Home Farm, Crakemarsh. She was held in high esteem by all who knew her.

William and Hannah's second daughter, Elizabeth Annie, often known as Lizzie, was the first of their brood to leave home when, on 6 April 1899, she married William Hidderley at St Peter's Church, Somersal. William was a son of Samuel and Sarah Hidderley, of *Bentley Hall*. He was the eldest brother of Hannah and Robert Hidderley, who both married Margaret's children, Owen John and Mary Poyser of Somersal Mill Farm.

Elizabeth Annie and William Hidderley farmed at *North Lodge Farm*, Doveridge, near Uttoxeter, where their first son William Jeffery was born on New Year's Eve, 1899. Later they farmed at *Agardsley Park*, Newborough,

William Hidderley

William and Elizabeth Annie (nee Jeffery) Hidderley with their first two children, Jeff and Elsie

Staffordshire and then at *Palmer Moor*, which is near to *Somersal Mill*.

Over the following seventeen years, the Hidderleys provided William and Hannah with nine grandchildren: William Jeffery, born 31 December 1899; Elsie Adeline on 28 May 1901; Walter on 5 December 1903; Edwin Samuel on 28 August 1905; Marjorie Elizabeth on 22 April 1907; Edith May on 8 April 1909; Winifred Mary on 12 August 1911; Charles Eric on 13 January 1916 and Dorothy on 17 February 1917.

William and Hannah's first grandchild, William Jeffery Hidderley, son of Elizabeth Annie and William Hidderley, was born on the last day of the nineteenth century, and was always known as Jeff. He was born with a profound hearing loss. His sister Elsie and brother Eric also suffered a hearing loss in childhood after contracting measles.

The decade of the 1930s was also to see many of the Hidderley cousins of the Princes marrying and establishing their own lives. In a number of instances they too continued the farming tradition extending the network of family farms across the borderlands of the Dove valley in Derbyshire and Staffordshire.

Six of Elizabeth Annie's nine children remained in farming. Walter married Nancy Wainwright and farmed at Hargate House, Hilton; Edwin (Ted) married Nora Shelley and farmed at Chapel House, Tutbury; Marjorie married Joe Bailey and farmed at Hill Farm, Newton Solney. Winifred (Win) married Robert (Henry) Riley and farmed at Whitewood Farm, Yoxall. Elsie and Charles (Eric) farmed at Palmer Moor, Doveridge.

Elizabeth and William Hidderley's eldest son, William Jeffery (Jeff), who was born on New Year's Eve 1899, was

the last of their children to marry. He married Evelyn Horsfield on 14 May 1949, in Ecclesfield, Sheffield and in the early 1950s, they had two children, Beryl and Philip. It is to their daughter, Beryl Page, (nee Hidderley) that I owe the copies of the wonderful collection of photographs of Elizabeth Jeffery Hidderley with her children, which were taken in the 1950s.

Beryl told me something of Elizabeth and William's daughter Edith, who became a nurse.

Auntie Edith married an actor and cartoonist. His name was Jay Jennings. He drew cartoons for national newspapers until he had a stroke. She was nursing him I gather. After the stroke he found drawing difficult but often played character parts in both TV and film. One of his claims to fame was that he played the tramp who died on the park bench in 'The Square' in the first episode of 'Neighbours' on TV.

I am also indebted to Elizabeth Hidderley's great niece, Peggy Halton (nee Poyser) for further information:

You asked me about Auntie Lizzie (Elizabeth) who was one of the daughters of William and Hannah Jeffery of Somersal House. Auntie Lizzie was present at my birth but she was a widow when I knew her. (William Hidderley died on the first of November 1930). *They had farmed at Agardsley Park Farm and her husband was William Hidderley, my grandmother's brother.*

His name was Jay Jennings.
He drew cartoons for national
newspapers until he had a stroke .....
.... One of his claims to fame was
that he played the tramp who died on
the park bench in 'The Square' in
the first episode of 'Neighbours'
on TV.

Speaking of the Hidderley daughters Peggy continued:

I believe Dorothy, the youngest daughter died young of diphtheria. The others were Edith, a nurse, Madge (Bailey) who lived at Newton Solney, and Win, the youngest girl, who moved to Cornwall. She married twice and had one son.

The eldest daughter, Elsie, never married and the youngest son, Eric, became a skilled cabinet maker.

Elizabeth Hidderley, died on 2 November 1965. The *UTTOXETER ADVERTISER* reported the following:

FUNERAL AT SOMERSAL HERBERT

The death occurred suddenly, while staying with her daughter at Pinner, Middlesex, of Mrs. Elizabeth Annie Hidderley, within a few days of her 90th birthday. She was the widow of Mr. William Hidderley, and the second daughter of the late Mr. and Mrs. William Jeffery, of Somersal. Both she and her husband belonged to very well-known farming families in Derbyshire. After their marriage in 1899, Mr. and Mrs. Hidderley farmed at Agardsley Park, Newborough for a number of years and later at Palmer Moor, Doveridge, where Mr. Hidderley died in 1930.

Mrs. Hidderley leaves four sons and three daughters, several of whom farm on the Derbyshire-Staffordshire border and two other daughters predeceased her. She also leaves 10 grandchildren and 14 great-grandchildren. After the death of her eldest daughter about five years ago, Mrs. Hidderley went to reside with her youngest daughter, Mrs. A. M. Laban at Daisy Bank Farm, Foston.

Apart from farming and family life Mrs. Hidderley had a great love for flowers and music. She was expert at both floral culture and arrangement. From the age of 12 up to the time of her marriage she was the organist at St Peter's Church, Somersal Herbert.

ABOVE *Elizabeth Annie (nee Jeffery) Hidderley with her children l. to r. Madge, Eric, Win, Ted, Jeff, Edith, Elsie, Walter. Elizabeth Annie's granddaughter, Beryl Page, daughter of her eldest son Jeffery Hidderley, thinks that these photographs were taken in the early 1950s and that the photographer was the youngest son, Eric Hidderley*

The immediate and extended family were well represented at the funerals of both sisters, Sarah Ann (nee Jeffery) Prince and Elizabeth Annie (nee Jeffery) Hidderley.

William and Hannah's eldest son, William Charles, was twenty when he took over at *Northfields Farm* in 1900. William Charles farmed *Northfields* for around twenty years. After his sister Sarah left to marry William Prince, his younger sister, Adeline, may have helped out with his housekeeping before she married Edwin Tipper in 1906.

William and Hannah with their children at Northfields Farm (Potter Somersal), circa 1909. L. to r. seated: Sarah Ann (Prince), William, Hannah, William Charles. L. to r. standing: John Frederick, Elizabeth Annie (Hidderley), Owen, Arthur Wood, Mary Adeline, Charles

William Charles married Mary Elizabeth Chadfield on 2 April 1907. Over the next seven years they provided William and Hannah with a further three grandchildren: Constance Mary (Connie) on 30 May 1908; Henry William on 26 August 1911 and Frank, born just before the outbreak of World War 1, on 20 July 1914

William and Hannah's grandson, ninety-eight year old Arthur, clearly had a very high regard for his Uncle William Charles. His own father, Arthur Wood Jeffery, died thirty years before his Uncle William of *Aston House*.

Arthur, who was seven years old when his Grandfather William died , continued recalling his memories for me:

William and May (Elizabeth Mary Chadfield was always known as May) *farmed at Northfields until around 1920 when they moved to Aston House, Sudbury. My grandparents* (William and Hannah) *stayed on at Somersal House. When grandfather died in 1916, Owen* (William and Hannah's youngest son) *took over at Somersal House. From there, Owen later went to the Common Farm at Anslow. I remember my grandfather at Somersal House.*

The wedding of William Charles Jeffery (aged 28) and Mary Elizabeth Chadfield, at Cubley Lodge in 1907. William and Hannah, parents of William Charles, are to his left and Mrs Chadfield is seated right. Two of the bridesmaids are Maude and Edith Frost. William Charles' brother Arthur Wood stands behind the bride and Owen to the left

LEFT *William Charles and May Jeffery with their daughter Connie and son Henry at Northfields c. 1913*

BELOW *Connie, Henry and Frank Jeffery c. 1918*

BOTTOM *May Jeffery and her children, Connie, Henry and Frank*

Mary Jeffery, William and Hannah's niece, of the *Home Farm*, West Broughton, also has fond memories of her uncle and aunt at *Aston House*:

As children (Mary was the youngest of six) *we used to be piled off to Aston House. Auntie May loved to have children around. She loved to give a party.*

Garden at Northfields Farm, Somersal. In the garden seat Henry Jeffery with his brother Frank far right. Their sister Connie is seated on the grass second from the left

Henry and Frank Jeffery c. 1924

William Charles and May Jeffery with Connie, Henry and Frank at Aston House c. 1928

Three and a half years following Hannah's death in February 1930, tragedy was to strike at the heart of this close knit family of William and Hannah Jeffery's descendants.

William and Hannah's eldest son, William Charles, had moved, with his wife May and their three children, Connie, Henry and Frank, from *Northfields Farm*, Somersal to *Aston House Farm*, Sudbury, in 1920. Thirteen years following their move, when they were well established in what remains a Jeffery family home, May developed cerebral meningitis and died suddenly, aged only forty-nine, on 29 September 1933. The family were devastated at their totally unexpected loss.

Their daughter, Connie, was twenty-five and shortly to be married: the invitations to her wedding had already been sent out. In the event, the wedding was postponed and Connie married three months later. Their son, Henry, was twenty-two and he too married six months after his

mother's death, providing a new mistress for *Aston House*. The youngest son, Frank, was only nineteen when his mother died.

May, in addition to being much loved by her family, was a prominent member in the local community in Sudbury. Her obituary and report of her funeral in the *UTTOXETER ADVERTISER* declared that:

Not only in the home she adorned but in every cottage of the district her sad end will mean a great loss. The village was in complete mourning for the funeral.

SUDBURY'S LOSS
SAD DEATH OF MRS MARY ELIZABETH JEFFERY
FUNERAL TRIBUTES

****

The residents of Sudbury as a whole were thrown into mourning by the death, which occurred on Wednesday of last week, after a short illness, of Mrs. Mary Elizabeth (May) Jeffery, the wife of Mr. William Jeffery, of Aston House Farm, Sudbury.

She was the daughter of the late Mr. and Mrs. Thomas Henry Chadfield, of Cubley. The parents of both Mr. and Mrs. Jeffery were at one time the oldest tenants on the Lord Vernon estates at Sudbury.

The deceased lady was only forty-nine years of age, and much sympathy is felt for her husband and family of two sons and one daughter.

Mrs. Jeffery was a local Manager of the Sudbury school, a prominent member of the Women's Institute, and, in fact, connected with every phase of Church and social life in the village. In private life, she was a very generous friend and a willing helper in times of sickness and trouble. Not only in the home she adorned, but in every cottage of the district her sad end will mean a great loss.

The village was in complete mourning for the funeral, which took place at Sudbury Church on Saturday afternoon. The service was conducted by the Rev. E. A. Shrubbs, of Sudbury, the service being choral. Mr. Berridge, of Uttoxeter, was the organist and the hymns 'Jesu lover of my soul' and 'The King of Love my Shepherd is' (her favourite) were sung.

Lord and Lady Vernon attended the service, together with representatives embracing every home in Sudbury and district.

The mourners were: Mr. W. Jeffery (husband), Miss Connie Jeffery (daughter), Mr. Frank Jeffery (son), Mr. Henry Jeffery (son), Mr. Joseph Chadfield (brother), Mrs. Joseph Chadfield (sister-in-law), Mr. Frank Chadfield (brother), Mrs. Frank Chadfield (sister-in-law), Miss Chadfield (niece), Mr. and Mrs. Offley Jeffery (cousins), Miss Goodall (cousin), Mr. and Mrs. W. Prince (cousins), Mr. Harold Goodall (cousin), Mr. and Mrs. E. Owen (cousins), Mrs. Brookes (cousin), Mrs. F. Goodall (cousin), Mrs. W. Bullock (cousin), Mrs. Allen (cousin), Billy, Vera and Lillian, Mr. and Mrs. W. Prince (sister-law and brother-in-law), Mrs. Hidderley (sister-in-law), Mr. and Mrs. E. Tipper (brother-in-law and sister-in-law), Mr. and Mrs. Arthur Jeffery (brother-in-law and sister-in-law), Mr. Fred Jeffery (brother-in-law), Mr. Owen Jeffery (brother-in-law), Mr. and Mrs. Foden (Liverpool), Mr. and Mrs. Sargeant, Mr. R. Sutton, Mr. and Mrs. Hellaby (Fauld), Mr and Mrs. Hellaby (Marston Montgomery)and Mr. and Mrs. Todd.

Nephews and cousins who acted as bearers were: Messrs. Walter Goodall, Frank Goodall, E. Hidderley and E. Tipper.

The grave was beautifully lined with evergreens and flowers by the head gardener and staff at Sudbury Hall, and the coffin was of waxed oak with brass appointments.

May Jeffery

WEDDING AT SUDBURY

OPPOSITE FAR RIGHT *Wedding of Henry and Vera Jeffery at Hanbury Church. Henry's father, William Charles and brother Frank, standing on the left. Henry's cousins, brides-maids, Marie Jeffery of the Home Farm, West Broughton, seated on the left and Edith Hidderley seated right*

There were a great many floral tributes from all of the above and the many other relatives and friends who filled the church. These included tributes from: *'All at the Riddings'; 'All at Bentley Fields'; 'Dolly and Ernest (Shirley Mill)'; 'Mr. and Mrs. Poyser, Somersal'* and many, many more.

There were other reports in the local papers including one which recorded:

The Jeffery family is well known in the district, notably at Somersal, where Mr. and Mrs. Jeffery farmed before going to Sudbury some years ago. Mrs. Jeffery was highly esteemed and took an active part in the affairs of the parish.

William and May's daughter Connie married in the New Year, three months following the sad loss of her mother. Her wedding was reported in the *UTTOXETER ADVERTISER*.

The capes and hems of the dresses were of primrose organdie, as were also their large picture hats. They wore shoes of primrose satin to tone with the dresses and elbow-length mitts of lemon silk and carried bouquets in pastel shades of tulips, pink, cream, yellow and mauve with pendants of amber and pearl.

The wedding was solemnised at Sudbury Parish Church between Mr. William Owen, son of Mr. and Mrs. R. Owen, of Offoxy, Tong (Salop), and Miss Constance May Jeffery, only daughter of Mr. William and the late Mrs. Jeffery, of Aston House, Sudbury. The Rev. E. A. Shrubbs officiated and the duties of best man were carried out by Mr. E. J. Owen (brother of the bridegroom), Messrs Henry and Frank Jeffery (brothers of the bride) acting as groomsmen.

The bride, given away by her father, was attired in a pictur-esque gown of white georgette and real lace. Her veil was of hand-embroidered Brussels net, over which she wore a Juliet cap of orange blossom. Her shoes were of white satin and she wore elbow-length white silk mitts. The two child bridesmaids, Miss Vera Jeffery (niece of the bride) and Miss Kathleen Brockley (niece of the bridegroom), acted as train-bearers for the bride who carried a sheath of lilies and lilies of the valley, with pendants of white heather.

The four bridesmaids, Miss Margaret Owen (sister of the bride-groom), and the Misses Edith Hidderley, Lillian Parkinson and N. Chatfield (cousins of the bride) were attired in dresses of floral ninon with pale primrose ground, the flowers shading from lemon to deep orange. The capes and hems of the dresses were of primrose organdie, as were also their large picture hats. They wore shoes of primrose satin to tone with the dresses and elbow-length mitts of lemon silk and carried bouquets in pastel shades of tulips, pink, cream, yellow and mauve with pendants of amber and pearl. The two little bridesmaids were attired in ankle-length dresses composed of frills of primrose organdie, and wore bronze ballet shoes and wreaths of bronze leaves and mimosa tied with pale green ribbon.

The service was fully choral and Miss M. Jackson presided at the organ.

Outside the church, the bride was handed a horse-shoe by a tiny onlooker. Owing to the recent death of the bride's mother, no reception took place, but the bride held an 'At Home', a day or two prior to the ceremony, when the numerous presents were on view

****

Within three months of his sister Connie's wedding, William Charles' son, Henry, was also married, on 3 April 1934. He brought his bride home to *Aston House*.

The wedding was also reported in the *UTTOXETER ADVERTISER*.

FARMING FAMILIES UNITED
MR H. W. JEFFERY AND MISS VERA SHELLEY
MARRIED AT HANBURY

Great interest was taken in the wedding at Hanbury Parish Church, on Tuesday afternoon, of Miss Vera Shelley, the younger daughter of Mr. and Mrs. William Shelley, of Rock House, Hanbury, who has been a teacher at the C. of E. Infants School, Hanbury, since her own school days. All her life, she has been a member of the church choir, and she has also been a teacher in the Sunday School. She is an active member of the local W.I. and been prominently associated with every form of social life in the village.

Mr. Henry William Jeffery, the bridegroom, is the elder son of Mr. W. C. Jeffery and the late Mrs. Jeffery, of Aston House, Sudbury. He is a member of the junior branch (Uttoxeter) of the National Farmers' Union.

The officiating clergy were the Revs. A. Cole M.A., (Vicar) and E. A. Shrubbs, Rector of Sudbury. The service was fully choral, Mr. H. Botham, the organist, playing bridal music and the hymns 'Lead us Heavenly Father' and 'O Perfect love' were sung.

Given away by her father, the bride wore a dress of cream chiffon velvet, with veil of hand-embroidered Brussels net, and halo of orange blossom. She had a necklace of pearls, the gift of the bridegroom and carried a bouquet of arum lilies, white carnations and lilies of the valley.

The bridesmaids were Miss Barbara Ward (of London, friend of the bride), Miss Nancy Hill (of Birmingham, cousin of the bride) and Miss E. Hidderley and Miss Marie Jeffery (cousins of the bridegroom). All wore dresses of gold ring velvet, with shoes and velvet gloves to match, and haloes of velvet leaves and flowers. Their necklaces were the gifts of the bridegroom and their bouquets were of mauve, pink and yellow tulips with pendant ribbons to match.

The best man was Mr. Frank Jeffery, the bridegroom's brother, and the churchwardens acted as groomsmen.

Mrs. Shelley, the bride's mother, wore a beige dress and matching coat, with a nigger-brown hat and shoes, and carried a spray of pink carnations.

Nearly a hundred guests attended the subsequent reception held at the Services Recreation Room, Hanbury.

Mr and Mrs Jeffery will reside at Aston House, Sudbury.

BELOW *The farmyard at Aston House outside the old farmhouse in the 1920s. The old house was used for the storage of grain and animals*

Aston House was built in 1861. An old farmhouse on a site nearer to the road continued to be used as farm buildings.

Vera wrote of her own wedding day:

The weather on our wedding day was typical of an early April day, rather cold but sunny mostly – it definitely shone on us when we came out of church and remained sunny the rest of the day and I was happy – the bride the sun shines on………… It was lovely when we came out of church because the bells began to peal and the sun was shining.

Following the wedding, William wrote to his son, Henry

Yes, the wedding went off very well and I trust fortune may smile on both of you as the sun shone on you that day. We had a dull day yesterday and a little rain but it is much better today. Cousin Cissie (Offley Jeffery's wife) says how well Frank performed his duties and altogether it was a very pretty wedding. You say you are very happy and fond of your wife and so you ought to be. I hope you may always be able to say that.

I personally have many happy recollections of visiting *Aston House*. Henry's father, William, was my father's first cousin, and Henry and Vera and my parents became good friends in addition to being part of the extended Jeffery family.

Over the years Vera wrote down her memories and her memoirs have been edited and published by her daughter Rosalie and husband Lew.[1] Vera wrote of arriving at *Aston House* as a bride. It was the home where she would spend the rest of her life and where their four children grew up.

I found life at Aston House, my new home, fascinating and happy and very busy. I seem to have married a house full of people apart from my husband! My father-in-law, brother-in-law, a maid and a housekeeper who were engaged to help when my mother-in-law died. We also had two young farm assistants living in. I had to 'settle down' – a phrase my father-in-law liked to use – in order to organise the running of the household. It wasn't easy. A woman came daily to clean the kitchens. I really needed good help and I was fortunate to have it.

Because Henry's mother had sadly died the September prior to our wedding in April his father stayed on and lived with us. He didn't want to go anywhere else.

I did have the opportunity of getting to know Henry's mother very well. I had the impression that she liked and 'approved' of me and she was happy that Henry and I were to be married, but sadly she didn't live to see it.

Henry had to be up at 6 am to milk so that the milk could be got away to London. It was taken every day to the local railway station ……………. Henry never expected me to work on the farm but during the day for him there would be much work for him to do on the farm – in the autumn the ploughing, in the spring sowing and then later harvesting. The hay harvest began in June and it was always a hair-raising time. We constantly prayed that it wouldn't rain when the hay had been cut until it was gathered in. In between harvests there was sheep shearing. After harvest it was the thrashing, when we had to feed a lot of men who came with the thrashing machine. I didn't like thrashing much. We gave them lots of porridge for breakfast and cold boiled bacon and potatoes. Then cold beef and apple pie for dinner. Feeding the farm men at harvest time was busy as they would all come in later for tea.

As I quote Vera's words, I can hear my own mother voicing comparable thoughts. They echo the experiences of all farmers' wives from the last century. Life would have been much the same for the many others of the family across Jefferyland.

Henry and Vera's four children, Christopher, Robert, Rosalie and Marilyn (always known as Lu), were all born at Aston House. Robert will continue to farm there until he retires in 2011.

[1]Written On My Heart: The Memoirs of Vera Jeffery 1908 – 2005. Privately published by Malcolm Lewis and Rosalie Vicars-Harris 2006

BELOW *The farmyard showing the unusually large steel hay barn probably built in the 1860s. It was demolished a hundred years later when the Derby road was first re-widened*

ABOVE RIGHT *Farm-workers around the animals' drinking trough in the Aston farmyard showing the old stable building, which still stands. Photograph taken by Connie Jeffery 1928*

BELOW *Henry Jeffery with his youngest daughter Lu at Aston House. Henry used horses to round up cattle for many years and Rosalie and Lu used to help on their ponies*

We gave them lots of porridge for breakfast and cold boiled bacon and potatoes. Then cold beef and apple pie for dinner. Feeding the farm men at harvest time was busy as they would all come in later for tea.

William Charles spent fifty years of his long life at *Aston House*, continuing there with Henry and Vera and their growing family until he died in 1970.

Vera wrote:

My father-in law lived with us for many years, in fact until he was 90 years old. When I first came to Aston he was a bit tyrannical which was perhaps understandable, as he had lost his wife only six months before. His standards were high and he wanted me to do everything for him just the way his wife would have done, but as time went by we became very good friends. He had been brought up in a strict way and maintained this attitude to the end of his life.

RIGHT *William Charles Jeffery with his cousin Offley Jeffery (left) from West Broughton at the wedding of his granddaughter Rosalie in 1965*

As a young girl I remember William well when visiting *Aston House* and also at local Agricultural Shows. He was highly regarded in the farming community and also the local community where he was a churchwarden and chairman of the Sudbury Parish Council.

William's youngest son Frank continued to make his home at *Aston House* for a number of years following Henry and Vera's marriage. Frank became a chartered accountant and practised in Derby. He married Marie Hilda Savidge on 20 July 1939 in Enfield, Middlesex. Their son Keith was born in 1942 and their twin daughters, Mary and Jean, in 1945. Sadly Frank's first wife Marie died on 28 November 1972 and Frank later married her great friend, Irene Scotland. Irene's husband,

His standards were high and he wanted me to do everything for him just the way his wife would have done, but as time went by we became very good friends.

ABOVE RIGHT *William Charles in retirement at Aston House*

RIGHT *Ninetieth birthday party of William Charles Jeffery, l. to r. Marie Jeffery (wife of Frank), Connie Owen (William's daughter), Frank (William's younger son), Henry (William's elder son), Billie Owen (Connie's husband). Vera Jeffery (Henry's wife)*

Portrait of William Charles Jeffery painted by his daughter-in-law Vera Jeffery

DEATH OF A VETERAN OF AGRICULTURE

Funeral at Sudbury

We regret to record the death in Burton General Hospital, at the advanced age of 90, of Mr. William C. Jeffery, of Aston House, Sudbury, a member of a well-known farming family.

He farmed originally at Somersal House, with his father, moving to North Fields Farm, Somersal, when he married and thence to Aston House, Sudbury, in 1920, where he lived until his death.

His wife, formerly Miss Elizabeth May Chadfield, of Cubley Lodge, Cubley, predeceased him in 1933.

He was a former Chairman of Sudbury Parish Council, and a former Churchwarden for 25 years at the Parish Church. He was also a School Manager.

In the 1939-45 War he was a member of the Derbyshire War Agricultural Executive Committee and was very proud to have his farm placed first in the Derbyshire County Farm Competition. He was a keen gardener and a lover of flowers.

He leaves a daughter, Mrs. W. H. Owen of Newport, Shropshire and two sons, Mr. H. W. Jeffery of Aston House, and Mr. Frank Jeffery, a chartered accountant in Derby, who lives in Uttoxeter Road, Mickleover.

****

An earlier report in the *ASHBOURNE NEWS* had described him as:

A good farmer combining the rare quality of a good gardener. .... He was a man who gave service to his fellow-farmers and the community in general being an original member of Ashbourne district agricultural committee and appointed to the agricultural executive committee during the war. He also supported the National Farmers Union.

Present in the church were a great many members of the extended family including Poysers, Hidderleys, Spencers, Hands and Hellabys together with Jefferys from the *Riddings*, West Broughton and Norbury.

a fighter pilot, was killed in wartime when his plane crashed into high ground in North Derbyshire. Marie had expressed a wish that Frank and Irene got together as Irene (known as Rene) had remained a close family friend. Frank and Rene married on 14 December 1974. Frank's daughter Mary emigrated with her husband Graeme Wilson to New Zealand where we have visited them. Frank's son Keith was only fifty-nine when, during a family holiday, he drowned tragically on 27 August 2001 at Holkham Bay, Norfolk. In his later years I came to know Frank well as we shared a joint interest in tracing our Jeffery family history. Very sadly, Frank died nine months before our Jeffery family reunion of 2008.

William Charles Jeffery of *Aston House* died on 29 May 1970. His obituary and funeral report were recorded on the front page of the *UTTOXETER ADVERTISER* of 10 June 1970.

BELOW *Frank Jeffery with his great granddaughter, Rebecca Louisa Stephens, 2007. Rebecca, granddaughter of Frank's late son Keith, is the great, great granddaughter of William and Hannah Jeffery*

William Charles Jeffery was old enough to have vivid memories of his grandmother Mary of the *Riddings* and also, to recall the visits made by his American uncles and cousins to their family in England

It was the first decade of the twenty-first century before William and Hannah's grandsons, Frank Jeffery, son of William Charles and May of *Aston House* and, Arthur Jeffery, son of Arthur and Louisa of *Windy Bank* and *Lower House* farms died.   Frank died on 22 October 2007 and Arthur on 16 February 2009.

One year after William's marriage to May Chadfield, William and Hannah's third son, Arthur Wood Jeffery married Louisa (always known as Louie) Tipper on 28 October 1908.

Arthur and Louie produced five more grandchildren for William and Hannah, two of whom were born after William's death. Their first child, Doris Mabel, was born in 1909 and their only son, Arthur John (who shared his memories with me before he died on 16 February 2009), was born on 11 August 1910. Ida May followed in 1911 and finally, over a decade later, Mary, on 28 February 1922 and her sister Constance Ada, on 31 December 1923. Constance, always known as Connie, has also shared her memories with me.

Before his marriage, Arthur had farmed with his father William at *Somersal House* but on his marriage to Louisa Tipper, he moved to *Moor Farm*, Amerton, near Tamworth in Staffordshire, where their first three children were born. Four years later, they moved back into Derbyshire and farmed firstly at *Windy Bank Farm*, which was close to both *Somersal House* and *Somersal Mill*, and secondly, after the death of his father at *Somersal House*, the family moved to *Lower House Farm*, Roston.

Arthur and Louie's son, Arthur, continued his recollections shared with me in the autumn of 2008:

William and Hannah with their children and grandchildren at Northfields Farm c. 1909. Back row standing l. to r. John Frederick Jeffery, Owen Edwin Jeffery, Charles Jeffery. Next row standing l. to r. William Hidderley junior, William Hidderley senior, William Prince, Louisa Jeffery (nee Tipper) holding Ida May, Arthur Wood Jeffery, Mary Elizabeth (May) Jeffery, Edwin (Ted) Tipper. Seated l. to r. Elizabeth Annie Hidderley with Winifred on her knee, Sarah Ann Prince with Dorothy May on her knee, Ida Prince, William Jeffery, Hannah Jeffery, William Charles Jeffery, Adeline Tipper with Ernest William on her knee. Children in front l. to r. Walter Hidderley, Edwin Hidderley, Edith May Hidderley, Arthur John Jeffery, William Prince, Doris Mabel Jeffery, Marjorie Elizabeth Hidderley, Henry William Jeffery, Connie May Jeffery, Elsie Adeline Hidderley, Mabel Tipper

ABOVE *Arthur Wood Jeffery and Louisa*

I was two years old when we went to Windy Bank and then, when I was seventeen, we went to Lower House Farm, Roston for twelve years.

Mary Jeffery, granddaughter of William's brother, John, who still lives at the *Home Farm*, West Broughton also recalled:

My oldest brother Wilson used to go and stay at Windy Bank Farm. They seemed to get on very well together. We always liked Arthur.

From the mid 1930s to the mid 1940s, whilst William Charles continued making his home with Henry and Vera's family at *Aston House*, the children of his brother, Arthur Wood Jeffery, the second of William and Hannah's surviving sons, were also marrying and establishing their own lives.

Arthur's only son, Arthur John, continued the farming tradition and, as he recalled his memories to me when I visited him before he died, I learnt something of his own life on the land.

ABOVE *Arthur and Louisa haymaking at Windy Bank Farm*

RIGHT *Arthur Wood and son Arthur John Jeffery*

BELOW *Arthur John and family*

BELOW LEFT *Arthur John and family, fruit harvest*

BELOW RIGHT *Ida and Mary, Windy Bank Farm*

When I was farming with my father at Lower House Farm, Roston, I was courting at the time. My father died on January the 4th, 1940 and I married three months later on March 25th. My wife (Margaret Smith) was the youngest of three girls and when we married I went and lived with them. The agent turned the farm over to me. That was Swinholme Farm on the outskirts of Roston. We had two children, Eileen and Dennis. This cottage I'm living in now goes along with the farm. Dennis's wife left him and later he married again. At that time, Dennis and his wife came here to this cottage and I continued on the farm The agent said he wanted to farm it himself and not let Dennis farm it. Later, he said he would take him on at a higher rent and Dennis accepted. He's still on Swinholme Farm. He has four children, a girl and a boy with his first wife and a girl and a boy with his second wife. I moved here (the cottage) twenty years ago. I didn't retire until the '80s. I remained as the tenant at the farm whilst I was living here.

Meanwhile, Arthur's four sisters, Doris Mabel, Ida May, Mary and Constance Ada (Connie) all married between 1935 and 1944 and, although remaining in the Roston and Norbury area, did not continue their lives in farming.

Arthur's youngest sister, Connie, who has also shared her memories with me, married William Bradley. Their youngest daughter, Elizabeth, married Neil Watson. Elizabeth has shared her own research into our joint family history with me and generously provided me with a number of family photographs.

Arthur's father, Arthur Wood Jeffery, died on 4 January 1940. He was only fifty-seven.

His obituary was reported in the *UTTOXETER ADVERTISER* of 10 January.

Arthur Jeffery with his youngest sister Connie at the Jeffery family reunion of 2008

When I was farming with my father at Lower House Farm, Roston, I was courting at the time.

DEATH OF MR. A.W. JEFFERY
Funeral at Somersal

The funeral of Mr. Arthur Wood Jeffery (57), of Lower House Farm, Roston, who died on Thursday, took place at Somersal Herbert on Monday afternoon, the Rev. A. J. Howden (Uttoxeter) conducting the service at Somersal Chapel.

Deceased was the second son of the late Mr. W. Jeffery, of Somersal House, Somersal and for some years had farmed at Windy Bank Farm, Somersal, and ten years ago he removed to Roston. While at Somersal he was a prominent member of the Wesley Methodist Church, being a chapel steward.

Among the mourners at the funeral were Mrs. A. Jeffery (widow), Mr. A. Jeffery (son), Misses M. and C. Jeffery (daughters), Mr. and Mrs. Leason (son-in-law and daughter), Mrs. Hidderley (sister), Mr. and Mrs. Prince (brother-in-law and sister), Mr. W. Jeffery, Sudbury (brother), Mr. and Mrs. F. Jeffery (brother and sister-in-law), Mr. and Mrs. Owen Jeffery (brother and sister-in-law), Mrs. Hellaby, Mr. E. Hellaby, Mr Spencer, Mr Offley Jeffery and Mr. W. Jeffery (West Broughton), Mr. and Mrs. Timmis, Miss Smith, Mrs. E. Prince and others.

His memorial in Somersal churchyard reads as follows:

In Loving Memory of
ARTHUR WOOD JEFFERY
Of Lower House, Roston
Died January 4, 1940
Aged 57 years
Peace perfect Peace

Also his Wife
LOUISA JEFFERY
Died July 6, 1980
Aged 92 years
Reunited

Arthur Wood Jeffery's wife, Louisa outlived her husband by forty years

Meanwhile, William and Hannah's youngest daughter, Adeline, like her sisters, had married into a farming family. Adeline married Edwin Tipper on 28 October 1906, at Somersal Methodist Church. They began their farming life together at *Newborough Hall Farm* close to *Agardsley Park* where Adeline's elder sister and husband, Elizabeth and William Hidderley, had been farming for seven years. Adeline and Edwin Tipper later moved to *Cross Plains Farm*, Needwood, Staffordshire where their children were born. They remained there until the farm was demolished to make way for the new aerodrome in World War 11.

Lower House Farm, Roston

Wedding of Adeline Jeffery to Edwin Tipper at Somersal House

Adeline and Edwin (Ted) Tipper produced two more grandchildren for William and Hannah. Mabel was born on 24 August 1908 and Ernest William on 21 May 1912. Their daughter, Mabel, married William Sutton and they too farmed at *Somersal House.* Mabel thus returned to her mother's and grandparent's old home and it was here that her father died in 1941.

꧁ ⁓⁓⁓⁓⁓ ꧂

Less than three years after his father's death, William and Hannah's third living son, Charles Henry, was taken into the Derby Infirmary where he was treated for appendicitis. He was apparently making good progress, when

Charles Henry Jeffery 1887-1919

peritonitis set in and he died on 5 February 1919, aged only thirty-one. He had been living with his sister and brother-in-law Elizabeth Annie and William Hidderley for some years before his death and had been engaged to be married to a Miss Beck.

Charles's death was reported in the *ASHBOURNE NEWS TELEGRAPH* of 14 February 1919.

SOMERSAL HERBERT
****

Death of Mr. Charles Henry Jeffery – The death of Mr. Charles Henry Jeffery, which occurred at the Derbyshire Royal Infirmary on Wednesday, caused much sorrow in the village. Deceased was class leader at Draycott-in-the-Clay Wesleyan Church. He was of a quiet but happy disposition, and his pleasant personality will be missed by all who knew him. He was highly respected by all and his Christian life will long be remembered by all who were near and dear to him. Mr. Jeffery had been living with Mr. Hidderley (his brother-in-law William and sister Elizabeth Annie) for the past three years. He went to Derby Infirmary to be treated for appendicitis, and was apparently making good progress towards recovery when peritonitis set in, causing his death in a short time. The funeral took place at Somersal on Saturday, the Wesleyan Church being filled with mourners and friends. The chief mourners were: Mother, Miss Beck, Mrs. Prince (Sarah Ann), Mrs. Hidderley (Elizabeth Annie) and Mrs. Tipper (Adeline) (sisters), William, Arthur, Fred and Owen (brothers) brothers-in-law and sisters-in-law, several uncles and aunts and cousins, and a large number of friends. The service was conducted by the Rev. T. C. Edwards and the Rev. J. B. Atkinson, circuit ministers. The Rev. Edwards spoke shortly about the deceased's life, and said how he was loved by all who knew him, and how he was valued in the Circuit as a local preacher. He was always willing to take a service when the appointed preacher was unable to take a service or to fulfil the duty. The hymns, 'God moves in a mysterious way' and 'Peace, perfect peace' were sung. A memorial service is to be held at Somersal on Sunday evening.

Charles was also buried in the little churchyard at Somersal and his memorial reads:

In Loving Memory of
CHARLES JEFFERY
Beloved son of the late William and
Hannah Jeffery
Of Somersal House
Who died February 5, 1919
Aged 31 years
Peace Perfect Peace

John Frederick, William and Hannah's fourth living son, and always known as Frederick or Fred, was farming with his father at *Somersal House* when the World War 1 broke out. Farming was a 'reserved occupation' but in 1915, he volunteered for the Army and was garrisoned in Yorkshire. He would later tell his son, (Frederick William) that he missed all the drafts overseas because he was:

'… the key tenor in the Garrison Glee Club'.

In fact, he served with the Royal Garrison Artillery on the Humber defences near Grimsby. John Frederick married Ethel Saint on 7 March 1916, at St John's, Alkmonton. When they married, late winter snow covered the ground in the churchyard. Frederick's younger brother, Owen, was his best man and Ethel's younger sister, Ada, was a bridesmaid at the wedding.

Following his demobilisation in 1919, he continued in farming, initially with his brother, Owen, at *Somersal House*. However, when Owen married in 1920, Frederick moved to a farm at Mackworth, Derby. In the years following William's death, Frederick and Ethel Jeffery produced five more grandchildren for Hannah: two sons were both born at *Somersal House* - William Frederick, on

6 September 1917 and John Edwin on 21 January 1919. Two daughters were born when their parents were farming at Mackworth, Derby - Dorothy Edith on 12 February 1921 and Vera Gwen on 30 March 1925. Unfortunately, under the difficult conditions prevailing after World War 1, Frederick's first farming project was not a success and the farm was sold early in 1926. The family then moved to a house in nearby Chaddesden where their youngest daughter, Ethel Freda, was born on 6 February 1927. Twelve years later, Freda was to succumb to meningitis and died on 3 April 1939.

Following the sale of the farm at Mackworth, Frederick was forced to find work outside of farming but early in 1927 the family fortunes took a turn for the better when he was appointed as general manager of the farms on the Duke of Rutland's Haddon estate. The family moved into *Bowling Green Farm*, close to the Manners home of *Haddon Hall*, and it was here that his young family spent their early formative years.

Frederick's eldest son, William Frederick, was ten years old when the family moved to *Bowling Green Farm*, on the Manners estate. His father hoped William Frederick would be a farmer but this was not to be. However, the move was to prove significant for this eldest son who, with his younger brother, went to the village school in Rowsley and joined the church choir. It was the organist at Rowsley Church who spotted his musical talent and persuaded his parents to have his voice trained. Also, the Vicar of Rowsley Church, who was a Governor at The Lady Manners School in Bakewell, persuaded Lady Manners, the Duchess of Rutland, to offer a Bursary to a local pupil for four years. William Frederick won this and it was here that both his musical and athletic talents were fully recognised.

The family spent five years at *Bowling Green Farm*, but when the Duke offered to lease the property as a tenancy, Frederick and Ethel Jeffery decided against it. The family came out of farming and moved to Eggington, in the south of the county, where Frederick became an agricultural representative for Levers and Fisons. It was at this stage that his son, William Frederick now aged fifteen and whose voice was beginning to crack, decided against becoming a boarder at Lady Manners School and moved in with his Uncle Owen at *Somersal House* although he certainly did not see his long term future in farming.

In February 1940, ten years after the family had moved from *Bowling Green Farm*, Haddon, William Frederick was called up for World War 11. In May 1942, he was drafted out to Africa and his war years included time spent in Kenya, Tanganyika and Northern Rhodesia. It was while he was posted to Nairobi that he met Ethne Maureen McCartney from Ireland. After the war ended, having decided to remain in East Africa, where he had taken up an appointment with a major oil company, they married, on 20 October 1945. Their two children were born in Africa: Irene Judith in Nairobi, Kenya and Denis Frederick in Kampala, Uganda.

For Irene's father, William Frederick Jeffery, his life in East Africa was a far cry from his schooldays in Derbyshire and the days of his youth when he had helped

Wedding of William Frederick Jeffery to Ethne McCartney in Nairobi

*Frederick and Ethel Jeffery
in their later years*

his Uncle Owen on the farm at *Somersal House*. Later, the family did return to England and William Frederick pursued his interest in discovering his own roots in Derbyshire. It is an interest that he passed on to his daughter Irene who, in recent years, I have come to know well through our shared interest in Jeffery family history. I am indebted to Irene for her generosity in sharing with me her own memories of her grandparents and parents.

In April 1920 Hannah, after her recent sad years of mourning following the deaths of both her husband and middle son Charles, had an occasion to celebrate. At Easter, on 5 April 1920, her youngest son Owen, who had been running the farm at *Somersal House* following his father's death, married Ada Saint.

Owen Jeffery and Ada Saint's wedding was reported in the *ASHBOURNE NEWS* for 23 April 1920.

RIGHT *Youngest son, Owen Jeffery in his twenties*

WEDDING AT ALKMONTON

On Easter Monday the little village church was the scene of a very pretty and interesting wedding. The contracting parties were Miss Ada Saint of Alkmonton and Mr. Owen E. Jeffery, youngest son of the late Mr. William Jeffery and Mrs. Hannah Jeffery, of Somersal House.

The bride, who was given away by her eldest brother, Mr. William Saint, was attired in ivory crepe de chine, trimmed most artistically with pearls and silk fringe, and wore an embroidered net veil with wreath of orange blossom and white heather. She carried a shower bouquet of white carnations and lilies of the valley, her sole ornament being a gold pendant set with pearls and aqua marine stones, the gift of the bridegroom.

There were four bridesmaids in attendance: Miss Olive Saint (sister of the bride) and the Misses Elsie Hidderley, Ida Prince and Mabel Tipper (nieces of the bridegroom).

The two elder bridesmaids wore blue crepe de chine with Brussels net cap and veil in place of the orthodox hat, and gold bracelets, the gift of the bridegroom. The two little girls looked very sweet in pale pink crepe de chine with net mob caps caught at the side with pink roses. They wore gold broaches, the gift of the bridegroom, and all carried bouquets of pink carnations, these also being the bridegroom's gift.

The office of groomsman was most ably filled by Mr. Ernest Wood of Marston.

The service, which was choral, was conducted by the Vicar, Rev. Dr. Dearden M.A. and the church was filled with friends and well wishers of both families. The two hymns 'The voice that breathed o'er Eden' and 'Thine for ever God of Love' were sung during the service, and Mendelssohn's Wedding March was played by Mrs. Dearden, who presided at the organ. After the ceremony, the guests, numbering between 70 and 80 were conveyed to Alkmonton House, where the reception was held by the bride's mother. Later the happy couple left for Derby, en route for Egremont, where the honeymoon was spent, the bride's travelling costume being navy-blue gabardine with fawn and blue straw hat and marabou shoulder wraps.

Wedding of Owen Jeffery and Ada Saint 1920

There followed a long list of gifts received and, in addition to those from Jefferys, Saints, Poysers, and Hidderleys, there were gifts from Websters, who are my mother's family. My mother's sister, Jessie, married Ada's brother, George Saint.

They had been married for nine years before their daughter, Audrey, was born, at *Somersal House*, on 27 January 1929. She was destined to be Hannah's twenty-eighth and last grandchild.

Earlier this year, I was delighted to be able to make contact with Audrey who is now living in South Africa. She has spent over fifty years in southern Africa. Thirty-six years ago, her parents, Owen and Ada Jeffery, joined her in Durban, South Africa.

LEFT *Owen Jeffery with his car*

BELOW *Owen Jeffery ploughing at Somersal House Farm*

Audrey wrote:

My father Owen was born in 1892. When his father, William, died in 1916, my father took over the running of Somersal House with his mother, Hannah. In 1920, he was 28 when he married Mum (Ada Saint) and continued to live at Somersal House. I was born at Somersal House in 1929. I'm not sure when my grandmother died, I was only a baby. (Hannah died on 14 February 1930).

In 1935 we moved to Anslow (The Common Farm). *Dad was still farming and in 1941 he went into partnership with a local farmer running a haulage business. He was still in farming as well until 1946 when they moved into a private residence in the Rolleston area. He was still in the haulage business and leased a portion of land from the new owner of the 'Common Farm', Anslow. He finally retired to Southport, Lancashire. I think that was 1961.*

In 1974, my parents came to Durban, South Africa for an extended holiday of four months and finally decided to emigrate in 1975 to join me, a brave move at 84 and 78 years.

I married in England in 1950 to Derek (Hall) *a Burtonian and an engineer. We lived in Walsall, St. Helens and lastly Bilston before emigrating to Ndola, Northern Rhodesia (Zambia) in 1954 where my husband was appointed Deputy Town Engineer. Our only child, Diane was born there in 1955. In 1959, we moved to Luanshya on the 'Copperbelt'. My husband decided to branch out into commerce and he was appointed Manager of Hulme Pipe Co. until 1962 when he was appointed to General Manager Central Africa and we moved to Salisbury, Southern Rhodesia (Harare). Another opportunity came along in 1965 with the same company which brought us to Durban, South Africa.*

Mum died here in her 98th year in 1995. It was 1982 when Dad died aged 90.

My father Owen was born in 1892. When his father, William, died in 1916, my father took over the running of Somersal House with his mother, Hannah. In 1920, he was 28 when he married Mum (Ada Saint) and continued to live at Somersal House. I was born at Somersal House in 1929. I'm not sure when my grandmother died, I was only a baby.

Owen Jeffery, the youngest son of William and Hannah, who died aged ninety on 19 August 1982 in South Africa, was the last of his generation. Owen's daughter Audrey, in South Africa, is one of the three remaining grandchildren of William and Hannah Jeffery. The other two are the younger daughters of Arthur and Louisa, Mary and Constance Ada.

At the time of Hannah's death, all of her seven surviving children were married with their own growing families.

Throughout the first half of the twentieth century, the Jeffery family home of *Somersal House* continued to feature significantly in the lives of William and Hannah's younger children, and their descendants.   It was 1975 before it was sold, having featured as a family home for three quarters of a century.

William and Hannah's story continues through the lives of their many great grandchildren and their descendants. Of their great grandchildren, there are a number who continue the farming tradition within Jefferyland. They include Dennis Jeffery, grandson of their son Arthur Wood Jeffery, who continues to farm at *Swinholme Farm* on the outskirts of Roston and also their great grandson Robert Jeffery who, following his father Henry and grandfather William, continues to farm at *Aston House*, Sudbury. When Robert retires in 2011 *Aston House Farm* will have been farmed by three generations of Jefferys for over ninety years.

ABOVE LEFT *Owen and Ada Jeffery, centre, 23 April 1970 in South Africa, celebrating their Golden Wedding with their daughter Audrey, left, and granddaughter Diane, right*

ABOVE RIGHT *Owen Jeffery with Ada in South Africa on his 90th birthday, 24 April 1982*

BELOW *Aston House in 1928 when John Arthur Jeffery and his family visited from America. John Arthur was the son of William's eldest brother Thomas who had emigrated in 1865*

JOHN JEFFERY
1848 – 1939

A Conflagration, a Secret and Discord

John Jeffery, the fifth of Thomas and Mary's fifteen children was born at the Riddings on 23 August 1848. He married Maria Wilson on 18 May 1880 and they had three children and eight grandchildren. John and Maria farmed at Somersal Mill for nine years and then, for fifty years, at the Home Farm, West Broughton, Derbyshire, where he bought a number of neighbouring farms and where his great grandsons remain farming to this day. John died on 7 October 1939. His long life took him through the reigns of five monarchs.

Descendants of John Jeffery

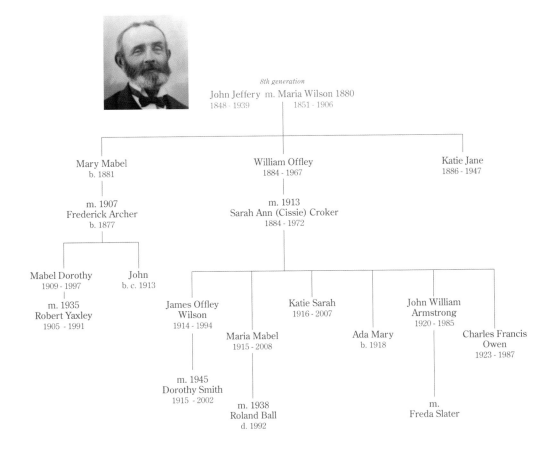

8th generation

John Jeffery m. Maria Wilson 1880
1848 - 1939   1851 - 1906

Mary Mabel
b. 1881

William Offley
1884 - 1967

Katie Jane
1886 - 1947

m. 1907
Frederick Archer
b. 1877

m. 1913
Sarah Ann (Cissie) Croker
1884 - 1972

Mabel Dorothy
1909 - 1997

John
b. c. 1913

m. 1935
Robert Yaxley
1905 - 1991

James Offley
Wilson
1914 - 1994

Maria Mabel
1915 - 2008

Katie Sarah
1916 - 2007

Ada Mary
b. 1918

John William
Armstrong
1920 - 1985

Charles Francis
Owen
1923 - 1987

m. 1945
Dorothy Smith
1915 - 2002

m. 1938
Roland Ball
d. 1992

m.
Freda Slater

John Jeffery 1848-1939
A Conflagration, a Secret and Discord

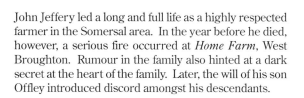

One of the best and most successful agriculturalists in the district.
Obituary of John Jeffery 1939

ABOVE LEFT *John Jeffery*

ABOVE RIGHT *John Jeffery in his twenties*

John Jeffery led a long and full life as a highly respected farmer in the Somersal area. In the year before he died, however, a serious fire occurred at *Home Farm*, West Broughton. Rumour in the family also hinted at a dark secret at the heart of the family. Later, the will of his son Offley introduced discord amongst his descendants.

John was Thomas and Mary's fifth child, born at the *Riddings* on 23 August 1848. At the time of his birth his four siblings were all under four years of age. He was seventeen by the time his youngest brother, Arthur, was born and the family was complete.

John outlived all of his brothers and sisters with the exception of his two youngest sisters, Clara and Ellen. Born in the middle of the nineteenth century, before the Crimean War, he lived to witness the outbreak of World War 11. He was destined, like his brothers, William and Owen, to continue the family farming tradition, firstly with his father and brothers at the *Riddings* and later, following his marriage, for nine years at *Somersal Mill* and for the last fifty years of his life, at the *Home Farm*, West Broughton.

John became particularly close to his younger brother George who was his junior by just over a year. Both brothers left home in their early twenties to work in Leeds. By this time, their elder brothers Thomas and Joseph had left for America and elder brother William had become their father's right hand man at the *Riddings*.

In 1871 the census revealed twenty-three-year-old John working at the Queens Hotel in Leeds whilst his younger brother, George, was employed at the Albion Hotel, Leeds. However, within a couple of years, John had returned to Derbyshire. It was probably following his elder brother William's marriage in 1873 that John returned to the *Riddings* in order to help his father and younger brother, nineteen-year-old Owen, on the farm.

On 18 May 1880 John married Maria Wilson. Maria, born in 1851, was the daughter of William and Jane (nee Berrisford) Wilson of *Mount Pleasant Farm*, Marston Montgomery, Derbyshire.

John and Maria started their farming life together at *Somersal Mill*. On the 1881 census they are shown here with their one-month-old daughter, Mary Mabel. This first daughter was known by her second name Mabel or sometimes, according to her niece Mary at the *Home Farm*, West Broughton, the diminutive May. At the time of the census in April 1881, two of John's younger sisters, twenty-four-year-old Fanny and nineteen-year-old Ellen

ABOVE *John's wife Maria*

LEFT *Maria's parents, William and Jane Wilson*

John's son, William Offley Jeffery c.1885

were visiting them. They would have been very welcome with a new baby in the home. There was one farm worker, Thomas Mousley, living in at the time. Three years later, John and Maria's son, William Offley, (always known as Offley) was born on 31 March 1884 and their youngest child, Katie Jane (known as Katie), arrived in 1886.

There is a story behind the name 'Offley' which John and Maria gave to their only son. It seems that Maria Wilson, before she married John, had been impressed by a man called Sir Offley Shaw. She promised herself that if ever she had a son she would call him Offley.

In 1889, John and Maria, with their young family, moved to nearby *Home Farm*, West Broughton. This was the time that John's eldest sister, Margaret, and her husband John Poyser, with their family of nine children, moved into *Somersal Mill*.

John's youngest granddaughter Mary who continues to live at the *Home Farm*, West Broughton, told me:

Grandpa was farming at the Mill Farm, Somersal. My grand-mother wasn't too smitten with it. Lord Vernon sent for my grandfather and said – 'I want you to move to Home Farm'. My grandfather's sister, Aunt Margaret Poyser, then went to the Mill Farm. I think their move there was something to do with Grandpa.

Also by 1899, as we have seen, John's brother and sister-in-law, William and Hannah, with their first six children, were well established at nearby *Northfields Farm*, Somersal. John and William's children and their Poyser cousins, grew up close together on these three neighbouring farms.

Grandpa was farming at the Mill Farm, Somersal. My grand-mother wasn't too smitten with it.

John Jeffery c.1905

ABOVE *Offley Jeffery c.1905*

ABOVE *John and Maria with their children at West Broughton.*
L. Katie Jane, centre Offley, r. Mabel c.1905

All of these pictures still hang today in the dining room of the
Home Farm, West Broughton. They were probably taken at
around the time of Offley's twenty-first birthday

These three families established firm roots in this part of
Jefferyland and their descendants remain there to this
day. John and Maria's descendants still farm the land of
Home Farm, West Broughton, together with that of three
neighbouring farms which were bought by John.

The 1891 census shows John and Maria, together with
ten-year-old Mabel, seven-year-old Offley and five-year-old
Katie at the *Home Farm*, West Broughton. It was a full
and busy household with four farm labourers living in on
the farm at this time: John Carter (29), George Blood
(13), John Talbot (20) and James Talbot (18).

The first few months of 1906 were very sad ones for
John. His mother's death at the *Riddings* on February 17
was followed a month later by that of his wife Maria on
15 March. Maria was only fifty-five and her children, in
their twenties, were on the threshold of their adult lives.
Mabel, at twenty-five, planned to marry Frederick Archer
the following year. Twenty-two-year-old Offley was already shouldering much of the work on the farm at West
Broughton and twenty-year-old Katie became a nurse.

LEFT *Offley*
Jeffery c.1905

Maria's obituary, in the local press, read as follows:

SUDBURY

We deeply regret to announce the death of Mrs. Jeffery, of the Home Farm, Sudbury, which took place on Monday, the 19th. ult. The deceased lady had been a great sufferer for some considerable time, and had throughout manifested a true Christian spirit. She was held in very high esteem throughout the neighbourhood. She had lived a very busy life, and was sustained throughout by her strong faith and confidence in the mercy and goodness of God. The funeral took place on Saturday, the 24th. ult. in Somersal Wesleyan Churchyard, with which Church the deceased was clearly identified. Before leaving the home, a short service was conducted by the Rev. J. T. Platt (Wesleyan minister). A large congregation had assembled at the church to pay their last respects to the deceased lady. The whole of the service was most impressively conducted throughout by the Circuit ministers, the Revs. J. Kendrew and J. T.Platt. Mr. Meakin, of Sudbury, presided at the organ and played The Dead March at the conclusion of the service. The hymns sung were 'On the Resurrection" and 'Jesu, Lover of my Soul', the latter, around the graveside. A large number of relatives followed. The bearers were nephews of the deceased viz: Messrs J. Hall, W. Dew, O.Poyser, T. Poyser, W. Jeffery and T. Holbrook.

The following sent wreaths – Husband and children, Mr. and Mrs. J. Wilson (Preston), Mr. and Mrs. Hall and family (Foremark), Mr. and Mrs. Webster (Chartley), Tom, Ida and May (Chartley), Wilson Smith (Holt Wood), Mr. and Mrs. Poyser and family (Shardlow), Mr. and Mrs. Jeffery and family (Somersal House), Mrs. Holbrook, Mrs. Spencer and Miss Jeffery (Riddings), Mr. and Mrs. Cook (Donnington Park), Mr. and Mrs. O. Jeffery and family (Bentley Fields), Mr. and Mrs. Hellaby (Bentley Hall) Mr. and Mrs. O. Poyser (Doveridge) Mr. T. and Miss Poyser (Longford). All at Castle Hayes Park and Miss Copestake, Mrs. Salisbury, Lizzie and Carrie, Mrs. Lann and Mrs. Bennett, Mr. and Mrs. Chadfield (Cubley Lodge), Hilda Allen and the Somersal Wesleyan Sunday School scholars.

John was only fifty-seven when Maria died. By the time he had reached sixty, it was his son, Offley, who had taken over the farm, although John maintained a keen interest in its running throughout his long life.

Maria had inherited *Deepmore Farm* at Doveridge from her parents and at some time before her death, John had bought *Brocksford House Farm*. He had been planning for their retirement there when his son Offley would take over at the *Home Farm*, West Broughton. John's grand-daughter Mary told me:

After he (John) *lost his wife, Auntie Katie went with him to Deepmore at Doveridge. Later Auntie Katie went into nursing. He had bought Brocksford House – he got it ready for them – and then his wife died before they could go.*

The year following his wife Maria's death, John's eldest daughter Maria Mabel married Frederick Archer in 1907. In 1911, sixty-two-year-old John with his son, twenty-seven-year-old Offley were at the *Home Farm* West Broughton and John's younger daughter, twenty-five-year-old Katie Jane, was their housekeeper. It was a full household with a cowman, a waggoner and a milk-boy, together with a domestic servant, all living in.

At some time after 1911, younger daughter Katie Jane left home to pursue her nursing career in Nottingham. John, therefore, was urgently in need of a housekeeper to run the busy farming household where, in addition to his son Offley, there continued to be up to four farm labourers and a domestic servant living in the house.

One can only speculate as to exactly how Cissie Croker, who was not from a local family, came to make her home at the *Home Farm*, West Broughton. It could be that John placed an advertisement in the national farming press. However it came about, it was the *Home Farm*, West Broughton where she was destined to spend the rest of her life.

Nurse Katie Jane Jeffery

Cissie, christened Sarah Ann, came from a family of farmers and small holders in the Fens. She was born on 18 February 1881, near Whaplode, Lincolnshire. Her father, James Croker, born in 1854 at Tydd Fen, Cambridgeshire, had a farm near Whaplode. Her mother, Sarah Ann Armstrong, born in 1858, was also from Whaplode. Cissie, who had two brothers and three sisters, was their second child. Named for both her mother and her maternal grandmother (Sarah Ann Richardson of Market Deeping, Lincolnshire), she appears to have been the only one of her family to leave Lincolnshire in the nineteenth and early twentieth century.

Following the end of World War 1, the great estates across the land were being broken up and individual farms purchased by their tenant farmers. The Vernon's Sudbury estate was no exception and a number of farms were sold by Lord Vernon. John Jeffery, who had already bought *Brocksford House Farm*, took the opportunity to purchase two more neighbouring farms: *Fiddlers Farm*

and *Flacketts Lane Farm* together with three nearby cottages. John placed *Fiddlers* and *Flacketts Lane* farms in the name of his son, Offley. Today, the land is all farmed by two of John's great grandsons, John and Peter Jeffery. John and Peter are the sons of John's grandson, also named John. His granddaughter, Mary, continues to live at *Home Farm*, West Broughton.

My father was always very close to his Jeffery uncles and aunts and most particularly to his cousins farming in the area. These included Offley Jeffery at the *Home Farm*, West Broughton, Tom Jeffery at the *Riddings* and Percy Spencer at *Bentley Fields*. In addition to the regularity with which they met at the Uttoxeter, Ashbourne and Derby markets, we would very frequently visit their homes. As a child I can recall visits to West Broughton and my sister Marjorie in particular remembers our Great Uncle John before he died in 1939. It was probably early in 1939 when we were visiting that she recalls:

I remember old John Jeffery. I remember being taken upstairs at West Broughton to see him in bed. He wasn't very well at the time. I remember him in his nightshirt. It was an iron bedstead with brass railings. I thought he was a very old man.

John's great nephew Geoff Jeffery, grandson of his brother the Reverend Joseph Jeffery, also remembers John. Geoff visited from America in 1939 when John was ninety-one and he recalls:

We talked with him for quite a while. His memory was excellent – much better than his hearing. He and Mrs Hellaby (John's sister Ellen) *tried to make me look like a Jeffery but couldn't find any typical features.*

John's granddaughter, Mary Jeffery, youngest daughter of Offley, also has very clear memories of meeting Geoff Jeffery in the summer of 1939. She also has many

His memory was excellent — much better than his hearing. He and Mrs Hellaby tried to make me look like a Jeffery but couldn't find any typical features.

I never knew him any other way than walking on sticks and yet he remained active, he didn't deteriorate. He'd been injured – kicked by an animal. He worked hard and you had to work hard for him. I think he liked to be where the family were and with the children.

memories of her grandfather and the closeness of the Jeffery family. Mary was twenty-one when her grandfather John died. She recalls:

I remember a particular occasion when Auntie Nellie (my grandmother Ellen) and Auntie Clara visited – I think it must have been my grandfather's birthday, August 23rd - we had a little party.

My father (Offley) used to take Auntie Nellie up to visit Auntie Clara at Snitterton Hall. He (Offley) used to stay at Snitterton Hall when he was younger. Grandpa (John) also used to spend time with his sister Polly's family (Spencers) at Bentley Fields.

Mary continued her memories of her grandfather John:

I never knew him any other way than walking on sticks and yet he remained active, he didn't deteriorate. He'd been injured – kicked by an animal. He worked hard and you had to work hard for him. I think he liked to be where the family were and with the children. He made his home here with us but he also used to spend extended periods of time at the Riddings and at Bentley Fields. I suppose he also went to Bentley Hall. He went for quite long spells to Bentley Fields and the Riddings. When the time came for him to be taken there he would have the horses with the 'Sunday best' vehicle.

John was clearly very much a family man and remained close to his brothers and sisters. Mary continued:

His sisters Auntie Polly and Auntie Nellie also used to visit him here on Wednesdays (Uttoxeter market day). I remember when Auntie Clara came here on Grandpa's birthday and when we visited her in Borrowash. I also remember when Uncle Owen was going to be buying Stydd Hall and Grandpa told cousin Dolly that it would be very isolated for her. I think Grandpa did quite a lot of business for his relatives. The Somersal House Jefferys – he did a lot to help them – I think some people thought he spent too much time there when his wife was working hard here. I also remember he was everlasting reckoning up in his head.

There's a story of when my grandfather and father lost the bull. They looked everywhere for it and one of the men on the farm said 'we've looked in all the ordinary places'. Grandpa then said – 'well, look in all the extraordinary places!' They found the missing bull – it had gone up a flight of stone steps.

Mary also recalled that:

Grandpa had very nice blue eyes. My sister Katie grew very much like him. It was quite noticeable.

I think I can detect a resemblance between John's granddaughter Katie and his mother Mary (nee Robinson) of the *Riddings*.

John's oldest brother, Thomas, who had emigrated to America in 1865, maintained regular contact with the *Riddings* and his siblings' families back home. On his relatively frequent visits to the *Riddings* he would also visit the *Home Farm*, West Broughton. After his death, in 1927, these visits were continued by Thomas's wife Jessie, together with Thomas and Maria's son and daughter-in-law, John Arthur (Art) and Myra, and their son, John. Later, Thomas's daughter and son-in-law, Adelaide and Lawrence Henderson also visited.

Mary remembers these visits of our American cousins:

I remember when Auntie Jessie visited. She came with Auntie Nellie. Auntie Jessie was interested in my eldest sister, Marie, going back with her. We were only schoolgirls (at Uttoxeter Girls' High School).

I remember a visit before that. There were two people and a son – that was before Auntie Jessie visited. Auntie Nellie came with them, I think they must have been staying at Bentley Hall – they were two smart gentlemen – one middle-aged and one in his

There's a story of when my grandfather and father lost the bull. They looked everywhere for it and one of the men on the farm said 'we've looked in all the ordinary places'. Grandpa then said – 'well, look in all the extraordinary places!' They found the missing bull – it had gone up a flight of stone steps.

John Jeffery - eightieth birthday 1928

prime. It would be John and Myra with their son John. (Thomas's son, wife and grandson from California). That visit was before Jessie's. I can visualise it now. I've seen a picture of them in front of Bentley Hall. I was maybe in my very early teens or maybe a little bit younger.

John (Art) and Myra, with their young son, John, did indeed visit in 1928, the year following the death of his father, Thomas, in Redlands, California. Mary would have been a ten-year-old at the time and the *'young man in his prime'*, who she so much admired, would have been her fifteen-year-old cousin John.

Thirty years later, both she and I recall the visit made by Adelaide (daughter of John's eldest brother Thomas) and her husband Lawrence in the summer of 1958 when we had a family party at the *Home Farm*, West Broughton. It was an occasion when I remember Mary's brothers telling me that I would forget my books and marry a farmer. Their forecast was not correct!

On 23 August 1929, when John celebrated his eightieth birthday with his family around him, he had his photograph taken.

Ten years later, shortly before John celebrated his ninetieth birthday, in the late summer of 1938, when both the hay and the corn harvest had been safely gathered in and Offley and Cissie had been planning to go on holiday, disaster struck in the form of a major fire on the farm. It was reported in the *UTTOXETER ADVERTISER* of 23 August 1938.

FIRE AT WEST BROUGHTON

Uttoxeter Brigade's Record 13 Hour Pumping

Mr. O. Jeffery, of the Home Farm, West Broughton, between Doveridge and Sudbury, had an unpleasant surprise when he returned from Derby market on Friday afternoon, and was disappointed in his intention of taking a holiday which he had planned to commence the following day. He found all his corn and hay blazing furiously and a Fire Brigade in attendance endeavouring to save his farm buildings.

The fire was discovered shortly before 2 o'clock by one of Mr. Jeffery's sons, and the Uttoxeter Fire Brigade received the alarm (by electric bells) about 2. 10 pm and by the time the rocket alarm was fired at 2. 20 the men and the engine were preparing to leave the fire-station for the scene of the fire.

On arrival, under Supt. G. A. Fox, the brigade found that an eight-bay Dutch barn was alight from end to end, and the flames were being fanned by a strong breeze. They were told that when the fire was discovered it was of very small proportions, but by the time the alarm had been given at the house it had reached alarming possibilities. The barn contained about 200 tons of this year's corn and old and new hay and only about 50 tons were saved. The cause of the fire is not known, but it has been definitely established that it was not due to spontaneous combustion. The barn is situated close to the cowsheds and granary and efforts were concentrated on preventing the fire reaching these and Mr. DeVille's farm 80 or 100 yards away where a seven-bay Dutch barn stands. Water was obtained from a nearby brook which was dammed up by the brigade and supplied just enough water to keep the motor engine, 'Mary Howitt' going. There was not a pint of water left when the engine finished pumping. Incidentally, the engine established a record for continuous pumping, being in operation for 13 hours without a break. Never at any fire has the brigade pumped (continuously or intermittently) for so long. At one time it was thought that other brigades would have to be sent for, but the Uttoxeter men, with the aid of a host of willing helpers from neighbouring farms, managed to get the fire under control. Enormous volumes of smoke were blown across the main road, and travelled for more than half a mile. The fire could be smelt beyond Aston, on the Derby side of Sudbury. The damage was covered by insurance.

The brigade returned to Uttoxeter at 9. 30 on Sunday evening.

Throughout his long and active life John kept a scrapbook entitled '*Literary Cuttings*' into which he pasted items he had been reading from a range of sources. His selection of those items which he considered worthy of preservation provides an interesting insight into his nature and character. They reflect the views and opinions of the man himself. Some of the cuttings were taken from a magazine entitled '*Great Thoughts*', which John clearly took on a regular basis, and some are from newspapers and other journals. The cuttings date from the later years of the nineteenth century up to the 1930s. The latter part of the scrapbook includes reports of family events: engagements, weddings and funerals. It is an eclectic but revealing mix. Illustrations of a few of the cuttings up to 1906 include:

Thoughts from W.E. Gladstone; The Demand for Farms; The last Judgement; Centenarians of the Year 1902; Land and Property Sales of 1902; Tolstoy's Famous Parable; Victor Hugo's Philosophy; Unionism in Yeaveley.

And:

Burning a Bedfellow – Extraordinary Assault Case from Doveridge; Sudbury Rural District Council; The Political Tyranny of Non-Conformity; Conflicting Sects and Voices in the Church; Commentary on George Eliot's Works and Canadian Cattle and British Farmers.

The last article mentioned may well have been pasted into the scrapbook with thoughts of his brother George, farming on the Canadian Prairies. The penultimate one may have been selected because there is reputed to be a family link with Mary Ann Evans (George Eliot). One short commentary is worthy of including in full as it provides interesting observations from the world of farming which, in many ways to this day, remains a world apart from those who live in urban environments.

THE FARMER AND
HIS CRITICS

It is perhaps inevitable that the most scathing criticisms of British agricultural methods should come from the towns. People who find it comparatively easy to make money in trade and commerce think it possible to do the same in cultivating the land. Without business traditions themselves they assume that the traditional practices of farming must necessarily be out of date; and where ways and manners of the agriculturalist differ from their own they take it for granted that they must be wrong.

From 1920 onwards, the cuttings are almost exclusively relating to family members with, in addition to engagements, weddings and funerals, there is a report with photographs on his son-in-law's farm.

In the late 1930s, John's health started to fail. It was on 7 October 1939, following a fulfilling life with his family, in farming, the local community and the Somersal Methodist Church, that he died at home, six weeks following his ninety-first birthday.

John lived during the reigns of five monarchs: Victoria, Edward V11, George V, Edward V111 and George V1. He was born in Victorian times, to parents who had married when William IV was on the throne, and whose grandfather was born in the year of the French Revolution when George III was the reigning monarch. The whole of his life had been spent on three farms in Derbyshire. His obituary declared that he was:

One of the most successful agriculturalists in the district and a generous and mostly anonymous contributor to many worthy causes

During his long life, he had witnessed not only significant changes in agricultural practices, but also, the sweeping social changes precipitated most particularly by the World War 1.

He lived to see two of his nephews, his brother William's son, Frederick, from *Somersal House* and his brother Owen's son, Thomas, from the *Riddings*, join up in World War 1, in the Army and Navy respectively. He also lived to see them both return safely home. By the time he died, Britain was again launched into another World War.

John's death was reported in the *ASHBOURNE NEWS*, the *UTTOXETER ADVERTISER* and the *DERBYSHIRE ADVERTISER*. It is the latter, which appeared on the front page on 13 October 1939 which is quoted here.

DEATH OF MR. JOHN JEFFERY

A NONOGENERIAN FARMER

Funeral at Somersal

Early to bed and early to rise' was the maxim adopted by Mr. John Jeffery, who passed away at the Home Farm, West Broughton, Sudbury, at the age of 91 years.

His birthplace, the Riddings Farm, Hungry Bentley, had been farmed by his ancestors for hundreds of years. He was one of a family of fifteen children, thirteen of whom lived to be over 70 years of age. Two sisters survive, being over 80 years and 70 years respectively.

About 60 years ago, he married Maria, the eldest daughter of Mr. and Mrs. Wilson, of Mount Pleasant Farm, Marston Montgomery. Mrs. Jeffery passed away 33 years ago, and of the marriage, one son, two daughters, eight grandchildren and two great grandchildren survive.

Mr. Jeffery, quite one of the best known and most successful agriculturalists in the district, commenced his farming career at Somersal Mill Farm, and about 50 years ago he took over the Home Farm at West Broughton.

When Mr. Offley Jeffery took over this farm about 31 years ago, his father continued to reside with him, and he took the keenest interest in the work of the farm until a short time before his death.

A Methodist all his life, Mr. Jeffery took a leading part, and was a generous contributor to the building of the Somersal Methodist Church.

Some years ago, Mr. Jeffery was a member of the Doveridge Parish Council. He was a generous and mostly anonymous contributor to many worthy objects.

THE FUNERAL

Conducted by the Rev. F. G. Howden, the funeral took place at Somersal Methodist Church by Mr. Howden, who gave a short address. Mrs. Fradley of Uttoxeter was the organist and the hymns 'Now the Labourer's task is O'er' and 'Peace, Perfect Peace' were sung.

The mourners were: Mr. W. O. Jeffery, son; Mrs. F. Archer and Miss K. Jeffery, daughters (Mary Mabel and Katie Jane); Mr. Wilson Jeffery, Mr. John Jeffery, Mr. Francis Jeffery and Mr. John Archer (grandsons); Mrs. R. Ball (Marie), Miss Katie Jeffery and Miss Mary Jeffery, grand-daughters; Mrs. Cook and Mrs. Hellaby, sisters (Clara and Ellen); Mr. W. Wilson, brother-in-law; Mrs. Owen Jeffery, sister-in-law; Mr. F. Archer, son-in-law; Mr. R. Ball, grandson-in-law; Mr. C. Poyser; Mr. A. Jeffery; Mr. O. Jeffery; Mr. T. Jeffery; Mr. E. Hellaby and Mr. P. S. Spencer, nephews; Mrs. Ball; Mrs. Prince; Miss Poyser; Mrs. Roberts and Mrs. Hand, nieces. Friends present included. T. Reeve, nurse; Mr. T. Webster; Mrs. Charles Blore; Mr. Sutton; Miss Allen; Mrs. O. Jeffery; Mrs. W. J. Hellaby; Mr. T. Smith and Mr. W. Wilson, tenants, Mr. and Mrs. E. J. De Ville, Mrs. E. De Ville, Somersal; Mrs. Smith; Mrs. F. J. Howden; Mrs. P. S. Spencer; Mr. C. Ball; Mr. J. Sant; Mr. H. Sant; Mr. Goodall; Mr, R. Goodall; Mr. Torr; Mr. Hand; Mr. R. Taylor; Mrs. H. Lane; Mr. R. F. Cowlishaw, solicitor; Mr. Frank Howard, representing Lord Vernon; Mr. Walter Salt; Mrs. Clark and Mrs. Slaney.

Mr. O. J. Poyser, Mr. C. Jeffery, Mr. E. Jeffery, Mr. W. J. Hellaby, all nephews of the late Mr. Jeffery, were the bearers.

Mrs. W.O.Jeffery was unable to attend owing to illness.

Was Cissie's indisposition a diplomatic one?

There were many floral tributes, including those from:

Cissie and grandchildren; Mabel, Fred, Dorothy, Jack, Bob and Great Grandchildren; Mabel, Katie and Offley; Marie and Rowland; sister Nellie and family; all at the Riddings; all at Deepmore; sister Clara and family…………..

and many, many more.

John was buried with his wife Maria at Somersal and their memorial reads:

IN LOVING MEMORY OF
MARIA
BELOVED WIFE OF JOHN JEFFERY
OF WEST BROUGHTON

Who died March 15th, 1906

Aged 55 years

"Trusting in Jesus"

ALSO JOHN JEFFERY
BELOVED HUSBAND OF THE ABOVE

Who died Oct. 7th, 1939

Aged 91 years

With Long Life Will I satisfy Him?
And Shew him my Salvation
The Blood of Jesus Christ
Cleanseth us from all sin

In his will, John Jeffery directed that his daughters, Mary Mabel and Katie Jane, inherit *Deepmore Farm*, Doveridge. *Deepmore* had been owned by their mother, Maria, and she had inherited it from her parents, William and Jane Wilson. His will also directed that:

Deepmore Farm shall not be sold until the death of the survivor of my said two Daughters

Also:

I give devise and bequeath the rest and residue of my real and personal estate unto and equally between my said three children viz. the said Mary Mabel Archer, William Offley Jeffery and Katie Jane Jeffery.

John and Maria's tomb-stone at Somersal

John Jeffery added three codicils to his will which seem to reflect some of his serious concerns regarding its execution. The codicils involved changing the Executors and Trustees. Initially, in 1931, he appointed his son Offley and his grandsons Wilson and John as the Trustees. Three years later, on 16 April 1934, the appointed Trustees were named as his son Offley, his daughter Mabel and his friend (and Solicitor) Charles Cowlishaw. Three days later, on 19 April 1934, a second codicil was signed which added two additional Trustees, namely his daughter Katie Jane and his nephew Arthur Poyser of *Somersal Mill*. Four months later, a third codicil directed that the trustees of the will should be his son, Offley and daughters Mabel and Katie together with his grandsons Wilson and John. This final codicil to his will, of August 1934, was signed five years before his death.

John and Maria Jeffery's children and their descendants

In 1907, the year following Maria's death, John's eldest daughter Mary Mabel, married farmer's son Frederick Archer. Frederick, born in 1877, was the second child of Samuel and Eliza Archer's family of four at *Castle Hayes Park*, Hanbury, Staffordshire. At the time of Frederick's birth, *Castle Hayes* was a large farm of 440 acres and Samuel Archer employed ten farm labourers. Their eldest son Frederick attended the Collegiate School for Boys in Belper, Derbyshire where, in 1891, he was one of twenty-three boarders. On leaving school, he worked with his father on the farm.

Frederick and Mabel Archer farmed at the *Seed Farm*, Stapleford and also at *New Farm*, Toton Lane, Stapleford, Nottinghamshire near the Derbyshire border. Their two children, John and Maria's first two grandchildren, were Mabel Dorothy born on 4 August 1909 and John who was born a few years later.

Grandchildren, Dorothy and John Archer

We came across Mr. Archer on his way to the milking shed, and he unhesitatingly gave us permission to inspect his farm buildings, cattle and land until he should be at liberty.

In John Jeffery's Scrapbook I came across a newspaper cutting from 'Our Agricultural Commissioner' entitled:

Seed Farm, Stapleford Occupied by Mr. Fred Archer

The article included photographs of his Shire horses and Friesian cattle and commented:

We came across Mr. Archer on his way to the milking shed, and he unhesitatingly gave us permission to inspect his farm buildings, cattle and land until he should be at liberty. We spent a very profitable hour and a half, and found on our return to the farmhouse that Mrs. Archer had kindly thought of the inner man, and hospitably entertained us to a sumptuous tea, during which we had a pleasant chat on agricultural prospects in general and Mr. Archer's farm in particular. We believe it is characteristic of the Derbyshire farmer that, where conditions appear to be the most difficult, the more determined is he to try and overcome these difficulties. ....

It is pleasant to meet with such a genial pair as Mr. and Mrs. Archer, who are probably two of the most enthusiastic and practical agriculturalist in the district.

Mabel and Fred Archer's daughter, Mabel Dorothy, who was always known as Dorothy, followed in her Aunt Katie's footsteps and trained as a nurse in Nottingham. In 1935, four years before her grandfather's death, Dorothy married the Rev. Robert Yaxley. Robert Yaxley, four years older than Dorothy was born on 23 March 1905. He became a Canon in the Church.

Grandfather John's scrapbook also provides a newspaper cutting on his granddaughter's engagement where Dorothy was described as 'the ideal nurse'.

A Woman Looks Around

The engagement is announced of Miss Dorothy Archer, of Stapleford, near Nottingham, and the Rev. Robert Yaxley of Sutton Coldfield, near Birmingham.

It is another romance between a clergyman and a nurse, and follows rapidly upon the recent interesting wedding at Annesley Woodhouse between the Rev. Albert Rose and Miss Ellen Baker, who also was a hospital nurse.

In the case of the Rev. Robert Yaxley and Miss Dorothy Archer, however, it has not sprung from contact in work.

Although Mr. Yaxley comes from Birmingham, he is well known and has many friends in the district around his fiancé's home.

He is the only son of Mr. and Mrs. W. Yaxley, and, curiously enough, Miss Archer is an only daughter. Her parents, Mr. and Mrs. W. Archer, live at a big farm on Toton Lane, just outside Stapleford, commanding an extensive view of the countryside around. At one time it must have been an isolated spot, but building operations have brought new houses quite close to it.

The Ideal Nurse

At the moment Miss Archer is not living at home, for her work as a nurse at the Nottingham General Hospital often keeps her away for several days at a time. With her slight build and serious grey eyes and quiet demeanour she radiates an efficiency and charm which one always hopes to find in a nurse.

She has been training for two years and she assures me that she is determined not to get married until she has completed her training, although this will not be for nearly three years.

Dorothy's younger brother, Mabel and Fred Archer's son John did not marry. He was remembered by Vivian Lowe (daughter of Offley and Cissie's eldest daughter Marie) as

A lovely jolly fellow. Very good looking. He did not marry.

A Woman Looks Around

BY
J.S.H.

THE engagement is announced of Miss Dorothy Archer, of Stapleford, near Nottingham, and the Rev. Robert Yaxley, of Sutton Coldfield, near Birmingham.

It is another romance between a clergyman and a nurse, and follows rapidly upon the recent interesting wedding at Annesley Woodhouse between the Rev. Albert Rose and Miss Ellen Baker, who also was a hospital nurse.

In the case of the Rev. Robert Yaxley

Miss Dorothy Archer and the Rev. Robert Yaxley.

and Miss Dorothy Archer, however, it has not sprung from contact in work.

Although Mr. Yaxley comes from Birmingham he is well known and has many friends in the district around his fiancee's home.

He is the only son of Mr. and Mrs. W. Yaxley, and, curiously enough, Miss Archer is an only daughter. Her parents, Mr. and Mrs. W. Archer, live at a big farm on Toton Lane, just outside Stapleford, commanding an extensive view of the countryside around. At one time it must have been an isolated spot, but building operations have brought new houses quite close to it.

It is another romance between a clergyman and a nurse.......In the case of the Rev. Robert Yaxley and Miss Dorothy Archer, however, it has not sprung from contact in work.

John Jeffery's younger daughter, Katie Jane, was also a nurse. She did not marry. She continued with her nursing at the Nottingham General Hospital and lived in Nottingham on her retirement.

Her great niece, Vivian Lowe, has vivid memories of her Great Aunt Katie:

Aunt Katie was absolutely unique! I believe she helped with the wounded in World War One. Did she go to France? I don't know. As long as I can remember she lived in Nottingham, a bungalow called Killarney with a big rockery. A man lived with her too but what his role was I did not think to ask! I recall she went to the Holy Land and rode on a camel – this was before most of us were contemplating going as far as London! She left 'Killarney' and moved to a little terraced house. She dabbed paint in all colours everywhere. The doors were dabbed – the walls too – it was like being in a mad house! I recall the ceiling in the front room. It was dark blue, covered in stars.

I remember how she used to send heavily highlighted copies of TV programme schedules which she meant the family to view. She was always sending instructions. A great believer in God and a member of a Penticostal Church in Nottingham.

Engagement of John's grand-daughter, Dorothy Archer

John's only son, William Offley Jeffery, was twenty-nine when he married Sarah Anne (Cissie) Croker in 1913. By this time, Offley had largely taken over the running of the *Home Farm*, West Broughton from his father John. Cissie had been housekeeper at the farm for around two years.

Offley farming

Offley and Cissie were married in the Wesleyan Methodist Church in Uttoxeter on 20 June 1913. It is a mystery and remains a secret as to why they were married in Uttoxeter and not at Somersal where the family worshipped and also why the witnesses to the marriage were not members of the family. It is rumoured within the family that Offley was coerced into marrying Cissie. The marriage certificate states that they are both aged twenty-nine. However, Cissie, who was born in February 1881, would have been thirty-two at the time of her marriage.

Their first child was born on 20 January 1914. He was christened James Offley Wilson: James after Cissie's father, who had died in March 1913, and Wilson after Offley's mother's family. However, the name he was always known by was Wilson.

Interestingly, Wilson was not born at the *Home Farm*, West Broughton. Cissie returned to her mother's home in Whaplade for the birth and she waited for six weeks to register her son's birth. Wilson was registered on 2 March 1914 in Holbeach, Lincolnshire which would

have been close to nine months after Offley and Cissie's marriage. The birth certificate states that her son was born at the Fen, Whaplode and the father's name is Offley William Jeffery. In registering the birth, Cissie managed to get her husband's names the wrong way around.

It was my cousin Frank Jeffery who first hinted to me that the circumstances of Wilson's birth were something of a mystery, especially as the birth occurred seven months after Cissie's marriage to Offley.

In March, Cissie returned to the *Home Farm*, West Broughton with her son Wilson who was now over six weeks old. The circumstances of Wilson's birth and the stories surrounding it remain a family secret to this day. However Wilson's son, another John Jeffery, has outlined the possibilities recounting the alternative allegations:

The first possibility is, that Old John Jeffery, my great grandfather had an affair with a maid (Sarah Croker) and Wilson (my father) was the result. Offley (Old John's son) was forced to marry Sarah. This seems very likely as James Offley Wilson, my father, did not look anything like his brothers and sisters. They were all rotund and large faced and my father was small, thin and totally different facially.

This leads to the second possibility which is very strange, but is still a local story. It transpires that Lord Vernon .... had an affair with a maid, Sarah Croker, and Wilson was again the result. Offley was asked by Lord Vernon to take responsibility and in return put into Home Farm. This is also possible as it is common knowledge that the last Lord Vernon and my father looked like twins, so much in fact that he was often taken for the Lord when walking in the village. .... The locals still call me Lordy occasionally, which always cheers me up.

It is very likely that one of these stories is true because my father was hidden away in Lincolnshire for three months when born. His birth certificate gives his birth on 20 Jan. 1914 but he was not registered until 2nd. March 1914. This ties up because he always thought his birthday was in March and so did we for many years.

Wilson's youngest sister Mary confirms that her brother's birthday was always celebrated in March:

We always celebrated it (his birthday) *on the third of March. I think he was born in January but I don't know the exact date.*

ABOVE LEFT *Six children of West Broughton. seated l. to r.*
Wilson, Francis; standing l. to r. Mary, Marie, Katie, John

ABOVE RIGHT *L. to r. Mary,*
John and Marie

RIGHT *L to r. standing –*
John, Marie, Katie, seated -
Mary

One year following Wilson's birth, Offley and Cissie's first daughter, Maria Mabel, was born on 28 January 1915. Maria Mabel was always known as Marie. Her sister Katie Sarah arrived the following year on 11 April 1916 and two years later, a third daughter, Ada Mary, arrived on 5 June 1918. Ada Mary was always known as Mary. The following year, John William Armstrong arrived in 1919 and finally, Charles Francis Owen, always known as Francis was born on 18 November 1923. All of these five children were born at the *Home Farm*, West Broughton.

Although Offley had taken over the major running of the farm from before his marriage, Grandfather John continued active both on the farm and in family life whilst his grandchildren were growing up at West Broughton. John's eldest granddaughter, Marie, married the year before he died and his youngest grandson, Francis, was nearly sixteen by this time. His youngest granddaughter, Mary, retains many memories of him which she has very generously shared with me.

Mary has also told me of her parents:

My Mother came to run this farmhouse. She came from Lincolnshire – Whaplode near Spalding. Mother had to have lots of help. I believe, with the children, there were thirteen people that she had to cater for – there were young men working on the farm and young girls living-in to help in the house. Mother had a real full house. My father worked very hard. He always went to Church on a Sunday and became a local preacher. Mother often used to entertain the preacher after the service. She liked cooking – she was a good cook. I remember the killing of the pigs – the pork and the curing of the bacon. When we were little we used to break up the salt for the curing of the bacon and the hams. Mother loved to make pork-pies and sausages – she could do most things out of a pig! She also used to make butter and she did make cheese for a while.

My father was very active for his years. We had a tennis court and he used to have a go at that. He loved horses – he was very horse-minded. He used to ride around the farm on his horse.

*In the summer time he'd do a bit of shooting – he'd bring home
some rabbits for the pot. He loved sheep-farming as well. He said
he was shepherding sheep – at lambing time – from the time he
was five years old.*

Mary's father Offley Jeffery was described in his
obituary as:

Of a genial and kindly nature he would help anyone.

And:

A man whose thinking was in advance of his times.

I too have fond memories of my father's cousin Offley
of West Broughton.

Of her brother Wilson, Mary recalled:

*Wilson went to Alleynes Grammar School. He started there as
a weekly boarder before there was a bus service into Uttoxeter.
He farmed at Brocksford House Farm.*

Wilson also farmed with his father and brothers at the
Home Farm, West Broughton before farming at *Brocksford
House Farm*. I discovered the following local news item
in John Jeffery's scrapbook which dated from some time
pre 1939.

SUDBURY FARMER AND THE PARTRIDGES

'I went out with the intention of shooting snipe, when the
partridges got up and I had a go at them' said James Offley
Wilson Jeffery, a farmer at the Home Farm, Sudbury, who was
summoned for killing game without a licence.

Albert Henry Victor Holden, a chauffeur in the employ of
Captain Verelst, of Oak Cottage, Sudbury said that on December
19 he was on land at Sudbury, when he heard a shot, and then
found Jeffery, who was carrying a gun and a brace of partridges.

PC Cope said Jeffery, when interviewed admitted he 'had a go'
at the birds. Jeffery had a gun licence but no game licence.

A fine of 10s and costs of 2s 6d were imposed.

LEFT *Katie Jeffery*

RIGHT *Wedding of
Marie Jeffery and
Rowland Ball
1949. Offley is
standing right of
the bride in the
picture and
Wilson far right.
Cissie is seated on
the left.*

This is the closest I have come to discovering any
criminal activity in researching the Jeffery family
story!

Of her other brothers and sisters, Mary recalled:

*My brother John worked on this farm and later so did Francis.
John was a very good farmer. Wilson wasn't so keen on it.
Wilson could farm but John was more active in the mechanical
way. With Francis – his health was against him. He was a very
nice and most kind man. He loved the animals – he was very
good with dairy cattle and sheep. His health broke down. He
was in Queen Elizabeth's Hospital in Birmingham for seven
weeks. He had a serious operation and lost a kidney.*

*My oldest sister Marie – she was rather artistic. Marie was a
pretty good scholar and a musician. She was good at Art and
Music. Katie was more interested in running the farm and the
domestic side of life. She liked helping on the farm and being
outside and gardening – and she liked doing embroidery.*

Only one of Offley and Cissie's daughters married. Their
eldest daughter, Marie, married Rowland Ball on 7 September 1938 at All Saints' Church, Sudbury. The wedding
was reported in the *UTTOXETER ADVERTISER*.

WEDDING AT SUDBURY
Ball – Jeffery

****

Well-known farming families in the Uttoxeter area were united by a wedding at All Saints Church, Sudbury on Wednesday. The bridegroom, Mr. Rowland Ball, who is a farmer at Upper Leigh, is the second son of Mr. and Mrs. C. Ball, of Felt House, Grindon, Leek. Miss Marie Jeffery is the eldest daughter of Mr. and Mrs. Offley Jeffery, of Home Farm, West Broughton, near Uttoxeter.

The bride's father, who comes of an old Methodist family, has been prominently identified with activities throughout the Uttoxeter district, holding various offices in the Uttoxeter Circuit, and is a local preacher of long-standing. He has also been actively identified with the work of the Uttoxeter branch of the National Farmer's Union of which he has been chairman and a member of various committees.

Given away by her father the bride wore a two-piece suit of coral cloque, a brown velvet hat with a long veil, brown shoes and a shoulder spray of cream roses. She was unattended. Her mother wore black georgette embroidered with gold on which was a spray of crimson carnations, and a black hat, while the bridegroom's mother had a brown and gold ensemble, a similar spray of carnations and a hat to tone.

A reception was held at the bride's home. The honeymoon is being spent in a tour of Wales and the west of England.

Mary Jeffery

Katie and Mary were always together. Katie was the most outgoing – the most forceful. Francis was a bit of a clown. Francis did not make a go of farming. Offley and John were the farmers.

sister Katie and his niece Vivian were bridesmaids. Wilson and Dorothy had wanted his youngest sister Mary as a bridesmaid but Katie insisted she should take her place much to their displeasure.

Vivian (nee Ball) Lowe recalls:

Mary was going to be one of the bridesmaids. At the last minute, for whatever reason, Katie was bridesmaid instead. She wore red velvet – I was in white velvet with red velvet bows down the front. I had a red velvet muff. I was four years old. I remember standing in the aisle at the cathedral but not much else. Wilson was my godfather which is why I guess I was chosen. He did not get on with Katie as I recall but that would not stop her from getting what she wanted.

Wilson and Dorothy's son, another John Jeffery, was born on 14 November 1947. Wilson farmed at *Brocksford*

Marie and Rowland Ball's daughter Vivian was born on 12 November 1940 and their son, Oliver on 28 September 1949.

My sister Marjorie has vivid memories of the Jeffery family at the *Home Farm*, West Broughton as she lived with them for a period in 1944.

I knew Katie and Mary well. I got on well with Katie – she had a bit of fun. I stayed there after the Explosion (Fauld Explosion of November 1944). *John was serious – a nice man – tall and well-built. Wilson was a much slighter build – he never seemed close to the rest of the family.*

Mrs. Offley – Cissie – was very hospitable – she looked after me when I stayed there. Offley was always full of fun – he was very nice and friendly. I used to see Marie in Uttoxeter. John was farming at Flacketts Lane. When I went to stay, Katie, Mary and Francis were still at home. Katie and Mary were always together. Katie was the most outgoing – the most forceful. Francis was a bit of a clown. Francis did not make a go of farming. Offley and John were the farmers.

It was nearly seven years after Marie's marriage that her brother, Wilson, married Dorothy Ellen Smith. They married in Derby Cathedral on 5 April 1945. Wilson's

Mary was going to be one of the bridesmaids. At the last minute, for whatever reason, Katie was bridesmaid instead. She wore red velvet – I was in white velvet with red velvet bows down the front. I had a red velvet muff. I was four years old.

LEFT *L. to r. Mary, Cissie and Katie Jeffery at a wedding*

ABOVE *Offley's son John William Armstrong Jeffery*

ABOVE *Offley with his sisters, l. Katie Jane and r. Mary Mabel*

House Farm. This was one of the farms which had been purchased by his grandfather, John, many years earlier. John lives in Kent and he e-mailed telling of his family:

I joined the army at aged 16 and served for 30 years and continuing the trade as an armourer. I now work for the RAF looking after the Queen's Colour Squadron and Royal Flight at Northolt.

In 1970 I married Pauline and we have three sons, Lee, Jean-Paul and Christian, producing eight grandchildren between them.

All my sons joined the army, Jean-Paul serving in two war zones in the Balkans.

Offley and Cissie's son John increasingly took over farming the land of *Home Farm*, West Broughton in addition

Four generations. Cissie is holding her great granddaughter, Marea with Marea's mother Vivian and Marea's grandmother Marie, 1967. Photograph taken in the dining room at Home Farm, West Broughton. The photograph on the wall in the background is of John and Maria and their three children.

to that of *Fiddlers Farm* and *Flacketts Lane Farm*. Offley was seventy-six when forty-year-old John married farmer's daughter Freda Slater in the spring of 1960. They married in Somersal Chapel and none of the family was present. John and Freda lived at *Fiddlers Farm* and continued managing the land of all three farms. Their sons, John and Peter Jeffery, continue the family farming tradition and have farmed the land of all three farms since their father John died in 1985.

Only three of Offley and Cissie's six children married. Although the management of the farms was increasingly shouldered by his son John, Offley remained active within the family and local community until shortly before his death.

In January 1967, Offley and Cissie became great grandparents. Their granddaughter Vivian Ball, daughter of Marie and Rowland Ball, had married David Lowe and the first of their three daughters, Marea, was born on 5 January 1967.

In April 1967, Offley had a fall and broke his hip. He spent the last month of his life in hospital. He died on 15 May 1967.

His obituary was reported by the *UTTOXETER ADVERTISER* of 17 May and his funeral was reported the following week.

Of a genial and kindly nature he would help anyone

DEATH OF MR. W. O. JEFFERY

WELL KNOWN SUDBURY FARMER

We regret to record the death in the Derbyshire Royal Infirmary last week, where he had been a patient for nearly a month, of Mr. William Offley Jeffery (83), of Home Farm, Sudbury, a very well-known and respected farmer and cattle dealer. Of a genial and kindly nature he would help anyone. He leaves a widow, three sons, (Mr. Francis Jeffery, Home Farm; Mr. John Jeffery, Fiddlers Farm and Flacketts-lane Farm; Mr. Wilson Jeffery, Brocksford House Farm) and three daughters (Misses Mary and Katie Jeffery, Home Farm; Mrs. M. Ball, of Ashbourne). He was the son of the late Mr. John Jeffery, who farmed at Home Farm after moving from Mill Farm, Somersal. Mr. W. O. Jeffery who had a fall and broke his thigh necessitating his removal to hospital, where pneumonia set in, had lived at Home Farm since he was five years of age.

Evidence at the inquest at Derby Infirmary on Wednesday of last week showed that death was due to natural causes – broncho-pneumonia, following a fracture of the right thigh and a verdict of "Death by Misadventure" was recorded by the Derby Coroner (Mr. R. H. Cleaver).

Evidence of identification was given by a cousin, Mr. Frank Jeffery, of Uttoxeter Road, Mickleover.

The 300 acre farm is mainly dairy, but Mr. Jeffery had some arable land. He kept Friesian and Hereford herds and also sheep, being particularly fond of the latter, and, in his younger days – before the horse was supplanted by the tractor – he bred Shires. He was fond of dealing.

He was an esteemed member of the Uttoxeter National Farmers' Union, and one of his recreations was music. He had quite a good bass voice.

A staunch Methodist he had been a local preacher for 60 years and was next to the oldest on the plan. He had also been a Circuit Steward. His wife had also taken a prominent part in Methodist affairs.

Offley Jeffery's funeral was reported in the *UTTOXETER ADVERTISER* of 24 May 1967.

LATE MR. W. O. JEFFERY FUNERAL AT SOMERSAL

The funeral for Mr. William Offley Jeffery, of the Home Farm, West Broughton, Sudbury, was held at Somersal Methodist Chapel where he had been a very regular worshipper and was conducted by the Rev. K. V. Fisher of Rocester. ....

.... An address was given by Rec. Cyril Armitage (Supt. Minister) who paid a gracious tribute to Mr. Jeffery's work for the Church and community and described as a man whose thinking was in advance of his times.

The mourners were: Mr. and Mrs. Wilson Jeffery, Mr. and Mrs. John Jeffery and Mr. Francis Jeffery (sons and daughters-in-law); Mr. and Mrs. R. T. Ball and Miss Mary Jeffery (son-in-law and daughters); Mr. and Mrs. D. Lowe and Mr. Oliver Ball (grandchildren); Mrs. M. M. Archer and Miss K. J. Jeffery (sisters); Mr. F. J. Archer and Rev. Canon and Mrs. R. W. Yaxley (nephews and niece) ....

Owing to indisposition, Mrs. S. Jeffery (widow) and Miss K. S. Jeffery (daughter) were unable to attend.

Included in the large congregation, many of whom could not get into the chapel, were the following relatives ....

Once again, Cissie was absent from a family funeral.

There followed a very, very long list of family and friends who had come to pay their last respects.

Cissie survived Offley by five years. Their memorial can be found at St Peter's, Somersal Herbert, where Offley had preached for many years.

IN
LOVING MEMORY
OF
WILLIAM OFFLEY JEFFERY
OF HOME FARM WEST BROUGHTON
METHODIST LOCAL PREACHER
FOR 30 YEARS
1884-1967
ALSO HIS BELOVED WIFE
SARAH ANN
1882-1972

CONSIDER THE LILIES OF THE
FIELD

At the time of Offley's death, he was farming 300 acres. This included the land of the *Home Farm*, as a tenant on the Vernon estate, and also the adjoining land of the farms which he owned: *Brocksford House Farm*, *Fiddlers Farm* and *Flacketts Lane Farm*. Offley's son John was the farmer of the family. He had managed the *Home Farm* together with *Fiddlers* and *Flacketts Lane* farms for many years before his father's death. After his marriage, he had moved into *Fiddlers Farm*. His brother, Wilson, had farmed *Brocksford House Farm* from the time of his marriage twenty-two years before Offley's death.

In his will, Offley endeavoured to be fair to all six children. He owned three farms and decided to leave them in shared ownership. His will bequeathed *Brocksford Farm* to Wilson and John; *Flacketts Lane* to Katie and Francis and *Fiddlers Farm* to Marie and Mary. Three cottages – one each – were also bequeathed to his daughters.

Wilson, with little interest in farming, sold most of the *Brocksford Farm* to John. He retained just the house and a little land. Marie also sold her share of *Fiddlers Farm* to John. Since the youngest son Francis was not capable of managing *Flacketts Lane Farm* John therefore took it over.

The will and subsequent arrangements appear to have seriously disconcerted Katie. As an executor she blocked probate of the will. What followed was ten long years of litigation and dispute and Queen's Counsel was consulted.

Again, I initially learnt something of the difficulties created by Katie from Frank Jeffery. Frank, Offley's cousin and an accountant, had also been an executor of the will. He also spoke, as we have seen, of the 'dark secret' at the heart of the family regarding Wilson's parentage. The reason Katie gave for holding up probate for so long was her apparent view that the will had not been fair to Francis. Her real motives may have been otherwise but have died with her. More distant relatives found Katie to be charming and good company. However, within the close family, she alienated her sister Marie and both her sisters-in-law. The manner in which she tried to exercise control over her siblings, even to the extent of attempting to select John's wife, deeply offended them. Indeed, they would never join her for family gatherings.

It is perhaps sad that one should end the long story of John Jeffery this way. But it is hardly surprising that in a family so large that there should not be some dark clouds.

I would like to pay a personal tribute to John Jeffery's youngest granddaughter Mary who continues to live in the home where she was born - the *Home Farm*, West Broughton. Mary has always welcomed me warmly and been outstandingly generous in sharing with me her wealth of family memories and in so doing has made a major contribution to the writing of the Jeffery family story.

OWEN JEFFERY
1852 – 1919

An Untimely Death

Owen Jeffery, the eighth of Thomas and Mary's fifteen children was born at the Riddings on 27 May 1852. Owen was almost forty-three when he married Hester Bannister on 16 April 1895. They had two children and six grandchildren. Owen farmed at the Riddings and Bentley Fields and also purchased Stydd Hall. He died at the Riddings on 14 December 1919. Two of his grandchildren remain at the Riddings. His descendants today are in Derbyshire and Canada.

Descendants of Owen Jeffery

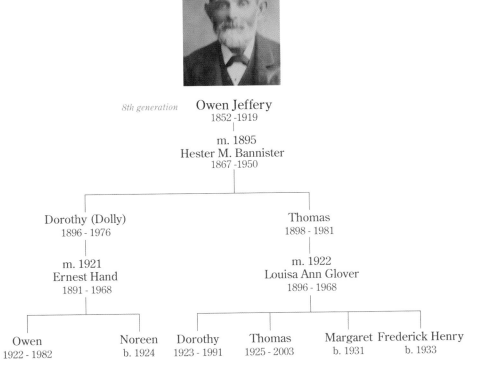

8th generation

Owen Jeffery
1852 -1919

m. 1895
Hester M. Bannister
1867 -1950

Dorothy (Dolly)
1896 - 1976

m. 1921
Ernest Hand
1891 - 1968

Thomas
1898 - 1981

m. 1922
Louisa Ann Glover
1896 - 1968

Owen
1922 - 1982

Noreen
b. 1924

Dorothy
1923 - 1991

Thomas
1925 - 2003

Margaret
b. 1931

Frederick Henry
b. 1933

Owen Jeffery 1852-1919
An Untimely Death

A successful agriculturalist and a frequent exhibitor at the Ashbourne Shire Horse Show. Of a quiet and unassuming disposition he was highly esteemed by all who knew him.

Obituary of Owen Jeffery 1939

Thomas and Mary's eighth child, Owen, born on 27 May 1852, was only twenty-three when he took over sole responsibility for farming the *Riddings*. He was the member of the family closely associated with three of the places of the Hungry Bentley heartland: the *Riddings*, *Bentley Fields* and *Stydd Hall*.

At the end of 1919 Owen died whilst in the process of purchasing *Stydd Hall* for his daughter Dolly and just before the *Riddings* was placed on the market by the Clews Estate. Owen's untimely death brought to his family and the trustees of his estate a major worry. It was left to the executors of Owen's estate to finalise the purchase of *Stydd Hall* for his daughter Dolly, and also to purchase the *Riddings*, for his son Tom. The realisation of a father's dream threatened to become a son's nightmare and the family's future was placed in jeopardy.

Owen's unmarried sisters, Elizabeth, Mary, Fanny, Clara and Ellen and his youngest brother, Arthur, were also still at the *Riddings* when their father died on 12 May 1876. The family had been joined by the children of their brother George so that Owen had become a father figure to three-year-old Mary Ellen and 'Little Willie' aged two.

Five years later the family was still together. The 1881 census recorded Owen's mother, Mary, as the head of the household and his sisters Mary and Clara, his brother Arthur and niece and nephew Mary Ellen and William at home. His sisters Ellen and Fanny were visiting his brother John and family at *Somersal Mill* and his sister Elizabeth was working away from home in a farming household near Duffield, Derbyshire.

Ten years later, the situation had changed. Owen's mother Mary was now seventy-three and the 1891 census showed Owen as the head of the household. All of his sisters, with the exception of the youngest, Ellen, had left home and his niece and nephew, Mary Ellen (18) and William (16) were growing up. His sister Fanny at this time was living with their married sister Clara and family. Both censuses record that there were still a

ABOVE *Owen Jeffery*

RIGHT *Owen Jeffery at Bentley Fields*

ABOVE *Owen haymaking at Bentley Fields*

number of both farm and household servants living-in at the *Riddings*.

Nineteen years after his father's death Owen married. He was almost forty-three when he married twenty-eight-year-old farmer's daughter, Hester Mary Bannister, on 16 April 1895 at the Zion Chapel in Ashbourne. His sister, Fanny and Hester's brother, Isaac, were witnesses to the wedding. On his marriage, he and Hester moved to live at neighbouring *Bentley Fields* farm and Owen farmed the 110 acres of *Riddings* land together with the adjoining 137 acres of *Bentley Fields*.

When Owen and Hester moved to *Bentley Fields* his seventy-seven-year-old mother Mary remained at the *Riddings*. With her, in 1901, were Owen's unmarried sister, Fanny and, his now widowed sister, Mary Spencer (see later) with her eleven-year-old son, Percy Spencer. His niece, Mary Ellen was staying with his elder sister Margaret at Shardlow.

Owen and Hester gave Mary at the *Riddings* two further grandchildren. Dorothy was born in 1 May 1896 and Thomas on 12 December 1898. They were always known in the family as Dolly and Tom and spent their early years at *Bentley Fields*.

The 1901 census shows Owen and Hester with four-year-old Dorothy and two-year-old Thomas living at *Bentley Fields*. Also at this time there were three farm workers living in, twenty-two-year-old waggoner Herbert Stone together with John Jeffery (20) and George Jeffery (17).

John and George Jeffery were the sons of Owen's cousin Thomas of *Bentley Cottage*. Thomas's father, William, was a younger brother of Thomas the 'Vile' (See THE PREDECESSORS). Additionally, the two young Frost sisters, Mary, 17 and Maud, 14, were general indoor domestic servants.

Dolly with her dolly c.1899

Owen's mother, Mary, was eighty-eight when she died on 17 February 1906. Her grandchildren, Dolly and Tom, were nine and seven. Owen and Hester with Dolly and Tom remained at *Bentley Fields* until 1914 when Owen's nephew, Percy Spencer, took over the farm and Owen returned with his family to the *Riddings*. Owen had farmed the land of both *Bentley Fields* and the *Riddings* for nearly twenty years.

During the early years of the twentieth century, Tom Jeffery and his cousins Percy Spencer and Jeff and Ernest Hellaby, like many of the family both before and since, attended Queen Elizabeth's Grammar School in Ashbourne. Tom's school reports, for the years 1911 to 1913 have survived in the archives and it is interesting to note that his first report in December 1911 revealed that he had made a first class start with his Latin. In the term ending 31 July 1912, his form master reported:

He has worked well and has made great strides during the year.
He is careless and often lazy over his music practice which seems
a pity when he seems fond of it. Nothing good is gained without
trouble.

It is of interest to note that in later years, it was his younger daughter Margaret who inherited his love of music although she was clearly more dedicated to her

ABOVE *Owen and Hester with Dolly and Tom c.1905*

RIGHT *Dolly at the village school- middle row, fifth from the left*

practising. Margaret today is the organist at St John's Church, Alkmonton.

Additionally, it is noteworthy that Tom's school reports reveal his interest in geography. In later years, it would be his elder daughter Dorothy who studied geography at university.

In Tom's final report for July 1913, his Headmaster, Mr William J. Butcher, wrote that:

ABOVE *Dolly at school – back row, extreme right*

ABOVE *Queen Elizabeth's School, Ashbourne from a print in the possession of Owen's granddaughter, Noreen Haselwood*

ABOVE *Dolly at school – back row, fourth from the left*

He has done well during his stay here. He has been industrious and obedient and his conduct has been good. We are sorry to lose him and wish him every success in the future.

Tom left school in the summer of 1913 to help his father Owen on the farm. He was not yet fifteen when, a year later, World War 1 broke out.

Dolly meanwhile, had attended a private school for young ladies in Ashbourne – Langley House School.

Towards the end of his life, Owen was evidently very interested in researching his Jeffery family history as evidenced by a request he made to the rector of Longford Church in the summer of 1913. A letter in the family archives, from the rector, dated 23 July 1913, records the following:

RIGHT *Dolly at Bentley Fields aged about fifteen*

Dear Mr Jeffery,

I am sorry for the delay. I have been collecting these names for some years, and the old registers are very difficult to make out. I don't think the list is a perfect one and if you wish any of the names followed up I will try and do it, provided you give me dates to guide me. You can also see the registers here by appointment.

I don't think there are entries before 1738, but the registers are carelessly kept in some years.

In some haste
I am yours truly,

J. Clewes Wilson

Owen's eldest granddaughter, Dorothy Jeffery, would follow up his interest many years later, as would his great niece Valerie!

World War 1 was to impact directly on Owen's family. His son Tom was eighteen in December 1916 and shortly afterwards he joined the Royal Navy. He returned safely and resumed his work in taking increased responsibility for the farm as Owen's health declined.

The end of the War, however, heralded a time of great social change. It was marked most particularly in the farming world by the break up of the landed estates. This created opportunities for tenant farmers to purchase their own farms and become owner occupiers. In 1919, Owen saw an opportunity to fulfil one of his long-held dreams when *Stydd Hall* came on the market. Shortly after his death, early in 1920, the Bentley Estate, owned by the Clews family, was broken up and the *Riddings* came on the market. It was the coincidental purchases of a father's dream and a son's imperative, so close to Owen's demise, that caused the family and trustees so much distress.

The land of *Stydd Hall* borders that of the *Riddings* and it had been the old home of his mother Mary nee Robinson Jeffery. Indeed, Robinsons had farmed at *Stydd* over a number of generations and there were many family links between Jefferys, Poysers and Robinsons with *Stydd Hall* throughout the nineteenth and twentieth centuries. These family links included the marriage of Richard

Robinson of *Stydd Hall* to Mary Jeffery of *Bentley Cottage Farm* in 1852; the marriage of Samuel Robinson of *Stydd Hall* to Ellen Poyser of Ellastone and schoolmistress at Yeaveley, in 1864 and even earlier the marriage of Owen's own parents, Mary Robinson and Thomas Jeffery in 1843. (See PART TWO: THE PREDECESSORS)

Stydd Hall has captured the imagination of a number of the great grandchildren of Thomas and Mary including myself. In researching the Jeffery family history for this book, I have endeavoured to capture the memories of all of those surviving great grandchildren. One of these is Mary Jeffery of the *Home Farm*, West Broughton, who is the granddaughter of Owen's brother, John. Mary recalled:

Stydd Hall was the home of our great grandmother wasn't it Valerie? You see, they would be neighbours (to the Riddings) *wouldn't they? I can remember visiting there as a child with my parents.* (Offley and Cissie Jeffery). *I can remember one visit, when Dolly and Ernest were there, and it was bluebell time and I had on a blue velvet dress with pearl buttons. I remember some very impressive steps, and there were gravestones. I would love to see Stydd Hall again.*

Stydd Hall

I can remember one visit, when Dolly and Ernest were there, and it was bluebell time and I had on a blue velvet dress with pearl buttons.

Stydd Hall is located in open fields down a lane. The lane today is no more than a rough and frequently muddy track. It is even more remote and isolated than the *Riddings*. Its setting is atmospheric: dramatic under a blue sky but creating a somewhat eerie feel under grey and leaden skies. It is a house full of history dating back to the time of Richard the Lionheart. This old Manor Hall of Yeaveley, was once the hub of village life. The Hall was originally a fortified medieval preceptory of the Knight's Hospitallers, founded in 1189 by the de Ferrers family. The brick and stone farmhouse, standing on the medieval stone foundations, is mainly Elizabethan or Jacobean in date with alterations carried out in the nineteenth and twentieth centuries. (See PART ONE: THE PLACES).

Owen had been in the process of purchasing *Stydd Hall* before he died. He was buying it for his daughter with a view to Dolly and her future husband, Ernest Hand, settling there when they married. Sadly, Owen died before the final arrangement for purchase had been completed and consequently it was his wife Hester and young son Tom, together with the trustees of Owen's estate, who included William Charles Jeffery, the son of his late older brother William, who were left with 'unfinished business'.

During the summer of 1919, Owen's health declined and his sister Ellen, who was now married and living with her husband William Hellaby and sons at neighbouring *Bentley Hall*, alerted her brothers in America to their brother's failing health. It is only Arthur's letters in response to Ellen's which have survived. (See PART THREE: THE PIONEERS). Arthur, *'the faithful little brother'*, in addition to writing to Owen in the months before his death, visited him before he died. Both he and his wife Margaret attended Owen's funeral.

Christmas 1919 would not be the happiest for those at the *Riddings* and *Bentley Fields* and others of this close-knit extended family. Owen died on 14 December 1919. His daughter, Dolly, was twenty-three. Two days before his father's death, his son Tom had reached his twenty-first birthday. Tom, like his father Owen before him, was to take over at the *Riddings* in his early twenties.

Owen was buried at Alkmonton on 17 December. His funeral was attended by a very large gathering of family and friends when ….

One of the largest gatherings seen in the village assembled to pay a last tribute.

Of a quiet and unassuming disposition, he was highly esteemed by all who knew him and his activities in the district will be much missed.

His death was reported in the *UTTOXETER ADVERTISER* under the heading:

DEATH OF MR OWEN JEFFERY
WELL KNOWN CUBLEY FARMER

and more fully in the local Ashbourne paper which reported:

DEATH OF MR OWEN JEFFERY

It is with deep regret we announce the death of Mr Owen Jeffery of the Riddings, Hungry Bentley, Derby, which took place at his residence on Sunday last. For some time past, Mr Jeffery had been in failing health, but notwithstanding his malady he managed to keep getting about up to a short time ago, when he was ultimately compelled to keep to his bed, and his illness increasing in severity, he passed away peacefully as stated. The late Mr Jeffery, who was 67 years of age, was a member of a family which had occupied that farm for about 200 years, having occupied it himself for the past 30 years. Of a quiet and unassuming disposition, he was highly esteemed by all who knew him and his activities in the district will be much missed. He was a trustee and prominent supporter of the Yeaveley Congregational Chapel, which he attended most regularly in all weathers and which will feel his loss most keenly. Another institution which will miss his kindly help and presence is the Earl Ferrers Lodge of Oddfellows, of which he was also trustee and was for many years a popular figure at the annual club feast. He was a successful agriculturalist and a frequent exhibitor at the Ashbourne Shire Horse Show. In Ashbourne and neighbourhood he was widely respected, and the deepest sympathy is extended to Mrs Jeffery and family and other bereaved relatives.

The funeral took place at Alkmonton on Wednesday, when one of the largest gatherings seen in the village assembled to pay a last tribute to the deceased. Service was first held in Yeaveley Chapel, conducted by the Rev. A. G. Bradford, Congregational minister, Ashbourne, who in the course of a few appropriate remarks, paid a high tribute to the memory of the deceased. The latter's favourite hymn, 'Jesu, lover of my soul' was sung and later the lengthy cortege proceeded to Alkmonton Church where a short service was conducted by the Rev. Dr. Dearden, and the hymns 'Peace, perfect peace' and 'Jesu, lover of my soul' were sung. The committal rites at the graveside were performed by the Rev Dr. Dearden, in the presence of a very large company. The family mourners were Mrs Jeffery (widow) (Hester), Mr T. Jeffery (son) (Tom), Miss D. Jeffery (daughter) (Dolly), Mr John Jeffery (brother), Mr Offley Jeffery (nephew), Mrs Spencer (sister) (Mary), Mr and Mrs P. Spencer (Percy and Mabel), Miss F. Jeffery (sister) (Fanny), Miss G. Jeffery, Miss E. Jeffery, Mrs W. Jeffery, Mr and Mrs W. Jeffery (Somersal) (William and Hannah), Mr and Mrs A. Jeffery (Arthur and Margaret from America), Mr and Mrs F. Jeffery, Mrs Prince, Mr and Mrs Tipper, Mrs Cook (sister, Borrowash) (Clara), Mr W. Cook (Milton), Mr J. Cook (Stretton), Mrs Holbrook (sister) (Elizabeth), Mr J. T. Holbrook, Mrs Poyser (sister) (Margaret), Miss Poyser, Mr F. Poyser (Shardlow), Mr O. Poyser (Somersal), Mr W. Poyser (Hemington), Mr T. Poyser (Market Dreighton), Mr Chas. Poyser (Sutton on the Hill), Mr F. Hunt (Derby), Mr J. Jeffery, and Mr and Mrs. H. Hellaby; Mr and Mrs R. Hellaby

Amongst the large company present were representatives of the Earl Ferrers Lodge of Oddfellows.

The names of a very great number of friends who attended the funeral were listed as were the bearers of the coffin, sons of his sisters and brother, namely:

The bearers were four nephews of the deceased: Messrs. Owen Poyser, William Jeffery (Somersal), Owen Jeffery (Sudbury) and W. Cook (Milton).

The names of his sister and brother-in-law, Ellen and William Hellaby and their young sons appear to have been omitted from the list above. This could have been because they were anxious to return to *Bentley Hall* where the family had been invited after the service and therefore their names were not recorded when the mourners left the church. The details do, however, include a very long list of the wreaths which were given, with some very touching messages, including from the *Bentley Hall* family where, in addition to Ellen and William Hellaby and the boys, Ellen's sister, Fanny, and her widowed sister, Elizabeth Holbrook, were also living.

The floral tributes were very beautiful and included: To my dear husband from his sorrowing wife, and children Tom and Dolly; in loving memory from his brother John and Mabel and Katie; to dear Owen, with love and deep grief from Sisters Fanny and Lizzie (Bentley Hall): to dear Owen with love and deepest sympathy from Sister Polly, (Mary) Percy and Mabel (Bentley Fields); to dear Owen with love and sympathy from Nellie, Will and the boys (Bentley Hall); to dear Owen with love and deep sympathy from Arthur, Clara and family (Borrowash); in ever

loving memory from all at Shardlow; to dear Uncle Owen from Mary Ellen, Charlie and the boys; in loving remembrance of dear Uncle Owen with love and deep grief from Offley and Cissie and family (West Broughton).

And there were many, many more from family and friends including one from:

In loving remembrance of a dear old Sunday School teacher from the teachers and scholars at Yeaveley Chapel.

Owen had clearly been much loved within the family and very highly regarded within the local community.

❦

The New Year of 1920 was a difficult one for the family at the *Riddings* as they adjusted to the loss of a much loved husband and father. The position was not made any easier for the family by the difficulties created by the purchase of *Stydd Hall*. It fell to Owen's executors to complete the purchase. Shortly afterwards, when the Clews family sold the Bentley Estate, in April 1920, the *Riddings* was bought privately by Owen's executors.

However, on 16 February 1921, the family were delighted to celebrate Dolly's marriage to Ernest Hand. The reception was held at the home of Dolly's Aunt Ellen and Uncle William Hellaby of *Bentley Hall* and the young couple then moved into *Stydd Hall*.

Bridal group at Bentley Hall. The bride Dorothy Jeffery and bridegroom Ernest Hand. On bride's side: seated far right, mother, Hester Jeffery; standing, brother, Thomas Jeffery; small bridesmaid, right: Marie Jeffery, daughter of Offley and Cissie Jeffery of West Broughton

The local Ashbourne paper reported the wedding.

Wedding of Dolly and Ernest
Hand – full group

WEDDING AT ALKMONTON
****

On Wednesday, the 16th inst., the pretty little village church of Alkmonton was the scene of a most interesting wedding, the contracting parties being Mr Ernest Hugo Hand, second son of the late Mr and Mrs Henry Hand of Tissington and nephew of Mrs Chadfield of Yeaveley House, Yeaveley, and Miss Dorothy Mary Jeffery, only daughter of the late Mr Owen Jeffery and Mrs Jeffery of the 'Riddings', Bentley.

The bride was dressed in ivory satin charmeuse, and wore a wreath of orange blossom and white heather with an embroidered veil lent by her mother. She carried a shower bouquet of carnations and lilies of the valley, the gift of the bridegroom, and was attended by four bridesmaids, Miss Beatrice Glover (cousin of the bride), Miss Marjorie Hand (sister of the bridegroom), Miss Marie Jeffery (cousin of the bride) and Miss Margaret Hand (niece of the bridegroom). The two elder bridesmaids wore dresses of mauve silk aeolienne de chine and black lace hats daintily trimmed with mauve. They also wore gold brooches, the gift of the bridegroom and carried bouquets of pink carnations. The two small attendants looked sweetly pretty in dresses of shell-pink crepe de chine, carrying baskets of pink flowers and maiden-hair fern and wearing pearl necklaces, the gift of the bridegroom. In place of the orthodox hats they wore wreaths of silver leaves.

The bride was given away by her only brother, Mr. T. Jeffery, and the duties of groomsman were most ably carried out by Mr Harry Chadfield of Yeaveley House.

The strains of the Bridal March (Lohengrin) accompanied the bride's entry into the church, the service being choral and conducted by the Rev. Dr. Dearden, vicar of the parish. The two hymns 'Lead us Heavenly Father' and 'Thine for ever God of love' were sung and Mendelssohn's Wedding March was played as the happy couple left the edifice – Mrs. Dearden officiating at the organ.

The church was well filled with friends and well wishers of the bride and bridegroom, and after the ceremony the guests were conveyed to Bentley Hall (kindly lent for the occasion by Mr and Mrs W. Hellaby, uncle and aunt of the bride) where the reception was held by the bride's mother, the guests numbering about 150. During the afternoon, the happy couple left from Derby en route for Eastbourne, where the honeymoon is being spent, amid showers of confetti and rice. The bride's travelling costume was of navy blue gabardine and black hat underlined with aquamarine silk.

Following this report was a very long list of the wedding gifts from the guests.

Ernest Hand was one of the ten children of Henry and Mary Hand of *Overfield Farm*, Tissington, Derbyshire where many generations of his Hand ancestors had farmed since 1650. Ernest had two brothers and seven sisters. Sadly, his younger brother, Henry, died on 23 March 1921 aged only twenty-seven. It is Henry's son, Henry Hand, who has recalled for me his childhood memories of visiting his cousins at both *Stydd Hall* and *Shirley Mill*, where Dolly and Ernest farmed.

On one of my own recent visits to Mary Jeffery at West Broughton she recalled her memories of Dolly and Ernest's wedding:

There's a picture around somewhere of when cousin Dolly and Ernest Hand married. They had the wedding (reception) *at Bentley Hall. Marie, my oldest sister was a bridesmaid. It should have been Katie, but she made a fuss and didn't want to*

*do it. The picture was taken outside Bentley Hall on their Wedding Day. There was another small bridesmaid from the Hand family. My parents (*Offley and Cissie) *went to the wedding.*

Dolly and Ernest moved into *Stydd Hall* on return from their honeymoon. Their son Owen, was born there on 23 March 1922 and their daughter Noreen on 16 February 1924.

The year following Dolly's marriage to Ernest Hand, her brother Tom married Louisa Glover of Yeaveley on 6 June 1922.

The wedding was reported in the *ASHBOURNE TELE-GRAPH* of Friday, 16 June 1922.

LOCAL WEDDINGS
JEFFERY-GLOVER

Considerable interest was evinced in the marriage which took place at Holy Trinity Church, Yeaveley, on the 6th inst. of Miss Louisa Ann Glover, second daughter of Mr and Mrs W. H. Glover of Malt House, Yeaveley, and Mr Thomas Jeffery, only son of the late Mr Owen Jeffery and Mrs Jeffery of the Riddings, Hungry Bentley. The ceremony was performed by the Rev. Dr. Dearden and the bride, who was given away by her father, wore a handsome dress of satin charmeuse with ninon and silver panels with orange blossom at waist, and also a veil with wreath of orange blossom and white heather. Her bouquet was composed of lilies, roses, lilies of the valley and maiden-hair fern. She was attended by four maids, Miss J. Glover (sister), Miss C. Jeffery (cousin of the bridegroom), Miss M. Glover and Miss J. Glover (nieces of the bride). The elder bridesmaids wore primrose crepe de chine, with waist of primroses and blue rosebuds, with black hats with primrose coloured flowers. Their bouquets were composed of sweet peas and roses, and they wore gold brooches the gifts of the bridegroom. The younger bridesmaids were attired in turquoise blue crepe de chine, with wreaths to match forming their head covering, and they carried baskets of cream roses and sweet peas, and wore silver brooches, the gifts of the bridegroom. The duties of best man were ably discharged by Mr. J. Hellaby (my father). The service was choral, Mrs Langford, being the efficient organist. Later the bride and bridegroom left for Scarborough for their honeymoon.

Wedding of Thomas Jeffery to Louisa Glover

ABOVE *Louisa (nee Glover) Jeffery*

LEFT *Bridal group at Tom and Louie's wedding. On the bridegroom's side: Tom's mother, Hester; Cousin Jeffery Hellaby*

There followed, a long list of the

Numerous handsome presents of which the happy couple were the recipients.

Tom and Louie's four children, Dorothy, Thomas, Margaret and Frederick were all born at the *Riddings* with the two elder children quite close in age to their cousins Owen and Noreen at *Stydd Hall*.

After Owen's death, his executors had been required to complete the purchase of *Stydd Hall*, which had been left in trust to his children and their descendants. This requirement had not placed Tom in an easy position, at the start of his married life, when he was endeavouring to build his own farming career at the *Riddings*. *Stydd Hall* was threatening to become something of an albatross around his neck. It was some years before the situation was resolved and *Stydd Hall* remains in Jeffery hands to this day.

Owen's grandson Owen and granddaughter Noreen spent their early childhood at *Stydd Hall* and their cousin Henry Hand would regularly come to stay with them.

ABOVE *Dolly and Ernest's son, Owen, at Stydd Hall c.1923*

Henry has recalled his memories below.

Some childhood memories of Stydd Hall

These are of visits there, courtesy of Auntie Dolly and Uncle Ernest, with my mother Molly, nee Edge, from our home at Ashbourne, during 1923-26, when I was just 2–5 years old. My father, Henry Hand, younger brother of Uncle Ernest, had died in 1921, four months before my birth.

Even then I was very sensitive to the distinctive history of Stydd, its remoteness, seclusion, and not least, its antiquities. I was afraid to go to bed alone, in the room directly above the front door, and likened the two circular panes of the window to 'Owl's Eyes'! Indeed, to me, nightly hooting of the owls was very scary and, to a lesser extent, the plethora of cuckoo calls by day.

I remember the ivy-covered Chapel ruin, then supported by large timbers; also the font with moss therein.

The moat (or was it a stew-pond?) in the wood above the Chapel had masses of primroses on its banks. From this same wood, I remember Uncle Ernest bringing in mistletoe and holly one Christmas.

Then there was a field known as Nuns Croft, the exact location of which I'm uncertain.

Across two (?) fields lay the Jeffery's farm, The Riddings, where Tom and Louie Jeffery lived. I have vivid memories of walking there from Stydd one summer evening, with Mother, Auntie Dolly, Uncle Ernest and Owen, and returning by the light of a lantern.

Dolly with her daughter Noreen c.1925

Within sight of Stydd Hall, towards Yeaveley, lay The Edishes, farmed by my Uncle Tom and Auntie Ethel Brassington, where I was to stay later on a couple of occasions. When Cousin Owen (Dolly and Ernest's son) became of school age, he had to walk from Stydd Hall, via The Edishes, to Yeaveley School, quite a way for his tender years.

I can recall riding in Uncle Ernest's milk cart with churns for collection by Nestles from a stand at the end of the lane on Darley Moor.

An unforgettable experience was falling into the midden in front of the cowsheds! Then being swilled off by the backyard pump by Auntie Dolly! Mind you, she was her usual gentle, understanding, warm-hearted self, an angel on this Earth if ever there was one.

Finally, I recall the smell of the oil lamps being lit in the evenings and that of the linoleum covering the stairs.

Around 1929, when Henry Hand's cousins Owen and Noreen were seven and five, Dolly and Ernest and their family moved from the beautiful, but very remote, *Stydd Hall* to farm at *Shirley Mill*. *Stydd Hall* meanwhile was farmed by tenant farmers, as it continues to be to this day. Henry recalls his memories of visiting the family at *Shirley Mill*.

Noreen at Stydd Hall c.1927

Memories of Shirley Mill

These are of wonderful times I spent there, with Uncle Ernest, Auntie Dolly, Owen and Noreen, during the 1930s and early 1940s after their move from Stydd Hall at the end of the 1920s.

Shirley Mill was an idyllically situated farmhouse and farm belonging to the Osmaston Manor Estate, beside the country road between the villages of Rodsley and Shirley. The Mill itself was no longer working although the building and wheel were partially intact although they were demolished later. It should have been renovated and preserved.

Through the adjacent meadows ran a sparkling brook which crossed the road until it was later bridged. It also fed the Mill dam at the rear of the house. Trout and eels were in it aplenty, and Owen and I once caught numerous lampreys, which we mistakenly transferred to the still waters of the dam. A couple of the village lads were dab hands at tickling the trout, which sometimes came out as eels!

The large Mill dam was the haunt of water-hens, coots, swans, wild geese and herons; and there were fish therein, including perch, which we caught on hand lines while fishing from the branches of alder trees! Auntie Dolly cooked the tasty perch for us. Owen made a diving board out of a plank, from which we had great fun diving into the deep end of the dam during the summer holidays. He also made rafts out of empty old drums etc., aboard which we sailed as pirates!

We once 'marooned' Noreen and Auntie Dolly's maid, Dorothy Warner, on one of the two islands in the dam we called Coot Island, the other being Swan Island. Needless to say we got into trouble for this as the girls were upset!

Auntie Dolly had chickens in coops near the dam and in the lower meadow, which she visited mornings and evenings, usually in her wellingtons.

I remember how well Aunty Dolly always fed us: including her famous cream-covered sherry trifles! She held open house for all and sundry, a more generous, warm-hearted, loving person I can't imagine. She once told me I was more like a son to her than a nephew, which thrilled me no end!

Auntie Dolly's mother, Owen Jeffery's wife Hester, was a lovely lady like her daughter and she was often at the Mill during the times I stayed there.

Shirley Mill

After Owen and Noreen left Shirley Village School, they went to Ashbourne Grammar, cycling to the main road to catch the bus, leaving their bikes at a Miss Derbyshire's house at the lane-end.

I liked to go to the farmyard, so well managed by Uncle Ernest, to see the animals, stables, cowsheds etc. At milking times, I liked to watch Uncle Ernest and his lads hand-milking the cows, when I was sometimes allowed to try my own hand.

In the fields at Harvest time we lunched on bread, cheese and homemade buns, slaking our thirst with Auntie Dolly's famous 'Masons' which was a non-alcoholic herb beer, kept cool in the hedge bottom.

Then there were those pleasant summer walks through the neighbouring Osmaston Manor woods.

Christmases at Shirley Mill were wonderful too. There was the children's party with invitations to the Spencers at Bentley Fields, and also to our relations at Church Farm and Gravelly Bank Farm at Yeaveley.

I remember one winter at the Mill when the dam froze over and it was sufficient to allow sliding and skating. I had learnt to skate on Ashbourne Fishpond so was able to demonstrate my skill on the dam!

I am sure I have many more memories of those never-to-be-forgotten times, but these must suffice.

Henry Hand would regularly also spend part of his summer holidays with his cousins Owen and Noreen when his Aunty Dolly took them for sea-side holidays to Sheringham, Norfolk, whilst his Uncle Ernest was busy with the harvest.

Boating above the Dam at Shirley Mill

Whilst Dolly and Ernest's family were growing up at *Stydd Hall* and *Shirley Mill*, Tom and Louie's family of four were also growing up at the *Riddings*. Their first children were Dorothy, born on 28 February 1923 and Thomas on 12 May 1925. Later, Margaret was born on 26 September 1931 and Frederick on 21 May 1933.

In the summer of 1928 Dolly and Tom's first cousin, John Arthur (Art) Jeffery with his wife Myra and their younger son John, visited the *Riddings*. Art was the only son of Owen's eldest brother Thomas who had died in California in 1927.

TOP RIGHT *Dolly with Noreen and Owen at Sheringham*

ABOVE *Cousins Noreen, Owen and Henry Hand on the beach at Sheringham*

BELOW *John Arthur Jeffery with his son John Arthur visiting the Riddings in 1928. L. to r. Tom, Louie and Hester Jeffery, William Hellaby (husband of Ellen Jeffery), John Arthur Jnr. and John Arthur Jeffery. Photo taken by Myra and loaned by John Arthur the third of California*

Dolly with son Owen and daughter Noreen at Sheringham

ABOVE LEFT *The Riddings in 1928*

ABOVE RIGHT *Tom and Louie's eldest daughter, Dorothy Jeffery*

LEFT *Tom and Louie's younger children, Margaret and Fred Jeffery at the Riddings*

I have many happy memories of my own childhood visits to the *Riddings* to visit my cousins. My father, Jeffery Hellaby, remained very close to his cousins Dolly and Tom and had a great love of his mother's old home of the *Riddings*.

Dorothy and her brother Tom, as their father had before them, went to Ashbourne Grammar School. Dorothy studied at Nottingham University and then went into teaching. She eventually became Dean of Women Students at the Teachers' Training College which is now a part of the University of Derby.

All of Owen and Hester's grandchildren knew their grandmother well and it is clear, when they recall their memories of her today, that she was much loved. She was also highly regarded within the wider family and Mary Jeffery at the *Home Farm*, West Broughton recalls:

I thought Auntie Hetty was a very nice lady. She was always happy-looking.

BELOW *Owen Hand, Owen Jeffery's grandson, in the Royal Air Force in the 1940s. Photo given to Owen Hand's American cousins in California*

Hester survived Owen by over thirty years. She died at the *Riddings* on 18 July 1950 and her death was reported in the *ASHBOURNE NEWS* of 27 July.

ABOVE *Hester with Ernest and Dolly Hand at an Agricultural Show*

LATE MRS. H. M. JEFFERY
Of the Riddings, Hungry Bentley

The funeral took place at Alkmonton Church on Friday, of Mrs. H. M. Jeffery, of the Riddings, Hungry Bentley.

Mrs. Jeffery, who was the widow of Mr. Owen Jeffery, was 83 years of age and her death occurred at her home on July 18th, after a short illness. She had lived in the parish of Hungry Bentley for fifty-five years.

The service at the church was conducted by the Rev. J. Naish. The organist was Miss Eley and the hymns 'Jesu, lover of my soul' and 'Peace, perfect peace'.

The coffin was of oak, with brass fittings and bore the inscription, 'Hester M. Jeffery: died July 18th, 1950; aged 83 years.'

The bearers were four of her nephews, Messrs. Ernest Hellaby, Harold Spencer, Jeffery Spencer and John Jeffery.

Family mourners: Mr. T. Jeffery (son) (Tom), Mrs. Hand (daughter) (Dolly), Mrs. Jeffery (daughter-in-law) (Louie), Mr. Hand (son-in-law) (Ernest), Mr. O. H. Hand (Owen), Mr. T. Jeffery (Tom), Mr. F. Jeffery (Fred), (grandsons), N. H. Hand (Noreen), D. M. Jeffery (Dorothy), M. A. Jeffery (Margaret) and Mrs. O. Hand (granddaughters). J. Hellaby (my father), Mrs. E. Hellaby, Mrs. H. Spencer, Mr W. Jeffery, Mrs. E. Tipper, Mr. and Mrs. Offley Jeffery, Miss K. Jeffery, Mr. C. Ball, Mr. and Mrs. O. Jeffery, Mrs. F. Jeffery, Mr. J. Cook, Mr. and Mrs. T. Dale.

Many more family and friends were listed as present in the church and contributed many wreaths.

The summer following her grandmother's death, Dorothy Jeffery left for America on a teaching exchange.

During the year 1951-52, whilst teaching at Niagara Falls, Dorothy was able to visit many Jeffery American cousins. She was the first Jeffery in the twentieth century to return the visits of the transatlantic members of the family.

TOP *Owen and Hester's granddaughter Noreen, 2009*

ABOVE *Owen and Hester's grandson Fred, 2008*

The following appeared in the *ASHBOURNE TELE-GRAPH* in August 1951.

AMERICAN EXCHANGE

****

ASHBOURNE FORMER PUPIL'S VISIT

A former pupil of Queen Elizabeth's Grammar School, Ashbourne, Miss Dorothy M. Jeffery will leave for America on Thursday week.

Miss Jeffery, after leaving Queen Elizabeth's, studied at University College, Nottingham, where she gained a B.Sc. Honours degree in Geography and her teaching diploma in Education.

Since 1948, she has been teaching Geography at Parkfield Cedars School, Derby and will be going to America under the Britain-United States scheme for the exchange of school teachers.

Miss Jeffery will exchange her place at Parkfield Cedars with Miss Lucy Massimillian, who is a teacher of Social Studies at Niagara Falls High School, where Miss Jeffery will remain for a year.

My own schoolgirl recollections of visiting the *Riddings* with my parents, on Dorothy's return at the end of the summer of 1952, remain crystal clear. I remember becoming absorbed as I listened to the stories of some of her experiences meeting our American cousins, the descendants of four of our grandmother's brothers. Years later, Dorothy gave me contact details of our American Jeffery cousins, which enabled me to visit many of them myself during our own educational exchange. Indeed, it is to Dorothy Jeffery of the *Riddings* that I owe much of my own inspiration and desire to discover more about the Jefferys and eventually to record their history.

MARY JEFFERY
1853 – 1936

The Dowager of Bentley Fields

Mary Jeffery, the ninth of Thomas and Mary's fifteen children was born at the Riddings on 18 September 1853. She married Herbert Spencer on 10 October 1888 and their only child Percival was born one year later. Mary was a widow from May 1891 until her death on 7 May 1936. The Riddings was her home for over fifty years and Bentley Fields, which remains the home of her great grandson, was her home for the last twenty-two years of her life. Mary's descendants are in Derbyshire and New Zealand.

Descendants of Mary Jeffery

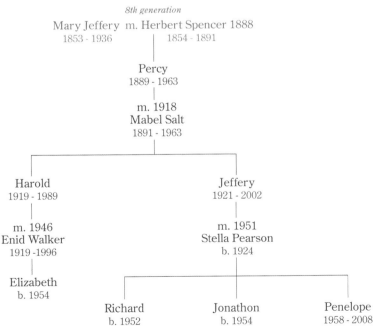

8th generation

Mary Jeffery m. Herbert Spencer 1888
1853 - 1936   1854 - 1891

Percy
1889 - 1963

m. 1918
Mabel Salt
1891 - 1963

Harold
1919 - 1989

m. 1946
Enid Walker
1919 -1996

Elizabeth
b. 1954

Jeffery
1921 - 2002

m. 1951
Stella Pearson
b. 1924

Richard
b. 1952

Jonathon
b. 1954

Penelope
1958 - 2008

Mary Jeffery 1853-1936
The Dowager of Bentley Fields

An active and familiar figure in the district, her willing help in all the movements for the welfare of the village are well known.

Obituary of Mary nee Jeffery, Spencer 1936

Bentley Fields was Mary's home throughout her later years. It was the home she made for her son Percy when, in 1914 he took over the farm from her brother Owen. When, four years later, Percy brought his bride home to *Bentley Fields*, Mary was the well established mistress of the house and somewhat loath to hand over the reins. Family stories of her high-handed ways have become legendary.

Mary, known within the family as Polly, was born at the *Riddings* on 18 September 1853. She was Thomas and Mary's ninth child and born into a family of two sisters and six brothers. She was just eighteen months old when her sister Sarah Ann was born and a twelve-year-old when her youngest brother Arthur arrived and her eldest brother left for America.

ABOVE *Mary Jeffery*

LEFT *Bentley Fields*

Mary was seventeen when her eldest sister, Margaret, married John Poyser. At this time, it was Mary, together with her elder sister nineteen-year-old Elizabeth, who offered the greatest support to their mother Mary in caring for their younger siblings and housekeeping at the *Riddings*. Both sisters were into their thirties before they married.

One of Mary's greatest friends throughout her girlhood was Rosamond Clews of *Littleover Old Hall*, near Derby. As a child, Rosamond would visit her grandparents who farmed at Yeaveley and walk across the fields to visit her friend Mary Jeffery at the *Riddings*. Mary's brother Charles became engaged to Rosamond but after his early death, she married Mary's brother Joseph. (See PART THREE: PIONEERS). Mary's niece, Rosamond and Joseph's daughter Florence, recorded:

Mother (Rosamond) *knew a great deal about the young family at the Riddings. The Clews and Jeffery families had known each other for many years. Rosamond Clews and Polly Jeffery were great friends.*

It seems highly probable that it was via this friendship with Rosamond that Mary came to know the Spencer family. Mary's brother Charles had worked as a grocer in Littleover before his tragic death in 1881 and Littleover was also one of the locations where the Spencers had a grocery business. Paintings of the Hollow and the Cottage in the Hollow, Littleover, still hang in the dining room at *Bentley Fields*. Interestingly, these Raymond Dearn paintings are dated 1888, which is the same year that Mary married Herbert Spencer.

Mary was thirty-five when she married Herbert Spencer on 10 October 1888 at the Independent Chapel, Yeaveley. The witnesses to the wedding were Mary's married brother John and her sister, Fanny. Herbert Spencer, born in 1854, was a grocer and the son of a grocer, John Spencer, of Littleover, Derbyshire. Mary and Herbert Spencer started their married life in Littleover and in 1891 they were living near to Herbert's parents John and Ann Spencer. Seventy-three-year-old John Spencer had retired from the grocery business and was living on his own means.

Mary and Herbert Spencer's son, Percival Stretton, always known as Percy, was born on 10 October 1889 exactly one year after their marriage. He was their only child and was born at Heanor, Derbyshire, where the Spencers also had a grocery business. He was never to remember his father: he was less than two years old when Mary's marriage was tragically cut short. Herbert Spencer was only thirty-seven when he died on 6 May 1891. Mary returned with her young son to the *Riddings* and it was here that Percy grew up. Mary's mother, Mary, now seventy-three, was welcoming yet another young child into the family home. Mary's sisters Fanny and Ellen, together with her brother Owen, who was running the farm, her niece Mary Ellen and her nephew William, were also still at home at the *Riddings*.

Although Mary with young Percy was eventually to make the *Riddings* her main home again, Mary Jeffery at the *Home Farm*, West Broughton, Mary Spencer's great niece recalled:

Auntie Polly brought Percy here for a spell – they lived here (Home Farm, West Broughton) *for a while. That was after her husband,* (Herbert Spencer) *died.*

Percy's daughter-in-law, Stella Spencer, who married Percy's younger son Jeffery, has also pointed out to me a house in Ashbourne where she said Mary lived for a short while. Stella has recorded:

Jeffery's father (Percy Spencer) was about eighteen months old when his father (Herbert Spencer) died. He had a grocery and provisions merchant's business in Heanor though according to records he died and was buried at Littleover. Following her husband's death, Percy's mother Mary came to live for a short while in Ashbourne on Clifton Road but after a time returned to her family home at the Riddings.

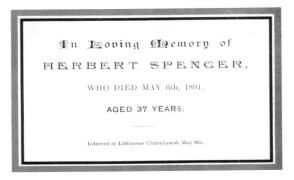

In Memoriam card - death of Herbert Spencer 6 May 1891

LEFT *Mary with her young son Percy and sister Elizabeth (right) at Bentley Fields*

BELOW *Mary with her sister Elizabeth (centre) and niece Dolly (left) at Bentley Fields*

BOTTOM *Percy Spencer ploughing at Bentley Fields*

By 1901 the *Riddings* household comprised eighty-three-year-old mother Mary as head of the household with her daughter Fanny, her widowed daughter Mary Spencer and grandson, eleven-year-old Percy. Mary's brother Owen, as we have seen, was now married and farming both the *Riddings* and *Bentley Fields* and Mary and her son Percy spent time on both farms.

In 1911 the *Riddings* household was reduced to three: fifty-seven-year-old Mary, her fifty-four-year-old unmarried sister Fanny and her twenty-one-year-old son Percy who was shown as a farm pupil.

Mary was sixty when she moved with her son Percy from the *Riddings* to *Bentley Fields*. Percy took over farming at *Bentley Fields* when his Uncle Owen and Aunt Hester Jeffery with his cousins Dolly and Tom returned to the *Riddings*. Percy spent the rest of his life at *Bentley Fields* and it is where his children and many of his grandchildren and great grandchildren have grown up.

Mary spent the last twenty-two years of her long life at *Bentley Fields*. From 1914 to 1918 she was the mistress of the house. Following her son's marriage in 1918, it was not always easy for either Mary or, most particularly, the new mistress of the house, Mabel. Mary was a strong character, exhibiting a certain degree of hauteur

Marriage of Percy Spencer to Mabel H. Salt

and in her later years she became somewhat difficult. Her grandsons, Harold and Jeffery, grew up with their grandmother as part of the family and stories are still told of her demanding ways.

On 11 June 1918, Percy married Mabel Henrietta Salt. Mabel, born in 1893, was the youngest daughter of Richard Fynney and Mary Salt. In 1901, the Salts were farming at *Huffen Heath*, Littleover. At the time of Mabel's marriage, the family were at the *Elms Farm*, Little Eaton, Derbyshire. (It is at Little Eaton where John Salt, a descendant of one of Mabel's brothers, today runs a hotel and golf course.)

The *ASHBOURNE TELEGRAPH* reported the wedding:

Wedding of Percy Spencer to Mabel Salt

INTERESTING DERBYSHIRE WEDDING

A very pretty wedding was solemnised on Tuesday June 11th at St Peter's Church, Little Eaton. The contracting parties were Mr. Percival Stretton Spencer of Bentley Fields, Brailsford and Miss Mabel Henrietta Salt of the Elms, Little Eaton. The ceremony was conducted by the Rev. W. C. Wilson (vicar of Alkmonton). Mr. Smith officiated at the organ and rendered suitable music. The bride, who was given away by her father, was attired in a pretty gown of white silk crepe, hand embroidered with tiny pearls, with veil surmounted by a wreath of orange blossom, the gift of the bridegroom, and was attended by four bridesmaids. The two elder ones (Miss Marion Salt, sister of the bride and Miss Dorothy Jeffery, cousin of the bridegroom) were attired in pretty gowns of pale blue crepe trimmed with primrose silk with pale blue georgette hats to match. They wore gold bangles, and carried bouquets of pink carnations, the gift of the bridegroom. The youngest bridesmaids, Misses Lilian and Elaine Hutchinson (nieces of the bride), were attired in pale pink silk crepe dressed with silk mob caps caught with tiny bunches of white daises. They each wore a string of pearls and carried pink roses and carnations, the gifts of the bridegroom. The duties of the best man were admirably carried out by Mr. Tom Jeffery (cousin of the bridegroom). After the ceremony a reception was held at the home of the bride where a number of relations were present. The bride and bridegroom were the recipients of many beautiful presents, including a handsome set of skunk furs, the gift of the bridegroom to the bride. The bride gave to the bridegroom a leather-lined travelling coat.

Percy and Mabel Spencer bridal group. Mary is standing on Percy's right.

In April 1920, when the Clews family sold the Bentley Estate, Percy Spencer bought *Bentley Fields*. (See PART ONE: PLACES).

Percy and Mabel provided Mary with two grandsons at *Bentley Fields*. Their first son, Harold Stretton Spencer, was born on 9 April 1919. A little over two years later, their second son, Percival Richard Jeffery Spencer, always known as Jeffery, was born on 24 October 1921.

LEFT *Harold Spencer c.1921*

RIGHT *Jeffery Spencer c.1924*

The youngest granddaughter of Mary's brother John, Mary Jeffery of the *Home Farm*, West Broughton, remembers her grandfather's sister Mary:

I remember Auntie Polly very well. I think they (her grandfather John and his sister Mary) were very close as brother and sister. She lived here a little while I believe with Percy after she lost her husband. She saw the boys (Harold and Jeffery) grow up. Auntie Nellie (my grandmother Ellen) and Auntie Polly used to be together quite a lot. She must have been a big help at Bentley Fields.

Jeffery Spencer, Mary's younger grandson, at the request of his own eldest granddaughter, has recorded something of his early life. On Jeffery's seventy-ninth birthday, his son Richard's daughter, Katrina, gave her grandfather a journal:

24th October 2000
It's your birthday today and I've given you a diary to note down all your memories from when you were a small boy to now and any day from now.
All my love,
Katrina.

LEFT *Harold and Jeffery Spencer at Bentley Fields c.1927*

RIGHT *Percy with Harold and Jeffery at the Riddings*

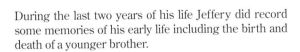

During the last two years of his life Jeffery did record some memories of his early life including the birth and death of a younger brother.

When I was four years old I woke one morning and went from my bedroom into my Mother's room. She was not there. I met Mrs Atkin who helped Mother. She told me Mum had gone to hospital to have a baby. So she had to look after us – me and my brother Harold. She was very nice. My Granny (Mary) was there but she spoilt Harold (not me). My Mother had another baby boy, but it was born dead. She was in hospital a long while (very poorly). When she came out she went to her Mother at Little Eaton for several months. We used to go with Dad to see her. When she came home she and I were very pleased. She called me her little Jeccy.

Jeffery also recorded memories of his school days and early years at *Bentley Fields.*

I loved living on the farm and never liked to leave it. I would not go out anywhere if I could help it. However, when I was five years old I started at Cubley School. I walked all the way ....When I got home from Cubley School I always called at Bentley Hall (the home of his Great Aunt Ellen Hellaby) *and asked for ...'My cheese as big as my bread please Auntie'. When my brother went to the Grammar School* (Queen Elizabeth's, Ashbourne) *at eleven years of age I would not go to Cubley anymore. They sent me to Longford where there was a good Head Teacher. I was then nine years-old and went to Longford on my bicycle .... I was the star pupil at Longford and at eleven years got a Scholarship to go to Ashbourne Grammar School which meant I could go free in those days. So I used to bike to Ashbourne with my brother and friend and others everyday, six miles and in all weathers. I loved the farm, especially the sheep and lambs. I used to rush home from school and also had a lot of homework to do.*

Love of sheep farming was in his blood.

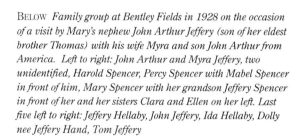

LEFT *Jonathan
Spencer with his
wife Lorna, son
Thomas and
daughter Kather-
ine with myself in
New Zealand in
February 1998*

Jeffery's love of sheep farming, inherited from his Jeffery great uncles, has been inherited by his eldest son Richard who has figured in and been one of the key advisers to the BBC in their recent production of a series of programmes entitled 'Victorian Farm'.

It is also interesting to note that Jeffery's second son Jonathan, now a veterinary surgeon in New Zealand, also keeps sheep.

BELOW *Family group at Bentley Fields in 1928 on the occasion of a visit by Mary's nephew John Arthur Jeffery (son of her eldest brother Thomas) with his wife Myra and son John Arthur from America. Left to right: John Arthur and Myra Jeffery, two unidentified, Harold Spencer, Percy Spencer with Mabel Spencer in front of him, Mary Spencer with her grandson Jeffery Spencer in front of her and her sisters Clara and Ellen on her left. Last five left to right: Jeffery Hellaby, John Jeffery, Ida Hellaby, Dolly nee Jeffery Hand, Tom Jeffery*

LEFT *Percy with his sons Harold and Jeffery c. 1933*

RIGHT *Mary in her later years*

Mary's grandsons Harold and Jeffery were nine and six years old when their Uncle John Arthur Jeffery with his wife and younger son John visited from America.

When Mary died aged eighty-two in 1936, her grandsons were in their teens. Her death, on 7 May 1936, was reported in the *ASHBOURNE TELEGRAPH*:

ALKMONTON BEREAVEMENT
MRS SPENCER

****

It is with regret we announce the death of Mrs. Spencer of Bentley Fields, Alkmonton, which took place on May 7th. Mrs. Spencer, who had attained the ripe old age of 82 years, had for many years been an active and familiar figure in the district, and her willing help in all movements for the welfare of the village and villagers are well known and will be much missed.

For over twenty years she had resided at Bentley Hall Fields, now the residence of her son, Mr. P. Spencer. Her husband predeceased her 45 years ago. The news of her death caused deep regret throughout the neighbourhood.

The funeral took place among manifestations of sincere regret at Alkmonton Church on May 11th, the Rev. W. B. Dearden officiating. The hymns 'Jesu lover of my soul' and 'Rock of Ages' were feelingly sung, and Mrs. Dearden, the organist, played appropriate voluntaries as the cortege entered and left the Church.

The principal mourners were Mr. and Mrs. P. S. Spencer, Harold and Jeffery Spencer, Mrs. Hellaby (sister Ellen), Mr. and Mrs. Cook (sister Clara and brother-in-law Arthur), Mrs. O. Jeffery (sister-in-law Hester), Mrs. T. Jeffery (sister-in –law Louisa), Mrs. Archer (Stapleford) (niece Mabel). Miss Jeffery (Notts) (niece Katie), Mrs. Prince (Crakemarsh) (niece Sarah Ann), Mr. Ball (Warrington) (nephew), Mr. and Mrs. E. Tipper (Cross Plains) (niece Adeline nee Jeffery), Mr. and Mrs. R. Salt (Little Eaton), Mr. F. Salt and Mr. F. B. Salt (Middleton Park), Mr. and Mrs. F. Jeffery, Mr. and Mrs. O. Jeffery, Mr. and Mrs. Hand (Shirley Mill), Mr. C. Poyser (Allestree), Mr. and Mrs. F. Poyser (Shardlow), Mr. J.Hellaby (Fauld), Mr. J. Cook (Stretton), Mr. J. Cook (Castle Donington) and many, many more ……..

Mary died shortly after I was born. My sister Marjorie can remember Great Aunt Polly when, in her later years her health had started to fail.

~~~~~~~~

Bentley Fields is a home which I would very regularly visit throughout the years of my girlhood. My very earliest memories of Percy and Mabel and the rambling old farm house stem from the summer of 1940. I recall staying there, together with my sister Marjorie, and playing in the attics with wonderful boys' toys that had long been outgrown by Harold and Jeffery. Walking across the fields to the *Riddings*, to see our cousins Dorothy, Tom, Margaret and Fred, is also one of my earliest memories. It seemed like a very long way for little legs!

Six years later I was a bridesmaid at Harold Spencer's wedding to Enid Walker on 29 April 1946 and eight years after their marriage I became godmother to their only daughter Elizabeth Anne who was born on 23 April 1954. One of the other bridesmaids at their wedding was Dorothy Jeffery, granddaughter of Mary Spencer's brother Owen of *Bentley Fields* and the *Riddings*. Harold and Enid farmed at nearby *Top House Farm*, Alkmonton before retiring and building a house closer to the church.

Percy and Mabel's younger son, Jeffery, married Stella Pearson on 18 July 1951. Stella, the third child of Stephen and Winifred Jane Pearson, was born on 7 December 1924. Stella's mother was a Spencer of Ashbourne and her parents had farmed in Derbyshire. Stella has written of her early life in Ashbourne and Leeds before her marriage to Jeffery:

December 1924. My mother and father were then farming at Wingerworth and my mother came to Ashbourne for my birth. When I was little more than a year old my parents sold up the farm and came to Ashbourne to join my grandfather in the bakery and confectionary business . . . . Reverting to my girlhood, we, as a family of six children, lived in the house behind and over the shop. (This is the Gingerbread Shop in St John's Street, Ashbourne).

When I was little more than a year old my parents sold up the farm and came to Ashbourne to join my grandfather in the bakery and confectionary business

Harold Spencer's wedding to Enid Walker. L. to r. Dorothy Jeffery, Valerie Hellaby, Jeffery Spencer

Jeffery Spencer, who continued farming with Shire Horses until the 1970s

Stella, like her husband Jeffery Spencer and both of his Jeffery cousins, Dorothy and Thomas Jeffery of the *Riddings* also went to the Queen Elizabeth's School in Ashbourne.

Her memories of her early life continue:

I stayed on at school into the sixth form after taking Higher School Certificate. It was during this time that I became very friendly with Dorothy Jeffery (of the *Riddings*).

Between 1943 and 1947 Stella trained as a nurse at Leeds General Infirmary and continued her nursing until her marriage to Jeffery Spencer in 1951.

Jeffery and Stella took over farming at *Bentley Fields* and their three children, Richard, Jonathan and Penelope were born there. Stephen Richard was born on 12 May 1952 and his brother Jonathan Jeffery arrived almost exactly two years later on 11 May 1954. The youngest of the family, their sister Penelope Mary, was born on 28 February 1958.

Percy Spencer, who had suffered from chronic arthritis for much of his life, and walked aided by sticks, died on 3 September 1963. His daughter-in-law Stella told me of how Percy, shortly before his death, walked in his fields where the lost village of Hungry Bentley lies and looked down towards the tranquil setting of the *Riddings* where he had spent his early life.

His obituary, recording his active public life, was reported in the *ASHBOURNE NEWS TELEGRAPH* of 12 September.

ALKMONTON FUNERAL OF MR. PERCY SPENCER

The church of St John at Alkmonton was filled to capacity on Saturday for the funeral of Mr. Percy Stretton Spencer of Bentley Grove, Alkmonton and many who were unable to find room in the church remained outside throughout the whole service.

Mr. Spencer, who was 73, died at his home on Tuesday.

He had been a member of the R.D.C. (Rural District Council) since 1934 as representative for Hungry Bentley and Alkmonton.

He was on the Board of Governors of Queen Elizabeth's Grammar School, Ashbourne from 1942 until 1958 and also served on the Food Control Committee from 1942 until 1954.

He was also a member of the old Mid-Derbyshire Guardians Committee and formerly served on the South Derbyshire Divisional Executive.

Mr. Spencer was a member of the Ashbourne Shire Horse Society and served on the Society's Council.

After leaving Queen Elizabeth's School, Ashbourne, Mr. Spencer went to help his uncle, the late Mr. Owen Jeffery, at Bentley Fields, Alkmonton and in 1914 took over the farm. He later went into partnership with his two sons and at the time of his death was still in partnership with one of his sons, Mr. Jeffery Spencer at Bentley Fields. His other son, Mr. Harold Spencer farms at Top House Farm, Alkmonton.

Mr. Spencer had been a churchwarden at Alkmonton Church for over 30 years.

Harold and Enid on the occasion of their Silver Wedding celebration, 1971, with Jeffery and Stella (left)

There followed a very long list of mourners of family and friends.

Percy's wife Mabel died just two months afterwards on 5 November 1963. Their younger son Jeffery, with his wife Stella and their young family continued farming at *Bentley Fields*.

Mary's grandson Harold died on 16 January 1989 and his wife, Enid, seven and a half years later on 16 June 1996. Her grandson Jeffery celebrated his Golden Wedding to Stella in 2001. Jeffery died on his eighty-first birthday, 24 October 2002.

Mary's great grandson Richard continues to farm at *Bentley Fields* where his father, grandfather and Great Uncle Owen Jeffery farmed before him. Richard married Rosemary Brown in 1972. Richard and Rosemary's son Simon will be the fifth generation to continue farming at *Bentley Fields*. Simon married Alison in 2008 and their son Oliver was born in 2009. Maybe Mary (nee Jeffery) Spencer's great, great, great grandson will be the sixth generation to farm at *Bentley Fields*.

Mary's great grandson Jonathan married Lorna Fox and emigrated to New Zealand where their son Thomas Morgan Jeffery Spencer was born in 1996 and their daughter Katherine in 1997. Her great granddaughter

Mary's great granddaughter, my goddaughter Elizabeth, on her twenty-first birthday, 1974, with my daughter Clare

Penny, a nurse, also emigrated to New Zealand with her husband Jon and young daughter Georgiana. It was in New Zealand that their second daughter Sally was born in 1998. Very sadly, Penny died in 2008. Mary's great, great granddaughter Katrina (Richard and Rosemary's daughter) has also emigrated with her partner to New Zealand and it is here where their son William, Mary's first great, great, great grandson was born.

CLARA JEFFERY
1857 – 1951

Longevity with Style

Clara Jeffery, the twelfth of Thomas and Mary's fifteen children was born at the Riddings on 20 September 1857. She married Arthur Cook on 21 March 1882 and they had five children and eight grandchildren. Clara and Arthur farmed in Derbyshire including at the Holly Bush and Snitterton Hall near Matlock and Donington Park in the south of the county. Clara was ninety-four when she died in Ashby de la Zouch, Leicestershire in 1951.

Descendants of Clara Jeffery

Clara Jeffery
1857 -1951

m. 1882
Arthur Cook
1854 -1938

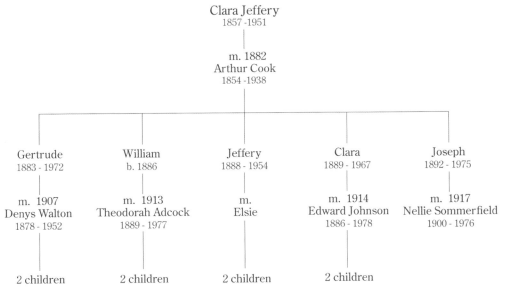

Gertrude	William	Jeffery	Clara	Joseph
1883 - 1972	b. 1886	1888 - 1954	1889 - 1967	1892 - 1975
m. 1907	m. 1913	m.	m. 1914	m. 1917
Denys Walton	Theodorah Adcock	Elsie	Edward Johnson	Nellie Sommerfield
1878 - 1952	1889 - 1977		1886 - 1978	1900 - 1976
2 children	2 children	2 children	2 children	

Clara Jeffery 1857-1951

Longevity with Style

Clara Jeffery in her early twenties around the time of her marriage, 1882

Clara, born on 20 September 1857, was Thomas and Mary's twelfth child and sixth daughter. She married quite young compared to her sisters who, with the exception of Margaret, were all in their thirties when they married. When Clara, aged twenty-four, married Arthur Cook on 21 March 1882 at St John's Church, Alkmonton, she left three older sisters at home at the *Riddings*. The witnesses to her wedding were her brother Owen and younger sister Ellen, together with Arthur Cook's brother Thomas and sisters Martha and Ann.

Apart from my grandmother, my Great Aunt Clara was the only one of Thomas and Mary's fifteen children who I met and I became very fond of her. I was four years old, living at *Fauld House Farm*, near Hanbury in Staffordshire, when eighty-three-year-old Clara came to stay with us during the bitterly cold and snowy winter of 1940–41. It was the second winter of World War II and my great aunt, who was living with her daughter, Clara Mabel Johnson, in Essex, came to stay with us to escape the London blitz.

I recall spending a great deal of time with my great aunt. She had the wonderful privilege of having a fire in her bedroom and consequently, apart from the large farmhouse kitchen, it was one of the warmest places in the house. I had only recently recovered from bronchial pneumonia and consequently my parents were happy for me to spend a lot of time in the warmth of Great Aunt Clara's room. She was always very welcoming and told great stories as we sat by the fire. My elder sister, Marjorie, also has vivid recollections of the time of Clara's visit but hers are of having to carry buckets of coal up to her bedroom for Great Aunt's fire!

Great Aunt Clara is associated with one of my earliest childhood memories. I have recounted the incident to my own granddaughters. Great Aunt and I were sitting by the open fire in the sitting room at *Fauld*. She had been telling me stories but the warmth of the fire had made her drowsy and she had fallen asleep. I recall wondering what would happen if I placed the wooden and cane stool, on which I was sitting, on the fire. At this point my childish curiosity overcame me. So, I proceeded to put the stool on the fire and stood entranced as the flames began to shoot around it. Clara continued sleeping as the stool made a wonderful blaze. It was still burning when my mother came into the sitting room. She gazed in horror at the blazing fire and what remained of the stool. I recall my own distress when my mother's wrath was initially vented on my lovely Aunt Clara for not watching what her great niece had been up to.

Clara's husband, Arthur Cook, was a farmer's son, born on 12 April 1854 in Bradnop in the Staffordshire Moorlands district and it was here that his parents, Thomas and Edith, farmed. However, at the time of his marriage he was farming in Blackwell in the parish of Taddington, northeast Derbyshire. Arthur was one of nine children: he had three sisters and five brothers. Simon Rawson, a great, great grandson of Clara and Arthur Cook has told me a wonderful story about Arthur Cook's great grandfather:

Arthur Cook in his later years

Arthur's great grandfather, Thomas Cook, 1749-1816, left the bulk of the estate to his eldest son, also a Thomas, Arthur's grandfather. Included in that will was a sum of £300 to another son, Joseph. It would seem that Joseph never got his money and some twenty-eight years later took the matter to Chancery. The solicitor involved knew Charles Dickens who shared the tale with him and Dickens included the bones of the story in 'Bleak House' (Jarndyce and Jarndyce lawsuit over a disputed will). *In the Cook case, however, nobody was ruined!*

Clara and Arthur farmed in northeast Derbyshire at the start of their married life and it was here, at Blackwell, that their first daughter, Gertrude Mary was born on 29 November 1883. Gertrude was two years old when her brother, William Arthur, was born on 19 February 1886. By the beginning of 1888 the family moved a

The solicitor involved knew Charles Dickens who shared the tale with him and Dickens included the bones of the story in 'Bleak House' (Jarndyce and Jarndyce lawsuit over a disputed will). In the Cook case, however, nobody was ruined!

little further north to farm near Spinkhill, southeast of Sheffield. It was here that their second son, John Thomas Jeffery, always known as Jeffery, was born on 11 January 1888. Seventeen months later, their second daughter, Clara Mabel, arrived on 28 May 1889.

Within two years of Clara Mabel's birth, the family was on the move again. They returned closer to 'home-ground' when they moved into *Holly Bush*, a sixteenth century coaching inn at Grangemill roughly half way between Ashbourne and Matlock. The *Holly Bush* was at this time an inn with a farm attached. It continued as both a hotel and a farm into the twentieth century: an article in the *DERBYSHIRE ADVERTISER* of 11 August 1911 reported:

Not to know the "Holly Bush" Hotel, that haven for tired wayfarers argues complete ignorance of west Derbyshire. Situated at the end of the lovely Via Gellia and at the junction of four roads leading respectively to Ashbourne, Buxton, Bakewell and Matlock, the charming little hostelry offers welcome, rest and refreshment to travellers from all parts of the country. But what may not be generally known is that the hotel is merely an adjunct to a farm of 204 acres, all good limestone land . . . . . . .On entering the house there is found everywhere that spotless daintiness typical of well-ordered English country life. Residential visitors are received . . . . A tiny bar is attached, a bijou affair, and so well ventilated that there is not the slightest odour recalling the presence of beer.

The Holly Bush Inn

Snitterton Hall as it is today, with the author seated

It was at this period that Arthur became a publican as well as a farmer. Recalling my childhood memories of Great Aunt Clara, she too would doubtless have ensured that her family maintained a – '*well ordered English country life*'. There are stories within the family that Clara refused to serve customers who she considered had already had more than she thought they should be drinking – this could mean more than a pint of beer! Simon Rawson told me that:

The story goes that Granny (his great grandmother Clara. Simon knew his grandmother as Nan) *used to tell the locals that they had enough to drink after just one glass.*

In 1891 thirty-three-year-old Clara with thirty-six-year-old Arthur were at the *Holly Bush* with their young family: Gertrude was now seven, her brothers William and Jeffery were five and three and her sister Clara Mabel was approaching her second birthday. Clara's sister Fanny was living with them and there were two farm servants living-in. It was whilst the family was at the *Holly Bush* that Clara's youngest son, Joseph, was born on 12 August 1892.

Clara and Arthur did not spend very long at the *Holly Bush*. Within four years they were on the move again. It seems probable that each move was occasioned by Arthur's desire to take on larger and larger farms. Judging by the photograph taken of Clara and Arthur with their five children at *Snitterton Hall*, it was probably

around 1895 when they moved to this beautiful old Hall which lies in the tiny village of Wensley, about a mile east of Matlock, Derbyshire.

The 1901 census shows the family at *Snitterton Hall*. The children were now aged between seventeen and eight. Living-in at the Hall were three men working on the farm and one house servant. Interestingly, one of the farm workers at this time was a cowman, Charles Ball. Charles married Clara's niece, Mary Ellen, in October 1902. They married from *Snitterton Hall* since Mary Ellen was living with her Aunt Clara at the time. (See PART THREE: THE PIONEERS).

At the time of the family's move to *Snitterton Hall* Clara and Arthur had a bathroom installed. This was quite advanced at the time. There is an interesting story

The builder was digging the foundations when he uncovered the skeleton of a young woman. That leads on to the story shortly after that Nan Johnson saw a ghost and jumped down a flight of stairs in fright.

BELOW *Clara and Arthur Cook and their children at Snitterton Hall. L. to r. William, Clara Mabel, Clara, Joseph, Arthur, Gertrude, Jeffery*

further to the installation of the bathroom. Clara Mabel's grandson, Simon Rawson told me the tale that his mother told him:

The builder was digging the foundations when he uncovered the skeleton of a young woman. That leads on to the story shortly after that Nan Johnson (Clara Mabel) *saw a ghost and jumped down a flight of stairs in fright.*

Simon continued:

I recall my mother relating the tale regarding the ghost and I seem to think it was more to do with Clara Mabel seeing her skirt and petticoat move as the 'ghost' moved along the landing.

Clara's great niece Mary Jeffery of the *Home Farm*, West Broughton also recalls her Great Aunt visiting and speaking of the bathroom they had at *Snitteron Hall*.

Auntie Clara was always a very elegant lady wasn't she Valerie? She liked to be smart. I remember when she visited and we were all sitting round the table she said – 'we've got carpet in our lavatory'. I thought that was terribly funny.

Mary Jeffery also recalled:

I once took mother and father (Offley and Cissie Jeffery of *Home Farm*, West Broughton) *up to see where the Cooks used to live. Grandpa* (Clara's brother John) *used to visit them when he was younger. He used to take Auntie Nellie* (Ellen) *up to see Auntie Clara at Snitterton Hall.*

It was probably whilst at *Snitterton Hall* that Clara certainly arranged for at least one of her children to learn the piano. However, as her daughter Clara Mabel was seventeen before she attained the Preparatory Grade, it doesn't indicate that she showed any great musical talent.

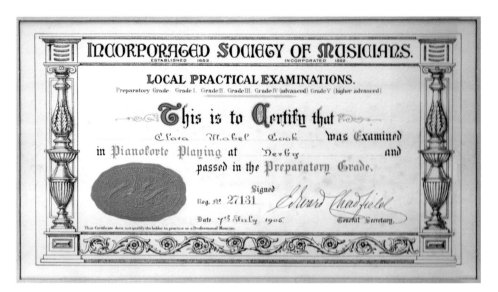

Clara Mabel's Piano Certificate

Some time before 1907, Clara and Arthur and their family moved from *Snitterton Hall* to Isley Walton, Castle Donington near Shardlow in the south of Derbyshire. The move meant they would be farming quite close to Clara's eldest sister Margaret and her husband John Poyser and family. Their move was to *Parkhouse Farm*, Donington Park, which is now a hotel.

Today the hotel advertises itself as a:

Seventeenth century farmhouse having a series of original brick and timber barns, sympathetically restored to create a beautiful collection of rooms ......

And many of the bedrooms have:

 ......breathtaking views across Breedon Hill and the surrounding countryside.

In 1907 Clara's eldest daughter Gertrude married from *Parkhouse Farm*, Donington Park which was regularly described simply as *Parkside* by the family. The 1911 census shows Clara and Arthur here with their two youngest sons, twenty-three-year-old Jeffery and eighteen-year-old Joseph. Living in at the time were three farm labourers - a cowman, a waggoner and a milk boy. There was also a live-in house servant.

RIGHT *Park Farmhouse, Donington Park from the rear*

BELOW *Park Farmhouse Hotel from the front*

LEFT *Wedding of Gertrude Cook and Denys Walton, 1907 at Donington Park*

BELOW *Family Wedding Group*

Park Farmhouse, Donington Park, was Clara and Arthur Cook's last farm up to the time of their retirement. Castle Donington is, of course, famed for its motor car racing track. It seems that Arthur kept sheep and was allowed to graze them on the grass around the race track on non-race days.

After Arthur retired from farming, he and Clara eventually bought a property called *Holme Leigh* in Ockbrook, Derbyshire.

However, at some point between their moving from Donington Park and settling at Ockbrook, the family spent some time in Borrowash, Derbyshire which is adjacent to Ockbrook. Clara was certainly at Borrowash

*Clara (left) with her
elder brother John
and youngest sister
Ellen in 1928*

at the time of her brother Owen's death in 1919 and she was still there in 1925, when her sister Fanny died as there was a floral tribute:

*To dear Fanny from Clara, Arthur and
Family (Borrowash).*

Many years later, when my father was driving through Borrowash, on the old road between Derby and Nottingham, he pointed out a large house which was up a short drive away from the road. He told me that that was where Great Aunt Clara had lived. Also, Clara's great niece Mary Jeffery of the *Home Farm*, West Broughton recalls visiting Clara at Borrowash.

*I'm not sure exactly when Arthur
and Clara left the farm but I think
this could have been their last farm up
to the point of Arthur's retirement.*

Clara was particularly close to her youngest sister Ellen who was closest to her in age. She did, however, remain in contact with all of her siblings and features in photographs taken when her eldest brother Thomas's son and grandson visited from America in 1928.

Simon Rawson wrote:

I'm not sure exactly when Arthur and Clara left the farm (Parkside, Donington Park) but I think this could have been their last farm up to the point of Arthur's retirement.

Arthur and Clara in later years purchased a property called Holme Leigh in Ockbrook. Arthur died there (aged sixty-five in 1938). *Clara, at some time as a widow, went to live with my grandmother i.e. her daughter, Clara Mabel Johnson nee Cook, in Essex. She may well have been there during the war years as I have a picture of my great grandmother Clara, my grandmother Clara Mabel and my mother taken at that time. My mother was dressed in her nurse's uniform.*
(Sadly this photograph has been impossible to reproduce here.)

Descendants of Clara Jeffery and Arthur Cook

Clara and Arthur Cook's eldest daughter, Gertrude, married Denys Walton on 11 June 1907. The marriage was registered in Shardlow and the reception was held at Clara and Arthur's home at Donington Park.

Denys Walton, born in 1878, was five years older than Gertrude. He was the son of Thomas Barron Walton and Elizabeth nee Ibbotson of Ashton on Mersey, Cheshire. How Gertrude came to meet him remains a mystery. They married at the Parish Church in Melbourne, Derbyshire. On their marriage certificate, Denys was described as an engineer and his father as a gentleman. Gertrude was one of the first of Thomas and Mary's grandchildren of the *Riddings* to move away from Derbyshire.

Gertrude and Denys's first daughter, Eileen May, was born on 31 May in 1909 in Barnet, Hertfordshire. By 1911 Gertrude and Denys were living at 86, Durham Road, East Finchley, Middlesex. Denys was described as a Civil Servant at the Board of India Patent Office. In addition to their one-year-old daughter, Eileen May, Gertrude's twenty-one-year-old sister, Clara Mabel Cook was living with them. Additionally, Gertrude had a living-in house servant, twenty-four-year-old Emily Sophia Wilson. Later that year, on 11 September, Gertrude and Denys's second daughter, Brenda Denise, was born.

At this time Clara and Arthur Cook's eldest son, twenty-five-year-old William Arthur was farming on his own in home territory. The 1911 census shows him at *The Clouds Farm*, Weston Underwood, Derbyshire. Weston Underwood lies about four miles northwest of Derby and around eight miles southeast of Ashbourne. Living at *The Clouds Farm* with William at this time were seventeen-year-old Arthur Tipping as cowman, nineteen-year-old Bert Roberts as waggoner and twenty-seven-year-old housekeeper, Gertrude Higginson.

Two years later, William married Theodora Adcock on 6 September 1913. Theodora was born on 7 June 1888 and was the daughter of Richard Orme Adcock who farmed in Melbourne, Derbyshire. William and Theodora provided Clara and Arthur with two more grandchildren: Kathleen Annie born on 4 July 1915 and Arthur Orme born on 19 September 1926.

Clara and Arthur's second son, Jeffery, married Elsie and gave Clara and Arthur two more grandchildren, Jeffery and Audrey. Clara's great grandson Simon Rawson has told me:

I recall my mother telling me that Jeffery had quite a cruel streak. I assume she heard that from Clara Mabel's comments to her about it.

Clara and Arthur Cook's second daughter, Clara Mabel, married Edward Clare Johnson on 30 March 1914. Their children were Benjamin Arthur Clare, born in 1915 and Margaret Jeffery, born on 16 June 1918.

Clara Mabel and Edward Clare Johnson were Simon Rawson's grandparents. Simon's mother, Margaret Jeffery Johnson, married Henry Keith Rawson on 4 June 1946 in Rayleigh, Essex. Simon is the only one of Clara's descendants I have been able to trace and I am greatly indebted to him for his help in piecing together their story.

Simon's grandparents, Clara Mabel and Edward Clare Johnson started farming in Derbyshire. They farmed at Findern near Derby and later, at *Bower Grange* and *Flamstead House*, Denby, Derbyshire. Later they moved to Rettenden, south east of Chelmsford, in Essex. Clara Mabel's husband was always known by his middle name of Clare.

Simon told me:

Clara Mabel's husband, Clare Johnson, my grandfather, was a stubborn man. This resulted in him moving the whole family from Derbyshire to Essex following a dispute regarding his Derbyshire farm and his not being prepared to back down. I think Flamstead, Denby was his last Derbyshire farm before he went down to Rettenden Grange in the mid to late 30s. I believe there was some disagreement with the landlord regarding a hike in the rent and that is what triggered the move to Essex. It was at Rettenden that he refused to plough in a particular way, I seem to recall my mother saying it was something to do with drainage. Clare was ploughing the way he always had done which was with gradient instead of the Ministry of Agriculture's preferred alignment of across the gradient.

Clara and Arthur Cook and family at Rettenden Grange Farm 1935. Seated l. to r. Clara, Arthur, Martha (Arthur's sister). Standing l. to r. Clara Mabel Johnson (nee Cook), Edward Clare Johnson, Margaret Jeffery Johnson, Benjamin Johnson (Clara's granddaughter and grandson), Margaret Johnson's Uncle John and Aunt Sissy

When my grandfather had to give up Rettenden, they moved to a property in Hockley, Essex. Clare actually finished up working for the Ministry of Agriculture during the war.

The last of Clara and Arthur Cook's children to marry was their youngest son, Joseph. On 15 March 1917 Joseph married Fanny Ellen Summerfield (Nellie). They farmed at *White House Farm*, Castle Donington close by Donington Park. In later years, they sold land for the building of Castle Donington (East Midlands) Airport in the 1960s.

Great Grandson Simon recalled:

I do not recall ever meeting William, Gertie or Jeffery but we used to meet Uncle Joe quite a bit. They were childless. They had the White House Farm in Castle Donington and we used to visit quite often. I remember my mother saying that it was Auntie Nellie's money which bought White House Farm and was always a little appalled that in the phone book it was Nellie's name rather than Uncle Joe's which was listed.

My Great Aunt Clara remained fit and active until well into her later years, as Simon Rawson recalls:

She must have been quite agile until old age as she used to walk for miles when she lived at Hockley with Nan and Grandpa.

It was here that Clara spent most of the war years apart from the period when she came to stay with us at *Fauld House Farm*. My father, Jeffery Hellaby, was Clara's nephew.

Clara later moved to live with her granddaughter Margaret and her husband Keith Rawson in Borrowash, Derbyshire. When Simon Rawson was born in 1949, Clara went to a care home in Ashby-de-la-Zouch, Leicestershire where she died on 5 January 1951.

Clara inherited the Jeffery longevity gene. She was one of three of the children of Thomas and Mary who lived to become nonagenarians. Her brother John had reached ninety-one and her sister Margaret had died at ninety-three in the late 1930s. However, Clara, at ninety-four was the longest lived of the fifteen children born at the *Riddings*. Born in the year of the Indian Mutiny when Queen Victoria was only twenty years into her long reign, Clara lived through five reigns. She died in the year of the Festival of Britain one year before Elizabeth became Queen.

E L L E N   J E F F E R Y
1862 – 1950

Mizpah

Ellen Jeffery, the fourteenth of Thomas and Mary's fifteen children was born at the Riddings on 6 January 1862. She married William Hellaby on 21 April 1897 and they had two sons and five grandchildren. Ellen and William farmed at Bentley Hall for almost thirty years before retiring to Ivy House, Marston Montgomery, Derbyshire. Ellen maintained contact with her pioneering brothers in America throughout her life. She died at Fullwood Farm, Hulland, Derbyshire, the home of her younger son, on 1 January 1950.

Descendants of Ellen Jeffery

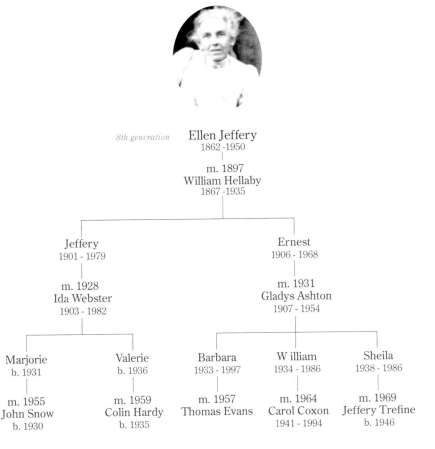

8th generation

Ellen Jeffery
1862 -1950

m. 1897
William Hellaby
1867 -1935

Jeffery
1901 - 1979

Ernest
1906 - 1968

m. 1928
Ida Webster
1903 - 1982

m. 1931
Gladys Ashton
1907 - 1954

Marjorie
b. 1931

Valerie
b. 1936

Barbara
1933 - 1997

William
1934 - 1986

Sheila
1938 - 1986

m. 1955
John Snow
b. 1930

m. 1959
Colin Hardy
b. 1935

m. 1957
Thomas Evans

m. 1964
Carol Coxon
1941 - 1994

m. 1969
Jeffery Trefine
b. 1946

Ellen Jeffery 1862 -1950

Mizpah

Ellen Jeffery was my grandmother and my mind is flooded with many very vivid memories of her. I have a ring which to me is very special and which never leaves the third finger of my right hand. It is a ring engraved with the mystical MIZPAH which is a Hebrew acronym meaning:

The Lord rest between me and thee whilst we are absent one from another.

It was, I have been led to understand, given to Ellen by her eldest brother Thomas, as a watchword following nearly a year in America keeping house for him after the death of his first wife Maria.

My grandmother, Ellen, was the fourteenth of Thomas and Mary's fifteen children. I was the fourth of her five grandchildren and, following the death of my grandfather, William Hellaby, she would spend the summers of the late 1930s and throughout the 1940s with us at *Fauld House*, the home of her eldest son, Jeffery Hellaby. It is perhaps inevitable that this chapter in the history of the Jeffery family becomes a personal memoir.

The date of 6 January, my grandmother's birthday, is one which refuses to be dislodged from my memory. Although she would spend the summers of her later years with us at *Fauld House Farm*, near Hanbury, my grandmother made her main home with her younger son, my Uncle Ernest and family at *Fullwood Farm*, Hulland. We would always visit and celebrate her birthday with a small family party. The date of 6 January 1942, however, was more significant as it was her eightieth birthday.

I vividly recall this celebration at *Fullwood Farm*. I was six at the time and my cousin Sheila, Ellen's youngest grand-daughter, only four. I remember our great excitement at being allowed to stay up so much later than we had ever done before and also being allowed a sip of port in order to drink her health. Before her big day Granny reminded me that it was also her eldest son's and eldest granddaughter's birthdays a few days before. She also told me that she looked forward to her ninetieth birthday when my father would have reached his half century and my sister, her majority. Sadly she missed this mile-stone by nearly two years.

Ellen Jeffery c.1876

Ellen, born on 6 January 1862, was Thomas and Mary's seventh and youngest daughter. At the time of her birth, her eldest sister, Margaret, was seventeen and her youngest brother, Charles, two years old. She was three when her mother gave birth to her last child, Ellen's younger brother Arthur. Ellen, always known in the family as Nell or Nellie was to spend the first thirty-five years of her life at the *Riddings*, the home for which she always had a very great affection. By the time she was four years old, her younger brother Arthur was a one year-old and her elder brothers Thomas and Joseph had left for America.

Ellen was only two and a half when her nine-year-old sister Sarah Ann died and, although she was probably too young to retain clear memories of this sister, she would recall the sadness around her in the family at that time. I personally was made aware of this by my father, who, following the early death of our own daughter, Sarah, told me of the death of his mother's sister Sarah nearly a hundred years before. Indeed, it was after the death of our daughter Sarah, that my father gave me his mother's MIZPAH ring.

By the time Ellen reached her tenth birthday she was aunt to two nieces and two nephews. Her brother George had brought his daughter, Mary-Ellen, born in 1872 and his son, William, born in 1874, back home to the *Riddings*, following the death of his first wife Sarah in 1874. (See PART THREE: THE PIONEERS). Ellen had a 'hands on' input into the bringing up of these first of her nieces and nephews. When they arrived at the *Riddings*, she was aged twelve and it would have seemed like gaining a new younger sister and brother. By the time Ellen left home to marry Mary-Ellen was a young woman. Another niece and another nephew who made her an aunt in her childhood were her sister Margaret's eldest son, Owen John, born in 1873 and her brother William's eldest daughter, Sarah Ann, born in 1874.

In 1876, when she was fourteen, Ellen lost her father, Thomas. Five years later, in 1881, her brother Charles died suddenly when he was only twenty-two years old. During the decade of the 1880s all of her remaining siblings, except Owen, married and left home.

By the final decade of the nineteenth century, twenty-nine-year-old Ellen was still at the *Riddings* with her thirty-eight-year-old brother, Owen as head of the household. Her mother, now seventy-three was living there on her 'own means' and it was Ellen who was running the house-hold. Also still at home were her niece, Mary-Ellen, now eighteen and her nephew, William, aged sixteen. There were two farm servants living-in at the time.

1892 was a year when tragedy struck on the other side of the Atlantic, over four thousand miles away in Minnesota, USA. Ellen's eldest brother, Thomas, lost his much loved wife Maria. It was a year which would demonstrate the strength of the family bonds which bridged space and time. Following Maria's death, Thomas, with his son John Arthur (Art) returned to visit the *Riddings* and when they returned home to Minneapolis, Ellen accompanied them. According to her niece Florence, daughter of her brother Joseph in Iowa, Ellen remained taking care of her brother's household for almost a year.

It was around the middle of the decade that William Hellaby first features in Ellen's life. Together with his

John and Ann Hellaby with their ten children at the Old Hall Farm, Yeldersley. John is wearing his Imperial Service Medal. Eldest son William is seated on the far right and his brother Jack who lost his life in World War l is standing behind him

father John he had worked the *Church Farm*, Osmaston, Derbyshire. William Hellaby then took over the *Cottage Farm*, the closest neighbouring farm to the *Riddings*. He also did some work for Owen who was now fully stretched running both the *Riddings* and *Bentley Fields* farms. There is a story that both Ellen, in her early thirties and her young niece Mary-Ellen, who was ten years younger, were both enamoured by the good looking William Hellaby. However, Ellen made it crystal clear that William Hellaby was not for Mary-Ellen but for her. She encouraged her instead to pay her attentions to Charles Ball.

Ellen was the last of the family of fifteen to leave the *Riddings* to marry. It was in the year of Queen Victoria's Golden Jubilee when, on 21 April 1897, Ellen Jeffery married William Hellaby in the Provident Independent Chapel at Yeaveley. Her niece, Mary-Ellen, who was a bridesmaid, married Charles Ball five years later! In Mary-Ellen's wedding photograph of the family, her Aunt Ellen is seen holding her first son in her arms, my father aged ten months.

William Hellaby, born on 26 February 1867 in Wyaston, Derbyshire was the eldest son of John and Ann Hellaby. His family had farmed in the Longford area for six generations. His father, John, in his later years, together with William's support, farmed at the *Church Farm* before retiring to the *Old Hall Farm*, Yeldersley, Derbyshire.

Recovering from this sad accident he obtained the appointment of rural postman, his round being from Ashbourne, through Osmaston, Edlaston, Wyaston, Rodsley and Yeaveley and back again to Ashbourne, a distance of seventeen miles daily.

John Hellaby met with a serious accident that made his life as a farmer extraordinarily difficult. He overcame this in a remarkable way. His obituary from the *ASHBOURNE NEWS* of 22 December 1916 gives an account:

He had the sad misfortune to meet with the most painful accident of losing the greater part of his left arm and the ends of the fingers of his right hand by a horsepower chopping machine. Recovering from this sad accident he obtained the appointment of rural postman, his round being from Ashbourne, through Osmaston, Edlaston, Wyaston, Rodsley and Yeaveley and back again to Ashbourne, a distance of seventeen miles daily. This round he performed for thirty years and was never once late.

John Hellaby's services were rewarded when he was awarded the Imperial Service Medal:

HONOUR FOR LOCAL POSTMAN

Amongst the list of the King's birthday Honours are a number of subordinate officers of the Civil Service, to whom the medal of the Imperial Service has been granted. One of those highly favoured recipients is Mr. John Hellaby of Osmaston who is, or rather was, one of the rural postmen of the Ashbourne District. Mr. Hellaby joined the postal service in 1877.

During those thirty years in performing his duties, he must have travelled more than 150, 000 miles. (By pony and trap).

The deceased gentleman succeeded his eldest son William as tenant of the *Church Farm*, Osmaston and later retired to *Yeldersley Old Hall Farm*.

When Ellen began her married life with William Hellaby at the *Cubley Cottage Farm*, she had not moved far from the *Riddings*. Thirty-five years old when she married, she was less than two weeks away from her fortieth birthday when, on 29 December 1901, her first son, William Jeffery, was born. It was quite dangerous to have a first child at that age at the beginning of the twentieth century. This first son, my father, was always known as Jeff. He was born in the year that Queen Victoria died and died in the year of her great, great granddaughter Elizabeth's Silver Jubilee.

It was at some time in the period 1902/1903 that Ellen and William, with their young son Jeffery, moved into

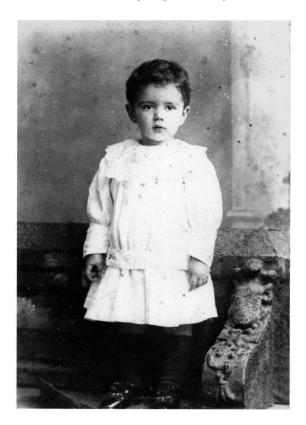

Ellen's eldest son, Jeffery Hellaby c.1903

Bentley Hall. Picture taken by John Arthur Jeffery, son of Ellen's brother Thomas, when he visited in 1928

Bentley Hall. It was here on 19 April 1906 that their second son, John Ernest, always known as Ernest, was born. Ellen was now aged forty-four and Ernest was her last child. My Uncle Ernest, on his marriage, twenty-six years later, continued farming at *Bentley Hall* and it was here where the two eldest of my Hellaby cousins were born.

In making *Bentley Hall* her home, my grandmother Ellen was returning to what had been the childhood home of her own grandmother, Elizabeth Oakden, over a hundred years before. (See PART ONE: THE PLACES). *Bentley Hall,* a house full of history, became the much loved home of my grandparents and father and uncle. Later it became home to my young cousins for some years.

Jeff and Ernest c.1911

Jeff and Ernest c.1915

BELOW *Ellen and William Hellaby with their sons, Jeff and Ernest c.1915*

ABOVE *Ellen with her sons, three of her sisters and two of her nieces at Bentley Fields c.1910-11. Standing in the middle l. to r. sisters Polly, Lizzie and Fanny; far left niece Dolly and far right niece Clara Mabel*

Ellen and William's sons, Jeffery and Ernest, like many of their Jeffery and Poyser cousins, went to Queen Elizabeth's Grammar School in Ashbourne. Jeffery's leaving certificate is dated 15 September 1914 and that of his cousin Tom Jeffery is 1913. The leaving certificates of both Ernest and his cousin Arthur Owen Poyser are dated September 1918. On leaving school, Ellen's sons both worked with their father on the farm. Just before Christmas in 1916, when Jeff was almost fifteen and Ernest only ten, their grandfather, John Hellaby, died on 9 December 1916 at *Yeldersley Old Hall Farm*. Floral tributes at his funeral included those from:

To our own dear father from Will and Nellie

and:

With love to Granddad from Jeffery and Ernest

It is interesting to note that when John Hellaby had signed his will on 17 June 1915, Ellen's nephew, Percy Spencer who had recently taken over farming at neighbouring *Bentley Fields*, was a witness to his signature.

Grandfather John Hellaby was spared knowing of the loss of one of his sons in World War 1. Jeff and Ernest's Uncle Jack lost his life in action. On 27 July 1917 the *ASHBOURNE NEWS* reported that he was feared killed and on 3 August officially reported his death at Ypres. Signaller John Hellaby of the Sherwood Foresters is buried in the Vlamertinghe New Military Cemetery, West Vlannderen, Belgium.

Jeffery Hellaby celebrated his twenty-first birthday on 29 December 1922 and his younger brother Ernest on 19 April 1927. William and Ellen arranged for their photographs to be taken.

When my father married in 1928, my grandfather, William Hellaby, was not ready to retire from farming at *Bentley Hall*. It was my father's younger brother who remained there and later started his married life at the Hall. My older sister Marjorie has vivid memories of the times she spent there with her cousins.

RIGHT *Ernest Hellaby 1927*

BELOW *Jeff Hellaby 1922*

When I was a child, my father often spoke of the home of his youth with very great affection. He spent his first twenty-six years at *Bentley Hall* and carried a photograph of his old home in his wallet until the day he died. I was always fascinated by the stories and rumours that it was haunted. He would never commit himself on the verity of these stories, merely giving a wry smile. However, having subsequently visited with the Copestakes, who made it their home until 2010, I am convinced that this house, with over 400 years of history as a family home, does retain some secrets. Indeed, they have shared with me some of their own interesting experiences. I have also learnt, from other members of the family, of strange experiences which have no rational explanation.

Although the story of the underground passage between *Bentley Hall* and *Stydd Hall* is improbable, the possibility of the 'hidden room' described by my sister Marjorie, could most certainly have been a Priest Hole.

My sister recalls playing with our cousin Barbara:

I stayed at Bentley Hall. I remember running along the landing ……… jumping down into the Priest Hole and having a real struggle getting out! I remember wondering – how are we going to get out of here?

At the time, Marjorie was four and Cousin Barbara, three. They were doing what children have done from time immemorial and been exploring where they had been expressly told not to go. But, in jumping down into the secret room, these two little girls were plunging back three hundred and fifty years into history. The Priest Hole where they found themselves may well have housed many Catholics up to the very highest level in the land. *Bentley Hall* played a part in the political intrigues of the sixteenth century and the story of those for whom *Bentley Hall* was home at this time is worthy of re-telling.

The Bentleys, like many of the nobility of Derbyshire in the sixteenth century, remained loyal to the Catholic faith. Edward Bentley became involved with Anthony Babington (1561-1586), a Derbyshire Catholic nobleman who, as a child had been a pageboy to Bess of Hardwick and later became a page in the service of Mary Stuart whilst she was Queen Elizabeth's prisoner in England. The Babington plot of 1586 was designed to kill Queen Elizabeth and free Queen Mary with a view to placing her on the throne. The plot was bungled and Babington, along with his fellow conspirators, was executed. Edward Bentley Esq. of Hungry Bentley was tried at the Old Bailey on a charge of high treason and convicted in 1586. He was attainted, his estate forfeited to the Crown and he himself paid the ultimate penalty with his life.

The sad demise of the last of the Bentleys of *Bentley Hall* may lend just a little credence to the highly fanciful legend that there was a plot to remove Mary Stuart from her imprisonment at nearby Tutbury Castle and hide her at *Bentley Hall*. According to the Barkers, who lived at the Hall between 1975 and 1981, it was even rumoured among the locals that she may have spent one night there on her way from imprisonment at Chatsworth to Tutbury.

He took him to a room which was called the armoury and when they were there he was shown a sword. The sword disappeared later after some workmen had been doing some work there.

Peggy Halton (nee Poyser) also reinforced the story of a secret room, which was on a different level, when she told me:

My father (Arthur Owen Poyser) *told me of when he visited his older cousin Jeff Hellaby at Bentley Hall. Your father Jeff took him up to a room which was disguised and on a different level – you had to jump down into it. He took him to a room which was called the armoury and when they were there he was shown a sword. The sword disappeared later after some workmen had been doing some work there.*

This story, with mention of a room called the armoury, is most particularly intriguing when recalling that Edmund

I remember going to Bentley Hall. . . . They've got two fine staircases haven't they? The old staircase interested me very much — it was a beautiful staircase — really rich oak.

Browne of *Bentley Hall* was implicated in a conspiracy against Oliver Cromwell in 1654 and that he was suspected of storing arms at the Hall. (See PART TWO: THE PREDECESSORS).

Mary Jeffery of the *Home Farm*, West Broughton also has her own childhood memories of *Bentley Hall,* the home of her Great Aunt Nellie and Great Uncle Will:

I remember going to Bentley Hall. Auntie Nellie must have been showing me around or something. They've got two fine staircases haven't they? The old staircase interested me very much – it was a beautiful staircase – really rich oak. There's a picture around somewhere of when cousin Dolly married Ernest Hand and Auntie Nellie had the reception there. My sister Marie was a bridesmaid.

My own first visits to *Bentley Hall* were as a babe in arms and a very young child when we would visit my uncle and aunt and young cousins. Clearly I have no recollection of these early visits. Although I have known the exterior all of my life, it was not until the 1960s when my father took me, together with our young daughter Clare, to see inside. I remember one of the things which made the greatest impact on me at the time was the sloping oak floor in what had been my father's bedroom. I also endeavoured to visualise the party which had been thrown in the drawing room in the west wing to celebrate my father's twenty-first birthday.

Ellen figured as a strong influence in the early lives of all of her grandchildren. She maintained very close contact with all of her family throughout her life. Her unmarried sister, Fanny, during her later years made her home at *Bentley Hall* and her widowed sister Elizabeth was also living there in 1919. Ellen was a regular visitor to the homes of her brothers and sisters and she often hosted them and their families at *Bentley Hall*. She also

Bentley Hall in 2008

maintained close contact with her brothers' families across the Atlantic. Not only have Marjorie and I, her granddaughters, retained our own clear memories but so have her great nieces and nephews. Her nephew Geoff Jeffery in America, grandson of her brother Joseph, has fond memories of her from his own first visit in 1939.

I remember particularly your grandmother (Ellen) conducting my tour of various members of the family. Percy Spencer provided the transportation. One of our stops was at the home of Jeffery Hellaby, where among others were two children, I listed them as being 6 and 1 years of age, but now it seems likely that they were 8 and 3 (what would a 20 yr- old college student know about children's ages?) I'm assuming the 3- year old was you? Incidentally your grandmother was a delightful person. She wanted me to see everyone possible during my visit, and she was a wonderful guide. (See PART THREE: THE PIONEERS)

My own childhood memories of my grandmother are of a reserved, somewhat austere person who did not reveal her emotions readily. She always appeared calm, sure and very much in control of her life. Indeed, as a little girl, I sometimes found her quite formidable as a particularly memorable incident illustrates. I was a child who loved to go barefoot (nothing changes!) and when my mother, having despaired because I always kicked off my shoes, bought me some lace-up boots, I threw a tantrum. My grandmother, without further ado, sat me on the kitchen table at *Fauld House*, shocking me into a realisation that maybe this was a battle that I was not going to win and laced me into the boots with a:

She won't kick those off in a hurry!

Ivy House where Ellen and William Hellaby retired

My mother's relationship with my grandmother was never an easy one, primarily because they were such very different personalities: Ellen's somewhat imperious and punctilious manner contrasted with my mother's more outgoing personality.

I remember my grandmother Ellen as a woman of very high standards, superbly organised, dainty and meticulous in all things and always immaculate in her grooming and dress. I can recall looking into the top drawer of her chest of drawers, in the bedroom which was always kept as hers when she lived with us, and seeing her many pairs of beautiful buttoned gloves neatly arranged by colour and fabric. High buttoned boots and neat shoes were in the cupboard. She kept her dressing table pristine and I recall the porcelain candle holder and snuffer which were always there. She would show me the fine stitching on her personally sewn lace-trimmed nightgowns and I knew I would never be able to emulate such beautiful needlework. In the attics upstairs at *Fauld House* there were large travel trunks where some of her beautiful old dresses were stored, including a beautiful ivory silk brocade evening gown embroidered with roses. The content of these old trunks provided a treasure trove for dressing up for my sister and me.

Ellen and William left *Bentley Hall* when their younger son, Ernest married in 1931. They moved to *Ivy House*, Marston Montgomery, Derbyshire.

My elder sister has more memories of our grandmother. She also has vivid memories of our Hellaby grandfather who died before I was born. Marjorie, when a young child of three and four years old, would stay with her grandparents at *Ivy House* and also visit their old home and our Hellaby cousins at *Bentley Hall*.

Marjorie recalled:

I used to go and stay at Marston with Granny and Granddad. I remember going down the pathway in their lovely garden – I then went all the way down the steps on my tricycle! I used to get up early and go and get the milk with Granddad every morning. I remember on the right hand side there were two outbuildings – he kept pigs there – and there was a woodshed. There was a long orchard and some land – he had sheep and calves there – and also beef cattle – young stock. I used to walk down into Marston with him – he was a wonderful man.

I remember his car with its leather seats and driving into Ashbourne a lot with Granny and Granddad. I used to go with Granny into the shoe shop and the men's clothes shop and also to the lovely flower shop. I remember the kitchen and the jar of humbugs. I was very close to my Granny. I was close to both of them.

I remember Granny was very particular about her dress. She was always very neat and organised. I think she was a very good cook. Her hair was always immaculate. I can see her now – in the double bed – her long white nightdresses – lace round the edges. She un-plaited her hair and re-plaited it every morning. I have her wonderful watch. It was given to me because I was the eldest grandchild.

Her hair was always immaculate. I can see her now – in the double bed – her long white nightdresses – lace round the edges. She un-plaited her hair and re-plaited it every morning.

Mary Jeffery of the *Home Farm*, West Broughton also recalled my grandparents, her Great Aunt Nellie and Great Uncle Will:

My earliest memories of seeing Auntie Nellie and Uncle Will were of when they'd visit here. I remember seeing a Ford car- we used to call them 'Tin Lizies'. Uncle Will was one of the earliest people to drive a car. We liked Uncle Will – he was jolly – a nice man – he made you laugh and forget your religion (sic).

Auntie Nellie and Auntie Polly (Mary Spencer) *would come and visit on a Wednesday and stay with Grandpa* (Ellen's brother John). *They also brought Jeff and Auntie Polly's son Percy* (Spencer) *with them. Uncle Will Hellaby and Jeff and Percy would go on to Uttoxeter market. Percy's wife Mabel would go with them. They would then return here* (*Home Farm*, West Broughton) *after the market and take Auntie Nellie and Auntie Polly back to Bentley Hall and Bentley Fields.*

I am also indebted to Bill Hellaby, son of my grandfather's youngest brother Harry Hellaby, who, before he died in 2006, shared with me his fond memories of my grandparents.

I remember many visits to Bentley Hall to see Uncle Will and Aunt Nellie. I recall staying there as a young boy around 1928 when we lived at Doles Farm, Clifton. He was a wonderful man - a grand chap was Uncle Will. Aunt Nellie was very kind and hospitable. I remember policemen visiting Bentley Hall because poachers had been shot there. My father helped them when they moved from Bentley Hall to Ivy House when your grandfather retired in 1931. I remember catching a Stevenson's bus and walking from the 'Cubley Stoop' (The Howard Arms Inn was always known as the Cubley Stoop) *to Marston Montgomery to visit them at Ivy House.*

Ellen and William Hellaby were delighted to host their nephew John Arthur Jeffery (son of Ellen's eldest brother Thomas) together with his wife Myra and son John Arthur at *Bentley Hall* when Thomas's son and grandson visited in 1928. During this visit, John Arthur met many members of the family including Ellen's newly married eldest son Jeffery and his wife Ida at *Fauld House*. The pictures on the right were taken during that visit and have been provided by John Arthur's grandson, John Arthur the third.

My grandfather, like his father and grandfather before him and my father after him, died of a heart attack. He

ABOVE *Fauld House 1928. L. to r. Ellen Hellaby, William Hellaby, Ida Hellaby, John Arthur Jeffery, Myra Jeffery*

ABOVE *Tutbury Castle 1928. L. to r. John Arthur Jeffery, William Hellaby, Ellen Hellaby, Myra Jeffery*

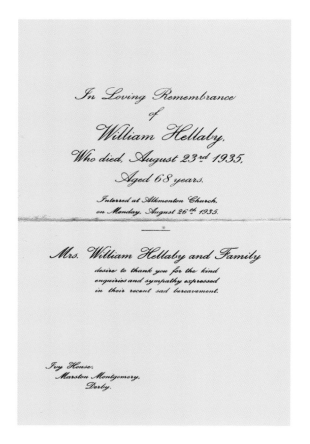

Memoriam Card

died on 23 August 1935 eight months before I was born. His death certificates states that the cause of death was myocarditis. My father was present at his death. His obituary recorded:

Few men were better known or held in such high esteem in the district, and the news of his death was received with profound regret throughout the district.

The *ASHBOURNE NEWS* of 29 August 1935 reported:

DEATH OF MR. W. HELLABY
FUNERAL AT ALKMONTON CHURCH
Many Sympathisers

It is with much regret we record the death of Mr. W. Hellaby of *Ivy House*, Marston Montgomery, which took place on Friday last. Few men were better known or held in such high esteem in the district, and the news of his death was received with profound regret throughout the district.

Mr. Hellaby, who was 68 years of age, resided at Bentley Hall, Alkmonton for 28 years and retired to Marston four years ago. For twenty years he was churchwarden of Alkmonton Church, and for the same period he acted as steward for the Cubley Methodist Church, carrying out his duties with a conscientiousness which was characteristic of his quiet unassuming disposition. He was a valuable official and both churches will feel his loss keenly.

He was the senior trustee of the Earl Ferrars Lodge of Oddfellows, of which he had been a member for very many years. He was elected president of the Brailsford Ploughing Match Committee for 1935 and was a member of the Ashbourne Shire Horse Society.

The funeral took place on Monday at Alkmonton Church where there was such a large gathering present that many were unable to get into the church.

The funeral was conducted by Dr. W. B. Dearden (Vicar of Alkmonton) and the Reverend E. A. Elliot (Vicar of Cubley). The hymns 'Abide with me' and 'Jesu lover of my soul' were sung.

The family mourners were Mrs. Hellaby (widow), Messrs. Jeffery and Ernest Hellaby (sons), Mrs. J. and Mrs. E. Hellaby (daughters in law), Messrs. R. Hellaby, G. Hellaby and H. Hellaby (brothers), Mrs. Housley, Mrs. F. Barnes, Mrs. A. A. Watkinson (sisters), Mrs. H. Hellaby (sister-in-law), and Mrs. F. Bainbridge (aunt).

The Earl Ferrars Lodge was well represented and the bretheren include Mr. F. Hellaby, the secretary.

Other relatives and friends present included .... (Almost 100 names were recorded). There were many floral tributes including one from his three grandchildren:

MARJORIE, BARBARA AND BILLIE

Ellen survived her husband by fifteen years. She made her home with her younger son Ernest and family at *Fullwood Farm*, Hulland. She also, as indicated, regularly spent her summers with her elder son Jeff and family at *Fauld House*.

Fauld House, home of Jeffery Hellaby and family. Ellen's eldest son Jeff farmed at Fauld House for twenty-seven years and it was my childhood home. It was also home to her eldest granddaughter Marjorie with her husband John Snow and became the early childhood home of Ellen's first three great granddaughters. It was where Ellen spent time in the summers of her later years

During the summer of 1949, when she was eighty-seven-years old, my grandmother's health began to decline. She remained active however and did not become seriously frail until shortly before her death. I recall the period between Christmas and New Year 1949–1950 very clearly. My parents spent most days at *Fullwood Farm*, Hulland and I was left in the care of my sister Marjorie.

Ellen died on 1 January 1950. It was my sister's birthday. Her obituary appeared in both the *ASHBOURNE NEWS* and the *ASHBOURNE TELEGRAPH*. It is the latter which is quoted:

A winsome personality which attracted a wide circle of friends.

My sister Marjorie and two elder cousins Barbara and Bill attended her funeral. My cousin Sheila and I were considered too young and remained at *Fullwood Farm*. I remember that it seemed like a very long time before everyone returned without my much loved grandmother Ellen.

DEATH OF MRS W. HELLABY
WELL KNOWN ALKMONTON RESIDENT

Many of our older readers, especially those in farming circles, will learn with regret of the death on January 1st of Mrs. W. Hellaby, who, with her late husband resided at *Bentley Hall*, Alkmonton for very many years.

Mrs. Hellaby had a winsome personality which attracted a wide circle of friends and her death will be deeply regretted by many. She outlived her husband by 15 years, and she leaves two sons. The funeral took place on January 5th at Alkmonton Church which she had attended for many years whilst she lived at *Bentley Hall*. The ceremony was conducted by the Vicar, the Rev. J. Naish, and the hymns, 'Jesu, lover of my soul' and 'Abide with Me' were feelingly sung.

The chief mourners were Mr. and Mrs. Jeffery Hellaby, Mr. and Mrs. Ernest Hellaby, Marjorie and Barbara Hellaby, Mrs. Cook (Sister Clara) and Mr. J. Cook, Mr. and Mrs. P. S. Spencer (Percy and Mabel), Mr. P. R. J. Spencer (Jeffery), Mrs. O. Hand (Dolly), Mr. and Mrs. T. Jeffery and family (the *Riddings*), Mr. W. Jeffery, Mr. Offley Jeffery, Mr. Frank Jeffery, Mrs. Roberts, Mrs. Houseley, Mr. G. Hellaby, Mr. Hellaby ……….. And many more.

Descendants of Ellen (nee Jeffery) and William Hellaby

Ellen's eldest son, Jeffery, married Ida Webster on 4 June 1928. They had first met at school. They were both weekly boarders at Queen Elizabeth's School, Ashbourne. My mother told the story of how she:

Had had my eye on him and was determined to ask him to dance at an end of term Christmas Dance but he was so shy!

Ida Olive Webster was the fifth child of Ralph and Olive (nee Robinson) Webster. Born at the *Common Farm*, Cubley, Ida was married from the home to which her parents retired, the *Hall Farm*, Stramshall near Uttoxeter. The *UTTOXETER AND ASHBOURNE TIMES* of Wednesday 6 June 1928 reported the wedding.

Had had my eye on him and was determined to ask him to dance at an end of term Christmas Dance but he was so shy!

FAR RIGHT *Family group at the wedding of Jeffery Hellaby and Ida Webster*

BELOW *Wedding of Jeffery Hellaby and Ida Webster. Ellen and William Hellaby are seen on the left*

WEDDINGS OF LOCAL INTEREST
HELLABY – WEBSTER

There were animated scenes in the quiet village of Stramshall on Monday, on the occasion of the marriage of Miss Ida Olive Webster, third daughter of Mr. and Mrs. R. Webster of Creighton House, Stramshall, to Mr. William Jeffery Hellaby, eldest son of Mr. and Mrs. William Hellaby of Bentley Hall, Longford, Derby. The ceremony was performed in Stramshall Church by the Rev. C. F. L. Barnwell (Vicar) assisted by the Rev. Dr. Dearden of Alkmonton, and there was a crowded attendance of friends. Miss Webster has for the past six years been an assistant mistress in the infants department at Longford School and on Thursday was presented by Mrs. Bourne (headmistress), on behalf of the scholars with a pair of oxidised candlesticks. She was also the recipient of presents from the staff. The bride, who was given away by her father, was attired in ivory georgette and wore a wreath and veil of orange blossoms and carried a shower bouquet of white carnations. She was attended by her sisters, Elsie May and Phyllis Margaret and Miss Betty Meakin, niece and Miss Joan Radford (cousin of the bridegroom). Miss E. M. Webster was attired in peach flowered georgette and Miss P. M. Webster in salmon georgette and the remaining two bridesmaids in blue silk. All wore close-fitting gold lace caps trimmed with foliage and shoes and stockings to match their dresses. The two first mentioned carried bouquets of golden tea roses, and the two latter baskets of forget-me-knots…………… Mr. Ernest Hellaby was best man……………

Ida joined Jeff at *Fauld House Farm*. Jeff and Ida Hellaby gave Ellen two granddaughters: my sister Marjorie was born on 1 January 1931 and I arrived on 22 April 1936. We grew up at Fauld: fortunately both of us were at school in Uttoxeter in November 1944 when the huge RAF 'Fauld Explosion' occurred. The underground bomb store of about 4000 tons of explosives, blew up. My parents and the farm were only saved by the low hill which interposed itself between the 'Dump' and the farm. My father ran along Fauld Lane to see what assistance he could render.

Three years after my parents married, Ellen's younger son, Ernest, married Gladys Ashton on 11 June 1931. The *ASHBOURNE NEWS* reported the wedding.

LONGFORD WEDDING
Mr. J. E. Hellaby Married to Miss Gladys Ashton

****

The wedding took place on Tuesday last week at St Chad's, Longford, of Miss Gladys Ashton, only daughter of the late Mr. and Mrs. Ashton, of Tissington, and Mr. John Ernest Hellaby, son of Mr. and Mrs Hellaby of *Bentley Hall*, Longford. The bride has resided with her uncle and aunt, Mr. and Mrs. Cottrell Waterfall of *Dairy House*, Alkmonton.

The bride who was given away by her uncle, Mr. C. Waterfall, wore an ankle length dress of ivory crepe suede with a coatee to match, and she wore a veil which was worn by her grandmother and mother. Her shower bouquet of pink carnations and cream roses was afterwards placed on her parents' grave at Tissington. The bridesmaids were Misses Margery and Joan Waterfall (cousins of the bride), whose dresses were ankle length, that of the former being of deep pink crepe suede whilst the younger attendant was attired in pale pink satin with ribbon frills on net. Both carried bouquets of pink and mauve sweet peas. The bridegroom's cousin, Mr. Owen Ball (grandson of George Jeffery) was best man.

ABOVE LEFT *Ellen's granddaughters Marjorie and Valerie Hellaby c.1938*

ABOVE RIGHT *Ernest and Gladys Hellaby with their children Barbara, Bill and Sheila*

LEFT *Ellen's eldest granddaughter Marjorie*

RIGHT *Jeff and Ida Hellaby at a family wedding*

BELOW *My twenty-first birthday. L. to r. Ida Hellaby, Jeffery Hellaby, Valerie Hellaby, Colin Hardy, Marjorie (nee Hellaby) Snow, John Snow*

Ernest and Gladys Hellaby gave Ellen three grandchildren, Barbara born in 1932, William, known as Bill, in 1934 and Sheila in 1938.

Ellen's eldest granddaughter Marjorie married John Snow of *Field House*, Marchington, Staffordshire on 2 April 1955. Their three daughters are Jennifer Anne

ABOVE *Jeff and Ida Hellaby, with their daughters Marjorie and Valerie, on the occasion of their Golden Wedding 6 June 1978*

LEFT *Ellen's second granddaughter Barbara Ellen Hellaby*

born on 14 May 1956, Susan Jane on 26 September 1957 and Gillian Noreen on 18 March 1959. These three great granddaughters of Ellen have provided four great, great granddaughter descendants: Sarah, Anna, Rachael and Georgia.

Ellen's granddaughter Valerie Hardy with her husband Colin and daughter Clare shortly before sailing for a year in America where they visited many of the descendants of Ellen's pioneering brothers

Ellen's granddaughter Valerie with her granddaughters Isabel and India 1998

I married Colin Hardy on 15 August 1959 at Hanbury. We had met over an atlas in a lecture theatre at the University of Leeds! Our three children were Clare Helen Mona born on 15 December 1963, Mark Jeffery on 3 May 1965 and Sarah Louise on 3 September 1966. Sadly, our son and youngest daughter died as infants. Our daughter Clare has provided Ellen's line with two great, great granddaughter descendants: Isabel and India de Bono.

The story of the descendants of Ellen's younger son, Ernest, is one of tragedy. Ernest's wife, Gladys, was only forty-seven when she died on 21 December 1954. Ernest died fourteen years later on 29 October 1968. He died eleven years before his elder brother Jeff and was only sixty-two. Both Ernest and Gladys died of cancer.

Their son Bill married Carole Coxon and had two sons, Mark and Simon. Their youngest daughter Sheila married Jeffery Trefine and had a daughter Fiona. Bill, his wife Carole and sister, Sheila, were all victims of cancer: Sheila was only forty-eight and Bill fifty-two when they died.

Their elder sister Barbara married Tom Evans and had a son Martin and a daughter Jane. They were later divorced. Barbara also died of cancer in 1997. Barbara's daughter Jane and Bill's son Mark have emigrated to Australia. Ellen now has Australian great, great grandchildren descendants.

Ellen was one of the lynch pins in building and maintaining the family bonds of what, by the middle of the twentieth century, was becoming a far flung family. Over seventy years after she had kept house for her brother Thomas in Minneapolis, her elder son Jeffery Hellaby and her third granddaughter (Valerie) were to visit many of her brothers' descendants across America.

Ellen's son Jeffery Hellaby in 1968 on board the SS France sailing for America to visit his daughter (myself) and family and also children and grandchildren of his Uncle, the Reverend Joseph Jeffery

VOIE SANS ISSUE

Those with no descendants

SARAH ANN JEFFERY

1855 – 1864

Affectionately remembered

It was quite remarkable that for Thomas and Mary's family of fifteen children born between 1844 and 1865 there was no infant mortality. Only one of their children, Sarah Ann, died in childhood.

Sarah Ann, born on 25 March 1855 was Thomas and Mary's tenth child and fourth daughter. When she died, just over nine years later on 15 June 1864, she was one of a family of fourteen. Her youngest sister, two-year-old Ellen, was probably too young to appreciate the impact of Sarah's death upon this tightly knit family. However, all of her remaining siblings had doubtless created their own special bond with their sister. Her elder brother William named his first daughter, born in 1874, Sarah Ann in memory of the sister who had died ten years previously.

Sarah Ann's death certificate states that the cause of death was cephalitis (inflammation of the brain) which she had suffered for thirteen days before she died.

Sarah Ann was buried at Longford. Her grave is next to that of her grandparents, Thomas and Margaret Jeffery, close to the door of the church. Her tombstone memorial records:

Affectionate Remembrance
of
Sarah Ann
Fourth daughter of Thomas and
Mary Jeffery
Riddings Farm Hungry Bentley
Who died June 15th 1864
Aged nine years

Shall not the Judge of all the
Earth Do Right GEN. XV111.25

Tombstone of Sarah Ann Jeffery, Longford Churchyard

CHARLES JEFFERY
1859 – 1881

Death keeps not calendar

Charles, born on 5 June 1859, was Thomas and Mary's fourteenth child and seventh son. He was almost seventeen when his father died. By that time it was clear that his elder brother, Owen, would take over at the *Riddings*.

Charles went into the grocery business in Littleover, near Derby. He did his apprenticeship with A. J. Pegge, grocer of the Strand in Derby who had a business in Littleover. Following his successful apprenticeship, Charles took over the Littleover business.

The 1881 census confirms that twenty-one-year-old Charles was a grocer and baker, employing one man and living on his own at Shepherd Street, Littleover. It was whilst he was in Littleover that he came to know Rosamond Clews more closely. (We have met Rosamond earlier in the PIONEERS section). Rosamond, living at *Littleover Old Hall* had for many years been a close friend of his elder sister Mary (Polly). Charles and Rosamond became engaged to be married. The marriage, however, was never to take place. Charles suffered a tragically sudden death aged only twenty-two years.

On the morning of Thursday 25 August 1881 Charles went as usual to his grocery shop in Littleover where he collapsed and died of heart failure. His death was reported in the *DERBY EVENING TELEGRAPH*:

AWFULLY SUDDEN DEATH OF A DERBY GROCER

Intelligence reaches us of the awfully sudden death of Mr. Charles Jeffery, grocer, while in his shop in Littleover. The deceased, who was a most respectable young man, aged only twenty-two years, was apprenticed with Mr. A. J. Pegge, grocer of the Strand, and recently took over the latter's Littleover business. Mr. Jeffery was apparently in his usual health until 10 o'clock this morning, when he suddenly dropped down and expired. Dr. Carter Whigg, who was called to see the deceased, expressed the opinion that death had ensued from heart disease.

Four days later on 29 August 1881 the *DERBY EVENING TELEGRAPH* reported:

THE SUDDEN DEATH AT LITTLEOVER

Mr. Coroner Whiston held an inquest at Littleover last (Friday) evening on the body of Charles Jeffery, aged 22, grocer and baker. The facts relating to Mr. Jeffery's sudden death have appeared in these columns. He was in his shop on Thursday, when he was observed to stagger and fall. Assistance was rendered him and Dr. Carter Whigg sent for. Death had, however, ensued before the doctor's arrival. Dr. Whigg gave it as his opinion that death was due to syncope, or failure of the heart's action, and a verdict was returned accordingly.

Charles is buried at Alkmonton and his memorial reads:

In
Affectionate Remembrance
of
Charles
Seventh son of
Thomas and Mary Jeffery
Who died suddenly August 25th
1881
Aged 22 years

Therefore be ye also ready for in such
an hour ye think not the Son of
Man Cometh.

ELIZABETH JEFFERY
1851 – 1923

Nothing is certain
but death and taxes

*Elizabeth aka
Lizzie Jeffery*

Elizabeth, born on 25 April 1851, was Thomas and Mary's seventh child and second daughter. In 1881, twenty-nine-year-old Elizabeth was living away from home. She was working as a housekeeper in a farming household at Horsley Woodhouse, near Derby.

Elizabeth was always known as Lizzie. She was almost thirty-four when she married a farmer's son, thirty-eight-year-old Thomas Holbrook, on 20 April 1885. The Holbrooks were farming in the Tutbury area in Staffordshire. Thomas, however, had gone into the grocery business. On his marriage certificate he was credited as a grocer and living close to Burton-on-Trent at Horninglow, Staffordshire.

Elizabeth and Thomas were married at the Parish Church in Somersal Herbert and her brother William and sister Fanny were witnesses to the marriage.

Their only child, John Thomas, was born the following year in 1886 and was registered in Burton-on-Trent, Staffordshire. Elizabeth and Thomas had sixteen years of married life together. Thomas was only fifty-four when he died in 1901.

In 1901 the widow Elizabeth and her fifteen-year-old son John were living at 31, Derby Road, Horninglow. John was working as an Engineers office boy. Ten years later they were still there and John was now a Customs and Excise Officer probably keeping an eye for the government on the Burton brewing industry.

Later, Elizabeth and her son John, who never married, moved to Barnsley.

Mary Jeffery at the *Home Farm*, West Broughton told me:

I do remember about Lizzie. It was an occasion when father and mother (Offley and Cissie) *were on holiday near Blackpool they met some people from Barnsley and discovered that John Holbrook was living in Barnsley. He had something to do with the Brewery and had moved from Burton to Barnsley. Mother wrote to him for quite a while. When John Holbrook was ill in hospital, Auntie Katie and father* (Katie Jeffery and her brother Offley) *went to see him and arranged for him to be brought down here. I just very faintly remember him being here. He was known to be a very good musician – a wonderful pianist. He didn't get married. Auntie Katie helped to organise his funeral at Alkmonton.*

Photographs of Lizzie at *Bentley Fields* with her sisters, nieces and nephews, reveal that, after her husband's death, she did spend time visiting family and in 1919 she was living with her sister and brother-in-law Ellen and William Hellaby at *Bentley Hall*. She was, however, with her son in Barnsley when she died, aged seventy-two on 21 May 1923. Both she and her son John, who died aged 68, on 10 January 1954, are buried at Alkmonton.

Elizabeth's memorial reads:

*In Loving Memory of
Elizabeth Holbrook
Wife of the late Thomas Holbrook
of Horninglow*

*Who died May 21 1923
Aged 72 years*

*Waiting for the coming of Our
Lord and saviour Jesus Christ*

FANNY JEFFERY
1856 – 1925

'Dear Fanny'

*Fanny Jeffery
c.1976*

In the spring of 1881, twenty-four-year-old Fanny was with her younger sister Ellen at *Somersal Mill*, the home of their brother John and his wife Maria. There was a new baby in the home, Fanny's new niece, Mary Mabel. Ten years later, Fanny was living with her sister Clara and her husband Arthur and their young family at the *Holly Bush*, Grangemill.

The *Riddings* remained Fanny's main home for most of her life and she was certainly there with her widowed sister Mary (Polly) and nephew Percy Spencer in 1911. She did, however, spend her final years with her sister

Fanny, born on 10 May 1856, was Thomas and Mary's eleventh child and fifth daughter.

Fanny did not leave the *Riddings* to marry. She did, however, spend time in the homes of her married siblings and became a much loved aunt to her many nephews, nieces and others in the family. Many years after her death, my cousin Jeffery Spencer, although he was only two-and-a-half when she died, had a distant memory of her and spoke of her with great affection.

Fanny at the Riddings

Fanny at Bentley Fields

Ellen at *Bentley Hall*. It was probably in 1914, when her sister Polly and nephew Percy moved to *Bentley Fields* and her brother Owen with his family returned to the *Riddings*, that Fanny moved to *Bentley Hall*.

Fanny died on 25 April 1925. The messages on the many floral tributes for her funeral were a testament to the love and affection which she had inspired within the family.

THE LATE MISS FANNY JEFFERY

The funeral took place at Alkmonton Church on Friday, August 28th of Miss Fanny Jeffery, fifth daughter of the late Thomas Jeffery of Riddings Farm, Hungry Bentley. She passed away after a long illness patiently born, on August 25th at *Bentley Hall*, the home of her sister, Mrs. Hellaby, with whom she had resided for several years.

The Rev. Dr. W. B. Dearden impressively conducted the service, the hymns 'Jesu lover of my soul' and 'Peace, perfect peace' being sung. The coffin was of un-polished English oak with brass appointments and name-plate inscribed:

Fanny Jeffery
Died August 25th 1925
Aged 69 years

The bearers were Messrs. O. Poyser, O. Jeffery, Wm. Jeffery and J. Cook (nephews).
The grave was tastefully lined with white flowers and evergreens. The mourners were Mr. J. Jeffery (brother), Mrs. Spencer, Mrs. Cook, Mrs. Hellaby (sisters), Mr. A. Cook, Mr. Wm. Hellaby (brothers-in-law), Mrs. Wm. Jeffery senr., Mrs. Owen Jeffery senr. (sisters-in-law), Mr. and Mrs. C. Ball, Miss K. Jeffery, Mr. and Mrs. P. Spencer, Mr. F. Jeffery, Mr. Jos. Cook, Mrs. Johnson, Mr. and Mrs. E. Hand, Mr. and Mrs. T. Jeffery, Mr. J. Hellaby, Mr. E. Hellaby, Mr. O. Jeffery (nephews and nieces), Mrs. Wibberley (cousin). Amongst others at the church were………………

There followed a list of many friends.

Below is a selection from the list of floral tributes which were sent:

To dear Fanny with love from Sister Margaret;
In fond remembrance from Brother John and family;
A token of love to dear Sister Fanny from Polly;
To dear Fanny from Clara, Arthur and Family (Borrowash);
A last token of love to dear Sister Fanny from Ellen and Will;
With love to dear Fanny from Sister Hannah and family;
With deepest sympathy and loving remembrance to dear Aunt Fanny from all at the Riddings;
To dear Aunt Fanny with love and fond remembrance from Percy and Mabel;
With fond love to dear Aunt Fanny from Jeffery and Ernest;
With love to Aunt Fanny from Charlie and Polly;
With loving sympathy from all at Mill Farm;
In loving remembrance of dear Auntie Fanny from Nelly and Polly (Poyser nieces);
With fondest love and deepest sympathy from Dollie and Ernest (Stydd Hall);
To dear Auntie from Offley and Cissie;
To Auntie Fanny with love from Harold;
To Auntie Fanny with love from little Jeffery

The last one listed was from the Jeffery Spencer who remembered her seventy-five years later. There were many more loving tributes to Fanny Jeffery who had clearly been much loved and held in such high regard by her family and friends.

APPENDICES

ADDENDUM TO THE STORY OF PIONEER
THOMAS JEFFERY
1845–1927

In mid-summer 2010, when the writing of this book was practically complete, I received some very exciting packages from America. John Arthur Jeffery from California, great grandson of pioneering Thomas, was very generously loaning me four old photograph albums which contained around three hundred family photographs dating from the late nineteenth and early twentieth centuries. John, who I had met in 1992 whilst staying with his parents John and Marion in Los Angeles, had inherited the albums from his parents, grand-parents and great aunt Adelaide.

The albums were crammed with many quality photo-graphs which I found totally irresistible and fascinating for the glimpse they provided of life in America for our ancestors at the time. They were a veritable treasure trove and I felt compelled to include at least some of the earliest ones within this book.

Some of these wonderful old pictures I have been able to incorporate within the story of John's great grand-father Thomas Jeffery in the section on the PIONEERS. A few of the other early ones, most dating from before pioneering Thomas's death in 1928, are included in this addendum.

Photographs included are of Thomas himself in his later years in California together with his second wife Jessie who he married in January 1894 and their daughter Adelaide born in December 1894. Additionally there are pictures of Thomas and Maria's son John Arthur (Art) Jeffery and his wife Myra, who he married in 1898. Also included are photographs of Thomas's three grand-children: Harold Whiting who was born in 1889; Dorothy Rose who was born in 1903 but who died in 1909 and John Arthur the second who was born in 1912 and who made a number of visits to Derbyshire.

LEFT *Thomas and Jessie with Art and Myra circa 1899*

ABOVE *Thomas's daughter-in-law Myra on the Pacific coast when visiting with Thomas and family circa 1902*

A<small>BOVE</small> *Thomas's daughter Adelaide on her pony at home at Redlands, California circa 1906*

R<small>IGHT</small> *Adelaide at Redlands circa 1906*

B<small>ELOW</small> *Thomas, Jessie and Adelaide - a family group outside 405 West Palm Avenue, Redlands circa 1906*

ABOVE *Art and Myra with friends. Myra and Cora were expectant mothers hence the 'Before' notations*

TOP RIGHT *Thomas's first two grandchildren Harold and Dorothy with their nurse at their Minneapolis home circa 1903*

RIGHT *Art with Harold and Dorothy circa 1906*

Art and Myra with their children would regularly visit Thomas, Jessie and Adelaide in Redlands, California to escape the bitter cold of Minnesota winters. The photo albums reveal that they also travelled quite widely both within the USA and abroad although it was not until after Thomas's death that they travelled with their youngest son to Derbyshire.

LEFT INSET *Thomas with his family at Arrowhead in the San Bernadino Mountains, California circa 1907*

BELOW LEFT AND RIGHT *Myra riding with Harold whilst visiting Thomas and Jessie in the Redlands area circa 1909*

RIGHT *Myra on the beach –
possibly at Santa Monica or
Santa Barbara circa 1910*

BELOW INSET *Myra with
horse and carriage at their
Minneapolis home - early
twentieth century*

RIGHT *Art and Myra's daughter Dorothy
circa 1906. (Dorothy died in 1909)*

BELOW LEFT *Art and Myra's son Harold circa 1910*

BELOW CENTRE *Art and Myra bathing circa 1909*

BELOW RIGHT *Art on a Mississippi paddleboat circa 1909*

LEFT *Myra, Adelaide and Harold in the gardens at Redlands circa 1910*

In 1911, Thomas's daughter Adelaide entered Smith College, University of Massachusetts. She graduated in 1915. In 1912, Thomas's last grandson, John Arthur the second was born. Young John, like his elder brother Harold, was introduced early to his grandfather's home at Redlands and the San Bernadino Mountains of California.

BELOW *Adelaide in her room at Smith College, University of Massachusetts*

ABOVE LEFT *Adelaide at home at Redlands circa 1911*

BELOW LEFT *Thomas's youngest grandson John with his mother Myra in the San Bernadino Mountains circa 1913 and* BELOW RIGHT *Setting out on a trip from Redlands. L. to r. Harold, Thomas, Jessie, John and Myra*

LEFT *Harold, John and Myra in the San Bernadino Mountains*

RIGHT *Young John Arthur Jeffery the second with his nurse at his grandfather Thomas's old house in Minneapolis circa 1913*

LEFT INSET *John Arthur the second circa 1914*

RIGHT *L. to r. Myra, Art, Jessie, Adelaide, Lawrence Henderson (Adelaide's husband). Picture taken by John Arthur the second following his graduation from the University of Pennslyvania in 1935*

BELOW *John at Ojai, California in the 1930s where he was probably visiting his cousin Clara nee Jeffery Miller, daughter of pioneer brother George*

Photographs in the four albums loaned by John Arthur Jeffery the third reveal that Thomas maintained contact with his younger brother Arthur (1865-1929), some of whose family also moved to California. There is, in addition, a photograph in one of the albums which is most particularly intriguing. It shows John Arthur Jeffery the second (1912-1993), Thomas's younger grandson when in his twenties, in a mountain area: on the picture is one word – Ojai. Ojai, California is where Thomas's brother George Jeffery's daughter Clara (born in Canada in 1886) was living with her husband Julius Miller when they were farming in the Ojai Valley in 1938.

It does seem highly likely that Thomas's grandson John was in touch with the family of his brother George Jeffery (1849-1927). It would be nice to know for sure - but I will have to leave that for others to pursue.

THE JEFFERY REUNION

AUGUST 2008

The Jeffery family reunion organised by Irene Jeffery which took place on 9 August 2008 was a wonderful opportunity for family members from across the world to meet with many relatives they had heard about but never met before. For many of those who had journeyed from far afield it was also an opportunity to discover something of Jefferyland – the land of their roots. In addition to the visits to Longford and Alkmonton churches and a number of family farms lunch was taken in an ancient local inn which had doubtless been frequented by earlier generations of Jefferys.

Among many other delightful touches, Irene arranged for family members to make their own written contributions to this memorable occasion and in her newsletter thanked everyone who wrote and in particular Dorothy Jeffery. Dorothy is married to Christopher Jeffery the great grandson of William Jeffery (1846-1916) and her quote 'seemed aptly to sum up the whole occasion':

'To everything there is a season and a time for every purpose under heaven – turn, turn, turn.' The Jeffery wheel has been turning and today's fantastic gathering is part of the harvest. Thank you for a wonderful day.

THE MAIN GROUP OF OVER 100 FAMILY MEMBERS AT THE CELEBRATORY DINNER FOR THE FAMILY REUNION

The *DERBY EVENING TELEGRAPH* reported the occasion as follows:

Report by Martin Naylor. Pictures: Leah McLaren

ONE BIG, HAPPY FAMILY FROM FOUR CORNERS OF THE GLOBE

Jeffery clan gather at ancestral home to celebrate their Derbyshire roots

More than a hundred members of a Derbyshire family gathered for huge reunion on Saturday. Some flew in from as far as New Zealand and Alaska and toured the Derbyshire countryside, discovering more about their ancestors and the land they used to farm.

They then joined generations of the Jeffery family, who have worked the land near Ashbourne for more than 300 years, for a huge party at the Quality Hotel, in Derby Road, Ashbourne, in the evening.

The reunion was the idea of cousins Irene Jeffery and Val Hardy who had spent two-and-a-half years contacting family members from across the globe.

Ms. Jeffery, 62, who now lives in London, said: "It has been such a lot of hard work but seeing everyone here together at last makes it all worthwhile. It's just so exciting that so many people from such far-flung places have all got together to celebrate the family name."

Mrs Hardy, who lives in Gloucestershire agreed. She said that four members of the Jeffery family emigrated to the USA in the 1860s. "One of them, Joseph, became a minister in Iowa and now it is just wonderful that we have some family members over from the USA here."

Representing North America for the Jeffery family was 63-year-old Michael Jeffery, who is a court judge in Barrow, Alaska – the USA's most northerly city. He had travelled to the UK with his wife,

Esther, and three children – Christina, 23, Nicole, 21, and Jordan, 19.

He said: "Everyone has been wonderful and it is so nice to meet family members who I never even knew about before. We have had a tremendous day and it has been really interesting seeing all of the old places where our ancestors lived and worked. Our thanks have got to go to Irene and Val for their hard work in organising this great reunion."

The group started Saturday's tour at St John's Church, in Alkmonton, where dozens of members of the Jeffery family used to worship and are buried in the churchyard.

The stained-glass window at the Church was paid for by the children of Thomas and Mary Jeffery, who lived in the village in the late 1800s and early 1900s.

From there they went to see Richard and Rosemary Spencer, descendants of the Jefferys, whose home, Bentley Fields Open Farm, in Alkmonton, has been in the family for more than 200 years. Mrs Spencer said: "I am used to having lots of people come and go at the farm but I have never had this many visitors before. It's our 34th wedding anniversary today so this is a double celebration for us.'

Tim Jeffery, of Caley Road, Dronfield, took his two children, Rebecca, 14, and David, 12 – to the reunion. The 47 year-old said: "I was supposed to be playing cricket for Matlock this afternoon but I couldn't miss out on this. It's a once-in-a-lifetime opportunity to get together with so many members of the family."

LEFT Three generations of Jeffery descendants from the UK, USA and New Zealand (NZ) in front of the East Window in Alkmonton Church. The right-hand panel of the window was donated by the Jeffery family and it reads:
'To the Glory of God
in memory of the late Thomas and Mary Jeffery
by their children 1907'

Of the smaller group photographs that follow, the first shows descendants of John Jeffery (1786-1864) who married Dorothy Smith in 1830; Fanny Jeffery (1817-1864) who married Thomas Hunt in 1835 (Fanny's daughter Mary emigrated to New Zealand) and John Jeffery (1830-1915) who married Ann Robinson in 1843.

The other six group photographs show the descendants of eight of the fifteen children of Thomas Jeffery (1823-1876) who married Mary Robinson in 1843. Five of these six photographs show the descendants (with spouses) of Thomas, William, Joseph, Mary and Ellen and the last one shows descendants of Margaret, John and Clara.

EARLY JEFFERY DESCENDANTS

LEFT Front Row l. to r: Gill le Bargy, Valerie Bennett, Brenda Garner, Margaret Walker, Kate O'Malley (NZ). Back Row l. to r: Gordon McClellan, Diane McClellan, Jane McKirdy, Alan Walker, Connor O'Malley (NZ), Philip O'Malley (NZ), Rose O'Malley (NZ)

THOMAS'S DESCENDANTS – FROM ALASKA, USA

LEFT *Seated l. to r: Michael Jeffery, Esther Jeffery Standing l. to r: Christina Jeffery, Jordan Jeffery, Nicole Jeffery*

BELOW *Seated Row l. to r: Terri Houghton, Betsy Barker, Geoff Jeffery, Sally Houghton, Janet Harrison. Standing l. to r: David Jeffery Houghton holding Henry Jeffery Houghton, Kenneth Houghton, Robert Harrison*

JOSEPH'S DESCENDANTS – ALL FROM USA EXCEPT FOR BETSY BARKER

WILLIAM'S DESCENDANTS

ABOVE *Front Row l. to r: Irene Jeffery, David Jeffery, Rebecca Jeffery, Constance Bradley, Irene Jeffery, Arthur Jeffery, George Simmons, Beatrice Simmons, Dorothy Jeffery.*
Second Row l. to. r: Beryl Page, Rosalie Vicars-Harris, Anna Wilson (NZ), Elizabeth Watson, Eileen Lyons, Alexandra Hall, Susan Hall, Angela Jeffery Collingwood, Mary Wilson (NZ),

Christopher Jeffery, Katie Simmons.
Third Row l. to r: Philip Hidderley, Elizabeth Jeffery Stephens, Rusty Ahearne, Peter McCarthy, Laura Galloway, Alec Galloway, Denis Jeffery, Maureen Galloway, Nigel Collingwood
Back Row l. to r: Robert Jeffery, Jonathan Simmons, Graeme Wilson (NZ), Roger Wilson (NZ), Tim Jeffery, Malcolm Lewis

MARY'S DESCENDANTS

RIGHT *Front Row l. to r: Thomas Jeffery Spencer (NZ), Katherine Spencer (NZ), Georgiana Davey (NZ), Sally Davey (NZ)*
Seated Row l. to r: Elizabeth Spencer, Rosemary Spencer, Stella Spencer, Lorna Spencer (NZ), Katrina Spencer (NZ)
Back Row l. to r: Jonathan Davey (NZ), Richard Spencer, Jonathan Spencer (NZ), Andrew Kaufman (NZ)

ELLEN'S DESCENDANTS

MARGARET(M), JOHN (J) AND CLARA'S (C) DESCENDANTS

ABOVE *Front Row l. to r: India and Isabel de Bono, Georgia Young*
Seated l. to r: Susan Snow, Clare de Bono, Valerie Hardy, Marjorie Snow, Gillian Young, Jennifer Snow
Back Row l. to r: Anna Critchlow, Sarah Critchlow, Michael de Bono, Colin Hardy, John Snow, Mark Young, Rachael Critchlow

LEFT *Front Row l. to r: Joanna Jeffery (J), Thomas Jeffery (J) and Amy Jeffery (J)*
Seated: Margaret Poyser (M), Margaret Hidderley (M), John Hidderley (M), Margaret (Peggy) Halton (M), Vivian Lowe (J)
Standing l. to r: Colin Poyser (M), Simon Rawson (C), Claire Tideswell (J), David Lowe (J).

POSTCRIPT

A GLOBAL FAMILY

The Jeffery family shares a similar history with that of many other yeoman farming families. Jefferys remained close to their heartland of Hungry Bentley for many centuries. However, significant events in the mid-nineteenth century, as a consequence of both the agricultural and industrial revolutions, introduced major changes. No longer could a large family, with many aspiring sons, be sustained on a single farm. Hence, there was dispersal to other farms in the locality, including the Somersal cluster, and also dispersal to the New World.

The twentieth century witnessed a second phase of emigration taking Jeffery descendants away from their Derbyshire roots in Hungry Bentley and the *Riddings*. This dispersal has been to New Zealand, Canada and South Africa as well as across the United Kingdom. Jeffery roots are in the land and although many of the family remain in a rural environment and farm in the Derbyshire and the Staffordshire borderlands, many more now live in towns and cities working as doctors, teachers, scientists, engineers, designers and managers.

It is in the particulars that the Jeffery family has its individuality. The paradox of history is that it is not just about the past. It concerns the present, which it has helped to shape and the future which it will influence. It is something of which I have been acutely aware in writing the Jeffery family story as I have walked in the footsteps of my ancestors. It is not just the personal and often remarkable stories of family members which gives it its own special flavour. It is that the family has remained so closely knit across both time and space: history and geography.

Each generation has nourished its affection for its Derbyshire roots. The links between the nineteenth-century pioneers and their descendants in the New World with family members in the Old World has been maintained through the generations.

Eighth generation pioneers Thomas, Joseph and Arthur Jeffery all returned to visit the *Riddings*. Their younger sister Ellen Jeffery reciprocated and travelled half way

Thirteen of the fifteen children of Thomas Jeffery (1823-1876) and Mary nee Robinson Jeffery (1817-1906) with their mother, spouses and grandchildren at the Riddings in 1882.
Standing l. to r: John Fanny, Arthur, Ellen, Joseph, Mary, George, Thomas, George's second wife Mary, Elizabeth, Owen, John Poyser (Margaret's husband), Clara, William.
Seated back row adults l. to r: Maria (John's wife) with their daughter Mary (aka May) on knee, John (younger brother of Father Thomas who had died in 1876), Mother Mary, Maria (Thomas's wife), Margaret, Hannah (William's wife) with their son William Charles on knee.
Front row children l. to r: Sarah Ann (William and Hannah's daughter), Owen Poyser (Margaret and John's son), John Arthur (Thomas and Maria's son), Elizabeth Annie (William and Hannah's daughter). Two children in front middle - George's children by his first wife Sarah, William and Mary Ellen

across America. Visits by ninth generation children of Pioneer Thomas Jeffery, John Arthur Jeffery and Adelaide Jeffery Henderson, were returned by Ellen's son Jeffery Hellaby when he met with his first cousins, the son and daughters of Pioneer Joseph Jeffery. In the tenth generation it was the turn of Joseph's grandson, Geoff Jeffery and Thomas's grandson, John Jeffery, to exchange visits with Owen's granddaughter Dorothy Jeffery and later, Ellen's granddaughter, myself. These have been followed up by those of the eleventh generation whose roots are in Hungry Bentley: Thomas Jeffery's great, great grandson Michael Jeffery from Alaska; Mary (nee Jeffery) Spencer's great grandson Jonathon Spencer now in New Zealand; William's great granddaughter Irene Jeffery and Ellen (nee Jeffery) Hellaby's great granddaughter Clare de Bono, London.

Nowhere was the closeness of this global family demonstrated more fully than in the summer of 2008 when over a hundred members of the family met together at a hotel in Ashbourne for a Jeffery reunion. Everyone appreciated a family tree which stretched the length of a corridor and a montage of family photographs covering over a hundred and fifty years. Few still retained the Jeffery name but most had Jeffery genes. Six of the remaining ten great grandchildren of Thomas and Mary Jeffery of the *Riddings* participated. The gathering was inspired by great, great granddaughter Irene Jeffery who carried most of the burden of organisation. It was recorded on both television and photographs. Four generations were present ranging from Arthur and Geoff Jeffery in their ninetieth and eightieth decades to five-month old Henry Houghton. They journeyed from Arctic Alaska, sub-tropical Georgia and the Antipodes. They came from the length and breadth of England: from the Scottish borders, Wales, London and the West Country. Naturally family members from Derbyshire and Hungry Bentley were there.

The family reunion provided an opportunity to visit Jeffery family farms including *Bentley Fields*, the *Home Farm*, West Broughton and *Aston House*, Sudbury. Alkmonton Church was visited and a service held at Longford Church to mark the gathering of the Jeffery family. The celebratory dinner in the evening ended when thanks to the organisers were offered and delight expressed in the occasion. None were more moving than those given by eleven-year-old Thomas Morgan Jeffery Spencer from New Zealand and nine-year-old

Henry Connolly Houghton, great, great, great grandson of Joseph Jeffery of the Riddings, with Isabel and India de Bono, great, great granddaughters of Ellen Jeffery of the Riddings, Hungry Bentley

India Valerie Natasha de Bono from London. Here was a glimpse of the future Jefferys.

I conclude with a fantasy. It is a fantasy which could relate to any one of the increasing number of descendants of Thomas and Mary Jeffery of the *Riddings*. It is that many years hence, Henry Houghton discovers this book and flips through its pages. His curiosity is aroused and his parents will relate how, as a babe in arms, he flew across the Atlantic with his parents, grandparents and great grandfather and was introduced to the Jeffery family in England. If Henry has inherited the Jeffery gene for travel and adventure he will follow his great grandfather. He will turn off the old Ashbourne turnpike and cross a couple of fields. Once there he will stop and gaze down across Jefferyland to the *Riddings*. Then another New World Jeffery will rediscover his roots in the land of Old Derbyshire.

And, who knows, if the Jeffery gene for longevity has been inherited, he may meet a very old lady who wrote the book that set him wondering.

NEW CONTRIBUTIONS

Memories, Thoughts, Impressions and Inspirations

Michael Jeffery

Looking Back at our 2008 Derbyshire Jeffery Family Reunion

It was so amazing to receive emails at our home in Utqiagvik (Barrow) in Arctic Alaska from our Jeffery relatives in the UK about a Jeffery reunion in the summer of 2008. At first, my wife Esther and I were not sure about it. Such a journey! Summertime is so busy! Would it conflict with our annual commercial salmon set net activities? Driving on the other side of the road?? Could Michael take all that time off from his judicial duties? But then, wow! What wonderful people to visit! Such an exciting family adventure! The chance of a lifetime! Our whole family got pretty excited! Soon we were on our way.

Esther is part Norwegian so we visited there first and then took a ferry across from Bergen to Newcastle Upon Tyne. We then rented a car and Michael had to get used to driving on the 'other' side of the road. Major highways were easier than the one lane roads where you drive off the road to let the other car go by.

We enjoyed a warm welcome at the hotel with such friendly Jeffery family from the UK and USA and beyond. We were blessed to experience *The Riddings* when we first arrived. We enjoyed so much meeting everyone and getting a sense of the generations of Jefferys in England and now across the globe. It was amusing to hear from so many that we all had to keep correcting people on the spelling of 'Jeffery'. The family dinner and photo session with the groups of Jefferys was fun to experience and the fellowship was wonderful!

After this lovely experience, we so appreciated the hospitality of Valerie and Colin Hardy and seeing the beautiful Cotswold area. With beautiful memories, we returned the vehicle (unscathed - phew!) and took our plane to the USA.

Michael Jeffery - great grandson of Thomas and Mary Jeffery of *The Riddings Farm*.
(see page 300 THOMAS'S DESCENDANTS)

LEFT
Michael and family with Margaret and Fred Jeffery at The Riddings. The author with her late husband right, with Isabel and India, granddaughters, on the wall.

Rosalie Vicars-Harris

'Written on our Hearts'

Having immersed myself so totally, as editor, in Val's account of our family's history, I could not help but be absorbed and fascinated by the detail and variety of adventures in the Jeffery story. What an intrepid and courageous lot our ancestors were!

As a descendant of William, one of the fifteen children of Thomas and Mary at The Ridddings, William Charles Jeffery, his grandson and my grandfather, farmed at Aston House, Sudbury. I and my three siblings belonged to the third generation of Jefferys there. Our father, Henry Jeffery, died in 1988 and our brother Robert Jeffery continued to farm at Aston House very successfully and converted it to to an organic farm. Robert's son, another William, did not continue the Jeffery farming tradition.

Vera Jeffery, Henry's wife and our mother, the matriach and custodian of family photos and their history, had created a beautiful home to which we all returned with our families every Easter and Christmas. In her own book, entitled 'Written On My Heart' she expressed the sentiment we all felt when we as a family had to give up Aston House. So it was with a heavy heart that Rob broke the news to us that on his retirement it could no longer be the focal point for the family - or a Jeffery farm.

On leaving Aston we all wrote down our thoughts about our lives there and a strong theme that came through was what a powerful and precious grounding growing up on the farm and being part of the Jeffery family there had been.

Val's book and the story of our ancestors and the wider family that it has revealed and introduced to us, has been an intriguing journey into our heritage. Having now a sense of how our immediate family fits into the bigger picture is both satifying and humbling. We value this hugely and hope that this book will be passed down and enjoyed by future generations.

Rosalie Vicars-Harris - great, great granddaughter of Thomas and Mary Jeffery of *The Riddings Farm*. (see page 301 WILLIAM'S DESCENDANTS) Aston House (see page 29)

LEFT *Rosalie*
ABOVE *Robert, Lu, Rosalie and Chris*

Richard Spencer

Thoughts

Now, my thoughts. I was very much aware in my formative years that Grandpa, Percy Spencer, thought the world of this farm and by the time I reached double figures, 10 years old, it had filtered through that just as my Dad would follow his father, so should I follow mine, Jeffery Spencer. Coming home from University I became totally involved in the farm.

Fortunately, when I married Rosemary she also had a very strong love of the land. This has grown stronger over the years and it is fair to say that caring for our piece of England is the driving force behind all we do. Our daughter Katrina, our son Simon and their respective families also have this awareness and that starting with great, great uncle Owen Jeffery, my eldest grandson Oliver, who will follow on after Simon, will be the sixth generation.

There is an Australian aboriginal word - I think 'kanyeewee' but I am not sure, which means love of land and family. The 'Jeffery' family book brought this emotion very much to the fore, and it will remain the driving force behind our continued caring for our little piece of England.

Richard Spencer - great nephew of Owen Jeffery and great, great, grandson of Thomas and Mary Jeffery of *The Riddings Farm*. (see pages 252 and 301 MARY'S DESCENDANTS)

BELOW
Richard and Rosemary Spencer, BENTLEY FIELDS FARM

Sally Houghton

Pride and Perseverance

It's nice to hear that you are writing another book about the Jefferys. I know it's quite an undertaking and I'm not sure how much I can add! It's hard to believe it's been almost 14 years since the reunion, but I have great memories from it. It was really lovely to meet Jefferys from so many different places. Actually being in England for the reunion where so many of my Jeffery ancestors came from was very satisfying. I think that knowing about my ancestors has given me a better sense of my own identity, in addition to a sense of pride. I'm proud that the Jefferys persevered through some pretty tough hardships that we don't have to deal with today. Everyday life was just harder in 'the old days'. And so many babies and young children died from disease and other causes. So much tragedy, and yet just knowing that they survived tell me that my family is, and has always been, strong and resilient.

Sally Houghton - great, great granddaughter of Thomas and Mary Jeffery of *The Riddings Farm*. (see page 300 JOSEPH'S DESCENDANTS)

Jenny Snow

Heritage

Just to say regarding my thoughts on a contribution to the revised edition of the Jeffery book, that, as a descendent of Ellen Jeffery, I am very proud of my heritage and equally proud to be included in such a well-researched book that contributes much to the rich tapestry of life!

Jenny Snow - great granddaughter of Ellen Hellaby (née Jeffery) and great, great granddaughter of Thomas and Mary Jeffery of *The Riddings Farm*. (see page 302 ELLEN'S DESCENDANTS)

Tom Spencer

Identity and Origins

To me it is not something I think about every day, or week, but in New Zealand we have a Maori concept called whaka-papa (FAR-KAR-PAR-PAR). Whakapapa is where you descend from, but also who you descend from and what you identify with. It's a powerful concept that is central to one's identity. I have a strong sense of identity, which I have drawn from the Jeffery reunion. Knowing where I come from is like having a safe place from which I can spring forward with confidence into whatever may come my way.

Tom Spencer - great, great, great grandson of Thomas and Mary Jeffery of The Riddings Farm. (See page 301 MARY'S DECENDANTS)

Gill Young

A Personal Insight

The main impact for us was meeting with the many distant family members. We think maybe relatives who attended the tour of Jefferyland homesteads and surrounding area will be able to have more input. We thought what a grand idea the tour was, but I personally wanted to make this visit with my mother, enlightened by her own personal stories.

Although she has always pointed out various places of interest on the way to Alkmonton Church to lay a wreath for grandad and granny, she eventually managed a day away from the business to take myself and Georgia on a guided tour, which you can imagine was brilliant. We visited The Riddings, Cottage Farm, Common Farm, Bentley Hall, Alkmonton Church, Ivy House, Dove House and West Broughton Farm - her personal account and remarkable memory made our day.

Gill Young - great, great granddaughter of Thomas and Mary Jeffery of *The Riddings Farm*. (see page 302 ELLEN'S DESCENDANTS)

India de Bono

The Time Spiral: A Poem for the Past

Time spins around us
Spiralling in a silver stream we never see.
But every so often
We are allowed glimpses into a past
we do not know.
It is coiled as tightly as a shell
and houses the gooey creature of Pertinence:
it slithers and writhes and slowly eats up Memory.
It is snails as it started
and in snails it will end.
Remembrance shot through me like lightning,
bolts of understanding and recollection for
the young girl who was once me
playing in found friendship with a cousin.
Snails. We were playing with snails.
Outside a house that was foreign to me but not my blood,
an echo of familiarity
Mud and memory
Snails.
How many snails had been born and died on their land?
A house of memorial
It began with snails
And so too it shall end.

LEFT *India aged 9*
BELOW *in 2019*

India de Bono - great, great, great granddaughter of Thomas and Mary Jeffery of *The Riddings Farm* was entranced by snails when visiting The Home Farm, West Broughton (page 27) on the day of the Jeffery reunion in August 2008.

Clare de Bono

Travels Through Time and Distance

Having grown up with the family stories and visited family farms as a child, it was amazing to read the family history back to 1630 through thirteen generations and four continents. At last I was able to join the dots and see how the patchwork fitted.

For me this was encapsulated in one particular picture on page 294. As a student in the 1980s I had the privilege to visit cousins (many times removed) in California as I travelled across the USA. At the time, they were just lovely people who looked after a hungry student, provided her with a washing machine and took her on the Rocky Mountain Railroad in Disneyland at midnight, screaming at the top of their lungs. Reading the book I learned about our shared forefathers and fell in love with the picture of three women on Santa Monica beach. This was a beach my cousins took me to, a beach I later visited through work as my US HQ was a stone's throw away - and here was a picture of Myra, one of my relatives, on the same beach over a hundred years before!

Thank you Mum for helping me join those dots, meet people across the world and understand 500 years of shared family history.

Myra on the beach, Santa Monica circa 1910

Clare - 2014

Clare de Bono - great, great granddaughter of Thomas and Mary Jeffery of *The Riddings Farm*.
(see page 302 ELLEN'S DESCENDANTS)

Author's Note

At the Jeffery family reunion of August 2008, I rashly announced that I would be writing a book. Just over two years later, breathing life into a vanished world, OLD DERBYSHIRE AND NEW WORLDS: THE JEFFERYS OF HUNGRY BENTLY was published.

When twelve years later I was encouraged to 'do something' with the book I resolved to produce a second edition or perhaps even a work of fiction based on the Jeffery story, or even a TV series. With these possible ways forward in mind it was suggested that I could start by writing a synopsis. However, I found this an extraordinarily frustrating exercise. How to précis, but still do justice to a compelling family saga originating in enigmatic historic settings dating from the days of Richard the Lionheart, Queen Elizabeth 1, Mary Queen of Scots and Bonnie Prince Charlie, which then went on to tell of the remarkable exploits of intrepid nineteenth century pioneering Jefferys in North America and New Zealand? Additionally it was a story taking Jefferys in the mid twentieth century to Kenya, the former Northern and Southern Rhodesia and eventually South Africa. Indeed a global family with Derbyshire roots as the reunion of 2008 encapsulated. Here was a story encompassing the massive social changes which commenced in the early nineteenth century and which continue with ever increasing momentum into the second decade of the twenty-first.

I eventually determined that the best way forward would be to invite contributions to a Second Edition: the response to my invitation proved very revealing, providing a number of inspirational and moving contributions and once again I found myself walking hand in hand with serendipity. The additional new data provided by Jeffery descendants in Canada, whose ancestors had emigrated in 1872, far exceeded what could be incorporated into this book. However, I trust that they will be encouraged, following their own reunion in 2015, which sadly I was unable to attend, to use that wealth of material to write their own story.

In writing this note I am reminded of an observation made by a good friend following the publication of the First Edition, when she emphasised that there is no such thing as an ordinary family: they are all extraordinary in their own way. I would like to think that recognition of this concept will encourage a wider readership way beyond those who have Jeffery roots in Derbyshire and that the reader will also be encouraged to grasp the hand of serendipity and become inspired to write their own family story.

Valerie Hardy - granddaughter of Ellen Jeffery, the fourteenth of the fifteen children of Thomas and Mary Jeffery of *The Riddings Farm*.